ST/ESA/SER/A/252

M-GOV

Department of Economic and Social Affairs
Population Division

WORLD MORTALITY REPORT 2005

United Nations
New York, 2006

DESA

The Department of Economic and Social Affairs of the United Nations Secretariat is a vital interface between global policies in the economic, social and environmental spheres and national action. The Department works in three main interlinked areas: (i) it compiles, generates and analyses a wide range of economic, social and environmental data and information on which States Members of the United Nations draw to review common problems and to take stock of policy options; (ii) it facilitates the negotiations of Member States in many intergovernmental bodies on joint course of action to address ongoing or emerging global challenges; and (iii) it advises interested Governments on the ways and means of translating policy frameworks developed in United Nations conferences and summits into programmes at the country level and, through technical assistance, helps build national capacities.

NOTE

The designations employed and the presentation of the material in this publication do not imply the expression of any opinion on the part of the Secretariat of the United Nations concerning the legal status of any country, territory, city or area or of its authorities, or concerning the delimitation of its frontiers or boundaries.

The designations of "more developed regions" and "less developed regions" are intended for statistical convenience and do not necessarily express a judgement about the stage reached by a particular country or area in the development process.

The term "country" as used in the text of this publication also refers, as appropriate, to territories or areas.

ST/ESA/SER.A/252
UNITED NATIONS PUBLICATION
Sales No. E.06.XIII.3
ISBN 92-1-151417-7

PREFACE

The Population Division of the Department of Economic and Social Affairs of the United Nations Secretariat is responsible for providing the international community with up-to-date and scientifically objective information about population and development. According to its mandate, the Population Division provides guidance on these issues to the United Nations General Assembly, the Economic and Social Council, and the Commission on Population and Development. It also undertakes regular studies on population levels and trends, population estimates and projections, population policies and population and development interrelationships.

In particular, the Population Division is concerned with the following substantive areas: the study of patterns of fertility, mortality, international and internal migration, including their levels, trends, and differentials, as well as their causes and consequences; analysis of mortality patterns as a function of age, sex, and cause of death; analysis of fertility patterns as a function of age and parity, and in terms of its proximate determinants (e.g., marriage, contraceptive use); estimates and projections of population size, spatial distribution, and age and sex structure; the documentation and analysis of population policies at the national and international levels; and the study of the relationship between socio-economic development and population change.

The work of the Population Division is published in a variety of formats, including electronically, in order to meet the needs of diverse audiences. These publications and materials are used by Governments, national and international organizations, researchers, social and economic planners, educators, and the general public.

This report is the first of its kind to be issued on topics related to mortality and health. It presents information on mortality risks, life expectancy, maternal mortality, HIV prevalence, and national policies with respect to such topics for 192 countries. The data are compiled from civil registration, population censuses, nationally representative sample surveys and, in the case of national policies, Governments' responses to United Nations inquiries and other sources.

For each country, available data on 19 indicators are presented in tabular form. In most cases, this information is provided for two dates (around 1970 and around 2000). In addition, time series of life expectancy at birth and the infant mortality rate from various sources are presented for each country in graphical form. Available estimates of these two indicators are compared on the graphs with estimates presented in *World Population Prospects: The 2004 Revision.*[†]

The Population Division gratefully acknowledges the assistance and cooperation of the United Nations Statistics Division, the World Health Organization, UNICEF, UNFPA, UNAIDS, the Council of Europe, EUROSTAT, ORC Macro, the International Programs Center of the U.S. Census Bureau, the Human Mortality Database (University of California at Berkeley and the Max Planck Institute for Demographic Research), and national statistical offices in providing the different data presented in this report.

This report as well as other population information can be accessed via the Internet on the official website of the United Nations Population Division, www.unpopulation.org. For further information concerning this publication, please contact the office of Ms. Hania Zlotnik, Director, Population Division, Department of Economic and Social Affairs, United Nations, New York, NY 10017, USA; telephone number +1 212-963-3179; fax number +1 212-963-2147.

[†] United Nations (2005). *World Population Prospects: The 2004 Revision* (CD-ROM Edition-Extended Dataset). New York: United Nations. Sales No. E.05.XIII.12.

CONTENTS

Explanatory Notes

A point (.) is used to indicate decimals.

Two dots (..) indicate that data are not available or are not separately reported.

Use of a hyphen (-) between years (for example, 1995-2000) signifies an inclusive period from 1 July of the first year to 30 June of the second year when referring to estimates from *World Population Prospects: The 2004 Revision*. When referring to estimates from civil registration, such use signifies an inclusive period from 1 January of the first year to 31 December of the second year. When used to refer to estimates from sample surveys, the exact date boundaries of the multi-year period can vary depending on the reference date of the survey.

Countries and areas are grouped geographically into six major areas: Africa; Asia; Europe; Latin America and the Caribbean; Northern America; and Oceania. The major areas are further divided into geographical regions. In addition, for statistical convenience, the regions are classified as belonging to either of two categories: more developed or less developed. The less developed regions include all of Africa, Asia (excluding Japan), and Latin America and the Caribbean, as well as Melanesia, Micronesia, and Polynesia. The more developed regions comprise Australia/New Zealand, Europe, Northern America, and Japan.

The following acronyms are used in the report:

AS	*Age Structure of Mortality in Developing Countries*[1]
COE	Council of Europe
CPS	Contraceptive Prevalence Survey(s)
DHS	Demographic and Health Survey(s)
DYB	United Nations *Demographic Yearbook*
GG	*Too Young to Die: Genes or Gender?*[2]
HFA	Health for All Database[3]
HIV/AIDS	Human Immunodeficiency Virus/Acquired Immunodeficiency Syndrome
HMD	Human Mortality Database[4]
IDB	International Data Base[5]
PVSR	United Nations *Population and Vital Statistics Report*
MICS	Multiple Indicator Cluster Survey(s)
UNPD	United Nations Population Division
WFS	World Fertility Survey(s)
WHO	World Health Organization

---

[1] United Nations (1986). *Age Structure of Mortality in Developing Countries*. New York: United Nations. ST/ESA/SER.R/66.

[2] United Nations (1998). *Too Young to Die: Genes or Gender?* New York: United Nations. Sales No. E.98.XIII.13.

[3] The Health for All Database (http://www.euro.who.int/hfadb) is maintained by the World Health Organization Regional Office for Europe (WHO Europe).

[4] The Human Mortality Database (http://www.mortality.org) is maintained by the University of California at Berkeley and the Max Planck Institute for Demographic Research (Rostock, Germany).

[5] The International Data Base is maintained by the U.S. Census Bureau (http://www.census.gov).

I. SCOPE, METHODOLOGY AND SOURCES

The main objective of this report is to compile and summarize available information about levels and trends of mortality and life expectancy for national populations. A related goal is to compare estimates from various sources to those derived by the United Nations Population Division as the baseline for its mortality projections, which are a key input for its biennial assessment of population prospects (see *World Population Prospects: The 2004 Revision*, United Nations, 2005).

Aside from a comparison of mortality data from different sources, the report permits an assessment of gaps in information. This exercise can provide crucial insights, especially given the ongoing efforts to combat child mortality and HIV/AIDS necessary to reach the United Nations Millenium Development Goals and the need for data to validate progress made in these areas.

Thus, this report presents a compilation of estimates of key mortality indicators for 192 countries and areas (hereafter referred to as "countries" for simplicity). This group includes all countries with a population of 100 000 or greater in the year 2000. Data are taken from a wide variety of sources. Emphasis is placed on official estimates of mortality indicators provided by countries to the United Nations, supplemented by estimates obtained from other databases, population censuses, and nationally representative surveys.

The *World Mortality Report 2005* provides a broad overview of mortality changes in all countries of the world during the latter half of the 20th century. It is the first report of its kind produced by the United Nations Population Division. Previous studies have analyzed levels and trends in mortality covering all regions of the world, and there have been other compendia of detailed mortality statistics. However, this report is the first attempt to document mortality levels and trends across the full age range for all countries of the world, also including an explicit comparison of mortality estimates from a variety of sources.

Given the ambitious scope of the project, it is perhaps inevitable that the final product has certain limitations, which should be acknowledged. The first issue concerns the amount of data analyzed. Although the report summarizes a vast body of data from many sources, the collection of mortality estimates presented here is not exhaustive. Most of the included data were already available in an electronic format (see section C. of this chapter, "Sources of mortality data"). Other collections of mortality data currently available only in print format will be computerized and incorporated into future versions of this report.

The second issue concerns the kinds of data included in the report. One major goal of this project was to compare mortality estimates used as the basis for the United Nations population projections, as published in *World Population Prospects: The 2004 Revision* (United Nations, 2005), to estimates derived from other sources. In most cases the data used for this comparison consist of official mortality estimates produced by national statistical agencies and published either in some government document or in the United Nations *Demographic Yearbook*. However, such data were not available for all countries and therefore some of the comparative estimates have been taken from other sources. Thus, the data presented here are not fully uniform in terms of their source, quality or manner of calculation.

Given these limitations, it is important to be cautious about the comparability of the mortality estimates presented here for different countries and time periods. Although this study provides an overview of historical mortality trends, it would be inappropriate to use these data for certain types of detailed comparative studies. Despite these limitations, this report provides a useful starting point for future studies of mortality levels and trends in all countries of the world.

A. OVERVIEW OF MORTALITY ESTIMATES

Data tables for each country (see Part IV of this report) present estimates of crude mortality rates, life expectancy, survival probabilities, and infant and child mortality rates. The estimates in the upper portion, Panel I, of the country profile tables are obtained mostly from non-United

Nations sources and usually refer to periods around 1970 and around 2000. Owing to data availability, in some cases the estimates refer to a year or period that is merely as close as possible to the two target dates.

The data in Panel I of each country profile table have been taken from various sources and have not been adjusted in any consistent fashion for coverage or other non-sampling errors. Therefore, the values of certain indicators, especially for countries with deficient data, may not match those published in *World Population Prospects: The 2004 Revision* (United Nations, 2005), since the latter have been adjusted, as needed, to ensure their consistency with information about other components of historical demographic change (e.g., fertility, migration) and to compensate for any deficiencies in the available data as assessed through demographic evaluation.

The lower portion, Panel II, of each country profile table includes indicators of mortality and health taken mostly from United Nations sources. For example, it provides estimates of life expectancy at birth and the "under-five mortality rate" (technically, the latter quantity equals the probability of dying between birth and exact age five) for two recent time periods, early 1990s and early 2000s. This part of the country profile table also presents recent estimates by United Nations organizations of maternal mortality and of the prevalence of HIV/AIDS, as well as the Government's reported views concerning levels of mortality in 1976 and 2003.

Figures for each country offer a graphical view of trends between 1950 and 2005 in life expectancy at birth and in infant mortality. These figures give the reader an overview of the estimates available from national statistical offices and other sources, and allow a comparison of these numbers to estimates prepared by the United Nations Population Division and published in *World Population Prospects: The 2004 Revision* (United Nations, 2005).

B. METHODS OF MORTALITY ESTIMATION

Mortality data for countries come from three main sources: civil registration, population censuses, and sample surveys. These three sources are complementary, particularly for detailed studies of mortality determinants and differentials. However, in the context of this report, they will be discussed in terms of their usefulness for producing national-level estimates of mortality by age and sex.

For the purpose of mortality estimation, *civil registration* refers to the legal documentation of deaths and the central compilation of death records. To measure mortality using this information, in most cases counts of deaths by age and sex are combined with comparable population estimates at the national level to produce age and sex-specific mortality rates, from which the standard life table indicators can be derived. For estimates of infant and child mortality, however, data on deaths up to age one or five are usually combined with registration data on live births to compute probabilities of death and survival directly, provided completeness of death and birth coverage is high.

When civil registration systems are complete and well-functioning, they provide an annual count of deaths by age and sex. Most countries in the more developed regions have had such systems in place for many years. As a result, a long, consistent time series of mortality indicators is available for such countries. However, many obstacles have prevented most developing countries from achieving full registration. For example, there may be little incentive to register deaths if death certificates are not needed for burial, insurance or inheritance purposes. Deaths of young children are particularly prone to omission, especially if the birth was not registered. It can be difficult to reach rural, nomadic or indigenous populations, and qualified personnel are often in short supply. Additionally, there may be problems with the flow of records from local registration offices to the responsible central agency.

The United Nations Statistics Division assigns a rating of complete, incomplete, or unknown completeness to civil registration data received from countries, based on the countries' own assessment of the completeness of registration. Data are considered complete when they represent 90 per cent or more of the events occurring in the specified year. In cases where the completeness rating changes over time, the United Nations Statistics Division assumes that the new rating applies to the entire time series of reported data. This convention is followed in the present publication.

In the absence of complete civil registration data, a few countries have established sample registration systems, surveillance systems, or annual demographic surveys to produce nationally representative estimates of mortality in situations where complete civil registration cannot be achieved. More commonly, periodic *censuses* and *surveys* are used to collect data allowing for the estimation of mortality.

One method for estimating mortality directly is to ask for retrospective reports of deaths in the household in a given reference period before a census or survey, and then to compute age-sex-specific mortality rates from the reported deaths and census population counts. Death reports collected by this method tend to be severely defective. Reasons include recall lapse, misunderstanding of the reference period, misreporting of age of the deceased, and dissolution of households after a death. However, a number of demographic methods are available to assess the completeness of reported deaths.

Measuring adult mortality through censuses and surveys is inherently difficult. Because adult deaths are relatively rare events, large sample sizes are necessary in order to obtain statistically reliable estimates, particularly when detailed breakdowns by age and sex are required. One set of methods attempts to gauge the level of adult mortality indirectly using questions on the survival of close relatives, such as parents or siblings. However, the mortality estimates produced by these methods represent average measures over a period of several years before the survey. Also, the method based on survival of parents is subject to an "adoption effect," that is, a tendency to report the status not of the biological parent, but of a foster or adoptive parent. Misreporting of respondents' ages can also affect the results. Mortality estimates produced through these methods are not included in the present report, unless they have been incorporated into official life tables reported by Governments to the

United Nations Statistics Division or in national statistical publications.

Estimates of adult mortality can also be derived from the population structures found in two consecutive censuses by examining the survival of cohorts from one census to the next. However, this method is sensitive to changes in the completeness of enumeration from one census to the next, and to the effects of in- or out-migration on the apparent survival rates.

By contrast, the measurement of child mortality via censuses and surveys has become quite well developed over the past several decades. Child mortality is measured through two main approaches: direct estimates through the collection of detailed maternity histories, and indirect estimation via tabulations of children ever born and children surviving for women of reproductive age (the so-called "Brass questions"). The collection of full maternity histories is very time-intensive and therefore is generally carried out only in dedicated demographic surveys with a strong focus on fertility and reproductive health. Ideally, the method collects information on births and deaths according to their exact time of occurrence, and thus allows for the computation of age-specific child mortality rates and direct estimates of trends over time. The method is subject to biases from omission of births (particularly of children who later died) and from systematic errors in the dating of births and deaths (Institute for Resource Development, 1990; United Nations, 1992).

Data for the second approach have been collected in a large number of censuses and surveys. In this case, proportions of children who have died among those ever born are tabulated as a function of mother's age (usually in five-year age groups). These proportions are converted into probabilities of dying before reaching certain childhood ages. By applying adjustment factors to correct for varying fertility schedules, these probabilities can be matched to levels of mortality from model life tables, from which conventional measures of infant and child mortality can be derived and assigned to reference dates preceding the census or survey. Estimates, particularly of infant mortality, can vary substantially depending on the model life table chosen.

This indirect method is subject to biases from the omission of children in the ever-born total; experience has shown that such omissions are more likely for children who have died or moved away. Misreporting of women's ages can also affect the resulting estimates of child mortality. Estimates based on the responses of younger women, particularly those aged 15-19 or 20-24, tend to be biased upward because a large proportion of births to these mothers are first births and tend to have higher mortality than births of higher orders. In addition, births to young mothers may be clustered in socio-economic groups that have higher child mortality. A detailed discussion of the Brass method for the estimation of mortality in childhood and its variants may be found in the *Step-by-Step Guide to the Estimation of Child Mortality* (United Nations, 1990).

C. SOURCES OF MORTALITY DATA

Mortality data presented here in the tables and graphs of the country profiles (see Part IV of this report) come from a variety of sources. This section provides an overview of these data sources. More detailed information about the data sources used for each country is listed in tables 1 and 2 (see Part II).

1. *Death counts and crude death rates*

Data on total deaths, deaths under age one, and the crude death rate, as shown in Panel I of the country profile tables, were obtained primarily from the *Demographic Yearbook* (United Nations, various years), the *Demographic Yearbook Historical Supplement* (United Nations, 1997), and the *Population and Vital Statistics Report* (United Nations, various years). Data were used only for those countries where death registration is reported to be complete. Note that the United Nations Statistics Division accepts countries' self-reports of the completeness of death registration; a recent study by the World Health Organization has shown that reported death totals for some of these countries may be deficient (WHO, n.d.).

For the earlier period (around 1970) death totals for several countries, specifically the successor states of the former Yugoslavia, Czechoslovakia, and the USSR, were not available in the *Demographic Yearbook* database. Totals for these countries were obtained from *Recent Demographic Developments in Europe* (Council of Europe, 2003).[1] For the more recent period (around 2000), if data available from national statistical office websites were more recent than those reported to the United Nations Statistics Division, these national sources were used.[2]

2. *Life expectancy and survival probabilities*

Estimates of life expectancy and probabilities of survival in the country profiles (Panel I of the tables, as well as the graphs) come primarily from official life tables provided by Governments to the United Nations Statistics Division, published by national statistical offices, or collected in the Human Life-Table Database.[3] Such life tables are most often calculated from vital registration data and official population estimates by age, but in some cases are based on data from censuses or surveys (see section B., "Methods of mortality estimation"). In addition, life tables were taken from sources that are not "official," but that produce life tables with no or only minor adjustments from death and population data provided by Governments. These sources include the Human Mortality Database, the Eurostat New Cronos database, and a set of life tables provided by the World Health Organization.

Lastly, some life tables were obtained from previous compilations of adjusted life tables,

---

[1] For the following countries, civil registration data for the earlier period were available from the Council of Europe: Albania (deaths under age one), Armenia, Azerbaijan, Bosnia and Herzegovina, Croatia, Czech Republic, Estonia, Georgia, Latvia, Lithuania, Republic of Moldova, Russian Federation, Serbia and Montenegro, Slovakia, and TFYR Macedonia.

[2] For the following countries, civil registration data that referred to a more recent year than data reported to the United Nations Statistics Division were obtained from national sources: Cape Verde, Costa Rica (population estimate used to compute crude death rate), Czech Republic, Denmark, Estonia (population estimate used to compute crude death rate), Latvia, Lithuania, Norway, Slovenia, Trinidad and Tobago (deaths under age one), United States Virgin Islands, and Venezuela (total deaths and crude death rate). Data for Guyana are from WHO.

[3] The Human Life-Table Database (www.lifetable.de) is maintained jointly by the Max Planck Institute for Demographic Research (Rostock, Germany), the University of California at Berkeley, and the Institut National d'Études Démographiques (Paris).

including a collection published earlier by the United Nations Population Division (United Nations, 1986) and the International Data Base of the U.S. Census Bureau. In selecting life tables from these sources, preference was given to tables based primarily on direct data from registration, censuses or surveys, rather than on model life tables.

In addition to the sources listed in the preceding paragraphs, some estimates of life expectancy at birth in the country profile tables and graphs were taken from sources that published only annual time series of life expectancy at birth, rather than full life tables. These include Government statistical publications and websites, the Health for All database produced by WHO Europe, the TransMONEE database produced by the UNICEF Innocenti Research Centre, and the report entitled *Recent Demographic Developments in Europe,* published by the Council of Europe (2003).

The specific sources used for each country are listed in table 1. In most cases, life expectancy estimates were taken directly from the e_x column of the source life table, whereas probabilities of survival were calculated by the United Nations Population Division from the l_x column of the source life table.

For the life expectancy graphs of the country profiles, estimates from several sources were combined when necessary to produce the most complete time series possible. In cases of disagreement between sources for a given year, all sources for a country were examined graphically and the source producing the most consistent time series was selected.

3. *Infant and under-five mortality*

The sources of infant and child mortality data in the table vary according to the development grouping of the country. For most developed countries, the estimates by sex in the table were calculated from survival values (l_x) in the life tables described in the previous paragraphs. The infant mortality rates (IMR) calculated in this manner may differ slightly from rates calculated directly from data on infant deaths and live births that are used in the graphs.

For most developing countries, estimates for the early period were produced by the United Nations Population Division in an earlier study using all available direct and indirect estimates of child mortality by sex (United Nations, 1998). For the later period, figures for developing countries are largely direct estimates from the most recent available Demographic and Health Survey and refer to the 10-year period before the survey. For a few developing countries, official life tables of sufficient quality were available to calculate the child mortality indicators in the later period. When estimates by sex were not available for the later period, estimates for both sexes combined are presented where possible.

The time series of IMR in the country profile graphs consists of estimates from civil registration, censuses, and surveys. IMRs based on civil registration data come from two United Nations publications, the *Demographic Yearbook* and the *Population and Vital Statistics Report* (both for various years). Where data are missing from these sources, they are supplemented by data from national publications and websites, the Health for All database, the TransMONEE database, and *Recent Demographic Developments in Europe* (Council of Europe, 2003), and other sources. Estimates derived from surveys and censuses up to around 1990 were obtained from *Child Mortality since the 1960s* (United Nations, 1992). Data for later censuses and surveys were obtained using DHS+ Statcompiler, directly from survey or census reports, and from secondary files provided by UNICEF. The specific sources used for each country are listed in table 2.

The direct and indirect methods used to estimate infant mortality produce a time series of estimates from an individual census or survey. However, for ease of interpretation, each survey or census is represented here by only one point on the country profile graph. For surveys with direct estimates based on maternity history data, including WFS, DHS and others, the point represents the average of estimates for the three 5-year periods preceding the survey date (in some cases, fewer periods were available).

Although indirect estimates based on children ever born and surviving from these surveys are not shown, they constitute an important check on the quality and consistency of the direct estimates. For surveys (MICS and some others) and censuses from which only indirect estimates were available, the point shown in the figure represents the estimate computed from maternal age group 25-29, rather than the full series of seven point estimates produced by the Trussell variant of the Brass method (United Nations, 1990). For detailed analyses of infant mortality, data users are urged to consult sources containing the full time series of direct and indirect estimates from each survey.

Note that in evaluating infant mortality estimates for the *World Population Prospects: The 2004 Revision* (United Nations, 2005), demographers at the United Nations considered the full series of both direct and indirect estimates from each data source, including variations resulting from alternative model life tables, and estimates were adjusted to be consistent with the other components of historical demographic change. For these reasons there may be discrepancies between the United Nations estimates and the consolidated survey and census estimates shown in the graph.

D. SUMMARY OF COMPARATIVE TABLES

The comparative tables (see Part III of this report) provide a worldwide overview of four selected indicators: life expectancy at birth, survival probability from age 15 to age 60, infant mortality, and child mortality. Data are drawn from Panel I of the country profile tables (see Part IV). Because these data are not adjusted or standardized, care should be taken in using them to draw inter-country comparisons regarding absolute levels and trends over time. They do, however, provide a convenient look at regional differentials in the availability of official estimates of mortality indicators, supplemented by other reliable estimates based upon empirical age-specific mortality rates from civil registration, censuses, or surveys. This summary represents an initial review, primarily of data that have been provided to international sources. At this time it has not been possible to perform a full review of country-specific publications, particularly those that are not available in electronic form. In addition, independent estimates from other

sources, such as journal articles or conference papers, are not included here.

The number of countries for which an estimate of life expectancy at birth (see table 3) was available decreased slightly between the earlier period and the later period. Africa, in particular, saw a decline in the availability of this indicator, as did Latin America and the Caribbean (concentrated specifically in the Caribbean), while in Oceania several more countries reported life expectancy in the later period than in the earlier period. In other major areas the number of countries with available estimates remained about the same between the two periods.

The availability of full life tables that permit the calculation of survival probabilities (table 4) is lower than the availability of life expectancy at birth alone. In addition, the availability of full life tables dropped considerably between the earlier period and the later period. This occurred, in part, because two of the major sources of life tables for the earlier period, the U.S. Census Bureau's International Data Base and the United Nations Population Division's *Age Structure of Mortality in Developing Countries* (United Nations, 1986), have not been updated in an equivalent way for life tables from the 1990s and 2000s. The lack of survival probability estimates is particularly notable in Africa.

Data in tables 5 and 6 focus on infant and under-five mortality by sex. For the earlier period (around 1970), data are shown for less developed countries only if they were included in an earlier publication (United Nations, 1998), which assessed the reliability of all census and survey estimates that were disaggregated by sex, and produced best estimates based upon these. In several cases, such a best estimate was made only for under-five mortality, and not for infant mortality. Some countries for which data are not shown in tables 5 and 6 may have had available estimates for both sexes combined; these are shown in the country profile graphs.

For the later period (around 2000), no analysis similar to United Nations (1998) has yet been undertaken to produce best estimates of child mortality by sex from the 1990s or 2000s;

the data to produce indirect estimates by sex from recent surveys, particularly DHS and MICS, are available but have not yet been systematically analyzed. For this reason, the data shown in tables 5 and 6 for less developed countries are taken from the most recent survey that produced direct estimates by sex, or from official estimates if such were available. These caveats complicate the analysis of the availability of estimates, but the general observation may be made that coverage of child mortality estimates is higher than that of life tables, and is particularly strong in Africa and other less developed regions. For the later period, estimates of infant and under-five mortality for both sexes combined are shown if disaggregated estimates by sex were not available

E. LAYOUT OF COUNTRY PROFILES

This section describes the layout of tables and graphs presented within the country profiles (see Part IV of this report).

1. Terminology and key concepts

The *annual number of deaths* refers to the number of deaths per year as recorded in the civil registration system of a country. Similarly, the *annual number of deaths under age one* refers to the number of deaths per year between birth and exact age one based on civil registration.

The *crude death rate* is the number of deaths over a given time period divided by the person-years lived over the same interval (usually approximated by the estimated population size at mid-interval, multiplied by the length of the interval). It is expressed here as the number of deaths per 1 000 person-years.

By definition, *life expectancy* is the average number of (remaining) years of life anticipated for a fictitious group of persons who are subject, hypothetically, to the mortality rates of a given year (or period) throughout their lives. Values of life expectancy can refer to any age. This report includes estimates of life expectancy at birth, at age 15, and at age 60, for males and females separately.

A *survival probability* refers to the probability of surviving to a given age, sometimes conditional on survival to some earlier age. Survival probabilities are presented here for the intervals from birth to age 15, from age 15 to age 60, and from age 60 to age 80. As with life expectancy, such quantities refer to a fictitious group of person who are subject, hypothetically, to the mortality rates of a given year (or period) throughout the age interval in question.

The *infant mortality rate* refers to the probability of dying within the first year of life. *Mortality from age 1 to age 4* refers to the probability that a newborn will die between exact age one and exact age five. The *under-five mortality rate* refers to the probability of dying between birth and exact age five. All three quantities are expressed here as deaths per 1 000 live births.

The *maternal mortality ratio* equals the number of maternal deaths (i.e., deaths due to pregnancy-related causes) per 100 000 live births.

The *number of HIV-infected persons* provides an estimate of the number of persons (at all ages) who are infected with the human immunodeficiency virus (HIV) at a given point in time. *Adult HIV prevalence* equals the percentage of adults aged 15 to 49 who are infected with HIV at some moment.

Government's view on life expectancy, *Government's view on under-five mortality*, and *Government's view of maternal mortality* are classified as "acceptable" or "unacceptable" based on inquiries made periodically by the United Nations Population Division. Similarly, *Government's level of concern about AIDS* is classified a "major concern," a "minor concern," or "not a concern." A designation of "major concern" or "minor concern" implies that the Government has expressed, respectively, "serious concern" or "some concern" about the level of HIV/AIDS or the risk that it poses to the country. A Government may also indicate that HIV/AIDS is "not a concern" for the country.

2. Format of tables and graphs

On the first page of each country profile, a large table presents various indicators of mortality and related topics. The second page of each profile contains two graphs, showing trends over time in two key indicators (life expectancy at birth and the infant mortality rate).

a. *Tables*

Panel I of each country profile table provides a snapshot of mortality as reported by national and other sources, including vital registration systems, population censuses, and nationally representative surveys. The first block of data, consisting of lines 3 to 5, presents reported counts of deaths at all ages and for infants alone, as well as the crude death rate. However, such information is included only for countries with relatively complete systems of death registration, as indicated in the most recent United Nations *Population and Vital Statistics Report*.

The second and third blocks, lines 6 to 13, present measures of expected longevity or survival derived from standard life tables. In these cases the data are presented separately by sex. The average length of life for the entire population is captured by life expectancy at birth, while the average longevity for adults and the elderly is given by life expectancy at ages 15 and 60, respectively. Also presented are estimates of the probability of survival between birth and age 15, between age 15 and age 60 and between age 60 and age 80. When compared over time, these survival probabilities reflect the relative magnitude of mortality changes in childhood, adulthood, and old age.

The fourth block, lines 14 to 17, shows changes over time in infant and child mortality by sex, as derived from various sources.

Panel II of each country profile table contains information about mortality and related topics from various United Nations organizations. The first block in Panel II, lines 19 to 25, shows mortality indicators for 1990-1995 and 2000-2005 produced by the United Nations Population Division and published in *World Population Prospects: The 2004 Revision* (United Nations, 2005). These estimates help to document recent mortality trends for countries that do not produce these indicators on their own. For countries that do produce such data, it can be useful to compare them with the United Nations estimates.

The second block in Panel II, lines 26 and 27, contains an estimate of the maternal mortality ratio for the year 2000, as produced jointly by the World Health Organization, UNICEF and UNFPA (2004). Comparable data for earlier years are not available.

The third block in Panel II, lines 28 to 30, presents the most recent published estimates of HIV prevalence, which refer to the year 2003 (UNAIDS, 2004). The first line gives the estimated total number of HIV infections in each country across all ages. The second line presents the prevalence of HIV in the adult population, that is, the percentage of persons aged 15 to 49 who are infected with HIV.

The fourth block of Panel II, lines 31 to 35, presents the views of Government on four topics: life expectancy, under-five mortality, maternal mortality, and HIV/AIDS. These views were collected by the United Nations Population Division as part of the Third (1976) and the Ninth (2003) Inquiry among Governments on Population and Development.

b. *Graphs*

The first graph for each country presents life expectancy estimates from 1950-1955 to 2000-2005 published by the United Nations Population Division in *World Population Prospects: The 2004 Revision* (United Nations, 2005). On the same graph, these United Nations estimates are compared to estimates from various alternative sources. Alternative estimates based on mortality rates derived from civil registration data, whether produced by Governments or by other organizations using such information are labelled "Registration." Estimates obtained from national statistical publications for countries that do not have complete registration data are labelled "Official." Likewise, estimates provided by countries to the United Nations Statistics Division and published (typically without alteration) in the United Nations *Demographic Yearbook* are also labelled "Official." Estimates from other sources are labelled "Other." See table 1 (in Part II) for more detailed information.

The second graph presents various estimates of the infant mortality rate for each country, including estimates for 1950-1955 through 2000-2005 produced by the United Nations Population Division. Alternative estimates based on relatively complete civil registration data are labelled accordingly; however, such information is not available for all countries. Countries with incomplete civil registration may publish official estimates of infant mortality, either independently or as part of official life tables. Such estimates are labelled "Official" in the graph.

Nationally representative sample surveys provide another important source of information about infant mortality. Many of these surveys were conducted as part of organized programmes of data collection, such as the World Fertility Survey (WFS), the Demographic and Health Survey (DHS), and the Multiple Indicator Cluster Survey (MICS). Although not centrally organized and coordinated in the same fashion, data collection under the auspices of a Contraceptive Prevalence Survey (CPS) often provides an additional source for estimates of infant mortality in many countries. Infant mortality estimates from one of these large collections of survey data are labelled individually by their acronym. Estimates derived from smaller survey programmes (e.g., Reproductive Health Survey, Pan Arab Project for Family Health), or from independent national efforts, are labelled "Survey."

Censuses provide another source of infant mortality estimates, derived mainly from questions on the number of children ever born and the number still living. The data points shown for individual surveys and censuses do not depict the full range of estimates produced from these sources using direct and indirect methods. See table 2 (in Part II) for more detailed information about the sources of data on infant and child mortality.

Differences between estimates of life expectancy at birth and infant mortality produced by the United Nations Population Division and those taken from other sources arise for a number of reasons. United Nations demographers evaluate the various estimates available, taking into consideration such factors as completeness of the data collected by national statistical systems, known biases in mortality estimation methods, and the range of estimates derived from different sources. Importantly, they also review the consistency of population trends implied by different mortality estimates with information about population size and other components of demographic change (e.g., fertility, migration) from various sources (e.g., censuses, birth registration).

REFERENCES

Institute for Resource Development (1990). *An assessment of DHS-I data quality. DHS Methodological Reports, No. 1.* Columbia, Maryland: Institute for Resource Development/Macro Systems, Inc.

Preston, S.H., P. Heuveline and M. Guillot (2001). *Demography: Measuring and Modeling Population Processes.* Oxford, UK: Blackwell Publishers, Ltd.

Council of Europe (2003). *Recent demographic developments in Europe 2003.*

Eurostat. *New Cronos Database.* http://epp.eurostat.cec.eu.int

Max Planck Institute for Demographic Research, University of California at Berkeley, and Institut National d'Études Démographiques. *Human Life-Table Database.* http://www.lifetable.de

ORC Macro (2005). *MEASURE DHS STATcompiler.* http://www.measuredhs.com

UNAIDS (2004). *2004 Report on the Global HIV/AIDS epidemic: 4th Global Report.* Geneva: UNAIDS.

UNICEF Innocenti Research Centre. *TransMONEE database – 2004 edition.* http://www.unicef-icdc.org/resources

United Nations (various years). *Demographic Yearbook.*

_____ (various years). *Population and Vital Statistics Report: Series A.* http://unstats.un.org/unsd/demographic/products/vitstats/seriesa2.htm

_____ (1983). *Manual X: indirect techniques for demographic estimation.* New York: United Nations. Sales No. E.83.XIII.2.

_____ (1984). *Data bases for Mortality Measurement.* New York: United Nations. Sales No. E.83.XIII.3

_____ (1986). *Age Structure of Mortality in Developing Countries.* New York: United Nations. ST/ESA/SER.R/66.

_____ (1990). *Step-by-step guide to the estimation of child mortality.* New York: United Nations. Sales No. E.89.XIII.9.

_____ (1992). *Child Mortality Since the 1960s: A Database for Developing Countries.* New York: United Nations. Sales No. E.92.XIII.10.

_____ (1997). *Demographic Yearbook Historical Supplement.* http://unstats.un.org/unsd/demographic/products/dyb/dybhist.htm

_____ (1998). *Too Young to Die: Genes or Gender?* New York: United Nations. Sales No. E.98.XIII.13.

_____ (2004). *World Population Policies 2003.* New York: United Nations. Sales No. E.04.XIII.3.

_____ (2005). *World Population Prospects: The 2004 Revision* (CD-ROM Edition-Extended Dataset). New York: United Nations. Sales No. E.05.XIII.12.

University of California, Berkeley, and Max Planck Institute for Demographic Research. *Human Mortality Database*. http://www.mortality.org

U.S. Census Bureau. *International Data Base*. http://www.census.gov/ipc/www/idbnew.html

World Health Organization (n.d.). *Statistical Information System. Table 3: Estimated completeness of mortality data for latest year*. http://www3.who.int/whosis/menu.cfm?path=whosis,inds,mort&language=english

World Health Organization Regional Office for Europe (WHO Europe). *European Health for All Database*. http://www.euro.who.int/hfadb

World Health Organization, UNICEF, and UNFPA (2004). *Maternal Mortality in 2000: estimates developed by WHO, UNICEF and UNFPA*. Geneva: World Health Organization.

II. DATA SOURCES

TABLE 1. SOURCES OF DATA ON LIFE EXPECTANCY AND SURVIVAL PROBABILITIES[a]

Country name	Earlier period	Later period
Afghanistan	..	..
Albania	DYB	DYB
Algeria	AS	DYB
Angola	..	..
Argentina	DYB	WHO
Armenia	HFA	DYB
Australia	HLD	National[b]
Austria	HMD	DYB
Azerbaijan	COE	DYB
Bahamas	DYB	DYB
Bahrain	DYB	DYB
Bangladesh	DYB	DYB
Barbados	DYB	..
Belarus	DYB; WHO	DYB
Belgium	DYB	National[c]
Belize	DYB	DYB
Benin	..	DYB
Bhutan	..	..
Bolivia	IDB	DYB
Bosnia and Herzegovina	..	DYB
Botswana	DYB	National[d]
Brazil	DYB	DYB
Brunei Darussalam	DYB	..
Bulgaria	HMD	HMD
Burkina Faso	..	..
Burundi	AS	..
Cambodia	..	..
Cameroon	IDB	..
Canada	DYB	DYB
Cape Verde	DYB	DYB
Central African Republic	..	..
Chad	..	..
Channel Islands	..	..
Chile	DYB	DYB
China	IDB	DYB
China, Hong Kong SAR	DYB	DYB
China, Macao SAR	..	DYB
Colombia	IDB	DYB
Comoros	..	..
Congo	..	..
Costa Rica	DYB	National[e]
Côte d'Ivoire	..	..
Croatia	WHO	Eurostat
Cuba	AS	DYB
Cyprus	DYB	DYB

TABLE 1. *(continued)*

Country name	Earlier period	Later period
Czech Republic	HMD	National[f]
Democratic People's Republic of Korea	..	..
Democratic Republic of the Congo	..	..
Democratic Republic of Timor-Leste	..	..
Denmark	DYB	National[g]
Djibouti	..	..
Dominican Republic	IDB	DYB
Ecuador	DYB	DYB
Egypt	AS	DYB
El Salvador	AS	DYB
Equatorial Guinea	DYB	..
Eritrea	..	..
Estonia	Eurostat	National[h]
Ethiopia	..	DYB
Fiji	DYB	National[i]
Finland	DYB	DYB
France	DYB	HMD
French Guiana	..	DYB
French Polynesia	..	National[j]
Gabon	..	..
Gambia	IDB	..
Georgia	WHO	DYB
Germany	HMD[k]	National[l]
Ghana	..	..
Greece	DYB	National[m]; Eurostat
Guadeloupe	DYB	DYB
Guam	DYB	Other[n]
Guatemala	DYB	DYB
Guinea	..	..
Guinea-Bissau	..	..
Guyana	IDB	..
Haiti	IDB	..
Honduras	AS	..
Hungary	DYB	DYB
Iceland	DYB	DYB
India	DYB	DYB
Indonesia	IDB	..
Iran (Islamic Republic of)	DYB	DYB
Iraq	IDB	DYB
Ireland	DYB	National[o]
Israel	DYB	DYB
Italy	DYB	National[p]

TABLE 1. *(continued)*

Country name	Earlier period	Later period
Jamaica	AS	DYB
Japan	DYB	DYB
Jordan	DYB	DYB
Kazakhstan	HFA	DYB
Kenya	DYB	..
Kuwait	DYB	DYB
Kyrgyzstan	HFA	DYB
Lao People's Democratic Republic	..	..
Latvia	HMD	HMD
Lebanon	..	..
Lesotho	..	DYB
Liberia	DYB	..
Libyan Arab Jamahiriya	..	..
Lithuania	HMD	HMD
Luxembourg	DYB	Eurostat
Madagascar	DYB	..
Malawi	DYB	DYB
Malaysia	IDB	DYB
Maldives	DYB	DYB
Mali	DYB	DYB
Malta	DYB	National[q]
Martinique	DYB	DYB
Mauritania	..	..
Mauritius	DYB	DYB
Mexico	DYB	WHO
Micronesia, Federated States of	..	DYB
Mongolia	..	DYB
Morocco	AS	DYB
Mozambique	..	..
Myanmar	..	..
Namibia	..	..
Nepal	DYB	National[r]
Netherlands	DYB	HMD
Netherlands Antilles	DYB	National[s]
New Caledonia	National[t]	DYB
New Zealand	DYB	HMD
Nicaragua	..	DYB
Niger	..	..
Nigeria	..	..
Norway	DYB	National[u]
Occupied Palestinian Territory	..	DYB
Oman	..	DYB

TABLE 1. *(continued)*

Country name	Earlier period	Later period
Pakistan	DYB	DYB
Panama	DYB	DYB
Papua New Guinea	..	National[v]
Paraguay	..	DYB
Peru	WHO	DYB
Philippines	WHO	DYB
Poland	HLD	National[w]
Portugal	DYB	Eurostat
Puerto Rico	DYB	DYB
Qatar	..	..
Republic of Korea	DYB	National[x]; DYB
Republic of Moldova	WHO	DYB
Réunion	DYB	DYB
Romania	WHO	DYB
Russian Federation	HMD	DYB
Rwanda	..	..
Saint Lucia	DYB	DYB
Saint Vincent and the Grenadines	DYB	..
Samoa	DYB	National[y]
Sao Tome and Principe	..	..
Saudi Arabia	..	..
Senegal	IDB	..
Serbia and Montenegro	WHO	Eurostat
Sierra Leone	IDB	..
Singapore	DYB	DYB
Slovakia	Eurostat; WHO	DYB
Slovenia	HLD	National[z]
Solomon Islands	DYB	National[aa]
Somalia	..	..
South Africa	IDB	DYB
Spain	DYB	HMD
Sri Lanka	DYB	National[bb]
Sudan	..	..
Suriname	DYB	..
Swaziland	DYB	DYB
Sweden	DYB	HMD
Switzerland	HMD	HMD
Syrian Arab Republic	DYB	..
Tajikistan	HFA	DYB
Thailand	DYB	National[cc]
The Fmr. Yugoslav Rep. of Macedonia	Eurostat; WHO	Eurostat
Togo	DYB	..
Tonga	..	National[dd]
Trinidad and Tobago	DYB	WHO

TABLE 1. *(continued)*

Country name	Earlier period	Later period
Tunisia	AS	DYB
Turkey	IDB	National[ee]
Turkmenistan	HFA	TransMONEE
Uganda	..	..
Ukraine	DYB; WHO	DYB
United Arab Emirates	..	..
United Kingdom	WHO	National[ff]
United Republic of Tanzania	IDB	..
United States of America	DYB	National[gg]
United States Virgin Islands	..	..
Uruguay	DYB	DYB
Uzbekistan	HFA	HFA
Vanuatu	..	National[hh]
Venezuela	DYB	DYB
Viet Nam	DYB	..
Western Sahara	..	..
Yemen	..	..
Zambia	DYB	..
Zimbabwe	..	DYB

NOTES:

[a] Where two sources are listed, the first refers to life expectancy and the second refers to survival probabilities.
[b] Australian Bureau of Statistics. Life tables, Australia 2001–2003. cat. no. 3302.0.55.001.
[c] Statistics Belgium (2005). Démographie mathématique: Tables de mortalité. http://statbel.fgov.be/pub/d2/p238y2003_fr.pdf
[d] Central Statistics Office. www.cso.gov.bw/html/tabdem04_dem1.html
[e] Instituto Nacional de Estadística y Censos. Tablas abreviadas de mortalidad. http://www.inec.go.cr/
[f] Czech Statistical Office. Complete life tables 2004. http://www.czso.cz/eng/edicniplan.nsf/p/4002-05
[g] Statistics Denmark. StatBank Denmark, Table HISB8. http://www.statbank.dk/statbank5a/default.asp?w=1280
[h] Statistical Office of Estonia. Statistical Database. Life expectancy by sex and age. http://pub.stat.ee/px-eb.2001/I_Databas/Population/01Population_indicators_and_composition/02Main_demographic_indicators/02Main_demographic_indicators.asp
[i] Bureau of Statistics. Key statistics: June 2004. http://www.spc.int/prism/country/fj/stats/Social/popn.htm
[j] Institute Statistique de Polynésia Française. Démographie. http://www.ispf.pf/(0e5kzau2cwzkifi4hehx5y55)/index.aspx?choix=stat
[k] Calculated by the Population Division from data on deaths and population by age and sex for East and West Germany.
[l] Federal Statistical Office. Sterbetafel 2002/2004. http://www.destatis.de/download/d/bevoe/sterbet04.xls
[m] National Statistical Service, www.statistics.gr/eng_tables/S201_SPO_5_TS_28_00_11_Y.htm
[n] Demmke, A., et al. (1997). Guam population profile. Noumea, New Calendonia: South Pacific Commission.
[o] Central Statistics Office (2004). Irish Life Tables No. 14 2001-2003. http://www.cso.ie/releasespublications/documents/births_d_m/current/irishlife.pdf
[p] ISTAT. Tavole di mortalità della popolazione italiana per provincia e regione di residenza - Anno 2002. http://demo.istat.it/tav2002/index.html
[q] National Statistics Office. Demographic Review 2003. http://www.nso.gov.mt/statdoc/document_view.aspx?id=344&backUrl=publication_catalogue.aspx

[r] Central Bureau of Statistics (2003). Population monograph of Nepal, Vol. II. http://www.cbs.gov.np/Population/Monograph/default_volume2.htm

[s] Central Bureau of Statistics. Population. http://www.central-bureau-of-statistics.an/population/population_

[t] Institut de la Statistique et des Etudes Economiques. Décès. http://www.isee.nc/tec/popsociete/popdeces.html

[u] Statistics Norway. Life tables 2004. http://www.ssb.no/english/subjects/02/02/10/dode_en/tab-2005-04-28-05-en.html

[v] National Statistical Office. Health statistics. http://www.spc.int/prism/country/pg/Stats/Pop_Soc_%20Stats/Social/Health/health.htm

[w] Central Statistical Office. Life tables of Poland 1995-2003. http://www.stat.gov.pl/english/dane_spol-gosp/ludnosc/trwanie/index.htm

[x] National Statistical Office. Abridged life tables. http://kosis.nso.go.kr/cgi-bin/sws_888.cgi?ID=DT_1B41&IDTYPE=3&A_LANG=2&FPUB=4&SELITEM=1.2

[y] Statistical Services Division, Ministry of Finance. Summary of population indicators. www.spc.int/prism/country/ws/stats/soc/Demographic.htm

[z] Statistical Office of the Republic of Slovenia (2004). Rapid Reports No 169: Population. www.stat.si

[aa] National Statistics Office. http://www.spc.int/prism/country/sb/stats/Social/Census1999.htm

[bb] Department of Census and Statistics. http://www.statistics.gov.lk/population/tables.pdf

[cc] National Statistical Office (1997). Report on the Survey of Population Change. Appendix Table 7.

[dd] Statistics Department. Tonga population census 1996: demographic analysis. http://www.spc.int/prism/country/to/stats/pdfs/census96/demo.pdf

[ee] State Institute of Statistics. Population and development indicators. http://nkg.die.gov.tr/en/goster.asp?aile=1

[ff] Government Actuary's Department. Interim life tables. http://www.gad.gov.uk/Life_Tables/Interim_life_tables.htm

[gg] National Centre for Health Statistics (2004). United States life tables, 2002. National vital statistics reports, Vol. 53, No. 6, p. 3. www.cdc.gov/nchs/data/nvsr/nvsr53/nvsr53_06.pdf.

[hh] National Statistics Office. Health indicators. http://www.spc.int/prism/country/vu/stats/Social/health_indicators.htm

TABLE 2. SOURCES OF DATA ON INFANT AND CHILD MORTALITY

Country name	Earlier period	Later period
Afghanistan	GG	..
Albania	DYB	DYB
Algeria	GG	DYB
Angola	..	MICS 2001
Argentina	GG	WHO
Armenia	..	DHS 2000
Australia	HLD	National[a]
Austria	HMD	DYB
Azerbaijan	..	Survey 2001[b]
Bahamas	DYB	DYB
Bahrain	DYB	DYB
Bangladesh	GG	DHS 2003-2004
Barbados	DYB	PVSR
Belarus	WHO	DYB
Belgium	DYB	National[c]
Belize	DYB	DYB
Benin	GG	DHS 2001
Bhutan	GG	Survey 2000[d]
Bolivia	GG	DHS 2003-2004
Bosnia and Herzegovina	..	DYB
Botswana	GG	MICS 2000
Brazil	GG	DHS 1996
Brunei Darussalam	..	PVSR
Bulgaria	HMD	HMD
Burkina Faso	GG	DHS 2003
Burundi	GG	MICS 2000
Cambodia	..	DHS 2000
Cameroon	GG	DHS 2004
Canada	DYB	DYB
Cape Verde	..	DYB
Central African Republic	GG	DHS 1994-1995
Chad	..	DHS 1996-1997
Channel Islands	..	DYB
Chile	GG	DYB
China	GG	Surveillance[e]
China, Hong Kong SAR	GG	DYB
China, Macao SAR	..	DYB
Colombia	GG	DHS 2000
Comoros	..	DHS 1996
Congo	GG	..
Costa Rica	GG	National[f]
Côte d'Ivoire	GG	DHS 1998-1999
Croatia	WHO	Eurostat
Cuba	GG	DYB
Cyprus	DYB	DYB

TABLE 2. (*continued*)

Country name	Earlier period	Later period
Czech Republic	HMD	National[g]
Democratic People's Republic of Korea	..	..
Democratic Republic of the Congo	..	MICS 2000
Democratic Republic of Timor-Leste	..	DHS 2003
Denmark	DYB	National[h]
Djibouti	..	Survey 2002[i]
Dominican Republic	GG	DHS 2002
Ecuador	GG	Survey 1999[j]
Egypt	GG	DHS 2000
El Salvador	GG	Survey 2002-2003[k]
Equatorial Guinea	..	MICS 2000
Eritrea	..	DHS 2002
Estonia	WHO	National[l]
Ethiopia	GG	DHS 2000
Fiji	DYB	National[m]
Finland	DYB	DYB
France	DYB	HMD
French Guiana	..	DYB
French Polynesia	..	National[n]
Gabon	..	DHS 2000
Gambia	..	MICS 2000
Georgia	WHO	Survey 1999[o]
Germany	HMD	National[p]
Ghana	GG	DHS 2003
Greece	DYB	Eurostat
Guadeloupe	DYB	DYB
Guam	DYB	PVSR
Guatemala	GG	DHS 1998-1999
Guinea	..	DHS 1999
Guinea-Bissau	..	MICS 2000
Guyana	DYB	MICS 2000
Haiti	GG	DHS 2000
Honduras	GG	Survey 2001[q]
Hungary	DYB	DYB
Iceland	DYB	DYB
India	GG	DHS 1998-1999
Indonesia	GG	DHS 2002-2003
Iran (Islamic Republic of)	..	DHS 2000
Iraq	GG	DYB
Ireland	DYB	National[r]
Israel	GG	DYB
Italy	DYB	National[s]

TABLE 2. (*continued*)

Country name	Earlier period	Later period
Jamaica	GG	DYB
Japan	HMD	DYB
Jordan	GG	DHS 2002
Kazakhstan	..	DHS 1999
Kenya	GG	DHS 2003
Kuwait	GG	DYB
Kyrgyzstan	..	DHS 1997
Lao People's Democratic Republic	..	Survey 2000[t]
Latvia	HMD	HMD
Lebanon	..	Survey 1996[u]
Lesotho	GG	Survey 2001[v]
Liberia	GG	..
Libyan Arab Jamahiriya	GG	..
Lithuania	HMD	HMD
Luxembourg	DYB	Eurostat
Madagascar	GG	DHS 2003-2004
Malawi	GG	DHS 2000
Malaysia	GG	DYB
Maldives	DYB	DYB
Mali	GG	DHS 2001
Malta	DYB	Eurostat
Martinique	DYB	DYB
Mauritania	GG	DHS 2000-2001
Mauritius	GG	DYB
Mexico	GG	WHO
Micronesia, Federated States of	..	Census 2000
Mongolia	..	Survey 1998[w]
Morocco	GG	DHS 2003-2004
Mozambique	GG	DHS 2003
Myanmar	GG	Survey 1999[x]
Namibia	GG	DHS 2000
Nepal	GG	DHS 2001
Netherlands	DYB	HMD
Netherlands Antilles	DYB	National[y]
New Caledonia	..	DYB
New Zealand	DYB	HMD
Nicaragua	GG	DHS 2001
Niger	GG	DHS 1998
Nigeria	GG	DHS 2003
Norway	DYB	National[z]
Occupied Palestinian Territory	..	DHS 2001
Oman	GG	Survey 1995[aa]

TABLE 2. (*continued*)

Country name	Earlier period	Later period
Pakistan	GG	Survey 2003[bb]
Panama	GG	DYB
Papua New Guinea	..	National[cc]
Paraguay	GG	Survey 2004[dd]
Peru	GG	DHS 2000
Philippines	GG	DHS 2003
Poland	HLD	National[ee]
Portugal	DYB	Eurostat
Puerto Rico	GG	DYB
Qatar	..	Survey 1998[ff]
Republic of Korea	GG	DYB
Republic of Moldova	WHO	DYB
Réunion	DYB	PVSR
Romania	WHO	DYB
Russian Federation	DYB	DYB
Rwanda	GG	DHS 2000
Saint Lucia	DYB	DYB
Saint Vincent and the Grenadines	DYB	DYB
Samoa	DYB	Survey 2000[gg]
Sao Tome and Principe	..	MICS 2000
Saudi Arabia	GG	Survey 1996[hh]
Senegal	GG	DHS 1999
Serbia and Montenegro	WHO	Eurostat
Sierra Leone	..	MICS 2000
Singapore	GG	DYB
Slovakia	WHO	DYB
Slovenia	HLD	National[ii]
Solomon Islands	..	Census 1999
Somalia	..	MICS 2000
South Africa	GG	DHS 1998
Spain	HMD	HMD
Sri Lanka	GG	DHS 1993
Sudan	GG	..
Suriname	DYB	PVSR
Swaziland	DYB	MICS 2000
Sweden	DYB	HMD
Switzerland	HMD	HMD
Syrian Arab Republic	GG	Survey 2001[jj]
Tajikistan	..	MICS 2000
Thailand	GG	Survey 1995-1996[kk]
The Fmr. Yugoslav Rep. of Macedonia	WHO	Eurostat
Togo	GG	DHS 1998
Tonga	..	National[ll]
Trinidad and Tobago	GG	WHO

TABLE 2. (*continued*)

Country name	Earlier period	Later period
Tunisia	GG	DYB
Turkey	GG	DHS 1998
Turkmenistan	..	DHS 2000
Uganda	GG	DHS 2000-2001
Ukraine	WHO	DYB
United Arab Emirates	GG	National[mm]
United Kingdom	WHO	National[nn]
United Republic of Tanzania	GG	DHS 1999
United States of America	DYB	National[oo]
United States Virgin Islands	..	DYB
Uruguay	GG	DYB
Uzbekistan	..	Survey 2002[pp]
Vanuatu	..	Census 1999
Venezuela	GG	DYB
Viet Nam	GG	DHS 2002
Western Sahara	..	..
Yemen	GG	DHS 1997
Zambia	GG	DHS 2001
Zimbabwe	GG	DHS 1999

NOTES:

[a] Australian Bureau of Statistics. Life tables, Australia 2001–2003. cat. no. 3302.0.55.001.

[b] Reproductive Health Survey 2001

[c] Statistics Belgium (2005). Démographie mathématique: Tables de mortalité. http://statbel.fgov.be/pub/d2/p238y2003_fr.pdf

[d] National Health Survey 2000

[e] Child Mortality Surveillance System

[f] Instituto Nacional de Estadística y Censos. Tablas abreviadas de mortalidad. http://www.inec.go.cr/

[g] Czech Statistical Office. Complete life tables 2004. http://www.czso.cz/eng/edicniplan.nsf/p/4002-05

[h] Statistics Denmark. StatBank Denmark, Table HISB8. http://www.statbank.dk/statbank5a/default.asp?w=1280

[i] Enquête Djiboutienne sur la Santé de la Famille 2002

[j] Encuesta Demográfica y de Salud Materna e Infantil 1999

[k] Encuesta Nacional de Salud Familiar 2002/03

[l] Statistical Office of Estonia. Statistical Database. Life expectancy by sex and age. http://pub.stat.ee/px-web.2001/I_Databas/Population/01Population_indicators_and_composition/02Main_demographic_indicators/02Main_demographic_indicators.asp

[m] Bureau of Statistics. Key statistics: June 2004. http://www.spc.int/prism/country/fj/stats/Social/popn.htm

[n] Institut Statistique de Polynésia Française. Démographie. http://www.ispf.pf/(0e5kzau2cwzkifi4hehx5y55)/index.aspx?choix=stat

[o] Reproductive Health Survey 1999

[p] Federal Statistical Office. Sterbetafel 2002/2004. http://www.destatis.de/download/d/bevoe/sterbet04.xls

[q] Encuesta Nacional de Epidemiología y Salud Familiar 2001

[r] Central Statistics Office (2004). Irish life tables No. 14 2001-2003. http://www.cso.ie/releasespublications/documents/births_d_m/current/irishlife.pdf

[s] ISTAT. Tavole di mortalità della popolazione italiana per provincia e regione di residenza - Anno 2002. http://demo.istat.it/tav2002/index.html

[t]   Reproductive Health Survey 2000
[u]   Maternal and Child Health Survey 1996
[v]   Demographic Survey 2001
[w]   Reproductive Health Survey 1998
[x]   National Mortality Survey 1999
[y]   Central Bureau of Statistics. Population. http://www.cbs.an/population/population_b8.asp
[z]   Statistics Norway. Life tables 2004. http://www.ssb.no/english/subjects/02/02/10/dode_en/tab-2005-04-28-05-en.html
[aa]   Family Health Survey 1995
[bb]   Demographic Survey 2003
[cc]   National Statistical Office. Health statistics.
       http://www.spc.int/prism/country/pg/Stats/Pop_Soc_%20Stats/Social/Health/health.htm
[dd]   Encuesta Nacional de Demografía y Salud Sexual y Reproductiva 2004
[ee]   Central Statistical Office. Life tables of Poland 1995-2003. http://www.stat.gov.pl/english/dane_spol-gosp/ludnosc/trwanie/index.htm
[ff]   Family Health Survey 1998
[gg]   Demographic and Vital Statistics Survey 2000
[hh]   Family Health Survey 1996
[ii]   Statistical Office of the Republic of Slovenia (2004). Rapid Reports No 169: Population. www.stat.si
[jj]   Family Health Survey 2001
[kk]   Survey of Population Change 1995-1996
[ll]   Statistics Department. Tonga population census 1996: demographic analysis.
       http://www.spc.int/prism/country/to/stats/pdfs/census96/demo.pdf
[mm]   Ministry of Planning. UAE in Figures 2003. http://www.uae.gov.ae/mop/UAE_figure/UAE_%2003.htm
[nn]   Government Actuary's Department. Interim Life Tables. http://www.gad.gov.uk/Life_Tables/Interim_life_tables.htm
[oo]   National Centre for Health Statistics (2004). United States life tables, 2002. National vital statistics reports, Vol. 53, No. 6, p. 3. www.cdc.gov/nchs/data/nvsr/nvsr53/nvsr53_06.pdf.
[pp]   Health Examination Survey 2002

III. COMPARATIVE TABLES

TABLE 3. LIFE EXPECTANCY AT BIRTH BY COUNTRY
(AS REPORTED IN NATIONAL AND OTHER SOURCES)

Country	Period	Life expectancy (years)		Period	Life expectancy (years)	
		Male	*Female*		*Male*	*Female*
Africa						
Eastern Africa						
Burundi	1970-1971	43.2	44.2	..	..	..
Comoros	..	..	..	..	..	..
Djibouti	..	..	..	..	..	..
Eritrea	..	..	..	..	..	..
Ethiopia	..	..	..	1994	49.8	51.8
Kenya	1969	46.9	51.2	..	..	..
Madagascar	1966	37.5	38.3	..	..	..
Malawi	1977	38.1	41.2	1992-1997	43.5	46.8
Mauritius	1971-1973	60.7	65.3	2002-2004	68.4	75.3
Mozambique	..	..	..	..	..	..
Réunion	1963-1967	55.8	62.4	2001	71.0	79.4
Rwanda	..	..	..	..	..	..
Somalia	..	..	..	..	..	..
Uganda	..	..	..	..	..	..
United Republic of Tanzania	1974	42.8	46.1	..	..	..
Zambia	1980	50.7	53.0	..	..	..
Zimbabwe	..	..	..	1990	58.0	62.0
Middle Africa						
Angola	..	..	..	..	..	..
Cameroon	1974	47.5	50.7	..	..	..
Central African Republic	..	..	..	..	..	..
Chad	..	..	..	..	..	..
Congo	..	..	..	..	..	..
Democratic Republic of the Congo	..	..	..	..	..	..
Equatorial Guinea	1981	44.9	47.8	..	..	..
Gabon	..	..	..	..	..	..
Sao Tome and Principe	..	..	..	..	..	..
Northern Africa						
Algeria	1969-1971	52.9	53.2	2000	72.5	74.2
Egypt	1965-1967	50.3	51.5	2001	65.6	67.4
Libyan Arab Jamahiriya	..	..	..	..	..	..
Morocco	1972	51.7	52.8	1987	63.7	66.4
Sudan	..	..	..	..	..	..
Tunisia	1968-1969	52.7	52.5	1995	69.6	73.1
Western Sahara	..	..	..	..	..	..
Southern Africa						
Botswana	1980-1981	52.7	59.3	2001	52.0	57.4
Lesotho	..	..	..	2001	48.7	56.3
Namibia	..	..	..	..	..	..
South Africa	1970	51.1	56.4	2004	49.9	52.9
Swaziland	1976	42.9	49.5	1997	58.0	63.0
Western Africa						
Benin	..	..	..	1992	51.8	56.8
Burkina Faso	..	..	..	..	..	..
Cape Verde	1979-1981	59.0	61.0	1990	63.5	71.3
Côte d'Ivoire	..	..	..	..	..	..
Gambia	1968-1973	32.3	35.7	..	..	..
Ghana	..	..	..	..	..	..
Guinea	..	..	..	..	..	..
Guinea-Bissau	..	..	..	..	..	..
Liberia	1971	45.8	44.0	..	..	..

TABLE 3. *(continued)*

Country	Period	Life expectancy (years)		Period	Life expectancy (years)	
		Male	*Female*		*Male*	*Female*
Mali	1976	46.9	49.7	1987	55.2	58.7
Mauritania	..	..	..	..	..	..
Niger..	..	..	..	..	..	..
Nigeria......................................	..	..	..	..	..	..
Senegal	1970	43.0	44.2	..	..	..
Sierra Leone	1974	32.9	35.8	..	..	..
Togo	1961	31.6	38.5	..	..	..
Asia						
Eastern Asia						
China	1973-1975	62.1	64.5	2000	69.6	73.3
China, Hong Kong SAR	1971	67.4	75.0	2003	78.5	84.3
China, Macao SAR..................	..	..	..	1993-1996	75.1	80.0
Dem. People's Rep. of Korea..............	..	..	..	..	..	..
Japan..	1970	69.3	74.7	2003	78.4	85.3
Mongolia	..	..	..	1996-2000	61.1	66.6
Republic of Korea	1970	59.8	66.7	2002	73.4	80.4
South-Central Asia						
Afghanistan	..	..	..	..	..	..
Bangladesh	1974	45.8	46.6	1994	58.7	58.3
Bhutan	..	..	..	..	..	..
India..	1961-1970	46.4	44.7	1993-1997	60.4	61.8
Iran (Islamic Republic of)......................	1973-1976	57.6	57.4	1996	66.1	68.4
Kazakhstan	1981	61.5	72.0	1997	59.0	70.2
Kyrgyzstan................................	1970	63.6	71.8	2002	64.4	72.1
Maldives	1982	53.4	49.5	1999	72.1	73.2
Nepal..	1981	50.9	48.1	2001	60.1	60.7
Pakistan	1976-1978	59.0	59.2	2001	64.5	66.1
Sri Lanka	1967	64.8	66.9	1991	68.9	73.6
Tajikistan..................................	1981	64.5	69.4	1991	67.6	73.2
Turkmenistan............................	1981	60.0	67.2	2002	64.9	71.8
Uzbekistan................................	1970	69.4	76.0	2002	67.6	72.5
South-Eastern Asia						
Brunei Darussalam	1970-1972	61.9	62.1	..	..	..
Cambodia	..	..	..	..	..	..
Dem. Rep. of Timor-Leste...................	..	..	..	..	..	..
Indonesia	1961-1971	37.4	40.0	..	..	..
Lao People's Democratic Republic.......	..	..	..	..	..	..
Malaysia	1970	58.6	62.1	2002	70.7	75.3
Myanmar	..	..	..	..	..	..
Philippines................................	1970	58.6	63.9	1991	63.1	66.7
Singapore..................................	1970	65.1	70.0	2003	76.9	80.9
Thailand....................................	1974-1975	57.6	63.6	1995-1996	70.0	75.0
Viet Nam	1979	63.7	67.9	..	..	..
Western Asia						
Armenia......................................	1970	69.9	75.8	2000	70.7	75.5
Azerbaijan	1977	65.5	73.4	2002	69.4	75.0
Bahrain	1976-1981	63.4	66.4	2001	73.2	76.2
Cyprus	1973	70.0	72.9	2002-2003	77.0	81.4
Georgia......................................	1981	66.8	74.7	2003	69.1	74.7
Iraq	1973-1974	59.9	59.9	1990	77.4	78.2
Israel..	1970	69.6	73.0	2003	77.7	81.9
Jordan..	1959-1963	52.6	52.0	2001	68.8	71.1
Kuwait.......................................	1970	66.4	71.5	1992-1993	71.8	73.3

TABLE 3. *(continued)*

Country	Period	Life expectancy (years)		Period	Life expectancy (years)	
		Male	*Female*		*Male*	*Female*
Lebanon..	..	..	..	..	..	..
Occupied Palestinian Territory.............	..	..	..	2001	70.5	73.6
Oman...	..	..	..	2002	72.2	75.4
Qatar...	..	..	..	..	..	..
Saudi Arabia.....................................	..	..	..	..	..	..
Syrian Arab Republic........................	1970	54.5	58.7	..	..	..
Turkey..	1974-1975	55.2	58.3	2003	66.4	71.0
United Arab Emirates........................	..	..	..	..	..	..
Yemen...	..	..	..	..	..	..
Europe						
Eastern Europe						
Belarus...	1970-1971	68.0	76.0	2002	62.3	74.1
Bulgaria..	1970	69.1	73.5	2003	68.9	76.0
Czech Republic.................................	1970	66.1	73.0	2004	72.5	79.0
Hungary..	1972	66.9	72.6	2003	68.3	76.5
Poland...	1970-1971	66.8	73.8	2004	70.7	79.2
Republic of Moldova..........................	1981	62.5	69.4	2002	64.4	71.7
Romania..	1970	65.7	70.2	2002	67.6	74.9
Russian Federation............................	1970	63.1	73.4	2004	58.9	72.3
Slovakia..	1970	66.7	72.9	2002	69.9	77.6
Ukraine...	1970-1971	67.0	74.0	2002-2003	62.6	74.1
Northern Europe						
Channel Islands.................................	..	..	..	..	..	..
Denmark..	1970-1971	70.7	75.9	2003-2004	75.2	79.9
Estonia..	1970	65.5	74.1	2003	66.0	76.9
Finland..	1971	65.9	74.2	2003	75.1	81.8
Iceland..	1971-1975	71.6	77.5	2002-2003	79.0	82.4
Ireland..	1970-1972	68.8	73.5	2001-2003	75.1	80.3
Latvia...	1970	65.7	74.2	2003	65.9	76.1
Lithuania..	1970	66.8	75.0	2003	66.5	77.8
Norway...	1971-1972	71.2	77.4	2004	77.5	82.3
Sweden...	1969-1973	72.0	77.3	2003	77.9	82.4
United Kingdom................................	1970	68.5	74.9	2001-2003	75.9	80.5
Southern Europe						
Albania...	1965-1967	64.9	67.0	2000	72.5	77.3
Bosnia and Herzegovina......................	..	..	..	1988-1989	69.2	74.6
Croatia..	1982	66.0	73.9	2000	70.5	77.8
Greece...	1970	70.1	73.6	2000	75.4	80.5
Italy..	1970-1972	69.0	74.9	2002	77.1	83.0
Malta..	1973	68.1	72.0	2003	76.4	80.4
Portugal..	1970	64.2	70.5	2002	73.8	80.5
Serbia and Montenegro......................	1982	67.8	72.6	2001	70.7	75.6
Slovenia..	1970-1972	65.9	73.4	2000-2002	72.3	80.2
Spain...	1970	69.7	75.0	2002	76.2	83.1
TFYR of Macedonia...........................	1970	65.6	67.6	2001	71.0	76.0
Western Europe						
Austria..	1970	66.5	73.4	2003	75.9	81.6
Belgium..	1968-1972	67.8	74.2	2003	75.9	81.7
France...	1971	68.5	76.1	2002	75.8	83.0
Germany...	1970	67.5	73.6	2002-2004	75.9	81.5
Luxembourg......................................	1971-1973	67.0	73.9	2002	74.9	81.5
Netherlands.......................................	1971	71.0	76.7	2003	76.2	80.9
Switzerland.......................................	1970	70.0	76.2	2003	77.9	83.1

TABLE 3. *(continued)*

Country	Period	Life expectancy (years)		Period	Life expectancy (years)	
		Male	Female		Male	Female
Latin America and the Caribbean						
Caribbean						
Bahamas	1969-1971	64.0	69.3	1989-1991	68.3	75.3
Barbados	1970-1980	67.2	72.5	..	..	..
Cuba	1969-1971	70.3	73.7	2001-2003	75.0	78.0
Dominican Republic	1965	52.6	56.0	1995-2000	69.9	73.1
Guadeloupe	1963-1967	62.5	67.3	2002	74.6	81.5
Haiti	1970-1971	47.6	48.3	..	..	..
Jamaica	1969-1971	65.8	70.1	2000-2002	72.8	76.5
Martinique	1963-1967	63.3	67.4	2002	75.4	82.2
Netherlands Antilles	1966-1970	58.9	65.7	1998-2002	72.1	78.7
Puerto Rico	1969-1971	69.0	75.2	2002	73.2	80.9
Saint Lucia	1959-1961	55.1	58.5	2002	72.0	76.7
Saint Vincent and the Grenadines	1959-1961	58.5	59.7	..	..	..
Trinidad and Tobago	1970	64.1	68.1	1997	68.0	73.0
United States Virgin Islands	..	..	..	..	..	..
Central America						
Belize	1980	69.9	71.8	1991	70.0	74.1
Costa Rica	1972-1974	66.3	70.5	2004	76.5	81.0
El Salvador	1970-1972	54.8	59.9	1995-2000	66.5	72.5
Guatemala	1972-1973	53.7	55.5	1995-2000	61.4	67.2
Honduras	1973-1975	50.2	54.3	..	..	..
Mexico	1970	59.4	63.4	1998	71.4	76.8
Nicaragua	..	..	..	2000-2005	67.2	71.9
Panama	1970	64.3	67.5	2000	72.2	76.8
South America						
Argentina	1969-1971	61.9	69.7	1997	69.8	77.4
Bolivia	1970-1975	46.0	49.0	1995-2000	59.8	63.2
Brazil	1960-1970	57.6	61.1	2002	67.3	74.9
Chile	1969-1970	60.5	66.0	2001-2002	74.4	80.4
Colombia	1973	57.1	60.8	2002-2007	69.6	75.7
Ecuador	1970-1975	57.4	60.5	2000-2005	71.3	77.2
French Guiana	..	..	..	2002	72.5	79.2
Guyana	1970	61.4	66.2	..	..	..
Paraguay	..	..	..	2000-2005	68.6	73.1
Peru	1970	53.6	57.6	1995-2000	65.9	70.9
Suriname	1980	64.7	71.0	..	..	..
Uruguay	1974-1976	65.7	72.5	2003	71.3	79.2
Venezuela	1974	64.5	69.4	1995-2000	68.6	74.5
Northern America						
Canada	1970-1972	69.3	76.4	2002	77.2	82.1
United States of America	1971	67.4	74.8	2002	74.5	79.9
Oceania						
Australia/New Zealand						
Australia	1970-1972	67.8	74.5	2001-2003	77.8	82.8
New Zealand	1970-1972	68.6	74.6	2003	77.0	81.4
Melanesia						
Fiji	1976	60.7	63.9	1996	64.5	68.7
New Caledonia	1981	62.8	70.8	2003	71.3	77.3
Papua New Guinea	..	..	..	2000	53.7	54.8
Solomon Islands	1980-1984	59.9	61.4	1999	60.6	61.6
Vanuatu	..	..	..	1999	65.6	69.0

TABLE 3. *(continued)*

Country	Period	Life expectancy (years)		Period	Life expectancy (years)	
		Male	*Female*		*Male*	*Female*
Micronesia						
Guam....................................	1979-1981	69.5	75.6	1988-1992	69.8	74.4
Micronesia, Federated States of...........	..	..	..	1991-1992	64.4	66.8
Polynesia						
French Polynesia	..	..	..	2004	71.5	76.7
Samoa...................................	1971	59.6	63.4	2001	71.8	73.8
Tonga...................................	..	..	..	1996	69.8	71.8

TABLE 4. SURVIVAL PROBABILITY FROM AGE 15 TO AGE 60 BY COUNTRY,
(AS REPORTED IN NATIONAL AND OTHER SOURCES)

Country	Period	Survival probability Male	Female	Period	Survival probability Male	Female
Africa						
Eastern Africa						
Burundi	1970-1971	0.51	0.58	..	..	..
Comoros	..	..	..	..	..	..
Djibouti	..	..	..	..	..	..
Eritrea	..	..	..	..	..	..
Ethiopia	..	..	..	..	..	..
Kenya	1969	0.61	0.67	..	..	..
Madagascar	1972	0.63	0.69	..	..	..
Malawi	1977	0.55	0.61	1992-1997	0.59	0.65
Mauritius	1971-1973	0.74	0.82	2002-2004	0.77	0.88
Mozambique	..	..	..	..	..	..
Réunion	1963-1967	0.62	0.78	..	..	..
Rwanda	..	..	..	..	..	..
Somalia	..	..	..	..	..	..
Uganda	..	..	..	..	..	..
United Republic of Tanzania	1974	0.58	0.64	..	..	..
Zambia	1980	0.64	0.69	..	..	..
Zimbabwe	..	..	..	1990	0.70	0.76
Middle Africa						
Angola	..	..	..	..	..	..
Cameroon	1974	0.59	0.65	..	..	..
Central African Republic	..	..	..	..	..	..
Chad	..	..	..	..	..	..
Congo	..	..	..	..	..	..
Democratic Republic of the Congo	..	..	..	..	..	..
Equatorial Guinea	1981	0.56	0.62	..	..	..
Gabon	..	..	..	..	..	..
Sao Tome and Principe	..	..	..	..	..	..
Northern Africa						
Algeria	1969-1971	0.76	0.80	2000	0.89	0.91
Egypt	1965-1967	0.73	0.82	2001	0.81	0.87
Libyan Arab Jamahiriya	..	..	..	..	..	..
Morocco	1972	0.70	0.70	..	..	..
Sudan	..	..	..	..	..	..
Tunisia	1968-1969	0.73	0.75	1995	0.84	0.90
Western Sahara	..	..	..	..	..	..
Southern Africa						
Botswana	1980-1981	0.65	0.76	..	..	..
Lesotho	..	..	..	..	..	..
Namibia	..	..	..	..	..	..
South Africa	1970	0.61	0.72	..	..	..
Swaziland	1976	0.53	0.66	..	..	..
Western Africa						
Benin	..	..	..	..	..	..
Burkina Faso	..	..	..	..	..	..
Cape Verde	..	..	..	1990	0.71	0.87
Côte d'Ivoire	..	..	..	..	..	..
Gambia	1968-1973	0.43	0.47	..	..	..
Ghana	..	..	..	..	..	..
Guinea	..	..	..	..	..	..
Guinea-Bissau	..	..	..	..	..	..
Liberia	1971	0.53	0.58	..	..	..

TABLE 4. *(continued)*

Country	Period	Survival probability Male	Survival probability Female	Period	Survival probability Male	Survival probability Female
Mali	1976	0.72	0.72	1987	0.75	0.77
Mauritania	..	..	..	..	..	..
Niger	..	..	..	..	..	..
Nigeria	..	..	..	..	..	..
Senegal	1970	0.64	0.64	..	..	..
Sierra Leone	1974	0.48	0.50	..	..	..
Togo	1961	0.35	0.50	..	..	..
Asia						
Eastern Asia						
China	1973-1975	0.78	0.81	..	..	..
China, Hong Kong SAR	1971	0.78	0.88	2003	0.91	0.96
China, Macao SAR	..	..	..	1993-1996	0.90	0.94
Dem. People's Rep. of Korea	..	..	..	..	..	..
Japan	1970	0.83	0.90	2003	0.90	0.96
Mongolia	..	..	..	1996-2000	0.69	0.78
Republic of Korea	1970	0.76	0.81	2001	0.85	0.94
South-Central Asia						
Afghanistan	..	..	..	..	..	..
Bangladesh	1974	0.60	0.60	1994	0.75	0.73
Bhutan	..	..	..	..	..	..
India	1961-1970	0.55	0.53	1993-1997	0.74	0.77
Iran (Islamic Republic of)	1973-1976	0.77	0.79	..	..	..
Kazakhstan	..	..	..	..	..	..
Kyrgyzstan	..	..	..	2002	0.71	0.86
Maldives	1982	0.71	0.60	1992	0.81	0.78
Nepal	1981	0.62	0.62	..	..	..
Pakistan	1976-1978	0.78	0.78	..	..	..
Sri Lanka	1967	0.80	0.85	..	..	..
Tajikistan	..	..	..	1991	0.81	0.87
Turkmenistan	..	..	..	..	..	..
Uzbekistan	..	..	..	..	..	..
South-Eastern Asia						
Brunei Darussalam	1970-1972	0.76	0.72	..	..	..
Cambodia	..	..	..	..	..	..
Dem. Rep. of Timor-Leste	..	..	..	..	..	..
Indonesia	1961-1971	0.43	0.47	..	..	..
Lao People's Democratic Republic	..	..	..	..	..	..
Malaysia	1970	0.69	0.75	2002	0.83	0.91
Myanmar	..	..	..	..	..	..
Philippines	1970	0.70	0.79	1991	0.76	0.81
Singapore	1970	0.77	0.86	2003	0.91	0.95
Thailand	1970	0.67	0.74	1995-1996	0.80	0.85
Viet Nam	..	..	..	..	..	..
Western Asia						
Armenia	..	..	..	1998	0.81	0.92
Azerbaijan	..	..	..	..	..	..
Bahrain	1976-1981	0.76	0.81	2001	0.89	0.92
Cyprus	1973	0.85	0.90	2002-2003	0.91	0.95
Georgia	1981	0.78	0.90	2003	0.80	0.91
Iraq	1973-1974	0.77	0.77	1990	0.86	0.94
Israel	1972	0.84	0.89	2003	0.91	0.95
Jordan	1959-1963	0.65	0.69	..	..	..
Kuwait	1970	0.80	0.89	1992-1993	0.86	0.91

TABLE 4. *(continued)*

Country	Period	Survival probability		Period	Survival probability	
		Male	*Female*		*Male*	*Female*
Lebanon..	..	..	..	..	..	..
Occupied Palestinian Territory............	..	..	..	..	..	..
Oman..	..	..	..	..	..	..
Qatar..	..	..	..	..	..	..
Saudi Arabia....................................	..	..	..	..	..	..
Syrian Arab Republic.......................	1970	0.73	0.80	..	..	..
Turkey...	1974-1975	0.75	0.79	..	..	..
United Arab Emirates........................	..	..	..	..	..	..
Yemen...	..	..	..	..	..	..
Europe						
Eastern Europe						
Belarus...	1981	0.72	0.89	2002	0.62	0.86
Bulgaria...	1970	0.82	0.90	2003	0.78	0.91
Czech Republic................................	1970	0.77	0.89	2004	0.84	0.93
Hungary...	1972	0.80	0.88	2002	0.74	0.89
Poland..	1970-1971	0.79	0.90	2004	0.79	0.92
Republic of Moldova........................	1981	0.70	0.83	2002	0.70	0.85
Romania...	1970	0.81	0.88	2002	0.76	0.89
Russian Federation...........................	1970	0.69	0.88	2004	0.53	0.83
Slovakia...	1982	0.76	0.90	2002	0.79	0.92
Ukraine..	1981	0.70	0.88	2002-2003	0.63	0.86
Northern Europe						
Channel Islands................................	..	..	..	..	..	..
Denmark...	1970-1971	0.84	0.89	2003-2004	0.88	0.93
Estonia...	1981	0.69	0.88	2003	0.70	0.89
Finland...	1971	0.74	0.90	2003	0.87	0.94
Iceland...	1971-1975	0.82	0.90	2001	0.92	0.95
Ireland...	1970-1972	0.82	0.88	2001-2003	0.89	0.94
Latvia...	1970	0.74	0.88	2003	0.70	0.88
Lithuania..	1970	0.75	0.89	2003	0.70	0.89
Norway..	1971-1972	0.85	0.93	2004	0.91	0.94
Sweden..	1969-1973	0.86	0.92	2003	0.92	0.95
United Kingdom...............................	1970	0.82	0.89	2001-2003	0.89	0.93
Southern Europe						
Albania..	1960-1961	0.82	0.88	2000	0.89	0.94
Bosnia and Herzegovina....................	..	..	..	1988-1989	0.80	0.90
Croatia...	1982	0.75	0.89	2000	0.82	0.93
Greece...	1970	0.88	0.92	1999	0.88	0.95
Italy...	1970-1972	0.83	0.91	2002	0.91	0.95
Malta...	1973	0.84	0.90	2003	0.92	0.95
Portugal...	1970	0.80	0.89	2002	0.85	0.94
Serbia and Montenegro.....................	1982	0.81	0.90	2001	0.82	0.90
Slovenia...	1970-1972	0.75	0.89	2000-2002	0.83	0.93
Spain...	1970	0.84	0.90	2002	0.88	0.95
TFYR of Macedonia.........................	1982	0.85	0.91	2001	0.84	0.92
Western Europe						
Austria...	1970	0.79	0.89	2003	0.88	0.94
Belgium...	1968-1972	0.81	0.89	2003	0.88	0.94
France..	1971	0.79	0.90	2002	0.86	0.94
Germany..	1970	0.81	0.89	2002-2004	0.88	0.94
Luxembourg.....................................	1971-1973	0.78	0.88	2002	0.88	0.94
Netherlands......................................	1971	0.84	0.92	2003	0.91	0.93
Switzerland......................................	1970	0.83	0.91	2003	0.91	0.95

TABLE 4. *(continued)*

Country	Period	Survival probability		Period	Survival probability	
		Male	*Female*		*Male*	*Female*
Latin America and the Caribbean						
Caribbean						
Bahamas	1969-1971	0.70	0.78	1989-1991	0.75	0.86
Barbados	1959-1961	0.79	0.83	..	..	..
Cuba	1969-1971	0.85	0.88	2001-2003	0.87	0.91
Dominican Republic	1965	0.63	0.69	1995-2000	0.83	0.88
Guadeloupe	1963-1967	0.72	0.80	2002	0.85	0.94
Haiti	..	..	..	..	..	..
Jamaica	1969-1971	0.78	0.83	2000-2002	0.82	0.87
Martinique	1963-1967	0.73	0.76	2002	0.88	0.95
Netherlands Antilles	1966-1970	0.69	0.79	..	..	..
Puerto Rico	1969-1971	0.79	0.89	2002	0.82	0.92
Saint Lucia	1959-1961	0.70	0.76	2002	0.79	0.89
Saint Vincent and the Grenadines	1959-1961	0.80	0.82	..	..	..
Trinidad and Tobago	1970	0.77	0.82	1997	0.78	0.85
United States Virgin Islands	..	..	..	..	..	..
Central America						
Belize	1980	0.83	0.88	1991	0.82	0.88
Costa Rica	1972-1974	0.81	0.87	2004	0.89	0.94
El Salvador	1970-1972	0.72	0.80	1995-2000	0.76	0.85
Guatemala	1972-1973	0.68	0.72	1995-2000	0.69	0.80
Honduras	1973-1975	0.63	0.71	..	..	..
Mexico	1970	0.70	0.78	1998	0.81	0.89
Nicaragua	..	..	..	2000-2005	0.77	0.85
Panama	1970	0.80	0.81	2000	0.86	0.91
South America						
Argentina	1969-1971	0.73	0.86	1997	0.81	0.90
Bolivia	1970-1975	0.67	0.69	1995-2000	0.73	0.78
Brazil	1960-1970	0.72	0.77	2002	0.75	0.87
Chile	1969-1970	0.71	0.82	1999	0.85	0.92
Colombia	1973	0.71	0.77	2002-2007	0.82	0.89
Ecuador	1970-1975	0.74	0.78	2000-2005	0.81	0.89
French Guiana	..	..	..	2002	0.83	0.92
Guyana	1959-1961	0.67	0.73	..	..	..
Paraguay	..	..	..	..	..	..
Peru	1970	0.74	0.79	1995-2000	0.80	0.87
Suriname	1980	0.75	0.85	..	..	..
Uruguay	1974-1976	0.78	0.88	2003	0.83	0.92
Venezuela	1974	0.76	0.84	1995-2000	0.81	0.89
Northern America						
Canada	1970-1972	0.81	0.90	2002	0.90	0.94
United States of America	1971	0.77	0.87	2002	0.86	0.92
Oceania						
Australia/New Zealand						
Australia	1970-1972	0.80	0.89	2001-2003	0.91	0.95
New Zealand	1970-1972	0.81	0.89	2003	0.90	0.93
Melanesia						
Fiji	1976	0.73	0.78	..	..	..
New Caledonia	..	..	..	2003	0.83	0.89
Papua New Guinea	..	..	..	..	..	..
Solomon Islands	..	..	..	..	..	..
Vanuatu	..	..	..	..	..	..

TABLE 4. *(continued)*

Country	Period	Survival probability		Period	Survival probability	
		Male	*Female*		*Male*	*Female*
Micronesia						
Guam	..	..	..	..	..	..
Micronesia, Federated States of	..	..	..	1991-1992	0.78	0.81
Polynesia						
French Polynesia	..	..	..	2004	0.85	0.91
Samoa	1971	0.71	0.77	..	..	..
Tonga	..	..	..	1996	0.84	0.89

TABLE 5. INFANT MORTALITY RATE BY SEX, BY COUNTRY
(AS REPORTED IN NATIONAL AND OTHER SOURCES)

Country	Period	Infant mortality rate (deaths per 1000 live births)			Period	Infant mortality rate (deaths per 1000 live births)		
		Male	Female	Total		Male	Female	Total
Africa								
Eastern Africa								
Burundi	1982	126	100	113	1997	..	..	127
Comoros	..	..	..	..	1986-1996	93	75	84
Djibouti	..	..	..	..	1997-2002	..	..	103
Eritrea	..	..	..	..	1992-2002	64	50	58
Ethiopia	..	..	..	..	1990-2000	124	101	113
Kenya	1973	96	86	91	1993-2003	84	67	76
Madagascar	1987	100	100	100	1993-2003	75	64	70
Malawi	..	..	..	..	1990-2000	117	108	113
Mauritius	1975	57	45	51	2002-2004	17	12	15
Mozambique	..	..	..	..	1993-2003	128	120	124
Réunion	1972-1976	48	36	42	2003	..	..	7
Rwanda	1973	140	123	132	1990-2000	123	112	117
Somalia	..	..	..	..	1996	..	..	140
Uganda	1983	113	104	109	1990-2000	93	86	89
United Republic of Tanzania	1978	124	109	117	1989-1999	118	97	108
Zambia	..	..	..	..	1991-2001	95	93	94
Zimbabwe	..	..	..	..	1989-1999	63	56	60
Middle Africa								
Angola	..	..	..	..	1997	..	..	150
Cameroon	1973	126	116	121	1994-2004	88	74	81
Central African Republic	..	..	..	..	1984-1994	109	94	102
Chad	..	..	..	..	1986-1996	120	100	110
Congo	1975	89	81	85	..	..	..	..
Democratic Republic of the Congo	..	..	..	..	1997	..	..	136
Equatorial Guinea	..	..	..	..	1996	..	..	110
Gabon	..	..	..	..	1990-2000	74	49	61
Sao Tome and Principe	..	..	..	..	1996	..	..	75
Northern Africa								
Algeria	1975	113	109	111	2000	36	33	35
Egypt	1975	139	139	139	1990-2000	55	55	55
Libyan Arab Jamahiriya	1975	101	99	100	..	..	..	..
Morocco	1972	122	111	117	1993-2003	51	37	44
Sudan	1973	109	91	100	..	..	..	..
Tunisia	1975	101	95	98	1995	34	27	31
Western Sahara	..	..	..	..	..	..	..	..
Southern Africa								
Botswana	1982	60	43	52	1996	..	..	61
Lesotho	1972	129	120	125	1998	..	..	76
Namibia	1987	75	64	70	1990-2000	45	34	40
South Africa	1987	50	40	45	1988-1998	49	35	42
Swaziland	1976	165	146	156	1996	..	..	86
Western Africa								
Benin	1975	143	127	135	1991-2001	98	92	95
Burkina Faso	1985	128	111	120	1993-2003	96	89	92
Cape Verde	..	..	..	..	1990	38	35	36
Côte d'Ivoire	1975	145	117	131	1988-1998	130	93	112
Gambia	..	..	..	..	1996	..	..	92
Ghana	1975	113	92	103	1993-2003	70	59	65
Guinea	..	..	..	..	1989-1999	112	101	107
Guinea-Bissau	..	..	..	..	1996	..	..	142
Liberia	1970	187	168	178	..	..	..	..

TABLE 5. *(continued)*

Country	Period	Infant mortality rate (deaths per 1000 live births)			Period	Infant mortality rate (deaths per 1000 live births)		
		Male	Female	Total		Male	Female	Total
Mali	1982	167	148	158	1991-2001	136	116	126
Mauritania	1975	114	104	109	1990-2000	75	59	67
Niger	1987	193	189	191	1988-1998	141	131	136
Nigeria	1975	128	108	118	1993-2003	116	102	109
Senegal	1973	171	148	160	1989-1999	74	66	70
Sierra Leone	..	..	..	..	1995	..	..	185
Togo	1983	109	94	102	1988-1998	89	71	80
Asia								
Eastern Asia								
China	1985	36	34	35	2003	..	..	26
China, Hong Kong SAR	1975	15	12	14	2003	2	2	2
China, Macao SAR	..	..	..	..	1993-1996	8	7	7
Dem. People's Rep. of Korea	..	..	..	..	..	..	..	..
Japan	1970	15	12	13	2003	3	3	3
Mongolia	..	..	..	..	1988-1998	81	57	69
Republic of Korea	1973	38	32	35	2001	6	6	6
South-Central Asia								
Afghanistan	1978	215	203	209	..	..	..	..
Bangladesh	1970	158	132	145	1994-2003	80	64	..
Bhutan	1983	111	103	107	2000	..	..	61
India	1977	116	124	120	1988-1998	75	71	73
Iran (Islamic Republic of)	..	..	..	..	2000	33	24	29
Kazakhstan	..	..	..	..	1989-1999	62	47	55
Kyrgyzstan	..	..	..	..	1987-1997	72	60	66
Maldives	..	..	..	..	1992	32	25	28
Nepal	1970	157	151	154	1991-2001	79	75	77
Pakistan	1975	114	101	108	2003	81	71	76
Sri Lanka	1975	51	41	46	1983-1993	31	20	25
Tajikistan	..	..	..	..	1997	..	..	95
Turkmenistan	..	..	..	..	1990-2000	83	60	72
Uzbekistan	..	..	..	..	1992-2002	67	59	63
South-Eastern Asia								
Brunei Darussalam	1970-1972	61	46	54	2004	..	..	9
Cambodia	..	..	..	..	1990-2000	103	82	93
Dem. Rep. of Timor-Leste	..	..	..	..	1998-2003	..	..	60
Indonesia	1970	120	91	106	1992-2002	46	40	43
Lao People's Democratic Republic	..	..	..	..	1995-1999	..	..	82
Malaysia	1975	36	28	32	2002	9	7	8
Myanmar	1982	99	77	88	1999	67	52	60
Philippines	1973	63	54	59	1993-2003	35	25	30
Singapore	1975	17	12	15	2003	3	2	3
Thailand	1972	110	90	100	1995-1996	27	25	26
Viet Nam	1985	40	34	37	1992-2002	25	25	25
Western Asia								
Armenia	..	..	..	..	1990-2000	46	42	44
Azerbaijan	..	..	..	..	1991-2000	84	78	81
Bahrain	1976-1981	53	49	51	2001	10	7	8
Cyprus	1973	25	31	27	2002-2003	4	4	4
Georgia	1981	33	26	29	1990-1999	48	32	41
Iraq	1973	86	77	82	1990	17	15	16
Israel	1975	24	20	22	2003	5	5	5
Jordan	1970	76	81	78	1992-2002	25	23	24
Kuwait	1975	39	33	36	1992-1993	13	10	11

TABLE 5. *(continued)*

Country	Period	Infant mortality rate (deaths per 1000 live births)			Period	Infant mortality rate (deaths per 1000 live births)		
		Male	*Female*	*Total*		*Male*	*Female*	*Total*
Lebanon	..	..	..	..	1991-1996	28	28	28
Occupied Palestinian Territory	..	..	..	..	1999-2003	27	22	24
Oman	1978	78	66	72	1985-1995	21	19	20
Qatar	..	..	..	..	1993-1998	..	..	10
Saudi Arabia	..	..	..	..	1992-1996	21	22	21
Syrian Arab Republic	1972	80	80	80	1996-2001	..	..	18
Turkey	1973	147	135	141	1988-1998	51	46	48
United Arab Emirates	..	..	..	..	2003	..	..	8
Yemen	1975	165	146	156	1987-1997	98	80	90
Europe								
Eastern Europe								
Belarus	1981	19	13	16	2002	8	7	8
Bulgaria	1970	31	23	27	2003	14	11	13
Czech Republic	1970	23	18	21	2004	4	3	4
Hungary	1972	37	29	33	2002	7	7	7
Poland	1970-1971	31	24	28	2004	7	6	7
Republic of Moldova	1981	40	29	35	2002	17	14	16
Romania	1970	51	42	47	2002	20	16	18
Russian Federation	1970	26	19	22	2004	13	10	12
Slovakia	1982	20	15	18	2002	7	8	8
Ukraine	1981	18	14	16	2002-2003	13	9	11
Northern Europe								
Channel Islands	..	..	..	..	1994	..	..	3
Denmark	1970-1971	17	11	14	2003-2004	5	4	4
Estonia	1981	19	15	17	2003	8	5	7
Finland	1971	15	11	13	2002	3	3	3
Iceland	1971-1975	14	9	11	2001	3	2	2
Ireland	1970-1972	21	17	19	2001-2003	7	5	6
Latvia	1970	22	14	18	2003	11	8	10
Lithuania	1970	22	17	20	2003	8	6	7
Norway	1971-1972	14	10	12	2004	3	3	3
Sweden	1969-1973	13	9	11	2003	4	3	3
United Kingdom	1970	21	16	19	2001-2003	6	5	5
Southern Europe								
Albania	1960-1961	80	85	83	2000	23	23	23
Bosnia and Herzegovina	..	..	..	..	1988-1989	20	17	19
Croatia	1982	22	15	19	2000	8	7	7
Greece	1970	42	35	39	1999	7	6	6
Italy	1970-1972	31	25	28	2002	5	4	4
Malta	1973	28	19	24	2002	5	3	4
Portugal	1970	63	53	58	2002	5	5	5
Serbia and Montenegro	1982	38	35	36	2001	15	11	13
Slovenia	1970-1972	26	22	24	2000-2002	6	4	5
Spain	1970	31	25	28	2002	5	4	4
TFYR of Macedonia	1982	51	49	50	2001	14	10	12
Western Europe								
Austria	1970	28	21	25	2002	5	3	4
Belgium	1968-1972	24	18	21	2003	4	3	3
France	1971	16	12	14	2002	5	4	4
Germany	1970	24	19	21	2002-2004	5	4	4
Luxembourg	1971-1973	20	14	17	2002	5	5	5
Netherlands	1971	14	11	12	2003	5	4	5
Switzerland	1970	17	13	15	2003	4	4	4

TABLE 5. *(continued)*

Country	Period	Infant mortality rate (deaths per 1000 live births)			Period	Infant mortality rate (deaths per 1000 live births)		
		Male	Female	Total		Male	Female	Total
Latin America and the Caribbean								
Caribbean								
Bahamas	1969-1971	39	31	35	1989-1991	22	16	19
Barbados	1959-1961	78	66	72	2002	..	..	14
Cuba	1975	31	25	28	2001-2003	7	6	6
Dominican Republic	1970	100	84	92	1992-2002	38	31	35
Guadeloupe	1963-1967	53	43	48	2002	8	6	7
Haiti	1970	158	141	150	1990-2000	97	83	89
Jamaica	1970	53	43	48	2000-2002	18	18	18
Martinique	1963-1967	48	43	46	2002	7	5	6
Netherlands Antilles	1966-1970	64	53	59	2003	..	..	9
Puerto Rico	1972	30	22	26	2002	10	8	9
Saint Lucia	1959-1961	110	104	107	2002	13	15	14
Saint Vincent and the Grenadines	1959-1961	118	113	115	2002	..	..	18
Trinidad and Tobago	1972	51	41	46	1997	21	18	20
United States Virgin Islands	..	..	..	..	1993	..	..	12
Central America								
Belize	1980	36	33	35	1991	35	35	35
Costa Rica	1972	56	44	50	2004	10	8	9
El Salvador	1980	97	82	90	1997-2002	26	22	24
Guatemala	1975	113	97	105	1988-1998	50	48	49
Honduras	1978	92	70	81	1996-2000	..	..	34
Mexico	1975	76	62	69	1998	21	17	19
Nicaragua	1980	103	83	93	1991-2001	39	32	35
Panama	1975	44	34	39	2000	22	19	21
South America								
Argentina	1970	63	53	58	1997	21	17	19
Bolivia	..	..	..	..	1993-2003	71	64	68
Brazil	1977	86	65	76	1986-1996	52	44	48
Chile	1972	73	62	68	1999	14	11	13
Colombia	1972	72	58	65	1990-2000	29	20	24
Ecuador	1975	82	70	76	1994-1999	37	24	30
French Guiana	..	..	..	..	2002	11	9	10
Guyana	1959-1961	59	50	55	1996	..	..	58
Paraguay	1975	54	52	53	..	..	..	..
Peru	1973	118	104	111	1990-2000	46	40	43
Suriname	1980	50	36	43	2002	..	..	15
Uruguay	1975	52	42	47	2003	17	12	14
Venezuela	1975	51	41	46	1995-2000	24	20	22
Northern America								
Canada	1970-1972	20	15	18	2002	6	5	5
United States of America	1971	21	17	19	2002	8	6	7
Oceania								
Australia/New Zealand								
Australia	1970-1972	19	15	17	2001-2003	6	4	5
New Zealand	1970-1972	18	15	16	2003	6	4	5
Melanesia								
Fiji	1976	37	28	33	1996	22	23	22
New Caledonia	..	..	..	..	2003	7	4	6
Papua New Guinea	..	..	..	..	2000	67	61	64
Solomon Islands	..	..	..	..	1999	..	..	66
Vanuatu	..	..	..	..	1999	27	26	27

TABLE 5. *(continued)*

Country	Period	Infant mortality rate (deaths per 1000 live births)			Period	Infant mortality rate (deaths per 1000 live births)		
		Male	Female	Total		Male	Female	Total
Micronesia								
Guam	1970	26	17	22	2004	..	..	12
Micronesia, Federated States of.......	..	..	..	..	2000	..	..	40
Polynesia								
French Polynesia	..	..	..	..	2004	4	4	4
Samoa	1971	71	55	64	2000	..	..	18
Tonga	..	..	..	..	1996	19	17	18

TABLE 6. UNDER-FIVE MORTALITY RATE BY SEX, BY COUNTRY
(AS REPORTED IN NATIONAL AND OTHER SOURCES)

Country	Period	Under-five mortality rate (deaths per 1000 live births)			Period	Under-five mortality rate (deaths per 1000 live births)		
		Male	Female	Total		Male	Female	Total
Africa								
Eastern Africa								
Burundi	1982	190	186	188	1997	..	..	196
Comoros	..	..	..	..	1986-1996	122	103	113
Djibouti	..	..	..	..	1997-2002	..	..	124
Eritrea	..	..	..	..	1992-2002	116	98	107
Ethiopia	1974	226	204	215	1990-2000	197	178	188
Kenya	1973	155	140	148	1993-2003	122	103	113
Madagascar	1987	166	162	164	1993-2003	117	106	111
Malawi	1975	317	309	313	1990-2000	207	199	203
Mauritius	1975	72	62	67	2002-2004	19	15	17
Mozambique	1982	284	275	280	1993-2003	181	176	178
Réunion	1972-1976	57	44	51	..	..	..	..
Rwanda	1973	233	213	223	1990-2000	215	198	207
Somalia	..	..	..	..	1996	..	..	237
Uganda	1983	190	172	181	1990-2000	164	150	157
United Republic of Tanzania	1978	205	186	196	1989-1999	172	150	161
Zambia	1973	179	171	175	1991-2001	176	160	168
Zimbabwe	1975	127	113	120	1989-1999	95	85	90
Middle Africa								
Angola	..	..	..	..	1997	..	..	249
Cameroon	1973	207	200	204	1994-2004	154	141	148
Central African Republic	..	..	..	..	1984-1994	165	152	159
Chad	..	..	..	..	1986-1996	213	189	201
Congo	1975	124	116	120	..	..	..	..
Democratic Republic of the Congo	..	..	..	..	1997	..	..	220
Equatorial Guinea	..	..	..	..	1996	..	..	183
Gabon	..	..	..	..	1990-2000	103	80	91
Sao Tome and Principe	..	..	..	..	1996	..	..	119
Northern Africa								
Algeria	1975	168	168	168	2000	42	39	40
Egypt	1975	200	217	208	1990-2000	69	70	69
Libyan Arab Jamahiriya	1975	146	146	146	..	..	..	..
Morocco	1972	183	179	181	1993-2003	59	48	54
Sudan	1973	170	156	163	..	..	..	..
Tunisia	1975	141	139	140	1995	40	34	37
Western Sahara	..	..	..	..	..	..	..	..
Southern Africa								
Botswana	1982	76	60	68	1996	..	..	76
Lesotho	1972	195	172	184	1998	..	..	106
Namibia	1987	92	87	90	1990-2000	67	54	60
South Africa	1987	72	61	67	1988-1998	66	48	57
Swaziland	1976	240	209	225	1996	..	..	122
Western Africa								
Benin	1975	238	218	228	1991-2001	162	163	163
Burkina Faso	1985	190	182	186	1993-2003	195	192	193
Cape Verde	..	..	..	..	1990	64	66	65
Côte d'Ivoire	1975	207	181	194	1988-1998	203	146	174
Gambia	..	..	..	..	1996	..	..	149
Ghana	1975	179	158	169	1993-2003	111	108	110
Guinea	..	..	..	..	1989-1999	202	188	195
Guinea-Bissau	..	..	..	..	1996	..	..	240
Liberia	1970	276	256	266	..	..	..	..

TABLE 6. (continued)

Country	Period	Under-five mortality rate (deaths per 1000 live births)			Period	Under-five mortality rate (deaths per 1000 live births)		
		Male	Female	Total		Male	Female	Total
Mali	1982	273	259	266	1991-2001	250	226	238
Mauritania	1975	170	164	167	1990-2000	110	94	102
Niger	1987	313	328	320	1988-1998	299	306	303
Nigeria	1975	207	188	198	1993-2003	222	212	217
Senegal	1973	277	265	271	1989-1999	150	141	145
Sierra Leone	..	..	..	..	1996	..	..	310
Togo	1983	167	167	167	1988-1998	156	132	144
Asia								
Eastern Asia								
China	1985	43	43	43	2003	..	..	30
China, Hong Kong SAR	1975	19	15	17	2003	4	3	4
China, Macao SAR	..	..	..	..	1993-1996	9	8	9
Dem. People's Rep. of Korea	..	..	..	..	..	..	..	..
Japan	1970	20	15	18	2003	4	4	4
Mongolia	..	..	..	..	1988-1998	106	78	92
Republic of Korea	1973	47	41	44	2001	8	7	7
South-Central Asia								
Afghanistan	1978	315	306	311	..	..	..	..
Bangladesh	1970	243	235	239	1994-2003	102	91	..
Bhutan	1983	181	175	178	2000	..	..	84
India	1977	179	195	187	1988-1998	98	105	101
Iran (Islamic Republic of)	..	..	..	..	2000	38	35	36
Kazakhstan	..	..	..	..	1989-1999	72	53	63
Kyrgyzstan	..	..	..	..	1987-1997	81	70	76
Maldives	1982	128	132	130	1992	51	34	43
Nepal	1970	231	231	231	1991-2001	105	112	108
Pakistan	1975	162	162	162	..	..	..	..
Sri Lanka	1975	71	63	67	1983-1993	38	27	32
Tajikistan	..	..	..	..	1997	..	..	122
Turkmenistan	..	..	..	..	1990-2000	101	76	88
Uzbekistan	..	..	..	..	1992-2002	78	72	75
South-Eastern Asia								
Brunei Darussalam	1970-1972	78	65	72	..	..	..	..
Cambodia	..	..	..	..	1990-2000	133	110	122
Dem. Rep. of Timor-Leste	..	..	..	..	1998-2003	..	..	83
Indonesia	1970	196	153	175	1992-2002	58	51	54
Lao People's Democratic Republic	..	..	..	..	1995-1999	..	..	107
Malaysia	1975	48	40	44	2002	12	10	11
Myanmar	1982	140	109	125	1999	85	68	78
Philippines	1973	81	75	78	1993-2003	48	34	42
Singapore	1975	19	15	17	2003	4	3	3
Thailand	1972	170	155	163	1995-1996	33	30	31
Viet Nam	1985	55	49	52	1992-2002	34	31	33
Western Asia								
Armenia	..	..	..	..	1990-2000	51	45	48
Azerbaijan	..	..	..	..	1991-2000	94	91	92
Bahrain	1976-1981	72	69	70	..	..	..	..
Cyprus	1973	28	36	32	2002-2003	5	6	6
Georgia	1981	40	33	36	1990-1999	53	35	45
Iraq	1973	121	109	115	1990	21	20	21
Israel	1975	28	24	26	2003	7	6	6
Jordan	1970	106	112	109	1992-2002	31	28	29
Kuwait	1975	47	41	44	1992-1993	15	12	14

TABLE 6. *(continued)*

Country	Period	Under-five mortality rate (deaths per 1000 live births)			Period	Under-five mortality rate (deaths per 1000 live births)		
		Male	Female	Total		Male	Female	Total
Lebanon	..	..	..	..	1991-1996	..	..	32
Occupied Palestinian Territory	..	..	..	..	1999-2003	32	25	28
Oman	1978	105	103	104	1985-1995	27	25	26
Qatar	..	..	..	..	1993-1998	..	..	15
Saudi Arabia	1980	89	76	83	1992-1996	30	27	29
Syrian Arab Republic	1972	111	116	113	1996-2001	..	..	20
Turkey	1973	187	187	187	1988-1998	61	58	60
United Arab Emirates	1980	33	26	30	2003	..	..	10
Yemen	1975	259	252	256	1987-1997	128	114	121
Europe								
Eastern Europe								
Belarus	1981	24	17	20	2002	12	9	11
Bulgaria	1970	36	27	31	2003	17	13	15
Czech Republic	1970	27	20	24	2004	5	4	5
Hungary	1972	40	32	36	2002	9	8	9
Poland	1970-1971	35	28	32	2004	9	7	8
Republic of Moldova	1981	49	37	43	2002	21	17	19
Romania	1970	60	51	56	2002	24	19	22
Russian Federation	1970	32	24	28	2004	16	13	15
Slovakia	1982	23	18	20	2002	9	9	9
Ukraine	1981	24	19	22	2002-2003	16	12	14
Northern Europe								
Channel Islands	..	..	..	..	..	..	..	..
Denmark	1970-1971	20	14	17	2003-2004	6	5	5
Estonia	1981	24	19	22	2003	11	7	9
Finland	1971	17	13	15	2002	4	3	4
Iceland	1971-1975	17	12	15	2001	4	3	3
Ireland	1970-1972	24	20	22	2001-2003	8	6	7
Latvia	1970	27	18	23	2003	14	11	12
Lithuania	1970	26	21	24	2003	10	7	9
Norway	1971-1972	18	12	15	2004	4	4	4
Sweden	1969-1973	15	11	13	2003	5	3	4
United Kingdom	1970	24	19	22	2001-2003	7	6	6
Southern Europe								
Albania	1960-1961	113	128	120	2000	28	28	28
Bosnia and Herzegovina	..	..	..	..	1988-1989	23	19	21
Croatia	1982	25	17	21	2000	9	8	9
Greece	1970	48	41	45	1999	8	7	7
Italy	1970-1972	34	28	31	2002	6	5	5
Malta	1973	30	23	26	2002	7	6	6
Portugal	1970	76	66	71	2002	7	6	7
Serbia and Montenegro	1982	43	39	41	2001	18	13	16
Slovenia	1970-1972	30	26	28	2000-2002	6	5	5
Spain	1970	35	28	32	2002	6	5	5
TFYR of Macedonia	1982	55	54	54	2001	16	12	14
Western Europe								
Austria	1970	32	25	29	2002	6	4	5
Belgium	1968-1972	28	21	24	2003	6	5	5
France	1971	19	15	17	2002	6	4	5
Germany	1970	29	22	25	2002-2004	5	5	5
Luxembourg	1971-1973	24	17	21	2002	7	6	7
Netherlands	1971	18	14	16	2003	6	5	6
Switzerland	1970	21	16	18	2003	5	5	5

TABLE 6. *(continued)*

Country	Period	Under-five mortality rate (deaths per 1000 live births)			Period	Under-five mortality rate (deaths per 1000 live births)		
		Male	*Female*	*Total*		*Male*	*Female*	*Total*
Latin America and the Caribbean								
Caribbean								
Bahamas	1969-1971	48	39	44	1989-1991	25	20	23
Barbados	1959-1961	94	79	87	..	..	..	..
Cuba	1975	37	30	34	2001-2003	9	7	8
Dominican Republic	1970	141	119	130	1992-2002	46	40	43
Guadeloupe	1963-1967	70	61	65	2002	9	6	8
Haiti	1970	226	224	225	1990-2000	143	132	138
Jamaica	1970	69	57	63	2000-2002	21	20	21
Martinique	1963-1967	65	61	63	2002	8	6	7
Netherlands Antilles	1966-1970	76	64	70	..	..	..	..
Puerto Rico	1972	35	26	31	2002	11	9	10
Saint Lucia	1959-1961	173	161	167	2002	15	16	15
Saint Vincent and the Grenadines	1959-1961	168	176	172	..	..	..	..
Trinidad and Tobago	1972	59	49	54	1997	24	21	23
United States Virgin Islands	..	..	..	..	..	..	..	..
Central America								
Belize	1980	49	50	49	1991	41	39	40
Costa Rica	1972	71	59	65	2004	11	9	10
El Salvador	1980	135	123	129	1997-2002	33	27	30
Guatemala	1975	156	148	152	1988-1998	64	65	65
Honduras	1978	123	103	113	1996-2000	..	..	45
Mexico	1975	101	89	95	1998	25	21	23
Nicaragua	1980	146	120	133	1991-2001	48	41	45
Panama	1975	59	48	54	2000	28	25	27
South America								
Argentina	1970	75	65	70	1997	24	20	22
Bolivia	1970	260	225	243	1993-2003	94	91	93
Brazil	1977	113	88	101	1986-1996	60	53	57
Chile	1972	90	76	83	1999	17	13	15
Colombia	1972	107	95	101	1990-2000	32	23	28
Ecuador	1975	123	116	120	1994-1999	45	33	39
French Guiana	..	..	..	..	2002	17	15	16
Guyana	1959-1961	79	68	74	1996	..	..	78
Paraguay	1975	73	66	70	..	..	..	..
Peru	1973	177	160	169	1990-2000	64	57	60
Suriname	1980	58	44	51	..	..	..	..
Uruguay	1975	59	49	54	2003	19	14	17
Venezuela	1975	64	54	59	1995-2000	43	26	35
Northern America								
Canada	1970-1972	24	18	21	2002	7	6	6
United States of America	1971	25	19	22	2002	9	8	8
Oceania								
Australia/New Zealand								
Australia	1970-1972	23	18	21	2001-2003	7	5	6
New Zealand	1970-1972	22	18	20	2003	7	6	6
Melanesia								
Fiji	1976	67	52	60	..	..	..	..
New Caledonia	..	..	..	..	2003	10	6	8
Papua New Guinea	..	..	..	..	..	..	..	..
Solomon Islands	..	..	..	..	..	..	..	..
Vanuatu	..	..	..	..	1999	..	..	33

TABLE 6. *(continued)*

Country	Period	Under-five mortality rate (deaths per 1000 live births)			Period	Under-five mortality rate (deaths per 1000 live births)		
		Male	*Female*	*Total*		*Male*	*Female*	*Total*
Micronesia								
Guam	..	..	..	..	..	..	..	..
Micronesia, Federated States of.......	..	..	..	..	..	..	..	..
Polynesia								
French Polynesia	..	..	..	..	2004	8	7	7
Samoa...	1971	95	76	86	..	..	..	..
Tonga..	..	..	..	..	1996	23	21	22

IV. COUNTRY PROFILES

Indicator	Period			
	Earlier year		Later year	

I. Data and estimates from national and other sources

General mortality

	Year	Value	Year	Value
Annual number of deaths *(thousands)*	..	..	..	..
Annual number of deaths under age one *(thousands)*	..	..	..	..
Crude death rate *(per 1 000 person-years)*	..	..	..	..

	Year	Male	Female	Year	Male	Female
Life expectancy *(years)*						
at birth..	..	..	..	..	..	..
at age 15..	..	..	..	..	..	..
at age 60..	..	..	..	..	..	..
Survival probability						
from birth to age 15.................................	..	..	..	..	..	..
from age 15 to age 60..............................	..	..	..	..	..	..
from age 60 to age 80..............................	..	..	..	..	..	..

Infant and child mortality

	Year	Male	Female	Both sexes	Year	Male	Female	Both sexes
Infant mortality rate *(per 1 000 live births)*	1978	215	203	209	..	..	..	..
Mortality from age 1 to age 4 *(per 1 000 live births)*	1978	128	130	129	..	..	..	..
Under-five mortality rate *(per 1 000 live births)*	1978	315	306	311	..	..	..	..

II. Data and estimates from United Nations sources

United Nations Population Division estimates

	1990-1995	2000-2005
Annual number of deaths *(thousands)*	361	525
Crude death rate *(per 1 000 person-years)*	20	20
Life expectancy at birth *(years)*		
Male...	45.3	45.8
Female..	45.9	46.3
Under-five mortality rate *(per 1 000 live births)*	257	252

Maternal mortality

	2000
Maternal mortality ratio *(deaths per 100 000 births)*	1 900

HIV/AIDS

	2003	[Low estimate - high estimate]
Number of HIV-infected persons, ...	..	..
Adult HIV prevalence *(percentage of adults 15-49)*	..	..

Policy views

	1976	2003
Life expectancy..	Unacceptable	Unacceptable
Under-five mortality..		Unacceptable
Maternal mortality..		Unacceptable
Level of concern about AIDS....................................		Major concern

Life Expectancy at Birth

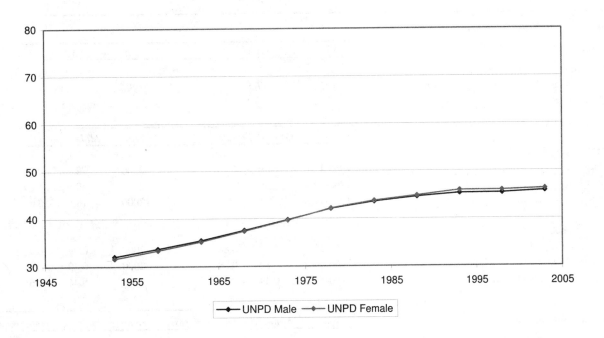

Infant Mortality Rate

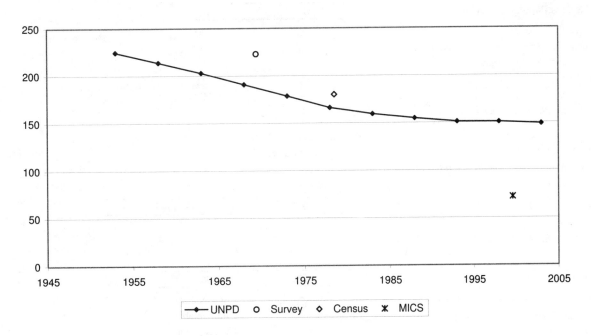

Indicator	Period				
	Earlier year			Later year	

I. Data and estimates from national and other sources

General mortality

	Year	Value		Year	Value	
Annual number of deaths *(thousands)*	1970	19.8		2004	17.7	
Annual number of deaths under age one *(thousands)*	1970	6.8		1998	0.9	
Crude death rate *(per 1 000 person-years)*	1970	9.3		2004	5.7	

	Year	Male	Female	Year	Male	Female
Life expectancy *(years)*						
at birth	1965-1967	64.9	67.0	2000	72.5	77.3
at age 15	1965-1967	58.0	61.3	2000	59.9	64.7
at age 60	1965-1967	18.1	20.0	2000	18.6	21.6
Survival probability						
from birth to age 15	1960-1961	0.88	0.86	2000	0.97	0.97
from age 15 to age 60	1960-1961	0.82	0.88	2000	0.89	0.94
from age 60 to age 80	1960-1961	0.44	0.55	2000	0.46	0.64

Infant and child mortality

	Year	Male	Female	Both sexes	Year	Male	Female	Both sexes
Infant mortality rate *(per 1 000 live births)*	1960-1961	80	85	83	2000	23	23	23
Mortality from age 1 to age 4 *(per 1 000 live births)*	1960-1961	36	46	41	2000	5	5	5
Under-five mortality rate *(per 1 000 live births)*	1960-1961	113	128	120	2000	28	28	28

II. Data and estimates from United Nations sources

United Nations Population Division estimates

	1990-1995	2000-2005
Annual number of deaths *(thousands)*	20	20
Crude death rate *(per 1 000 person-years)*	6	6
Life expectancy at birth *(years)*		
Male	68.9	70.9
Female	74.9	76.7
Under-five mortality rate *(per 1 000 live births)*	47	34

Maternal mortality

	2000
Maternal mortality ratio *(deaths per 100 000 births)*	55

HIV/AIDS

	2003	[Low estimate - high estimate]
Number of HIV-infected persons,	..	..
Adult HIV prevalence *(percentage of adults 15-49)*	..	..

Policy views

	1976	2003
Life expectancy	Unacceptable	Acceptable
Under-five mortality		Unacceptable
Maternal mortality		Unacceptable
Level of concern about AIDS		Major concern

Life Expectancy at Birth

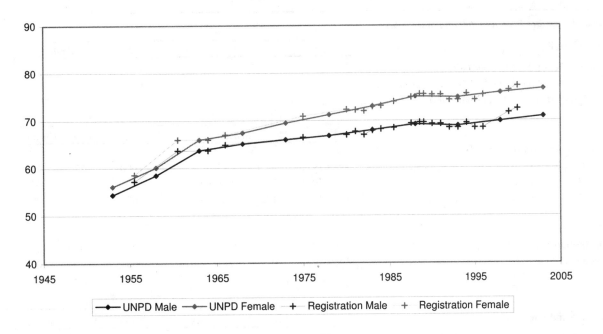

Infant Mortality Rate

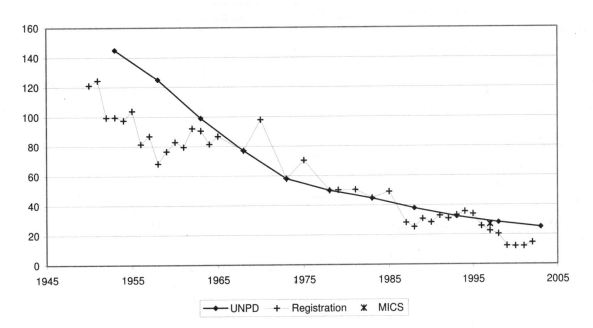

Indicator	Period				
	Earlier year			Later year	

I. Data and estimates from national and other sources

General mortality

	Year	Value		Year	Value
Annual number of deaths *(thousands)*	..	..		..	..
Annual number of deaths under age one *(thousands)*	..	..		..	..
Crude death rate *(per 1 000 person-years)*	..	..		..	..

	Year	Male	Female	Year	Male	Female
Life expectancy *(years)*						
at birth...	1969-1971	52.9	53.2	2000	72.5	74.2
at age 15..	1969-1971	54.4	55.6	2000	61.0	62.5
at age 60..	1969-1971	17.3	17.8	2000	19.9	20.7
Survival probability						
from birth to age 15..	1969-1971	0.75	0.75	2000	0.95	0.96
from age 15 to age 60......................................	1969-1971	0.76	0.80	2000	0.89	0.91
from age 60 to age 80......................................	..	..	..	2000	0.57	0.61

Infant and child mortality

	Year	Male	Female	Both sexes	Year	Male	Female	Both sexes
Infant mortality rate *(per 1 000 live births)*	1975	113	109	111	2000	36	33	35
Mortality from age 1 to age 4 *(per 1 000 live births)*	1975	62	67	64	2000	6	5	6
Under-five mortality rate *(per 1 000 live births)*	1975	168	168	168	2000	42	39	40

II. Data and estimates from United Nations sources

United Nations Population Division estimates

	1990-1995	2000-2005
Annual number of deaths *(thousands)*	163	159
Crude death rate *(per 1 000 person-years)*	6	5
Life expectancy at birth *(years)*		
Male...	66.6	69.7
Female..	69.4	72.2
Under-five mortality rate *(per 1 000 live births)*	61	41

Maternal mortality

	2000
Maternal mortality ratio *(deaths per 100 000 births)*	140

HIV/AIDS

	2003	*[Low estimate - high estimate]*
Number of HIV-infected persons, ...	9 100	[3 000 - 18 000]
Adult HIV prevalence *(percentage of adults 15-49)*	0.1	[<0.2]

Policy views

	1976	2003
Life expectancy..	Unacceptable	Unacceptable
Under-five mortality..		Unacceptable
Maternal mortality..		Unacceptable
Level of concern about AIDS..................................		Minor concern

Life Expectancy at Birth

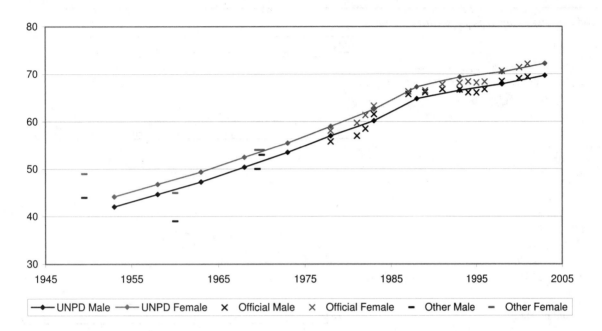

Infant Mortality Rate

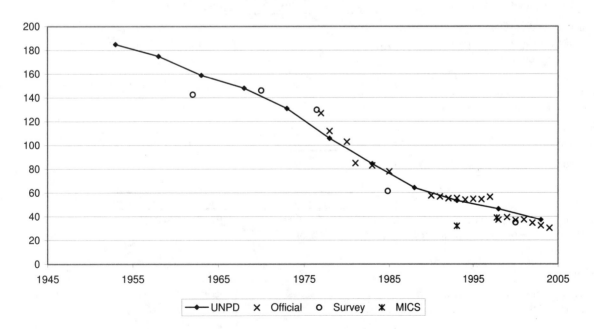

Indicator	Period							
	Earlier year				*Later year*			

I. Data and estimates from national and other sources

General mortality

	Year	Value			Year	Value		
Annual number of deaths *(thousands)*	..	..			..	..		
Annual number of deaths under age one *(thousands)*	..	..			..	..		
Crude death rate *(per 1 000 person-years)*	..	..			..	..		

	Year	Male	Female		Year	Male	Female	
Life expectancy *(years)*								
at birth...	..	..	..		..	..	..	
at age 15...	..	..	..		..	..	..	
at age 60...	..	..	..		..	..	..	
Survival probability								
from birth to age 15..	..	..	..		..	..	..	
from age 15 to age 60..	..	..	..		..	..	..	
from age 60 to age 80..	..	..	..		..	..	..	

Infant and child mortality

	Year	Male	Female	Both sexes	Year	Male	Female	Both sexes
Infant mortality rate *(per 1 000 live births)*	..	..	..	..	1997	..	..	150
Mortality from age 1 to age 4 *(per 1 000 live births)*	..	..	..	..	..	..	..	..
Under-five mortality rate *(per 1 000 live births)*	..	..	..	..	1997	..	..	249

II. Data and estimates from United Nations sources

United Nations Population Division estimates

	1990-1995	*2000-2005*
Annual number of deaths *(thousands)*	277	332
Crude death rate *(per 1 000 person-years)*	24	22
Life expectancy at birth *(years)*		
Male..	38.1	39.2
Female...	41.7	42.2
Under-five mortality rate *(per 1 000 live births)*	270	245

Maternal mortality

	2000
Maternal mortality ratio *(deaths per 100 000 births)*	1 700

HIV/AIDS

	2003	*[Low estimate - high estimate]*
Number of HIV-infected persons, ...	240 000	[97 000 - 600 000]
Adult HIV prevalence *(percentage of adults 15-49)*	3.9	[1.6 - 9.4]

Policy views

	1976	*2003*
Life expectancy...	..	Unacceptable
Under-five mortality..		Unacceptable
Maternal mortality..		Unacceptable
Level of concern about AIDS..................................		Major concern

Life Expectancy at Birth

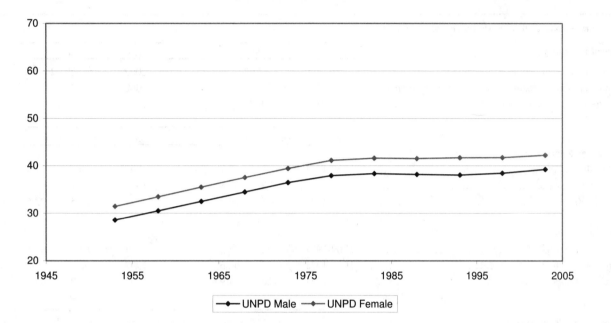

Infant Mortality Rate

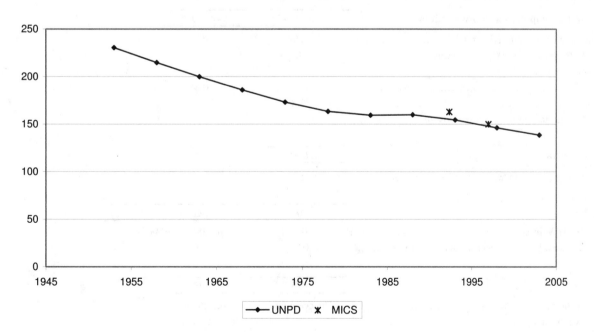

Indicator	Period				
	Earlier year			Later year	

I. Data and estimates from national and other sources

General mortality

	Year	Value		Year	Value	
Annual number of deaths *(thousands)*	1970	222.2		2002	291.2	
Annual number of deaths under age one *(thousands)*	1970	32.2		2002	11.7	
Crude death rate *(per 1 000 person-years)*	1970	9.3		2002	7.7	

	Year	Male	Female	Year	Male	Female
Life expectancy *(years)*						
at birth..	1969-1971	61.9	69.7	1997	69.8	77.4
at age 15...	1969-1971	52.3	59.8	1997	56.7	64.2
at age 60...	1969-1971	14.5	19.3	1997	17.5	22.5
Survival probability						
from birth to age 15...	1969-1971	0.92	0.93	1997	0.97	0.98
from age 15 to age 60...	1969-1971	0.73	0.86	1997	0.81	0.90
from age 60 to age 80...	1969-1971	0.26	0.49	1997	0.42	0.65

Infant and child mortality

	Year	Male	Female	Both sexes	Year	Male	Female	Both sexes
Infant mortality rate *(per 1 000 live births)*	1970	63	53	58	1997	21	17	19
Mortality from age 1 to age 4 *(per 1 000 live births)*	1970	13	13	13	1997	4	3	3
Under-five mortality rate *(per 1 000 live births)*	1970	75	65	70	1997	24	20	22

II. Data and estimates from United Nations sources

United Nations Population Division estimates

	1990-1995	2000-2005
Annual number of deaths *(thousands)*	276	291
Crude death rate *(per 1 000 person-years)*	8	8
Life expectancy at birth *(years)*		
Male...	68.6	70.6
Female..	75.8	78.1
Under-five mortality rate *(per 1 000 live births)*	28	17

Maternal mortality

	2000
Maternal mortality ratio *(deaths per 100 000 births)*	82

HIV/AIDS

	2003	[Low estimate - high estimate]
Number of HIV-infected persons, ...	130 000	[61 000 - 210 000]
Adult HIV prevalence *(percentage of adults 15-49)*	0.7	[0.3 - 1.1]

Policy views

	1976	2003
Life expectancy...	Unacceptable	Acceptable
Under-five mortality..		Unacceptable
Maternal mortality..		Unacceptable
Level of concern about AIDS...................................		Major concern

Life Expectancy at Birth

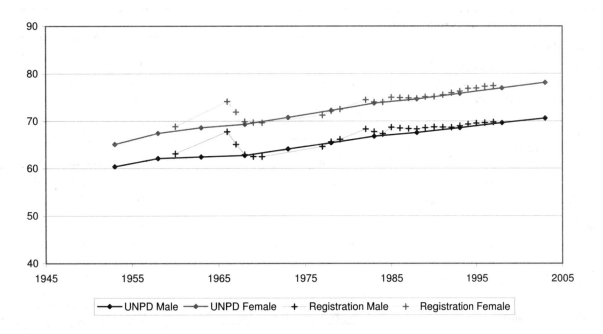

Infant Mortality Rate

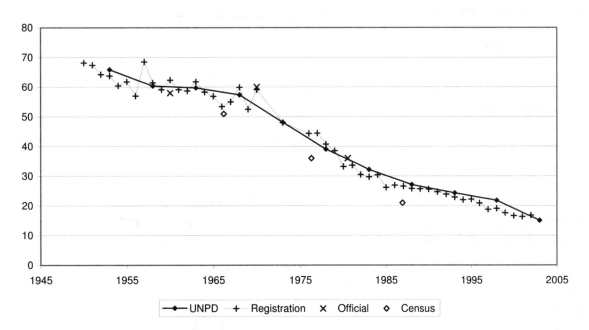

Indicator	Period					
	Earlier year			Later year		

I. Data and estimates from national and other sources

General mortality

	Year	Value		Year	Value	
Annual number of deaths *(thousands)*	1970	12.8		2003	26.0	
Annual number of deaths under age one *(thousands)*	1970	1.5		2003	0.4	
Crude death rate *(per 1 000 person-years)*	1970	5.2		2003	8.1	

	Year	Male	Female	Year	Male	Female
Life expectancy *(years)*						
at birth..	1970	69.9	75.8	2000	70.7	75.5
at age 15..	..	..	..	2000	57.2	61.8
at age 60..	..	..	..	2000	16.8	19.1
Survival probability						
from birth to age 15...	..	..	..	1998	0.97	0.98
from age 15 to age 60...	..	..	..	1998	0.81	0.92
from age 60 to age 80...	..	..	..	1998	0.42	0.53

Infant and child mortality

	Year	Male	Female	Both sexes	Year	Male	Female	Both sexes
Infant mortality rate *(per 1 000 live births)*	..	..	..	..	1990-2000	46	42	44
Mortality from age 1 to age 4 *(per 1 000 live births)*	..	..	..	..	1990-2000	5	3	4
Under-five mortality rate *(per 1 000 live births)*	..	..	..	..	1990-2000	51	45	48

II. Data and estimates from United Nations sources

United Nations Population Division estimates

	1990-1995	2000-2005
Annual number of deaths *(thousands)*	28	27
Crude death rate *(per 1 000 person-years)*	8	9
Life expectancy at birth *(years)*		
Male...	65.3	67.9
Female..	72.1	74.6
Under-five mortality rate *(per 1 000 live births)*	49	35

Maternal mortality

	2000
Maternal mortality ratio *(deaths per 100 000 births)*	55

HIV/AIDS

	2003	[Low estimate - high estimate]
Number of HIV-infected persons, ...	2 600	[1 200 - 4 300]
Adult HIV prevalence *(percentage of adults 15-49)*	0.1	[0.1 - 0.2]

Policy views

	1976	2003
Life expectancy..	..	Acceptable
Under-five mortality..		Acceptable
Maternal mortality..		Unacceptable
Level of concern about AIDS...................................		Major concern

Life Expectancy at Birth

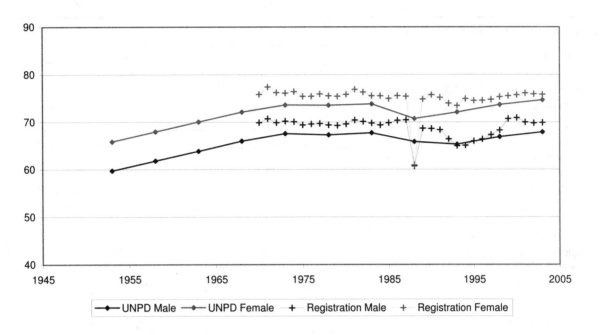

Infant Mortality Rate

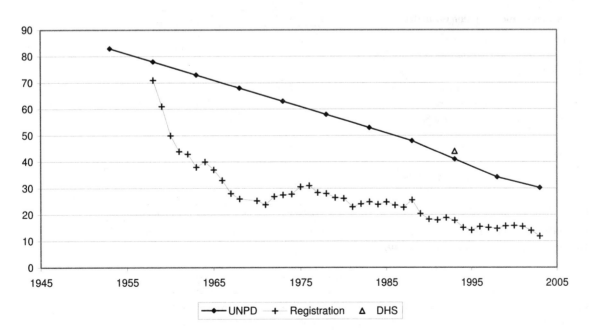

Indicator	Period			
	Earlier year		Later year	

I. Data and estimates from national and other sources

General mortality

	Year	Value	Year	Value
Annual number of deaths *(thousands)*	1970	113.0	2003	131.2
Annual number of deaths under age one *(thousands)*	1970	4.6	2003	1.2
Crude death rate *(per 1 000 person-years)*	1970	9.0	2003	6.6

	Year	Male	Female	Year	Male	Female
Life expectancy *(years)*						
at birth..	1970-1972	67.8	74.5	2001-2003	77.8	82.8
at age 15..	1970-1972	54.8	61.2	2001-2003	63.4	68.4
at age 60..	1970-1972	15.4	19.7	2001-2003	21.6	25.3
Survival probability						
from birth to age 15...	1970-1972	0.97	0.98	2001-2003	0.99	0.99
from age 15 to age 60.......................................	1970-1972	0.80	0.89	2001-2003	0.91	0.95
from age 60 to age 80.......................................	1970-1972	0.30	0.51	2001-2003	0.59	0.74

Infant and child mortality

	Year	Male	Female	Both sexes	Year	Male	Female	Both sexes
Infant mortality rate *(per 1 000 live births)*	1970-1972	19	15	17	2001-2003	6	4	5
Mortality from age 1 to age 4 *(per 1 000 live births)*	1970-1972	4	3	4	2001-2003	1	1	1
Under-five mortality rate *(per 1 000 live births)*	1970-1972	23	18	21	2001-2003	7	5	6

II. Data and estimates from United Nations sources

United Nations Population Division estimates

	1990-1995	2000-2005
Annual number of deaths *(thousands)*	121	132
Crude death rate *(per 1 000 person-years)*	7	7
Life expectancy at birth *(years)*		
Male..	74.7	77.6
Female..	80.6	82.8
Under-five mortality rate *(per 1 000 live births)*	8	6

Maternal mortality

	2000
Maternal mortality ratio *(deaths per 100 000 births)*	8

HIV/AIDS

	2003	[Low estimate - high estimate]
Number of HIV-infected persons, ...	14 000	[6 800 - 22 000]
Adult HIV prevalence *(percentage of adults 15-49)*	0.1	[0.1 - 0.2]

Policy views

	1976	2003
Life expectancy..	Acceptable	Acceptable
Under-five mortality...		Acceptable
Maternal mortality...		Acceptable
Level of concern about AIDS....................................		Major concern

Life Expectancy at Birth

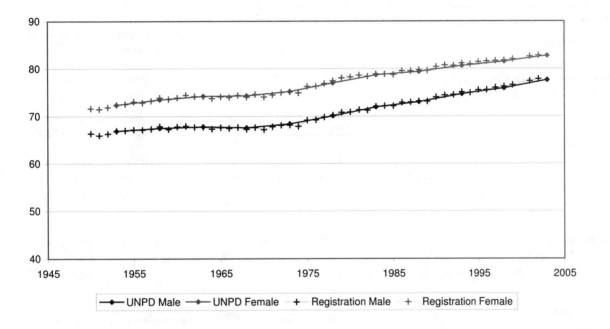

Infant Mortality Rate

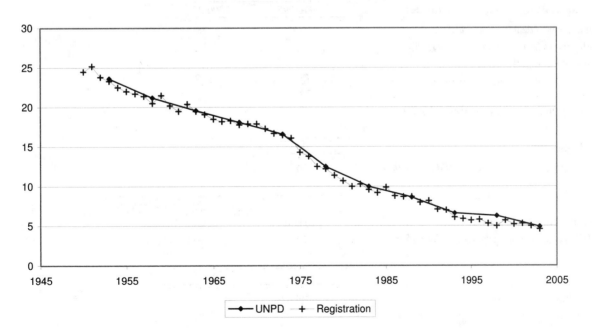

Indicator	Period					
	Earlier year			Later year		

I. Data and estimates from national and other sources

General mortality

	Year	Value			Year	Value	
Annual number of deaths *(thousands)*	1970	98.8			2003	77.2	
Annual number of deaths under age one *(thousands)*	1970	2.9			2003	0.3	
Crude death rate *(per 1 000 person-years)*	1970	13.2			2003	9.5	

	Year	Male	Female	Year	Male	Female
Life expectancy *(years)*						
at birth...	1970	66.5	73.4	2003	75.9	81.6
at age 15...	1970	54.1	60.5	2003	61.5	67.1
at age 60...	1970	14.8	18.8	2003	20.2	24.1
Survival probability						
from birth to age 15..	1970	0.96	0.97	2003	0.99	0.99
from age 15 to age 60..	1970	0.79	0.89	2003	0.88	0.94
from age 60 to age 80..	1970	0.28	0.47	2003	0.54	0.72

Infant and child mortality

	Year	Male	Female	Both sexes	Year	Male	Female	Both sexes
Infant mortality rate *(per 1 000 live births)*	1970	28	21	25	2002	5	3	4
Mortality from age 1 to age 4 *(per 1 000 live births)*	1970	4	4	4	2002	1	1	1
Under-five mortality rate *(per 1 000 live births)*	1970	32	25	29	2002	6	4	5

II. Data and estimates from United Nations sources

United Nations Population Division estimates	1990-1995	2000-2005
Annual number of deaths *(thousands)*	82	78
Crude death rate *(per 1 000 person-years)*	10	10
Life expectancy at birth *(years)*		
Male...	72.7	75.9
Female..	79.2	81.7
Under-five mortality rate *(per 1 000 live births)*	8	6

Maternal mortality

	2000
Maternal mortality ratio *(deaths per 100 000 births)*	4

HIV/AIDS

	2003	[Low estimate - high estimate]
Number of HIV-infected persons, ...	10 000	[5 000 - 16 000]
Adult HIV prevalence *(percentage of adults 15-49)*	0.3	[0.1 - 0.4]

Policy views

	1976	2003
Life expectancy...	Acceptable	Acceptable
Under-five mortality..		Acceptable
Maternal mortality..		Acceptable
Level of concern about AIDS...................................		Minor concern

Life Expectancy at Birth

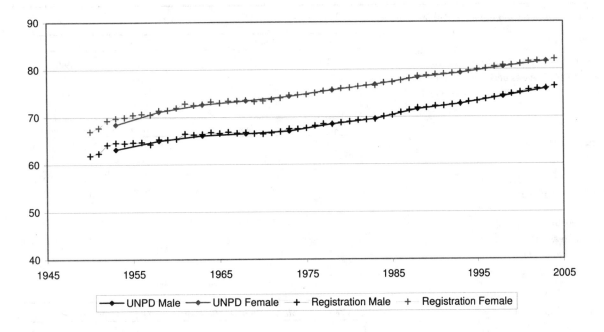

Infant Mortality Rate

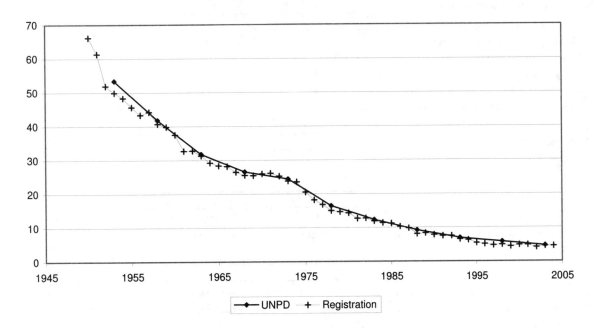

Indicator	Period				
	Earlier year			Later year	

I. Data and estimates from national and other sources

General mortality

	Year	Value		Year	Value	
Annual number of deaths *(thousands)*	1970	34.5		2003	49.0	
Annual number of deaths under age one *(thousands)*	1970	5.2		2003	1.5	
Crude death rate *(per 1 000 person-years)*	1970	6.7		2003	6.0	

	Year	Male	Female	Year	Male	Female
Life expectancy *(years)*						
at birth..	1977	65.5	73.4	2002	69.4	75.0
at age 15..	..	..	..	2002	56.6	61.5
at age 60..	..	..	..	2002	16.8	19.4
Survival probability						
from birth to age 15................................	..	..	..	..	..	..
from age 15 to age 60..............................	..	..	..	..	..	..
from age 60 to age 80..............................	..	..	..	..	..	..

Infant and child mortality

	Year	Male	Female	Both sexes	Year	Male	Female	Both sexes
Infant mortality rate *(per 1 000 live births)*	..	..	..	..	1991-2000	84	78	81
Mortality from age 1 to age 4 *(per 1 000 live births)*	..	..	..	..	1991-2000	10	13	11
Under-five mortality rate *(per 1 000 live births)*	..	..	..	..	1991-2000	94	91	92

II. Data and estimates from United Nations sources

United Nations Population Division estimates

	1990-1995	2000-2005
Annual number of deaths *(thousands)*	57	58
Crude death rate *(per 1 000 person-years)*	8	7
Life expectancy at birth *(years)*		
Male..	62.2	63.2
Female..	69.5	70.5
Under-five mortality rate *(per 1 000 live births)*	98	91

Maternal mortality

	2000
Maternal mortality ratio *(deaths per 100 000 births)*	94

HIV/AIDS

	2003	*[Low estimate - high estimate]*
Number of HIV-infected persons, ...	1 400	[500 - 2 800]
Adult HIV prevalence *(percentage of adults 15-49)*	<0.1	[<0.2]

Policy views

	1976	2003
Life expectancy..	..	Acceptable
Under-five mortality..		Unacceptable
Maternal mortality..		Unacceptable
Level of concern about AIDS..................................		Minor concern

Life Expectancy at Birth

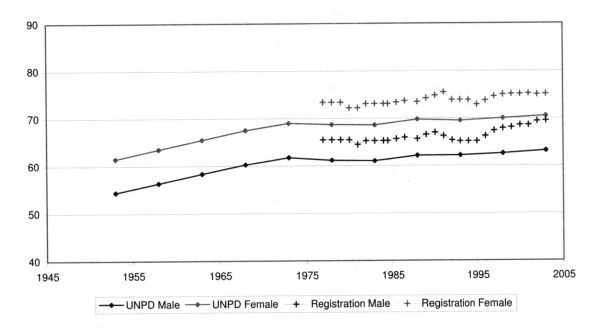

Infant Mortality Rate

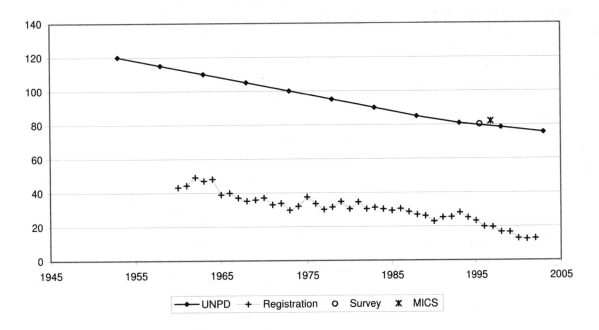

Indicator	Period				
	Earlier year			Later year	

I. Data and estimates from national and other sources

General mortality

	Year	Value		Year	Value
Annual number of deaths *(thousands)*	1970	1.1		2001	1.6
Annual number of deaths under age one *(thousands)*	1970	0.2		2001	0.0
Crude death rate *(per 1 000 person-years)*	1970	6.5		2001	5.6

	Year	Male	Female	Year	Male	Female
Life expectancy *(years)*						
at birth	1969-1971	64.0	69.3	1989-1991	68.3	75.3
at age 15	1969-1971	52.6	57.4	1989-1991	55.1	61.6
at age 60	1969-1971	16.7	19.7	1989-1991	18.2	21.6
Survival probability						
from birth to age 15	1969-1971	0.95	0.96	1989-1991	0.97	0.98
from age 15 to age 60	1969-1971	0.70	0.78	1989-1991	0.75	0.86
from age 60 to age 80	1969-1971	0.37	0.50	1989-1991	0.44	0.57

Infant and child mortality

	Year	Male	Female	Both sexes	Year	Male	Female	Both sexes
Infant mortality rate *(per 1 000 live births)*	1969-1971	39	31	35	1989-1991	22	16	19
Mortality from age 1 to age 4 *(per 1 000 live births)*	1969-1971	10	9	9	1989-1991	3	3	3
Under-five mortality rate *(per 1 000 live births)*	1969-1971	48	39	44	1989-1991	25	20	23

II. Data and estimates from United Nations sources

United Nations Population Division estimates

	1990-1995	2000-2005
Annual number of deaths *(thousands)*	2	2
Crude death rate *(per 1 000 person-years)*	7	7
Life expectancy at birth *(years)*		
Male	63.5	66.2
Female	72.7	72.7
Under-five mortality rate *(per 1 000 live births)*	26	16

Maternal mortality

	2000
Maternal mortality ratio *(deaths per 100 000 births)*	60

HIV/AIDS

	2003	[Low estimate - high estimate]
Number of HIV-infected persons,	5 600	[3 200 - 8 700]
Adult HIV prevalence *(percentage of adults 15-49)*	3	[1.8 - 4.9]

Policy views

	1976	2003
Life expectancy	Unacceptable	Unacceptable
Under-five mortality		Unacceptable
Maternal mortality		Acceptable
Level of concern about AIDS		Major concern

Life Expectancy at Birth

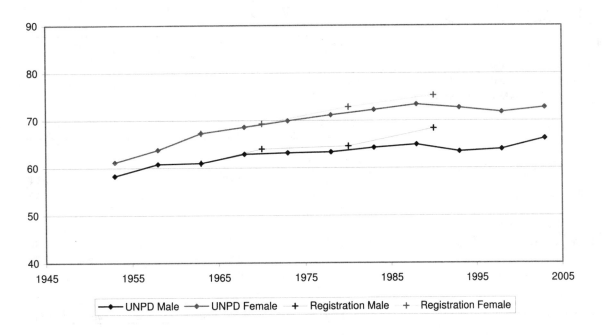

Infant Mortality Rate

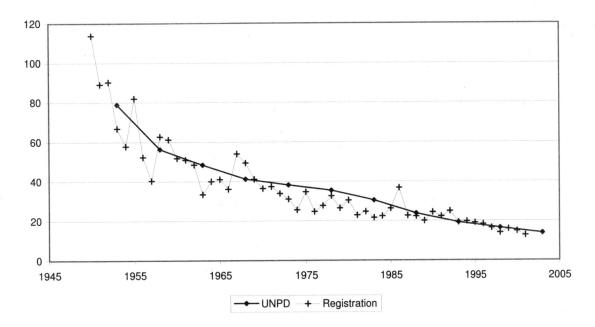

Indicator	Period				
	Earlier year			Later year	

I. Data and estimates from national and other sources

General mortality

	Year	Value		Year	Value
Annual number of deaths *(thousands)*	..	..		..	..
Annual number of deaths under age one *(thousands)*	..	..		..	..
Crude death rate *(per 1 000 person-years)*	..	..		..	..

	Year	Male	Female	Year	Male	Female
Life expectancy *(years)*						
at birth..	1976-1981	63.4	66.4	2001	73.2	76.2
at age 15..	1976-1981	53.9	56.9	2001	59.5	62.1
at age 60..	1976-1981	15.9	17.8	2001	17.8	19.6
Survival probability						
from birth to age 15...................................	1976-1981	0.92	0.92	2001	0.98	0.99
from age 15 to age 60.................................	1976-1981	0.76	0.81	2001	0.89	0.92
from age 60 to age 80.................................	1976-1981	0.33	0.42	..	..	..

Infant and child mortality

	Year	Male	Female	Both sexes	Year	Male	Female	Both sexes
Infant mortality rate *(per 1 000 live births)*	1976-1981	53	49	51	2001	10	7	8
Mortality from age 1 to age 4 *(per 1 000 live births)*	1976-1981	19	21	20	..	..	..	..
Under-five mortality rate *(per 1 000 live births)*	1976-1981	72	69	70	..	..	..	..

II. Data and estimates from United Nations sources

United Nations Population Division estimates

	1990-1995	2000-2005
Annual number of deaths *(thousands)*	2	2
Crude death rate *(per 1 000 person-years)*	4	3
Life expectancy at birth *(years)*		
Male..	69.9	72.9
Female..	74.0	75.8
Under-five mortality rate *(per 1 000 live births)*	26	17

Maternal mortality

	2000
Maternal mortality ratio *(deaths per 100 000 births)*	28

HIV/AIDS

	2003	[Low estimate - high estimate]
Number of HIV-infected persons, ...	<600	[200 - 1 100]
Adult HIV prevalence *(percentage of adults 15-49)*	0.2	[0.1 - 0.3]

Policy views

	1976	2003
Life expectancy..	Unacceptable	Acceptable
Under-five mortality..		Unacceptable
Maternal mortality..		Unacceptable
Level of concern about AIDS..		Minor concern

Life Expectancy at Birth

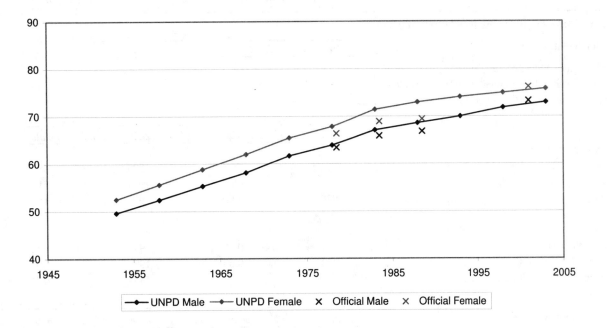

Infant Mortality Rate

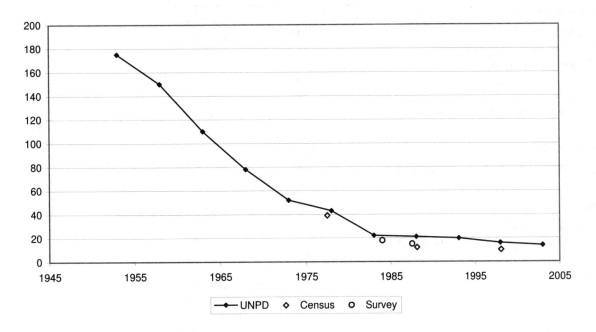

Indicator	Period				
	Earlier year			Later year	

I. Data and estimates from national and other sources

General mortality

	Year	Value		Year	Value	
Annual number of deaths *(thousands)*	..	..		..	..	
Annual number of deaths under age one *(thousands)*	..	..		..	..	
Crude death rate *(per 1 000 person-years)*	..	..		..	..	

	Year	Male	Female	Year	Male	Female
Life expectancy *(years)*						
at birth..	1974	45.8	46.6	1994	58.7	58.3
at age 15..	1974	46.3	46.1	1994	53.0	51.4
at age 60..	1974	14.4	14.0	1994	15.1	15.0
Survival probability						
from birth to age 15..	1974	0.74	0.76	1994	0.86	0.87
from age 15 to age 60..	1974	0.60	0.60	1994	0.75	0.73
from age 60 to age 80..	..	..	..	1994	0.27	0.26

Infant and child mortality

	Year	Male	Female	Both sexes	Year	Male	Female	Both sexes
Infant mortality rate *(per 1 000 live births)*	1970	158	132	145	1994-2003	80	64	..
Mortality from age 1 to age 4 *(per 1 000 live births)*	1970	101	119	110	1994-2003	24	29	..
Under-five mortality rate *(per 1 000 live births)*	1970	243	235	239	1994-2003	102	91	..

II. Data and estimates from United Nations sources

United Nations Population Division estimates

	1990-1995	2000-2005
Annual number of deaths *(thousands)*	1 228	1 078
Crude death rate *(per 1 000 person-years)*	11	8
Life expectancy at birth *(years)*		
Male...	55.8	61.8
Female...	57.0	63.4
Under-five mortality rate *(per 1 000 live births)*	124	79

Maternal mortality

	2000
Maternal mortality ratio *(deaths per 100 000 births)*	380

HIV/AIDS

	2003	*[Low estimate - high estimate]*
Number of HIV-infected persons, ...	..	[2 500 - 15 000]
Adult HIV prevalence *(percentage of adults 15-49)*	..	[<0.2]

Policy views

	1976	2003
Life expectancy...	Unacceptable	Unacceptable
Under-five mortality..		Unacceptable
Maternal mortality..		Unacceptable
Level of concern about AIDS...................................		Major concern

Life Expectancy at Birth

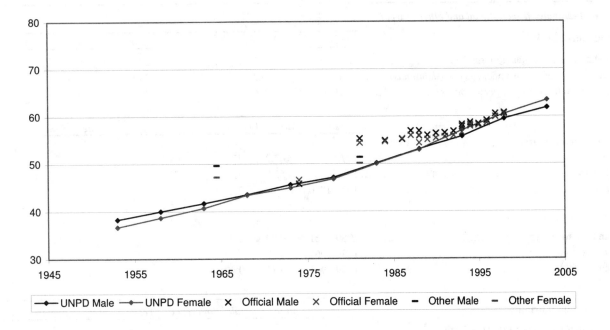

Infant Mortality Rate

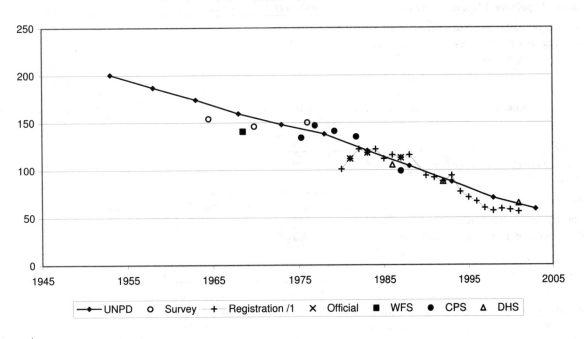

[1] Refers to sample registration

Indicator	Period					
	Earlier year				**Later year**	

I. Data and estimates from national and other sources

General mortality

	Year	Value			Year	Value
Annual number of deaths *(thousands)*	1970	2.1			2002	2.3
Annual number of deaths under age one *(thousands)*	1970	0.2			2002	0.1
Crude death rate *(per 1 000 person-years)*	1970	8.6			2002	8.4

	Year	Male	Female	Year	Male	Female
Life expectancy *(years)*						
at birth...	1970-1980	67.2	72.5	..	..	..
at age 15..	1970-1980	55.8	59.8	..	..	..
at age 60..	1970-1980	16.8	20.8	..	..	..
Survival probability						
from birth to age 15...	1959-1961	0.90	0.92	..	..	..
from age 15 to age 60..	1959-1961	0.79	0.83	..	..	..
from age 60 to age 80..	1959-1961	0.33	0.48	..	..	..

Infant and child mortality

	Year	Male	Female	Both sexes	Year	Male	Female	Both sexes
Infant mortality rate *(per 1 000 live births)*	1959-1961	78	66	72	2002	..	..	14
Mortality from age 1 to age 4 *(per 1 000 live births)*	1959-1961	17	15	16	..	..	..	..
Under-five mortality rate *(per 1 000 live births)*	1959-1961	94	79	87	..	..	..	..

II. Data and estimates from United Nations sources

United Nations Population Division estimates

	1990-1995	2000-2005
Annual number of deaths *(thousands)*	2	2
Crude death rate *(per 1 000 person-years)*	10	9
Life expectancy at birth *(years)*		
Male..	71.4	71.1
Female...	77.6	78.3
Under-five mortality rate *(per 1 000 live births)*	16	12

Maternal mortality

	2000
Maternal mortality ratio *(deaths per 100 000 births)*	95

HIV/AIDS

	2003	[Low estimate - high estimate]
Number of HIV-infected persons, ...	2 500	[700 - 9 200]
Adult HIV prevalence *(percentage of adults 15-49)*	1.5	[0.4 - 5.4]

Policy views

	1976	2003
Life expectancy...	Acceptable	Acceptable
Under-five mortality..		Acceptable
Maternal mortality..		Acceptable
Level of concern about AIDS....................................		Major concern

Life Expectancy at Birth

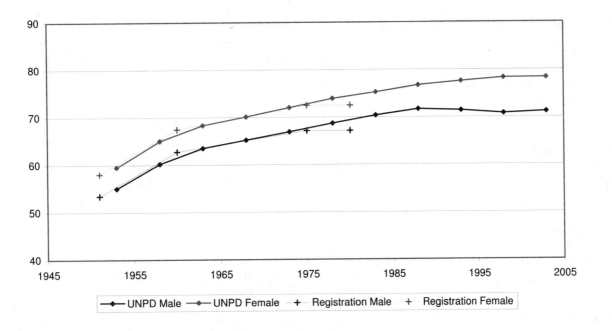

Infant Mortality Rate

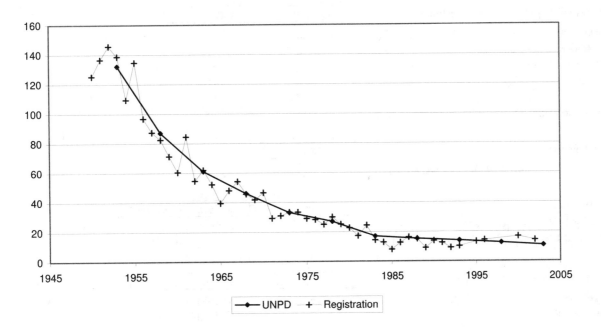

Indicator	Period				
	Earlier year			Later year	

I. Data and estimates from national and other sources

General mortality

	Year	Value		Year	Value
Annual number of deaths *(thousands)*	1970	69.0		2003	143.2
Annual number of deaths under age one *(thousands)*	1970	2.7		2003	0.7
Crude death rate *(per 1 000 person-years)*	1970	7.6		2003	14.5

	Year	Male	Female	Year	Male	Female
Life expectancy *(years)*						
at birth..	1970-1971	68.0	76.0	2002	62.3	74.1
at age 15..	..	..	..	2002	48.2	60.0
at age 60..	..	..	..	2002	13.4	19.1
Survival probability						
from birth to age 15...........................	1981	0.97	0.98	2002	0.98	0.99
from age 15 to age 60.........................	1981	0.72	0.89	2002	0.62	0.86
from age 60 to age 80.........................	1981	0.36	0.57	2002	0.24	0.50

Infant and child mortality

	Year	Male	Female	Both sexes	Year	Male	Female	Both sexes
Infant mortality rate *(per 1 000 live births)*	1981	19	13	16	2002	8	7	8
Mortality from age 1 to age 4 *(per 1 000 live births)*	1981	5	3	4	2002	4	3	3
Under-five mortality rate *(per 1 000 live births)*	1981	24	17	20	2002	12	9	11

II. Data and estimates from United Nations sources

United Nations Population Division estimates

	1990-1995	2000-2005
Annual number of deaths *(thousands)*	127	143
Crude death rate *(per 1 000 person-years)*	12	14
Life expectancy at birth *(years)*		
Male..	64.3	62.4
Female...	74.7	74.0
Under-five mortality rate *(per 1 000 live births)*	17	18

Maternal mortality

	2000
Maternal mortality ratio *(deaths per 100 000 births)*	35

HIV/AIDS

	2003	[Low estimate - high estimate]
Number of HIV-infected persons, ...	..	[12 000 - 42 000]
Adult HIV prevalence *(percentage of adults 15-49)*	..	[0.2 - 0.8]

Policy views

	1976	2003
Life expectancy...	Unacceptable	Unacceptable
Under-five mortality..		Acceptable
Maternal mortality..		Unacceptable
Level of concern about AIDS....................................		Major concern

Life Expectancy at Birth

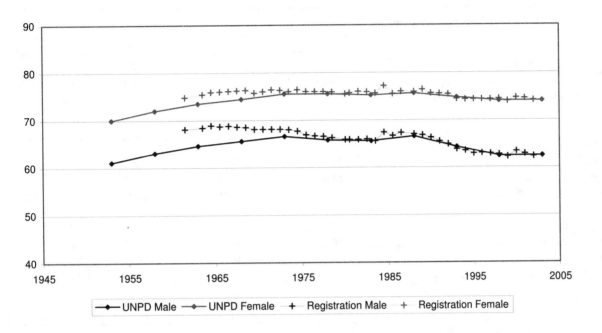

Infant Mortality Rate

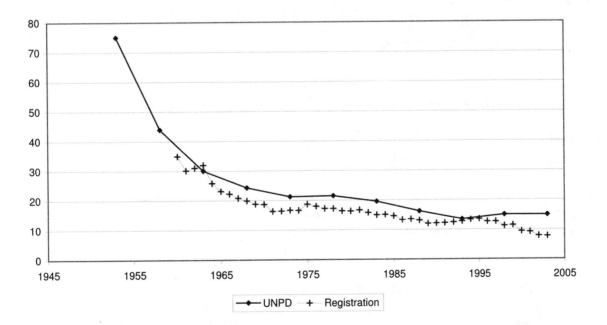

Belgium

Indicator	Period			
	Earlier year		Later year	

I. Data and estimates from national and other sources

General mortality

	Year	Value	Year	Value
Annual number of deaths *(thousands)*	1970	118.7	2004	101.9
Annual number of deaths under age one *(thousands)*	1970	3.0	2004	0.5
Crude death rate *(per 1 000 person-years)*	1970	12.3	2002	10.2

	Year	Male	Female	Year	Male	Female
Life expectancy *(years)*						
at birth	1968-1972	67.8	74.2	2003	75.9	81.7
at age 15	1968-1972	55.0	61.0	2003	61.4	67.1
at age 60	1968-1972	15.2	19.2	2003	20.2	24.4
Survival probability						
from birth to age 15	1968-1972	0.97	0.98	2003	0.99	0.99
from age 15 to age 60	1968-1972	0.81	0.89	2003	0.88	0.94
from age 60 to age 80	1968-1972	0.30	0.49	2003	0.54	0.72

Infant and child mortality

	Year	Male	Female	Both sexes	Year	Male	Female	Both sexes
Infant mortality rate *(per 1 000 live births)*	1968-1972	24	18	21	2003	4	3	3
Mortality from age 1 to age 4 *(per 1 000 live births)*	1968-1972	4	3	4	2003	2	1	2
Under-five mortality rate *(per 1 000 live births)*	1968-1972	28	21	24	2003	6	5	5

II. Data and estimates from United Nations sources

United Nations Population Division estimates

	1990-1995	2000-2005
Annual number of deaths *(thousands)*	105	103
Crude death rate *(per 1 000 person-years)*	10	10
Life expectancy at birth *(years)*		
Male	73.3	75.7
Female	80.0	81.9
Under-five mortality rate *(per 1 000 live births)*	11	6

Maternal mortality

	2000
Maternal mortality ratio *(deaths per 100 000 births)*	10

HIV/AIDS

	2003	[Low estimate - high estimate]
Number of HIV-infected persons,	10 000	[5 300 - 17 000]
Adult HIV prevalence *(percentage of adults 15-49)*	0.2	[0.1 - 0.3]

Policy views

	1976	2003
Life expectancy	Acceptable	Acceptable
Under-five mortality		Acceptable
Maternal mortality		Acceptable
Level of concern about AIDS		Minor concern

Life Expectancy at Birth

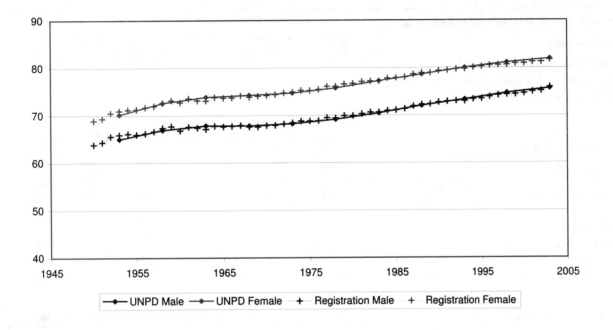

Infant Mortality Rate

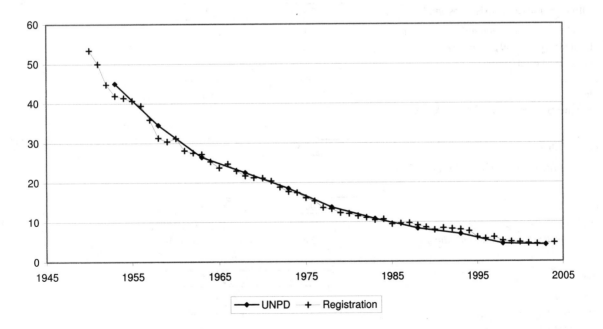

Indicator	Period				
	Earlier year			Later year	

I. Data and estimates from national and other sources

General mortality

	Year	Value		Year	Value	
Annual number of deaths *(thousands)*	..	..		..	..	
Annual number of deaths under age one *(thousands)*	..	..		..	..	
Crude death rate *(per 1 000 person-years)*	..	..		..	..	

	Year	Male	Female	Year	Male	Female
Life expectancy *(years)*						
at birth	1980	69.9	71.8	1991	70.0	74.1
at age 15	1980	58.8	60.8	1991	58.2	62.3
at age 60	1980	19.4	20.1	1991	18.9	21.5
Survival probability						
from birth to age 15	1980	0.95	0.95	1991	0.95	0.96
from age 15 to age 60	1980	0.83	0.88	1991	0.82	0.88
from age 60 to age 80	1980	0.51	0.57	1991	0.51	0.63

Infant and child mortality

	Year	Male	Female	Both sexes	Year	Male	Female	Both sexes
Infant mortality rate *(per 1 000 live births)*	1980	36	33	35	1991	35	35	35
Mortality from age 1 to age 4 *(per 1 000 live births)*	1980	14	17	15	1991	6	4	5
Under-five mortality rate *(per 1 000 live births)*	1980	49	50	49	1991	41	39	40

II. Data and estimates from United Nations sources

United Nations Population Division estimates

	1990-1995	2000-2005
Annual number of deaths *(thousands)*	1	1
Crude death rate *(per 1 000 person-years)*	5	5
Life expectancy at birth *(years)*		
Male	71.3	69.5
Female	73.8	74.5
Under-five mortality rate *(per 1 000 live births)*	45	41

Maternal mortality

	2000
Maternal mortality ratio *(deaths per 100 000 births)*	140

HIV/AIDS

	2003	[Low estimate - high estimate]
Number of HIV-infected persons,	3 600	[1 200 - 10 000]
Adult HIV prevalence *(percentage of adults 15-49)*	2.4	[0.8 - 6.9]

Policy views

	1976	2003
Life expectancy	..	Acceptable
Under-five mortality		Unacceptable
Maternal mortality		Unacceptable
Level of concern about AIDS		Major concern

Life Expectancy at Birth

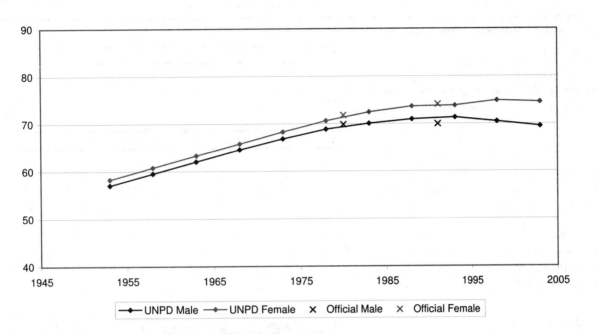

Infant Mortality Rate

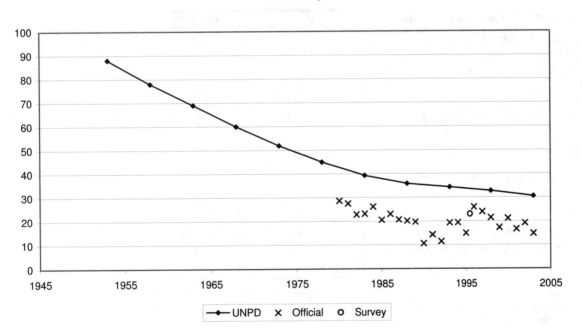

Indicator	Period				
	Earlier year			Later year		

I. Data and estimates from national and other sources

General mortality

	Year	Value		Year	Value
Annual number of deaths *(thousands)*	..	..		..	..
Annual number of deaths under age one *(thousands)*	..	..		..	..
Crude death rate *(per 1 000 person-years)*	..	..		..	..

	Year	Male	Female	Year	Male	Female
Life expectancy *(years)*						
at birth	..	..	..	1992	51.8	56.8
at age 15	..	..	..	1992	49.1	53.0
at age 60	..	..	..	1992	15.2	16.9
Survival probability						
from birth to age 15	..	..	..	..	..	..
from age 15 to age 60	..	..	..	..	..	..
from age 60 to age 80	..	..	..	..	..	..

Infant and child mortality

	Year	Male	Female	Both sexes	Year	Male	Female	Both sexes
Infant mortality rate *(per 1 000 live births)*	1975	143	127	135	1991-2001	98	92	95
Mortality from age 1 to age 4 *(per 1 000 live births)*	1975	111	104	108	1991-2001	72	79	75
Under-five mortality rate *(per 1 000 live births)*	1975	238	218	228	1991-2001	162	163	163

II. Data and estimates from United Nations sources

United Nations Population Division estimates

	1990-1995	2000-2005
Annual number of deaths *(thousands)*	80	101
Crude death rate *(per 1 000 person-years)*	14	13
Life expectancy at birth *(years)*		
Male	52.2	53.0
Female	54.7	54.5
Under-five mortality rate *(per 1 000 live births)*	183	161

Maternal mortality

	2000
Maternal mortality ratio *(deaths per 100 000 births)*	850

HIV/AIDS

	2003	[Low estimate - high estimate]
Number of HIV-infected persons,	68 000	[38 000 - 120 000]
Adult HIV prevalence *(percentage of adults 15-49)*	1.9	[1.1 - 3.3]

Policy views

	1976	2003
Life expectancy	Unacceptable	Unacceptable
Under-five mortality		Unacceptable
Maternal mortality		Unacceptable
Level of concern about AIDS		Major concern

Life Expectancy at Birth

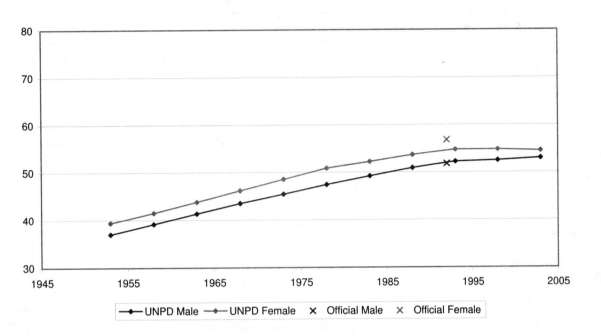

Infant Mortality Rate

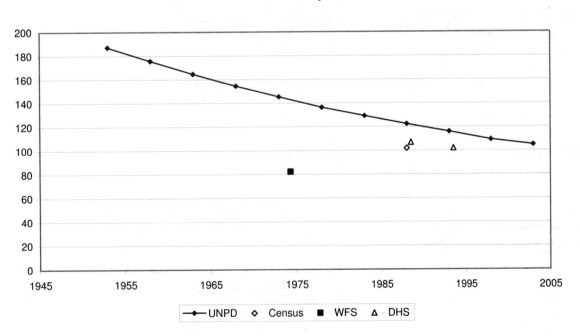

Indicator	Period			
	Earlier year		Later year	

I. Data and estimates from national and other sources

General mortality

	Year	Value	Year	Value
Annual number of deaths *(thousands)*	..	..	..	..
Annual number of deaths under age one *(thousands)*	..	..	..	..
Crude death rate *(per 1 000 person-years)*	..	..	..	..

	Year	Male	Female	Year	Male	Female
Life expectancy *(years)*						
at birth...	..	..	..	..	..	..
at age 15..	..	..	..	..	..	..
at age 60..	..	..	..	..	..	..
Survival probability						
from birth to age 15...	..	..	..	..	..	..
from age 15 to age 60...	..	..	..	..	..	..
from age 60 to age 80...	..	..	..	..	..	..

Infant and child mortality

	Year	Male	Female	Both sexes	Year	Male	Female	Both sexes
Infant mortality rate *(per 1 000 live births)*	1983	111	103	107	2000	..	..	61
Mortality from age 1 to age 4 *(per 1 000 live births)*	1983	79	80	80	..	..	..	..
Under-five mortality rate *(per 1 000 live births)*	1983	181	175	178	2000	..	..	84

II. Data and estimates from United Nations sources

United Nations Population Division estimates

	1990-1995	2000-2005
Annual number of deaths *(thousands)*	21	18
Crude death rate *(per 1 000 person-years)*	12	9
Life expectancy at birth *(years)*		
Male...	54.9	61.5
Female..	57.1	63.9
Under-five mortality rate *(per 1 000 live births)*	129	84

Maternal mortality

	2000
Maternal mortality ratio *(deaths per 100 000 births)*	420

HIV/AIDS

	2003	*[Low estimate - high estimate]*
Number of HIV-infected persons, ...	..	..
Adult HIV prevalence *(percentage of adults 15-49)*	..	..

Policy views

	1976	2003
Life expectancy..	Unacceptable	Unacceptable
Under-five mortality..		Unacceptable
Maternal mortality..		Unacceptable
Level of concern about AIDS...................................		Major concern

Life Expectancy at Birth

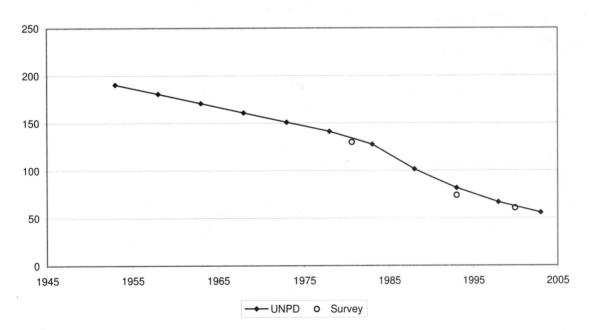

Infant Mortality Rate

Indicator	Period				
	Earlier year			Later year	

I. Data and estimates from national and other sources

General mortality	Year	Value		Year	Value
Annual number of deaths *(thousands)*	..	..		..	..
Annual number of deaths under age one *(thousands)*	..	..		..	..
Crude death rate *(per 1 000 person-years)*	..	..		..	..

	Year	Male	Female	Year	Male	Female
Life expectancy *(years)*						
at birth	1970-1975	46.0	49.0	1995-2000	59.8	63.2
at age 15	1970-1975	48.7	49.9	1995-2000	52.2	55.2
at age 60	1970-1975	14.3	14.9	1995-2000	15.9	17.6
Survival probability						
from birth to age 15	1970-1975	0.71	0.75	1995-2000	0.89	0.90
from age 15 to age 60	1970-1975	0.67	0.69	1995-2000	0.73	0.78
from age 60 to age 80	1970-1975	0.22	0.27	1995-2000	0.32	0.39

Infant and child mortality	Year	Male	Female	Both sexes	Year	Male	Female	Both sexes
Infant mortality rate *(per 1 000 live births)*	..	..	..	..	1993-2003	71	64	68
Mortality from age 1 to age 4 *(per 1 000 live births)*	..	..	..	..	1993-2003	25	29	27
Under-five mortality rate *(per 1 000 live births)*	1970	260	225	243	1993-2003	94	91	93

II. Data and estimates from United Nations sources

United Nations Population Division estimates	1990-1995	2000-2005
Annual number of deaths *(thousands)*	71	72
Crude death rate *(per 1 000 person-years)*	10	8
Life expectancy at birth *(years)*		
Male	58.3	61.8
Female	61.8	66.0
Under-five mortality rate *(per 1 000 live births)*	100	72

Maternal mortality	2000
Maternal mortality ratio *(deaths per 100 000 births)*	420

HIV/AIDS	2003	[Low estimate - high estimate]
Number of HIV-infected persons,	4 900	[1 600 - 11 000]
Adult HIV prevalence *(percentage of adults 15-49)*	0.1	[0.0 - 0.2]

Policy views	1976	2003
Life expectancy	Unacceptable	Unacceptable
Under-five mortality		Unacceptable
Maternal mortality		Unacceptable
Level of concern about AIDS		Minor concern

Life Expectancy at Birth

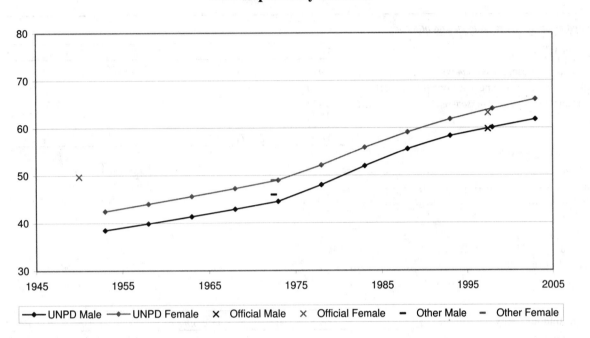

Infant Mortality Rate

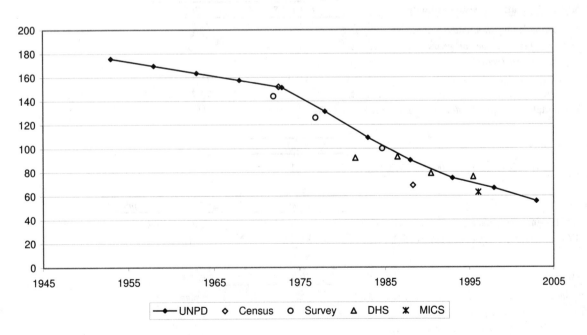

Indicator	Period					
	Earlier year			Later year		

I. Data and estimates from national and other sources

General mortality

	Year	Value		Year	Value	
Annual number of deaths *(thousands)*	1970	26.4		2004	31.7	
Annual number of deaths under age one *(thousands)*	1970	5.5		2004	0.2	
Crude death rate *(per 1 000 person-years)*	1970	7.2		2004	8.3	

	Year	Male	Female	Year	Male	Female
Life expectancy *(years)*						
at birth..	..	..	..	1988-1989	69.2	74.6
at age 15..	..	..	..	1988-1989	56.1	61.2
at age 60..	..	..	..	1988-1989	16.4	19.1
Survival probability						
from birth to age 15..	..	..	..	1988-1989	0.97	0.98
from age 15 to age 60......................................	..	..	..	1988-1989	0.80	0.90
from age 60 to age 80......................................	..	..	..	1988-1989	0.36	0.48

Infant and child mortality

	Year	Male	Female	Both sexes	Year	Male	Female	Both sexes
Infant mortality rate *(per 1 000 live births)*	..	..	..	..	1988-1989	20	17	19
Mortality from age 1 to age 4 *(per 1 000 live births)*	..	..	..	..	1988-1989	3	2	3
Under-five mortality rate *(per 1 000 live births)*	..	..	..	..	1988-1989	23	19	21

II. Data and estimates from United Nations sources

United Nations Population Division estimates

	1990-1995	2000-2005
Annual number of deaths *(thousands)*	27	34
Crude death rate *(per 1 000 person-years)*	7	9
Life expectancy at birth *(years)*		
Male..	69.5	71.3
Female...	75.1	76.7
Under-five mortality rate *(per 1 000 live births)*	20	16

Maternal mortality

	2000
Maternal mortality ratio *(deaths per 100 000 births)*	31

HIV/AIDS

	2003	[Low estimate - high estimate]
Number of HIV-infected persons, ...	900	[300 - 1 800]
Adult HIV prevalence *(percentage of adults 15-49)*	<0.1	[<0.2]

Policy views

	1976	2003
Life expectancy..	..	Unacceptable
Under-five mortality..		..
Maternal mortality..		..
Level of concern about AIDS................................		Major concern

Life Expectancy at Birth

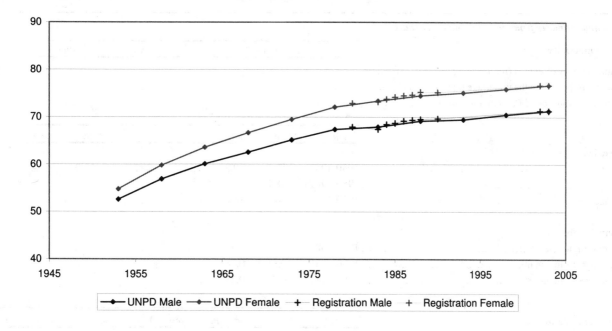

Legend: UNPD Male — UNPD Female — + Registration Male — + Registration Female

Infant Mortality Rate

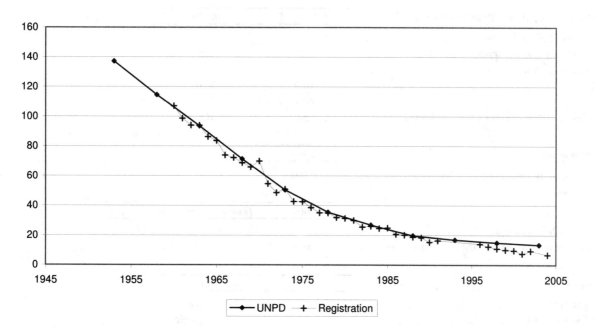

Legend: UNPD — + Registration

Indicator	Period				
	Earlier year			Later year	

I. Data and estimates from national and other sources

General mortality

	Year	Value		Year	Value	
Annual number of deaths *(thousands)*	..	..		..	..	
Annual number of deaths under age one *(thousands)*	..	..		..	..	
Crude death rate *(per 1 000 person-years)*	..	..		..	..	

	Year	Male	Female	Year	Male	Female
Life expectancy *(years)*						
at birth	1980-1981	52.7	59.3	2001	52.0	57.4
at age 15	1980-1981	48.2	53.0	..	..	..
at age 60	1980-1981	14.3	16.0	..	..	..
Survival probability						
from birth to age 15	1980-1981	0.83	0.87	..	..	..
from age 15 to age 60	1980-1981	0.65	0.76	..	..	..
from age 60 to age 80	1980-1981	0.25	0.33	..	..	..

Infant and child mortality

	Year	Male	Female	Both sexes	Year	Male	Female	Both sexes
Infant mortality rate *(per 1 000 live births)*	1982	60	43	52	1996	..	..	61
Mortality from age 1 to age 4 *(per 1 000 live births)*	1982	17	17	17	..	..	..	..
Under-five mortality rate *(per 1 000 live births)*	1982	76	60	68	1996	..	..	76

II. Data and estimates from United Nations sources

United Nations Population Division estimates

	1990-1995	2000-2005
Annual number of deaths *(thousands)*	10	44
Crude death rate *(per 1 000 person-years)*	7	25
Life expectancy at birth *(years)*		
Male	61.7	36.0
Female	66.6	37.1
Under-five mortality rate *(per 1 000 live births)*	62	106

Maternal mortality

	2000
Maternal mortality ratio *(deaths per 100 000 births)*	100

HIV/AIDS

	2003	[Low estimate - high estimate]
Number of HIV-infected persons,	350 000	[330 000 - 380 000]
Adult HIV prevalence *(percentage of adults 15-49)*	37.3	[35.5 - 39.1]

Policy views

	1976	2003
Life expectancy	Unacceptable	Unacceptable
Under-five mortality		Unacceptable
Maternal mortality		Unacceptable
Level of concern about AIDS		Major concern

Life Expectancy at Birth

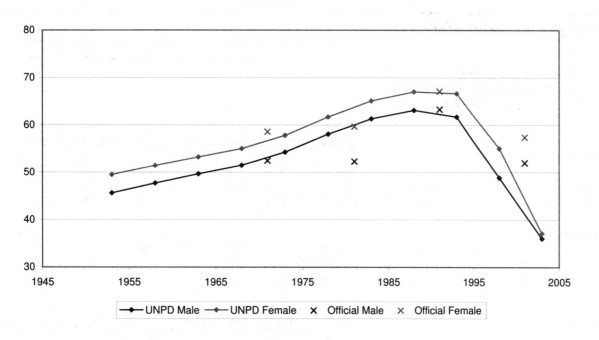

Infant Mortality Rate

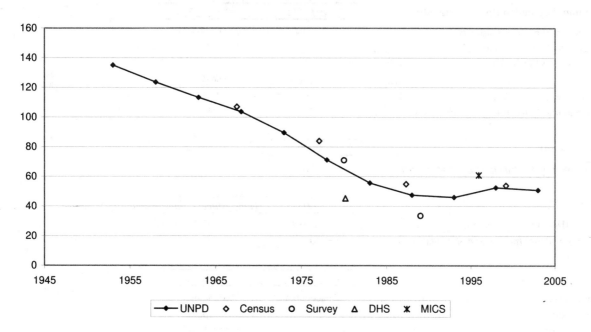

Indicator	Period					
	Earlier year			Later year		

I. Data and estimates from national and other sources

General mortality

	Year	Value		Year	Value	
Annual number of deaths *(thousands)*	..	..		..	..	
Annual number of deaths under age one *(thousands)*	..	..		..	..	
Crude death rate *(per 1 000 person-years)*	..	..		..	..	

	Year	Male	Female	Year	Male	Female
Life expectancy *(years)*						
at birth..	1960-1970	57.6	61.1	2002	67.3	74.9
at age 15..	1960-1970	51.5	54.2	2002	55.3	62.4
at age 60..	1960-1970	15.0	16.6	2002	19.0	21.9
Survival probability						
from birth to age 15..	1960-1970	0.86	0.88	2002	0.96	0.97
from age 15 to age 60...	1960-1970	0.72	0.77	2002	0.75	0.87
from age 60 to age 80...	1960-1970	0.30	0.38	2002	0.45	0.57

Infant and child mortality

	Year	Male	Female	Both sexes	Year	Male	Female	Both sexes
Infant mortality rate *(per 1 000 live births)*	1977	86	65	76	1986-1996	52	44	48
Mortality from age 1 to age 4 *(per 1 000 live births)*	1977	30	24	27	1986-1996	9	9	9
Under-five mortality rate *(per 1 000 live births)*	1977	113	88	101	1986-1996	60	53	57

II. Data and estimates from United Nations sources

United Nations Population Division estimates

	1990-1995	2000-2005
Annual number of deaths *(thousands)*	1 084	1 186
Crude death rate *(per 1 000 person-years)*	7	7
Life expectancy at birth *(years)*		
Male..	63.1	66.4
Female..	70.9	74.4
Under-five mortality rate *(per 1 000 live births)*	56	35

Maternal mortality

	2000
Maternal mortality ratio *(deaths per 100 000 births)*	260

HIV/AIDS

	2003	*[Low estimate - high estimate]*
Number of HIV-infected persons, ...	660 000	[320 000 - 1 100 000]
Adult HIV prevalence *(percentage of adults 15-49)*	0.7	[0.3 - 1.1]

Policy views

	1976	2003
Life expectancy..	Unacceptable	Acceptable
Under-five mortality..		Unacceptable
Maternal mortality..		Unacceptable
Level of concern about AIDS....................................		Major concern

Life Expectancy at Birth

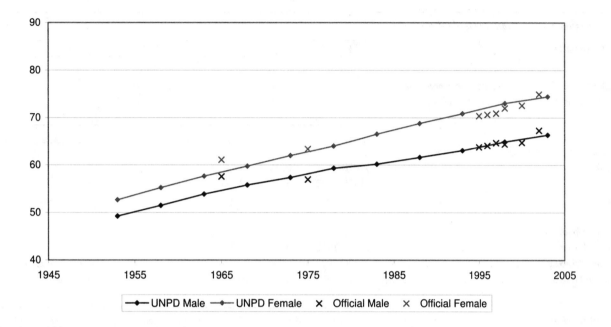

Infant Mortality Rate

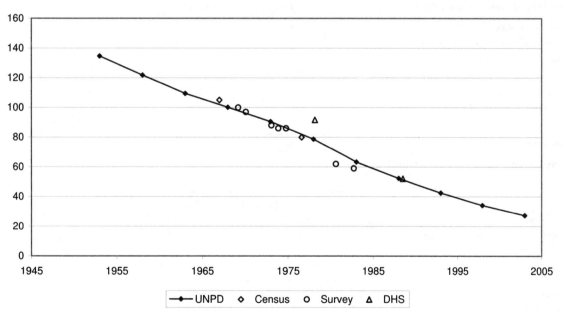

Indicator	Period					
	Earlier year			Later year		

I. Data and estimates from national and other sources

General mortality

	Year	Value			Year	Value	
Annual number of deaths *(thousands)*	1970	0.7			2004	1.0	
Annual number of deaths under age one *(thousands)*	1970	0.2			2004	0.1	
Crude death rate *(per 1 000 person-years)*	1970	5.5			2004	2.8	

	Year	Male	Female		Year	Male	Female
Life expectancy *(years)*							
at birth..	1970-1972	61.9	62.1		..	..	..
at age 15..	1970-1972	53.0	52.0		..	..	..
at age 60..	1970-1972	14.3	14.9		..	..	..
Survival probability							
from birth to age 15...	1970-1972	0.91	0.92		..	..	..
from age 15 to age 60...	1970-1972	0.76	0.72		..	..	..
from age 60 to age 80...	1970-1972	0.27	0.25		..	..	..

Infant and child mortality

	Year	Male	Female	Both sexes	Year	Male	Female	Both sexes
Infant mortality rate *(per 1 000 live births)*	1970-1972	61	46	54	2004	..	..	9
Mortality from age 1 to age 4 *(per 1 000 live births)*	1970-1972	19	20	19	..	..	..	..
Under-five mortality rate *(per 1 000 live births)*	1970-1972	78	65	72	..	..	..	..

II. Data and estimates from United Nations sources

United Nations Population Division estimates

	1990-1995	2000-2005
Annual number of deaths *(thousands)*	1	1
Crude death rate *(per 1 000 person-years)*	3	3
Life expectancy at birth *(years)*		
Male..	72.4	74.2
Female..	77.1	78.9
Under-five mortality rate *(per 1 000 live births)*	9	7

Maternal mortality

	2000
Maternal mortality ratio *(deaths per 100 000 births)*	37

HIV/AIDS

	2003	[Low estimate - high estimate]
Number of HIV-infected persons, ...	<200	[<400]
Adult HIV prevalence *(percentage of adults 15-49)*	<0.1	[<0.2]

Policy views

	1976	2003
Life expectancy...	..	Acceptable
Under-five mortality...		Acceptable
Maternal mortality..		Acceptable
Level of concern about AIDS...................................		Minor concern

Life Expectancy at Birth

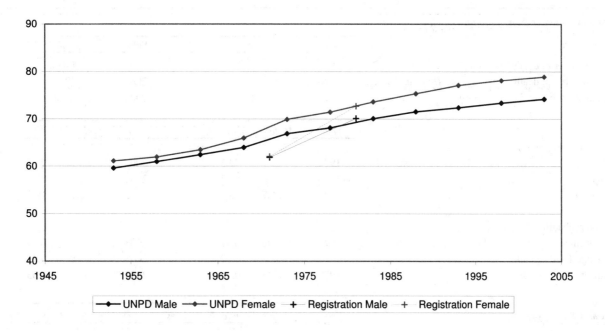

Legend: UNPD Male — UNPD Female — + Registration Male + Registration Female

Infant Mortality Rate

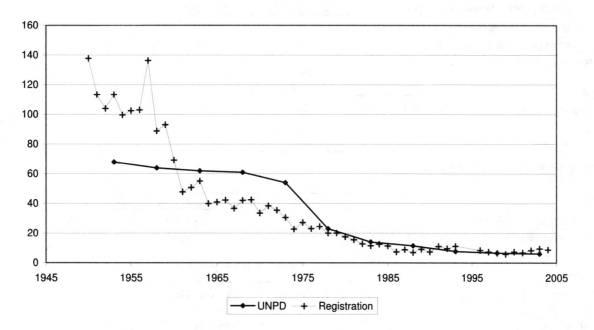

Legend: UNPD + Registration

Indicator	Period					
	Earlier year			Later year		

I. Data and estimates from national and other sources

General mortality

	Year	Value		Year	Value	
Annual number of deaths *(thousands)*	1970	77.1		2004	110.1	
Annual number of deaths under age one *(thousands)*	1970	3.8		2004	0.8	
Crude death rate *(per 1 000 person-years)*	1970	9.1		2004	14.2	

	Year	Male	Female	Year	Male	Female
Life expectancy *(years)*						
at birth..	1970	69.1	73.5	2003	68.9	76.0
at age 15..	1970	57.0	60.7	2003	55.3	62.1
at age 60..	1970	16.7	18.8	2003	16.1	19.9
Survival probability						
from birth to age 15..	1970	0.96	0.97	2003	0.98	0.98
from age 15 to age 60..	1970	0.82	0.90	2003	0.78	0.91
from age 60 to age 80..	1970	0.34	0.46	2003	0.35	0.53

Infant and child mortality

	Year	Male	Female	Both sexes	Year	Male	Female	Both sexes
Infant mortality rate *(per 1 000 live births)*	1970	31	23	27	2003	14	11	13
Mortality from age 1 to age 4 *(per 1 000 live births)*	1970	5	4	5	2003	2	2	2
Under-five mortality rate *(per 1 000 live births)*	1970	36	27	31	2003	17	13	15

II. Data and estimates from United Nations sources

United Nations Population Division estimates

	1990-1995	2000-2005
Annual number of deaths *(thousands)*	109	112
Crude death rate *(per 1 000 person-years)*	13	14
Life expectancy at birth *(years)*		
Male...	67.6	68.8
Female..	74.7	75.6
Under-five mortality rate *(per 1 000 live births)*	20	17

Maternal mortality

	2000
Maternal mortality ratio *(deaths per 100 000 births)*	32

HIV/AIDS

	2003	[Low estimate - high estimate]
Number of HIV-infected persons, ...	<500	[<1 000]
Adult HIV prevalence *(percentage of adults 15-49)*	<0.1	[<0.2]

Policy views

	1976	2003
Life expectancy...	Acceptable	Unacceptable
Under-five mortality...		Unacceptable
Maternal mortality..		Acceptable
Level of concern about AIDS....................................		Major concern

Life Expectancy at Birth

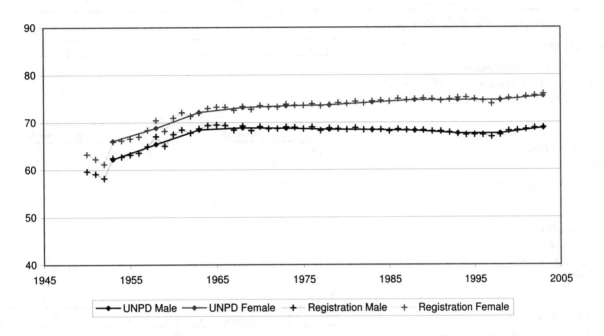

Infant Mortality Rate

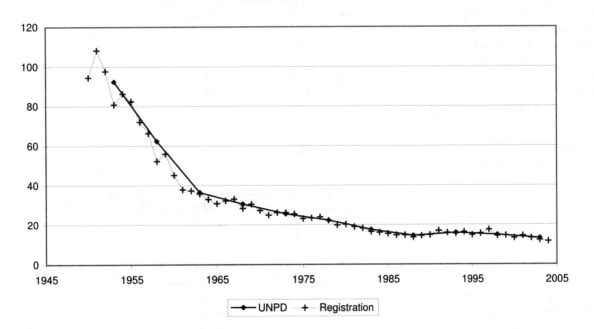

Indicator	Period							
	Earlier year				*Later year*			

I. Data and estimates from national and other sources

General mortality

	Year	*Value*			*Year*	*Value*		
Annual number of deaths *(thousands)*	..	..			..	..		
Annual number of deaths under age one *(thousands)*	..	..			..	..		
Crude death rate *(per 1 000 person-years)*	..	..			..	..		

	Year	*Male*	*Female*		*Year*	*Male*	*Female*	
Life expectancy *(years)*								
at birth..	..	..	..		..	..	..	
at age 15..	..	..	..		..	..	..	
at age 60..	..	..	..		..	..	..	
Survival probability								
from birth to age 15....................................	..	..	..		..	..	..	
from age 15 to age 60..................................	..	..	..		..	..	..	
from age 60 to age 80..................................	..	..	..		..	..	..	

Infant and child mortality

	Year	*Male*	*Female*	*Both sexes*	*Year*	*Male*	*Female*	*Both sexes*
Infant mortality rate *(per 1 000 live births)*	1985	128	111	120	1993-2003	96	89	92
Mortality from age 1 to age 4 *(per 1 000 live births)*	1985	71	79	75	1993-2003	110	113	111
Under-five mortality rate *(per 1 000 live births)*	1985	190	182	186	1993-2003	195	192	193

II. Data and estimates from United Nations sources

United Nations Population Division estimates

	1990-1995	*2000-2005*
Annual number of deaths *(thousands)*	171	211
Crude death rate *(per 1 000 person-years)*	19	17
Life expectancy at birth *(years)*		
Male..	45.3	46.7
Female...	48.4	48.1
Under-five mortality rate *(per 1 000 live births)*	208	196

Maternal mortality

	2000
Maternal mortality ratio *(deaths per 100 000 births)*	1 000

HIV/AIDS

	2003	*[Low estimate - high estimate]*
Number of HIV-infected persons, ...	300 000	[190 000 - 470 000]
Adult HIV prevalence *(percentage of adults 15-49)*	4.2	[2.7 - 6.5]

Policy views

	1976	*2003*
Life expectancy...	Unacceptable	Unacceptable
Under-five mortality...		Unacceptable
Maternal mortality...		Unacceptable
Level of concern about AIDS..................................		Major concern

Life Expectancy at Birth

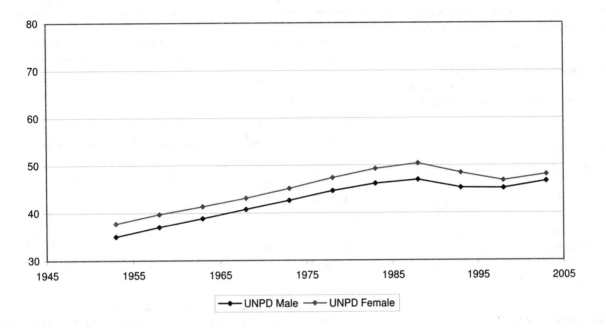

Infant Mortality Rate

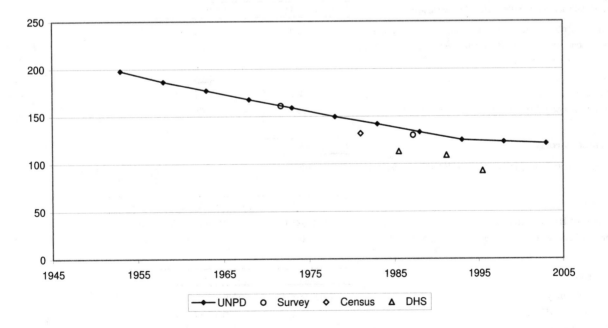

Indicator	Period			
	Earlier year		Later year	

I. Data and estimates from national and other sources

General mortality

	Year	Value	Year	Value
Annual number of deaths *(thousands)*	..	..	..	..
Annual number of deaths under age one *(thousands)*	..	..	..	..
Crude death rate *(per 1 000 person-years)*	..	..	..	..

	Year	Male	Female	Year	Male	Female
Life expectancy *(years)*						
at birth..	1970-1971	43.2	44.2	..	..	..
at age 15...	1970-1971	47.5	46.8	..	..	..
at age 60...	1970-1971	22.3	15.9	..	..	..
Survival probability						
from birth to age 15...........................	1970-1971	0.68	0.70	..	..	..
from age 15 to age 60.........................	1970-1971	0.51	0.58	..	..	..
from age 60 to age 80.........................	..	..	..	..	..	..

Infant and child mortality

	Year	Male	Female	Both sexes	Year	Male	Female	Both sexes
Infant mortality rate *(per 1 000 live births)*	1982	126	100	113	1997	..	..	127
Mortality from age 1 to age 4 *(per 1 000 live births)*	1982	74	96	85	..	..	..	..
Under-five mortality rate *(per 1 000 live births)*	1982	190	186	188	1997	..	..	196

II. Data and estimates from United Nations sources

United Nations Population Division estimates

	1990-1995	2000-2005
Annual number of deaths *(thousands)*	125	132
Crude death rate *(per 1 000 person-years)*	21	19
Life expectancy at birth *(years)*		
Male..	40.5	42.5
Female..	44.4	44.4
Under-five mortality rate *(per 1 000 live births)*	220	187

Maternal mortality

	2000
Maternal mortality ratio *(deaths per 100 000 births)*	1 000

HIV/AIDS

	2003	*[Low estimate - high estimate]*
Number of HIV-infected persons, ...	250 000	[170 000 - 370 000]
Adult HIV prevalence *(percentage of adults 15-49)*	6	[4.1 - 8.8]

Policy views

	1976	2003
Life expectancy..	Unacceptable	Unacceptable
Under-five mortality..		Unacceptable
Maternal mortality..		Unacceptable
Level of concern about AIDS..................................		Major concern

Life Expectancy at Birth

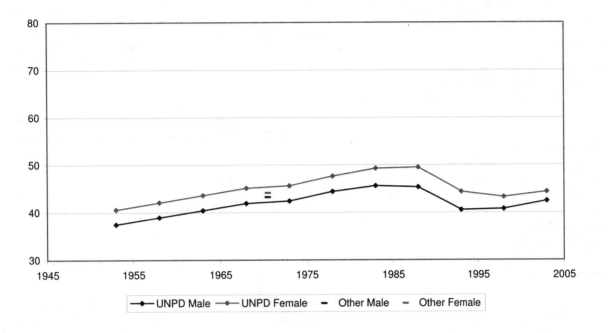

Infant Mortality Rate

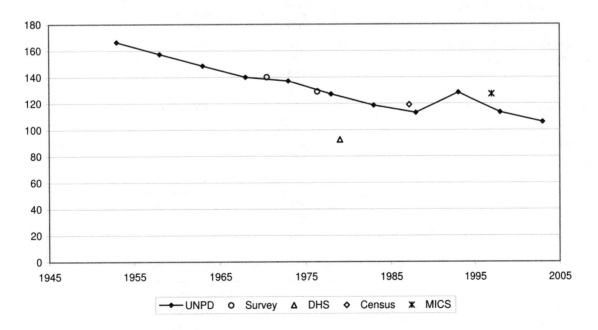

Indicator	Period			
	Earlier year		Later year	

I. Data and estimates from national and other sources

General mortality

	Year	Value	Year	Value
Annual number of deaths *(thousands)*	..	..	..	..
Annual number of deaths under age one *(thousands)*	..	..	..	..
Crude death rate *(per 1 000 person-years)*	..	..	..	..

	Year	Male	Female	Year	Male	Female
Life expectancy *(years)*						
at birth...	..	..	..	..	..	..
at age 15..	..	..	..	..	..	..
at age 60..	..	..	..	..	..	..
Survival probability						
from birth to age 15..	..	..	..	..	..	..
from age 15 to age 60..	..	..	..	..	..	..
from age 60 to age 80..	..	..	..	..	..	..

Infant and child mortality

	Year	Male	Female	Both sexes	Year	Male	Female	Both sexes
Infant mortality rate *(per 1 000 live births)*	..	..	..	..	1990-2000	103	82	93
Mortality from age 1 to age 4 *(per 1 000 live births)*	..	..	..	..	1990-2000	34	30	32
Under-five mortality rate *(per 1 000 live births)*	..	..	..	..	1990-2000	133	110	122

II. Data and estimates from United Nations sources

United Nations Population Division estimates

	1990-1995	2000-2005
Annual number of deaths *(thousands)*	131	145
Crude death rate *(per 1 000 person-years)*	12	11
Life expectancy at birth *(years)*		
Male...	52.9	52.1
Female..	56.9	59.6
Under-five mortality rate *(per 1 000 live births)*	170	140

Maternal mortality

	2000
Maternal mortality ratio *(deaths per 100 000 births)*	450

HIV/AIDS

	2003	[Low estimate - high estimate]
Number of HIV-infected persons, ...	170 000	[100 000 - 290 000]
Adult HIV prevalence *(percentage of adults 15-49)*	2.6	[1.5 - 4.4]

Policy views

	1976	2003
Life expectancy...	Unacceptable	Unacceptable
Under-five mortality..		Unacceptable
Maternal mortality...		Unacceptable
Level of concern about AIDS.....................................		Major concern

Life Expectancy at Birth

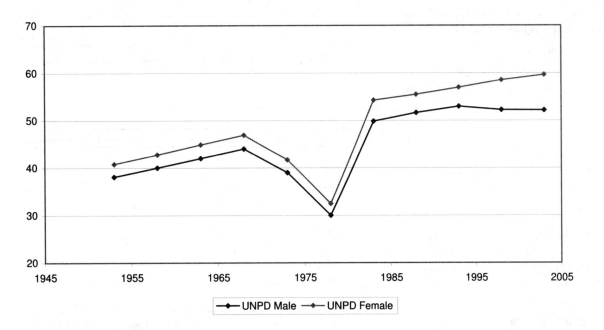

Infant Mortality Rate

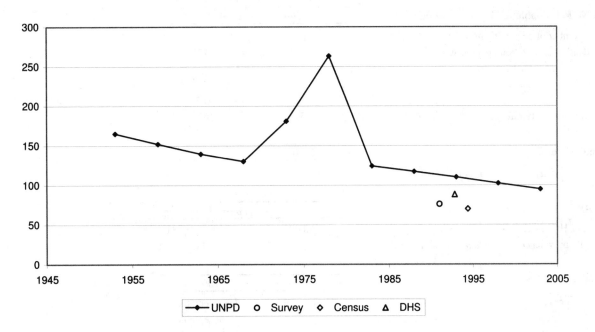

Indicator	Period				
	Earlier year			Later year	

I. Data and estimates from national and other sources

General mortality

	Year	Value		Year	Value	
Annual number of deaths *(thousands)*	..	..		..	..	
Annual number of deaths under age one *(thousands)*	..	..		..	..	
Crude death rate *(per 1 000 person-years)*	..	..		..	..	

	Year	Male	Female		Year	Male	Female
Life expectancy *(years)*							
at birth	1974	47.5	50.7		..	..	..
at age 15	1974	46.0	48.3		..	..	..
at age 60	1974	12.9	14.4		..	..	..
Survival probability							
from birth to age 15	1974	0.77	0.79		..	..	..
from age 15 to age 60	1974	0.59	0.65		..	..	..
from age 60 to age 80	1974	0.20	0.26		..	..	..

Infant and child mortality

	Year	Male	Female	Both sexes	Year	Male	Female	Both sexes
Infant mortality rate *(per 1 000 live births)*	1973	126	116	121	1994-2004	88	74	81
Mortality from age 1 to age 4 *(per 1 000 live births)*	1973	92	96	94	1994-2004	73	72	72
Under-five mortality rate *(per 1 000 live births)*	1973	207	200	204	1994-2004	154	141	148

II. Data and estimates from United Nations sources

United Nations Population Division estimates

	1990-1995	2000-2005
Annual number of deaths *(thousands)*	179	269
Crude death rate *(per 1 000 person-years)*	14	17
Life expectancy at birth *(years)*		
Male	50.3	45.1
Female	53.8	46.5
Under-five mortality rate *(per 1 000 live births)*	154	163

Maternal mortality

	2000
Maternal mortality ratio *(deaths per 100 000 births)*	730

HIV/AIDS

	2003	[Low estimate - high estimate]
Number of HIV-infected persons,	560 000	[390 000 - 810 000]
Adult HIV prevalence *(percentage of adults 15-49)*	6.9	[4.8 - 9.8]

Policy views

	1976	2003
Life expectancy	Unacceptable	Unacceptable
Under-five mortality		Unacceptable
Maternal mortality		Unacceptable
Level of concern about AIDS		Major concern

Life Expectancy at Birth

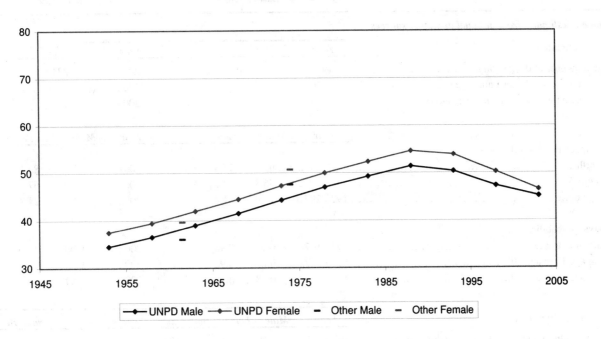

Infant Mortality Rate

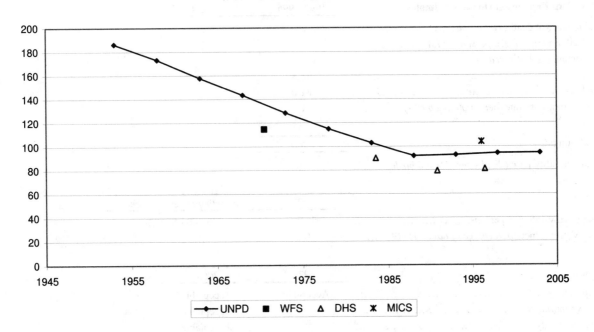

Indicator	Period						
	Earlier year				Later year		

I. Data and estimates from national and other sources

General mortality

	Year	Value			Year	Value	
Annual number of deaths *(thousands)*	1970	156.0			2004	234.6	
Annual number of deaths under age one *(thousands)*	1970	7.0			2002	1.8	
Crude death rate *(per 1 000 person-years)*	1970	7.3			2004	7.3	

	Year	Male	Female		Year	Male	Female
Life expectancy *(years)*							
at birth..	1970-1972	69.3	76.4		2002	77.2	82.1
at age 15...	1970-1972	56.3	63.0		2002	62.9	67.7
at age 60...	1970-1972	17.0	21.4		2002	21.1	24.8
Survival probability							
from birth to age 15.......................................	1970-1972	0.97	0.98		2002	0.99	0.99
from age 15 to age 60......................................	1970-1972	0.81	0.90		2002	0.90	0.94
from age 60 to age 80......................................	1970-1972	0.38	0.58		2002	0.57	0.71

Infant and child mortality

	Year	Male	Female	Both sexes	Year	Male	Female	Both sexes
Infant mortality rate *(per 1 000 live births)*	1970-1972	20	15	18	2002	6	5	5
Mortality from age 1 to age 4 *(per 1 000 live births)*	1970-1972	4	3	3	2002	1	1	1
Under-five mortality rate *(per 1 000 live births)*	1970-1972	24	18	21	2002	7	6	6

II. Data and estimates from United Nations sources

United Nations Population Division estimates

	1990-1995	2000-2005
Annual number of deaths *(thousands)*	201	226
Crude death rate *(per 1 000 person-years)*	7	7
Life expectancy at birth *(years)*		
Male..	74.8	77.3
Female..	81.0	82.4
Under-five mortality rate *(per 1 000 live births)*	8	6

Maternal mortality

	2000
Maternal mortality ratio *(deaths per 100 000 births)*	6

HIV/AIDS

	2003	[Low estimate - high estimate]
Number of HIV-infected persons, ...	56 000	[26 000 - 86 000]
Adult HIV prevalence *(percentage of adults 15-49)*	0.3	[0.2 - 0.5]

Policy views

	1976	2003
Life expectancy..	Acceptable	Acceptable
Under-five mortality...		Acceptable
Maternal mortality...		Acceptable
Level of concern about AIDS..................................		Major concern

Life Expectancy at Birth

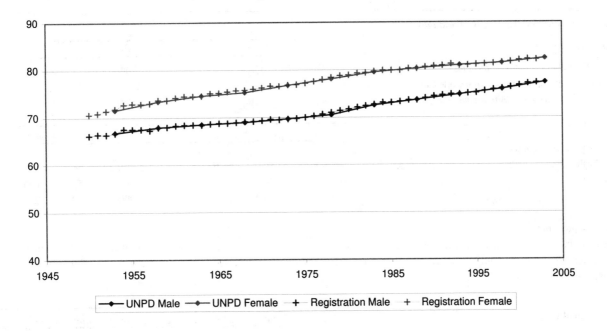

Legend: UNPD Male — UNPD Female — + Registration Male + Registration Female

Infant Mortality Rate

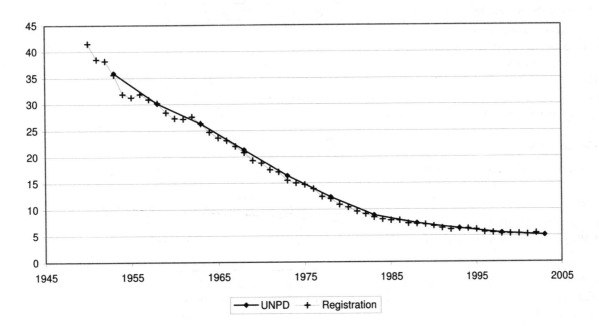

Legend: UNPD + Registration

I. Data and estimates from national and other sources

Indicator	Period					
	Earlier year			Later year		

General mortality

	Year	Value			Year	Value		
Annual number of deaths *(thousands)*	1970	2.9			1999	2.8		
Annual number of deaths under age one *(thousands)*	1970	0.9			1999	0.4		
Crude death rate *(per 1 000 person-years)*	1970	10.8			1999	6.6		

	Year	Male	Female		Year	Male	Female	
Life expectancy *(years)*								
at birth	1979-1981	59.0	61.0		1990	63.5	71.3	
at age 15	1979-1981	49.7	51.0		1990	53.7	62.0	
at age 60	1979-1981	8.4	8.7		1990	19.4	22.5	
Survival probability								
from birth to age 15		..	..	..	1990	0.92	0.92	
from age 15 to age 60		..	..	..	1990	0.71	0.87	
from age 60 to age 80		..	..	..	1990	0.49	0.58	

Infant and child mortality

	Year	Male	Female	Both sexes	Year	Male	Female	Both sexes
Infant mortality rate *(per 1 000 live births)*	..	..	..	..	1990	38	35	36
Mortality from age 1 to age 4 *(per 1 000 live births)*	..	..	..	..	1990	27	32	30
Under-five mortality rate *(per 1 000 live births)*	..	..	..	..	1990	64	66	65

II. Data and estimates from United Nations sources

United Nations Population Division estimates

	1990-1995	2000-2005
Annual number of deaths *(thousands)*	3	3
Crude death rate *(per 1 000 person-years)*	8	5
Life expectancy at birth *(years)*		
Male	63.5	66.8
Female	69.0	73.0
Under-five mortality rate *(per 1 000 live births)*	56	36

Maternal mortality

	2000
Maternal mortality ratio *(deaths per 100 000 births)*	150

HIV/AIDS

	2003	[Low estimate - high estimate]
Number of HIV-infected persons,	..	..
Adult HIV prevalence *(percentage of adults 15-49)*	..	..

Policy views

	1976	2003
Life expectancy	Unacceptable	Acceptable
Under-five mortality		Unacceptable
Maternal mortality		..
Level of concern about AIDS		..

Life Expectancy at Birth

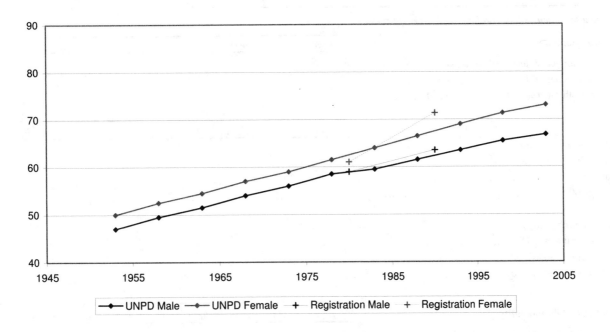

Infant Mortality Rate

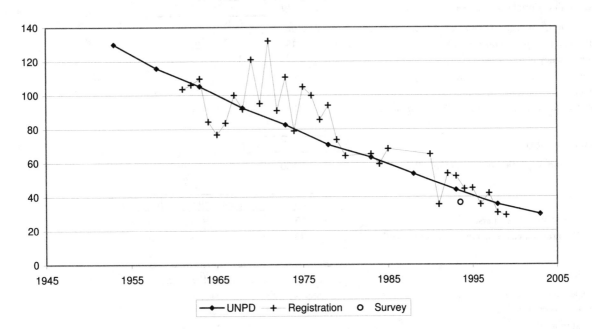

Indicator	Period			
	Earlier year		*Later year*	

I. Data and estimates from national and other sources

General mortality

	Year	Value	Year	Value
Annual number of deaths *(thousands)*	..	..	..	..
Annual number of deaths under age one *(thousands)*	..	..	..	..
Crude death rate *(per 1 000 person-years)*	..	..	..	..

	Year	Male	Female	Year	Male	Female
Life expectancy *(years)*						
at birth..............	..	..	..	..	..	..
at age 15..............	..	..	..	..	..	..
at age 60..............	..	..	..	..	..	..
Survival probability						
from birth to age 15..............	..	..	..	..	..	..
from age 15 to age 60..............	..	..	..	..	..	..
from age 60 to age 80..............	..	..	..	..	..	..

Infant and child mortality

	Year	Male	Female	Both sexes	Year	Male	Female	Both sexes
Infant mortality rate *(per 1 000 live births)*	..	..	..	..	1984-1994	109	94	102
Mortality from age 1 to age 4 *(per 1 000 live births)*	..	..	..	..	1984-1994	63	64	63
Under-five mortality rate *(per 1 000 live births)*	..	..	..	..	1984-1994	165	152	159

II. Data and estimates from United Nations sources

United Nations Population Division estimates

	1990-1995	2000-2005
Annual number of deaths *(thousands)*	58	87
Crude death rate *(per 1 000 person-years)*	18	22
Life expectancy at birth *(years)*		
Male..............	44.0	38.5
Female..............	49.6	40.3
Under-five mortality rate *(per 1 000 live births)*	181	176

Maternal mortality

	2000
Maternal mortality ratio *(deaths per 100 000 births)*	1 100

HIV/AIDS

	2003	*[Low estimate - high estimate]*
Number of HIV-infected persons, ...	260 000	[160 000 - 410 000]
Adult HIV prevalence *(percentage of adults 15-49)*	13.5	[8.3 - 21.2]

Policy views

	1976	2003
Life expectancy..............	Unacceptable	Unacceptable
Under-five mortality..............		Unacceptable
Maternal mortality..............		Unacceptable
Level of concern about AIDS..............		Major concern

Life Expectancy at Birth

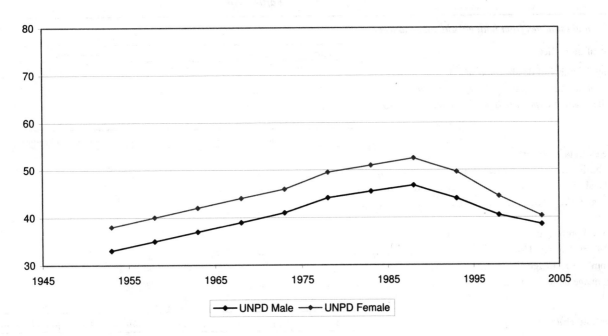

Infant Mortality Rate

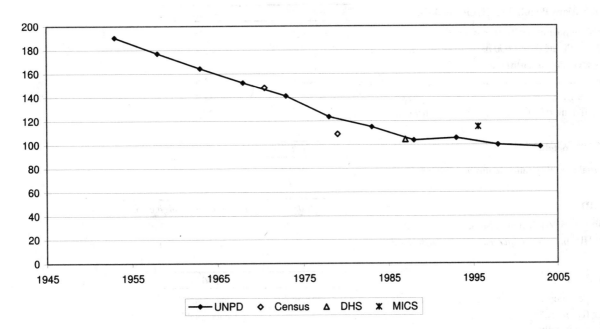

Indicator	Period			
	Earlier year		Later year	

I. Data and estimates from national and other sources

General mortality

	Year	Value		Year	Value
Annual number of deaths *(thousands)*	..	..		..	..
Annual number of deaths under age one *(thousands)*	..	..		..	..
Crude death rate *(per 1 000 person-years)*	..	..		..	..

	Year	Male	Female	Year	Male	Female
Life expectancy *(years)*						
at birth...	..	..	..	..	..	..
at age 15...	..	..	..	..	..	..
at age 60...	..	..	..	..	..	..
Survival probability						
from birth to age 15.................................	..	..	..	..	..	..
from age 15 to age 60...............................	..	..	..	..	..	..
from age 60 to age 80...............................	..	..	..	..	..	..

Infant and child mortality

	Year	Male	Female	Both sexes	Year	Male	Female	Both sexes
Infant mortality rate *(per 1 000 live births)*	..	..	..	..	1986-1996	120	100	110
Mortality from age 1 to age 4 *(per 1 000 live births)*	..	..	..	..	1986-1996	106	99	103
Under-five mortality rate *(per 1 000 live births)*	..	..	..	..	1986-1996	213	189	201

II. Data and estimates from United Nations sources

United Nations Population Division estimates

	1990-1995	2000-2005
Annual number of deaths *(thousands)*	125	181
Crude death rate *(per 1 000 person-years)*	19	20
Life expectancy at birth *(years)*		
Male...	44.3	42.5
Female...	48.1	44.8
Under-five mortality rate *(per 1 000 live births)*	207	203

Maternal mortality

	2000
Maternal mortality ratio *(deaths per 100 000 births)*	1 100

HIV/AIDS

	2003	*[Low estimate - high estimate]*
Number of HIV-infected persons, ...	200 000	[130 000 - 300 000]
Adult HIV prevalence *(percentage of adults 15-49)*	4.8	[3.1 - 7.2]

Policy views

	1976	2003
Life expectancy...	Unacceptable	Unacceptable
Under-five mortality..		Unacceptable
Maternal mortality..		Unacceptable
Level of concern about AIDS..................................		Major concern

Life Expectancy at Birth

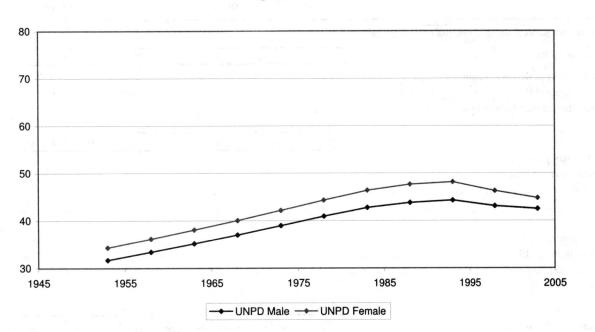

Infant Mortality Rate

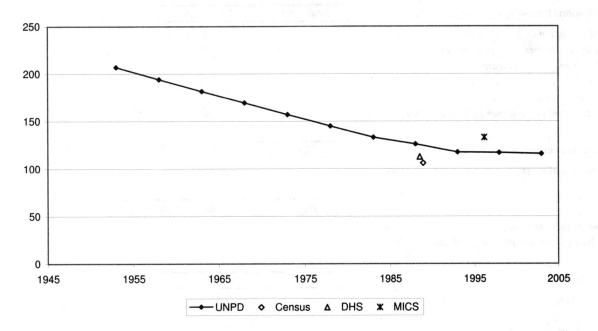

Indicator	Period				
	Earlier year			Later year	

I. Data and estimates from national and other sources

General mortality

	Year	Value		Year	Value
Annual number of deaths *(thousands)*	1970	1.5		1994	1.4
Annual number of deaths under age one *(thousands)*	1970	0.0		1994	0.0
Crude death rate *(per 1 000 person-years)*	1970	12.3		1994	9.7

	Year	Male	Female	Year	Male	Female
Life expectancy *(years)*						
at birth	..	..	..	..	..	..
at age 15	..	..	..	..	..	..
at age 60	..	..	..	..	..	..
Survival probability						
from birth to age 15	..	..	..	..	..	..
from age 15 to age 60	..	..	..	..	..	..
from age 60 to age 80	..	..	..	..	..	..

Infant and child mortality

	Year	Male	Female	Both sexes	Year	Male	Female	Both sexes
Infant mortality rate *(per 1 000 live births)*	..	..	..	..	1994	..	..	3
Mortality from age 1 to age 4 *(per 1 000 live births)*	..	..	..	..	..	..	..	..
Under-five mortality rate *(per 1 000 live births)*	..	..	..	..	..	..	..	..

II. Data and estimates from United Nations sources

United Nations Population Division estimates

	1990-1995	2000-2005
Annual number of deaths *(thousands)*	2	1
Crude death rate *(per 1 000 person-years)*	12	10
Life expectancy at birth *(years)*		
Male	74.4	75.9
Female	79.1	80.8
Under-five mortality rate *(per 1 000 live births)*	7	6

Maternal mortality

	2000
Maternal mortality ratio *(deaths per 100 000 births)*	..

HIV/AIDS

	2003	*[Low estimate - high estimate]*
Number of HIV-infected persons,	..	..
Adult HIV prevalence *(percentage of adults 15-49)*	..	..

Policy views

	1976	2003
Life expectancy	..	..
Under-five mortality		..
Maternal mortality		..
Level of concern about AIDS		..

Life Expectancy at Birth

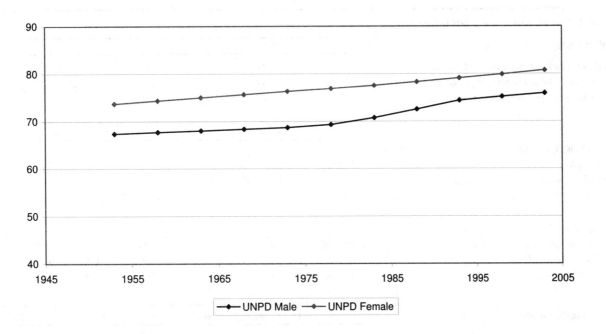

Infant Mortality Rate

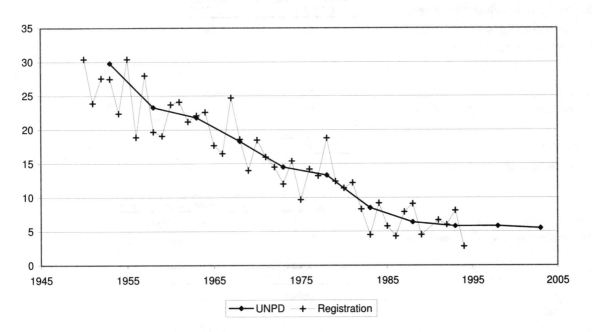

Indicator	Period				
	Earlier year			Later year	

I. Data and estimates from national and other sources

General mortality

	Year	Value		Year	Value
Annual number of deaths *(thousands)*	1970	83.0		2002	81.1
Annual number of deaths under age one *(thousands)*	1970	20.6		2002	2.0
Crude death rate *(per 1 000 person-years)*	1970	8.7		2002	5.2

	Year	Male	Female	Year	Male	Female
Life expectancy *(years)*						
at birth................	1969-1970	60.5	66.0	2001-2002	74.4	80.4
at age 15................	1969-1970	51.9	57.4	2001-2002	60.4	66.3
at age 60................	1969-1970	15.5	18.1	2001-2002	20.1	23.7
Survival probability						
from birth to age 15............	1969-1970	0.90	0.91	1999	0.98	0.98
from age 15 to age 60............	1969-1970	0.71	0.82	1999	0.85	0.92
from age 60 to age 80............	1969-1970	0.31	0.42	1999	0.46	0.61

Infant and child mortality

	Year	Male	Female	Both sexes	Year	Male	Female	Both sexes
Infant mortality rate *(per 1 000 live births)*	1972	73	62	68	1999	14	11	13
Mortality from age 1 to age 4 *(per 1 000 live births)*	1972	17	15	16	1999	3	2	3
Under-five mortality rate *(per 1 000 live births)*	1972	90	76	83	1999	17	13	15

II. Data and estimates from United Nations sources

United Nations Population Division estimates

	1990-1995	2000-2005
Annual number of deaths *(thousands)*	76	79
Crude death rate *(per 1 000 person-years)*	6	5
Life expectancy at birth *(years)*		
Male...	71.5	74.8
Female...	77.4	80.8
Under-five mortality rate *(per 1 000 live births)*	17	10

Maternal mortality

	2000
Maternal mortality ratio *(deaths per 100 000 births)*	31

HIV/AIDS

	2003	[Low estimate - high estimate]
Number of HIV-infected persons, ...	26 000	[13 000 - 44 000]
Adult HIV prevalence *(percentage of adults 15-49)*	0.3	[0.2 - 0.5]

Policy views

	1976	2003
Life expectancy...	Acceptable	Acceptable
Under-five mortality...		Acceptable
Maternal mortality..		Acceptable
Level of concern about AIDS..................................		Major concern

Life Expectancy at Birth

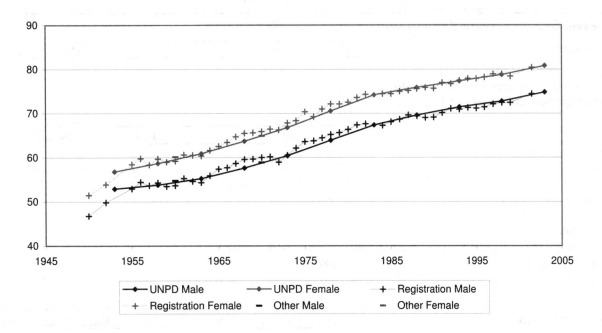

Infant Mortality Rate

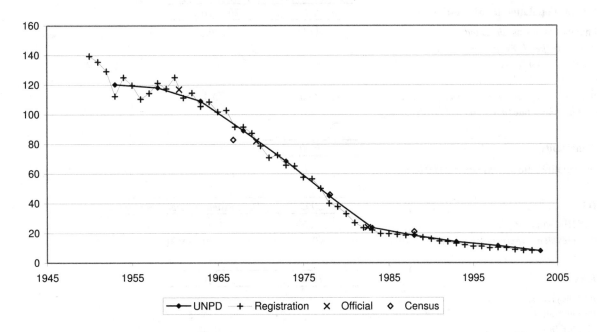

Indicator	Period			
	Earlier year		Later year	

I. Data and estimates from national and other sources

General mortality

	Year	Value	Year	Value
Annual number of deaths *(thousands)*	..	..	..	..
Annual number of deaths under age one *(thousands)*	..	..	..	..
Crude death rate *(per 1 000 person-years)*	..	..	..	..

	Year	Male	Female	Year	Male	Female
Life expectancy *(years)*						
at birth..	1973-1975	62.1	64.5	2000	69.6	73.3
at age 15..	1973-1975	54.0	56.4	..	..	..
at age 60..	1973-1975	15.1	17.2	..	..	..
Survival probability						
from birth to age 15..	1973-1975	0.90	0.90	..	..	..
from age 15 to age 60..	1973-1975	0.78	0.81	..	..	..
from age 60 to age 80..	1973-1975	0.29	0.39	..	..	..

Infant and child mortality

	Year	Male	Female	Both sexes	Year	Male	Female	Both sexes
Infant mortality rate *(per 1 000 live births)*	1985	36	34	35	2003	..	..	26
Mortality from age 1 to age 4 *(per 1 000 live births)*	1985	8	9	8	..	..	..	..
Under-five mortality rate *(per 1 000 live births)*	1985	43	43	43	2003	..	..	30

II. Data and estimates from United Nations sources

United Nations Population Division estimates

	1990-1995	2000-2005
Annual number of deaths *(thousands)*	8 681	8 795
Crude death rate *(per 1 000 person-years)*	7	7
Life expectancy at birth *(years)*		
Male...	66.5	69.8
Female..	70.0	73.3
Under-five mortality rate *(per 1 000 live births)*	56	41

Maternal mortality

	2000
Maternal mortality ratio *(deaths per 100 000 births)*	56

HIV/AIDS

	2003	[Low estimate - high estimate]
Number of HIV-infected persons, ...	840 000	[430 000 - 1 500 000]
Adult HIV prevalence *(percentage of adults 15-49)*	0.1	[0.1 - 0.2]

Policy views

	1976	2003
Life expectancy...	Unacceptable	Acceptable
Under-five mortality..		Acceptable
Maternal mortality..		Acceptable
Level of concern about AIDS....................................		Major concern

Life Expectancy at Birth

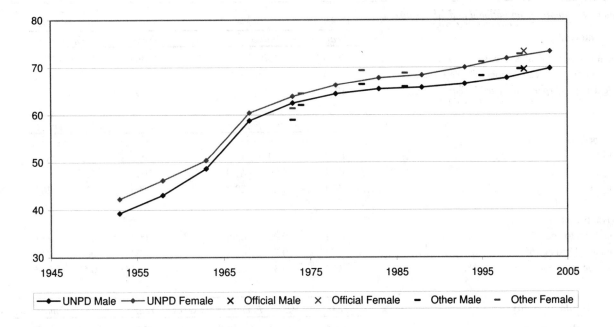

Infant Mortality Rate

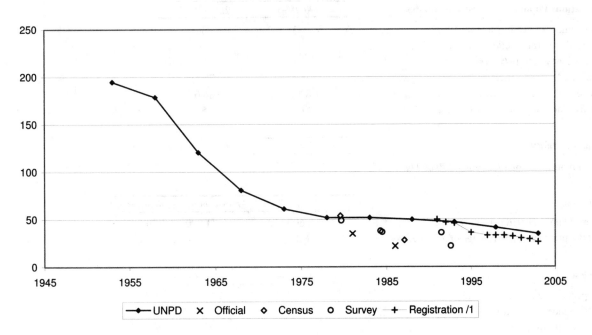

[1] Refers to the Child Mortality Surveillance System

Indicator	Period					
	Earlier year			Later year		

I. Data and estimates from national and other sources

General mortality

	Year	Value		Year	Value	
Annual number of deaths *(thousands)*	1970	20.0		2004	36.6	
Annual number of deaths under age one *(thousands)*	1970	1.5		2004	0.1	
Crude death rate *(per 1 000 person-years)*	1970	5.1		2004	5.3	

	Year	Male	Female	Year	Male	Female
Life expectancy *(years)*						
at birth..	1971	67.4	75.0	2003	78.5	84.3
at age 15..	1971	54.6	61.9	2003	63.9	69.6
at age 60..	1971	15.5	20.7	2003	21.9	26.2
Survival probability						
from birth to age 15....................................	1971	0.97	0.98	2003	0.99	1.00
from age 15 to age 60..................................	1971	0.78	0.88	2003	0.91	0.96
from age 60 to age 80..................................	1971	0.30	0.55	2003	0.58	0.76

Infant and child mortality

	Year	Male	Female	Both sexes	Year	Male	Female	Both sexes
Infant mortality rate *(per 1 000 live births)*	1975	15	12	14	2003	2	2	2
Mortality from age 1 to age 4 *(per 1 000 live births)*	1975	3	3	3	2003	2	1	1
Under-five mortality rate *(per 1 000 live births)*	1975	19	15	17	2003	4	3	4

II. Data and estimates from United Nations sources

United Nations Population Division estimates

	1990-1995	2000-2005
Annual number of deaths *(thousands)*	33	36
Crude death rate *(per 1 000 person-years)*	6	5
Life expectancy at birth *(years)*		
Male..	75.5	78.6
Female...	81.0	84.6
Under-five mortality rate *(per 1 000 live births)*	6	5

Maternal mortality

	2000
Maternal mortality ratio *(deaths per 100 000 births)*	..

HIV/AIDS

	2003	[Low estimate - high estimate]
Number of HIV-infected persons, ...	2 600	[1 300 - 4 400]
Adult HIV prevalence *(percentage of adults 15-49)*	0.1	[<0.2]

Policy views

	1976	2003
Life expectancy...	..	..
Under-five mortality..		..
Maternal mortality..		..
Level of concern about AIDS................................		..

Life Expectancy at Birth

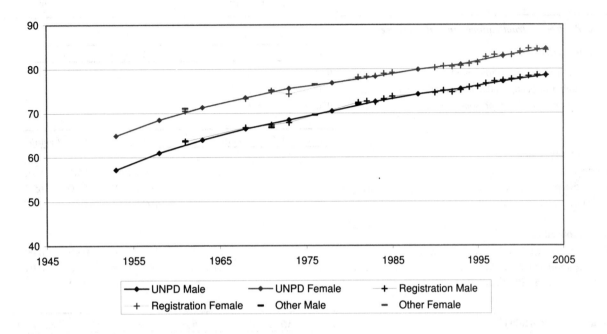

Infant Mortality Rate

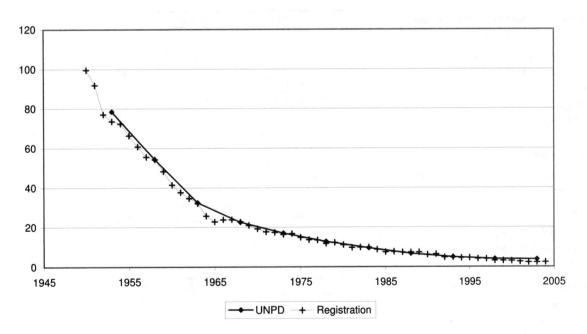

Indicator	Period					
	Earlier year			Later year		

I. Data and estimates from national and other sources

General mortality

	Year	Value		Year	Value	
Annual number of deaths *(thousands)*	1970	1.5		2003	1.5	
Annual number of deaths under age one *(thousands)*	1970	0.1		2003	0.0	
Crude death rate *(per 1 000 person-years)*	1970	6.2		2003	3.3	

	Year	Male	Female	Year	Male	Female
Life expectancy *(years)*						
at birth	..	..	..	1993-1996	75.1	80.0
at age 15	..	..	..	1993-1996	61.0	65.7
at age 60	..	..	..	1993-1996	19.2	22.7
Survival probability						
from birth to age 15	..	..	..	1993-1996	0.99	0.99
from age 15 to age 60	..	..	..	1993-1996	0.90	0.94
from age 60 to age 80	..	..	..	1993-1996	0.49	0.64

Infant and child mortality

	Year	Male	Female	Both sexes	Year	Male	Female	Both sexes
Infant mortality rate *(per 1 000 live births)*	..	..	..	..	1993-1996	8	7	7
Mortality from age 1 to age 4 *(per 1 000 live births)*	..	..	..	..	1993-1996	1	1	1
Under-five mortality rate *(per 1 000 live births)*	..	..	..	..	1993-1996	9	8	9

II. Data and estimates from United Nations sources

United Nations Population Division estimates

	1990-1995	2000-2005
Annual number of deaths *(thousands)*	2	2
Crude death rate *(per 1 000 person-years)*	5	4
Life expectancy at birth *(years)*		
Male	75.2	77.8
Female	79.8	82.0
Under-five mortality rate *(per 1 000 live births)*	11	8

Maternal mortality

	2000
Maternal mortality ratio *(deaths per 100 000 births)*	..

HIV/AIDS

	2003	[Low estimate - high estimate]
Number of HIV-infected persons,	..	..
Adult HIV prevalence *(percentage of adults 15-49)*	..	..

Policy views

	1976	2003
Life expectancy	..	..
Under-five mortality		..
Maternal mortality		..
Level of concern about AIDS		..

Life Expectancy at Birth

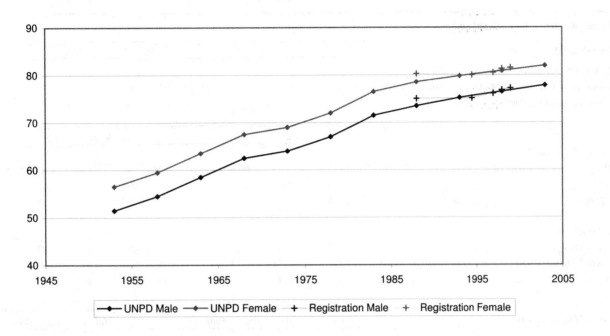

Infant Mortality Rate

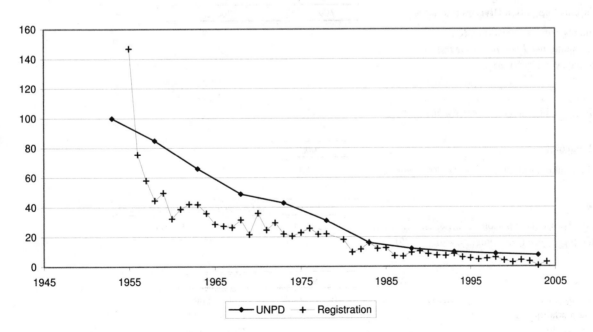

Colombia

Indicator	Period				
	Earlier year			Later year	

I. Data and estimates from national and other sources

General mortality

	Year	Value		Year	Value
Annual number of deaths *(thousands)*	..	..		..	..
Annual number of deaths under age one *(thousands)*	..	..		..	..
Crude death rate *(per 1 000 person-years)*	..	..		..	..

	Year	Male	Female	Year	Male	Female
Life expectancy *(years)*						
at birth...	1973	57.1	60.8	2002-2007	69.6	75.7
at age 15..	1973	50.8	54.1	2002-2007	57.3	63.2
at age 60..	1973	14.6	16.1	2002-2007	18.8	21.8
Survival probability						
from birth to age 15...	1973	0.86	0.88	2002-2007	0.96	0.97
from age 15 to age 60...	1973	0.71	0.77	2002-2007	0.82	0.89
from age 60 to age 80...	1973	0.27	0.35	2002-2007	0.45	0.57

Infant and child mortality

	Year	Male	Female	Both sexes	Year	Male	Female	Both sexes
Infant mortality rate *(per 1 000 live births)*	1972	72	58	65	1990-2000	29	20	24
Mortality from age 1 to age 4 *(per 1 000 live births)*	1972	38	29	39	1990-2000	4	3	4
Under-five mortality rate *(per 1 000 live births)*	1972	107	95	101	1990-2000	32	23	28

II. Data and estimates from United Nations sources

United Nations Population Division estimates

	1990-1995	2000-2005
Annual number of deaths *(thousands)*	237	239
Crude death rate *(per 1 000 person-years)*	6	5
Life expectancy at birth *(years)*		
Male..	64.3	69.2
Female...	73.0	75.3
Under-five mortality rate *(per 1 000 live births)*	47	33

Maternal mortality

	2000
Maternal mortality ratio *(deaths per 100 000 births)*	130

HIV/AIDS

	2003	[Low estimate - high estimate]
Number of HIV-infected persons, ...	190 000	[90 000 - 310 000]
Adult HIV prevalence *(percentage of adults 15-49)*	0.7	[0.4 - 1.2]

Policy views

	1976	2003
Life expectancy..	Unacceptable	Unacceptable
Under-five mortality..		Unacceptable
Maternal mortality...		Unacceptable
Level of concern about AIDS....................................		Major concern

Life Expectancy at Birth

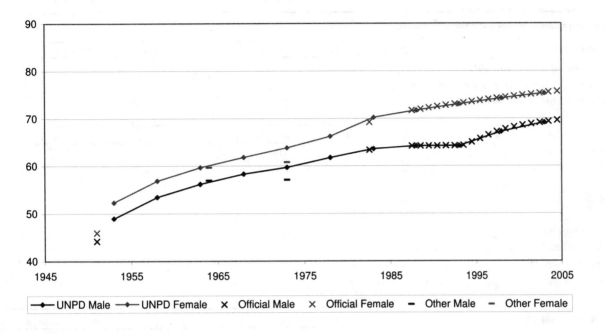

Infant Mortality Rate

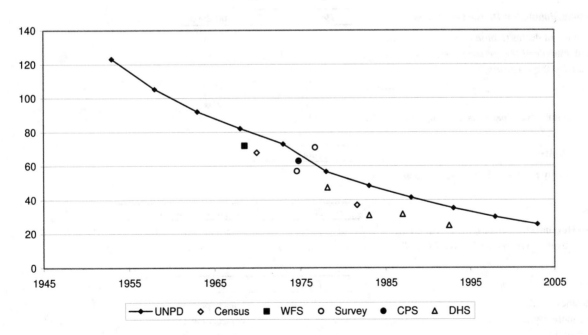

Indicator	Period							
	Earlier year				Later year			

I. Data and estimates from national and other sources

General mortality

	Year	Value			Year	Value		
Annual number of deaths *(thousands)*	..	..			..	..		
Annual number of deaths under age one *(thousands)*	..	..			..	..		
Crude death rate *(per 1 000 person-years)*	..	..			..	..		

	Year	Male	Female		Year	Male	Female	
Life expectancy *(years)*								
at birth...	..	..	..		..	..	..	
at age 15..	..	..	..		..	..	..	
at age 60..	..	..	..		..	..	..	
Survival probability								
from birth to age 15..	..	..	..		..	..	..	
from age 15 to age 60..	..	..	..		..	..	..	
from age 60 to age 80..	..	..	..		..	..	..	

Infant and child mortality

	Year	Male	Female	Both sexes	Year	Male	Female	Both sexes
Infant mortality rate *(per 1 000 live births)*	..	..	..	..	1986-1996	93	75	84
Mortality from age 1 to age 4 *(per 1 000 live births)*	..	..	..	..	1986-1996	32	31	32
Under-five mortality rate *(per 1 000 live births)*	..	..	..	..	1986-1996	122	103	113

II. Data and estimates from United Nations sources

United Nations Population Division estimates

	1990-1995	2000-2005
Annual number of deaths *(thousands)*	6	6
Crude death rate *(per 1 000 person-years)*	10	7
Life expectancy at birth *(years)*		
Male..	56.1	60.9
Female...	59.9	65.1
Under-five mortality rate *(per 1 000 live births)*	113	77

Maternal mortality

	2000
Maternal mortality ratio *(deaths per 100 000 births)*	480

HIV/AIDS

	2003	[Low estimate - high estimate]
Number of HIV-infected persons, ...	..	..
Adult HIV prevalence *(percentage of adults 15-49)*	..	..

Policy views

	1976	2003
Life expectancy..	Unacceptable	Unacceptable
Under-five mortality...		Unacceptable
Maternal mortality...		Unacceptable
Level of concern about AIDS.....................................		Major concern

Life Expectancy at Birth

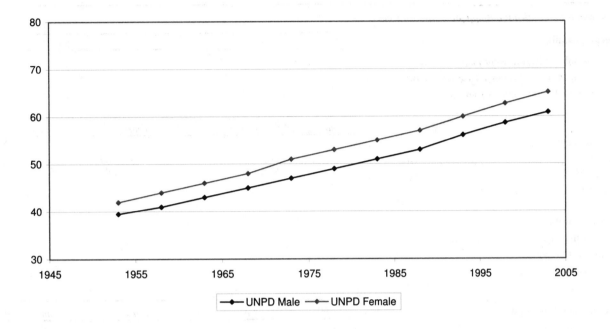

Infant Mortality Rate

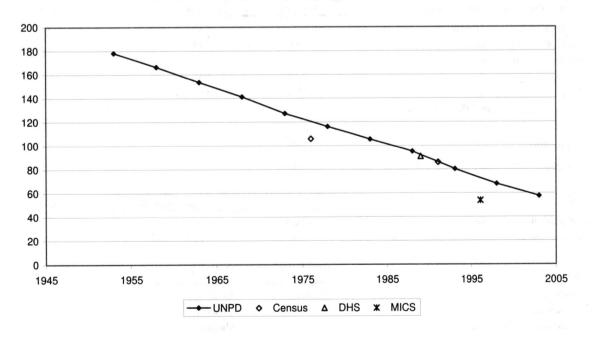

Indicator	Period			
	Earlier year		Later year	

I. Data and estimates from national and other sources

General mortality

	Year	Value	Year	Value
Annual number of deaths *(thousands)*	..	..	..	..
Annual number of deaths under age one *(thousands)*	..	..	..	..
Crude death rate *(per 1 000 person-years)*	..	..	..	..

	Year	Male	Female	Year	Male	Female
Life expectancy *(years)*						
at birth..	..	..	..	..	..	..
at age 15...	..	..	..	..	..	..
at age 60...	..	..	..	..	..	..
Survival probability						
from birth to age 15...............................	..	..	..	..	..	..
from age 15 to age 60............................	..	..	..	..	..	..
from age 60 to age 80............................	..	..	..	..	..	..

Infant and child mortality

	Year	Male	Female	Both sexes	Year	Male	Female	Both sexes
Infant mortality rate *(per 1 000 live births)*	1975	89	81	85	..	..	..	..
Mortality from age 1 to age 4 *(per 1 000 live births)*	1975	38	38	38	..	..	..	..
Under-five mortality rate *(per 1 000 live births)*	1975	124	116	120	..	..	..	..

II. Data and estimates from United Nations sources

United Nations Population Division estimates

	1990-1995	2000-2005
Annual number of deaths *(thousands)*	35	49
Crude death rate *(per 1 000 person-years)*	13	13
Life expectancy at birth *(years)*		
Male..	50.4	50.6
Female...	55.6	53.1
Under-five mortality rate *(per 1 000 live births)*	113	108

Maternal mortality

	2000
Maternal mortality ratio *(deaths per 100 000 births)*	510

HIV/AIDS

	2003	[Low estimate - high estimate]
Number of HIV-infected persons, ...	90 000	[39 000 - 200 000]
Adult HIV prevalence *(percentage of adults 15-49)*	4.9	[2.1 - 11.0]

Policy views

	1976	2003
Life expectancy..	Unacceptable	Unacceptable
Under-five mortality...		Unacceptable
Maternal mortality..		Unacceptable
Level of concern about AIDS....................................		Major concern

Life Expectancy at Birth

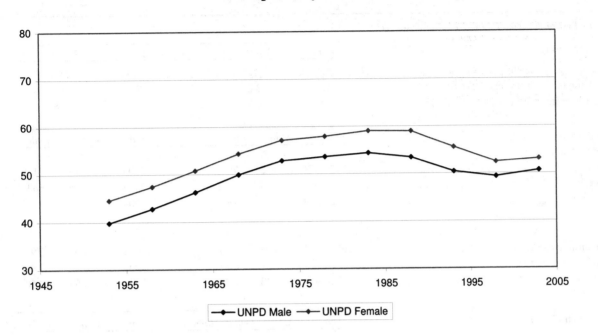

Infant Mortality Rate

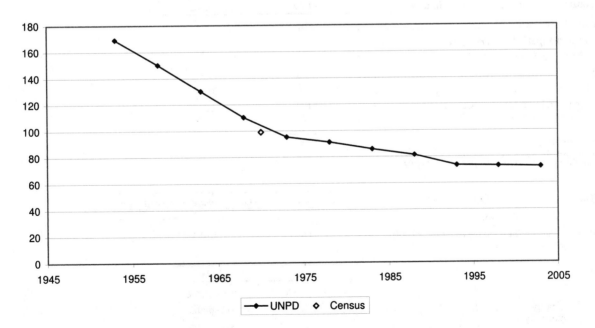

Indicator	Period				
	Earlier year			Later year	

I. Data and estimates from national and other sources

General mortality

	Year	Value		Year	Value
Annual number of deaths *(thousands)*	1970	11.5		2004	15.9
Annual number of deaths under age one *(thousands)*	1970	3.6		2004	0.7
Crude death rate *(per 1 000 person-years)*	1970	6.7		2004	3.8

	Year	Male	Female	Year	Male	Female
Life expectancy *(years)*						
at birth..	1972-1974	66.3	70.5	2004	76.5	81.0
at age 15...	1972-1974	56.5	60.0	2004	62.6	66.9
at age 60...	1972-1974	17.4	19.2	2004	21.6	24.2
Survival probability						
from birth to age 15...	1972-1974	0.93	0.94	2004	0.99	0.99
from age 15 to age 60...	1972-1974	0.81	0.87	2004	0.89	0.94
from age 60 to age 80...	1972-1974	0.40	0.48	2004	0.59	0.68

Infant and child mortality

	Year	Male	Female	Both sexes	Year	Male	Female	Both sexes
Infant mortality rate *(per 1 000 live births)*	1972	56	44	50	2004	10	8	9
Mortality from age 1 to age 4 *(per 1 000 live births)*	1972	15	16	16	2004	1	1	1
Under-five mortality rate *(per 1 000 live births)*	1972	71	59	65	2004	11	9	10

II. Data and estimates from United Nations sources

United Nations Population Division estimates

	1990-1995	2000-2005
Annual number of deaths *(thousands)*	14	16
Crude death rate *(per 1 000 person-years)*	4	4
Life expectancy at birth *(years)*		
Male..	74.0	75.8
Female...	78.6	80.6
Under-five mortality rate *(per 1 000 live births)*	17	12

Maternal mortality

	2000
Maternal mortality ratio *(deaths per 100 000 births)*	43

HIV/AIDS

	2003	[Low estimate - high estimate]
Number of HIV-infected persons, ...	12 000	[6 000 - 21 000]
Adult HIV prevalence *(percentage of adults 15-49)*	0.6	[0.3 - 1.0]

Policy views

	1976	2003
Life expectancy...	Acceptable	Acceptable
Under-five mortality..		Acceptable
Maternal mortality..		Acceptable
Level of concern about AIDS...................................		Major concern

Life Expectancy at Birth

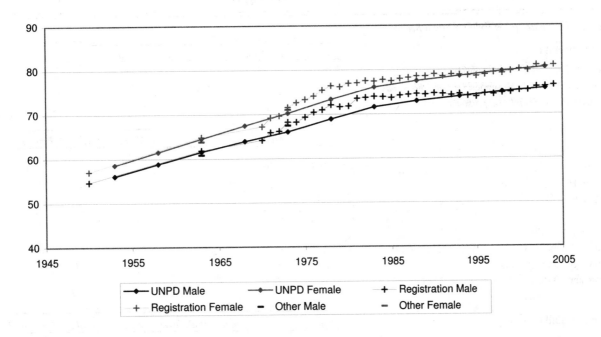

Infant Mortality Rate

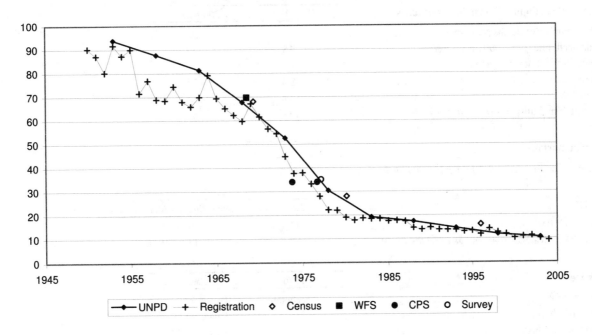

Indicator	Period							
	Earlier year				Later year			

I. Data and estimates from national and other sources

General mortality

	Year	Value			Year	Value		
Annual number of deaths *(thousands)*	..	..			..	..		
Annual number of deaths under age one *(thousands)*	..	..			..	..		
Crude death rate *(per 1 000 person-years)*	..	..			..	..		

	Year	Male	Female		Year	Male	Female	
Life expectancy *(years)*								
at birth...	..	..	..		..	..	..	
at age 15..	..	..	..		..	..	..	
at age 60..	..	..	..		..	..	..	
Survival probability								
from birth to age 15...	..	..	..		..	..	..	
from age 15 to age 60...	..	..	..		..	..	..	
from age 60 to age 80...	..	..	..		..	..	..	

Infant and child mortality

	Year	Male	Female	Both sexes	Year	Male	Female	Both sexes
Infant mortality rate *(per 1 000 live births)*	1975	145	117	131	1988-1998	130	93	112
Mortality from age 1 to age 4 *(per 1 000 live births)*	1975	73	72	72	1988-1998	83	58	71
Under-five mortality rate *(per 1 000 live births)*	1975	207	181	194	1988-1998	203	146	174

II. Data and estimates from United Nations sources

United Nations Population Division estimates

	1990-1995	2000-2005
Annual number of deaths *(thousands)*	204	297
Crude death rate *(per 1 000 person-years)*	15	17
Life expectancy at birth *(years)*		
Male..	48.4	45.2
Female...	52.4	46.8
Under-five mortality rate *(per 1 000 live births)*	177	189

Maternal mortality

	2000
Maternal mortality ratio *(deaths per 100 000 births)*	690

HIV/AIDS

	2003	[Low estimate - high estimate]
Number of HIV-infected persons, ...	570 000	[390 000 - 820 000]
Adult HIV prevalence *(percentage of adults 15-49)*	7	[4.9 - 10.0]

Policy views

	1976	2003
Life expectancy..	Unacceptable	Unacceptable
Under-five mortality...		Unacceptable
Maternal mortality..		Unacceptable
Level of concern about AIDS....................................		Major concern

Life Expectancy at Birth

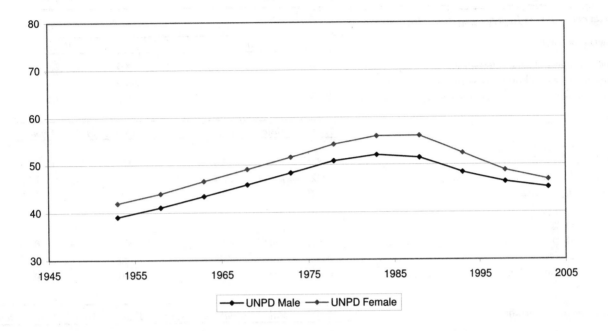

Infant Mortality Rate

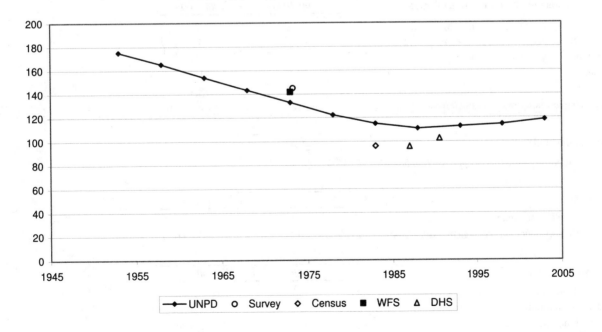

Indicator	Period				
	Earlier year			Later year	

I. Data and estimates from national and other sources

General mortality

	Year	Value		Year	Value	
Annual number of deaths *(thousands)*	1970	44.1		2003	52.6	
Annual number of deaths under age one *(thousands)*	1970	2.1		2003	0.3	
Crude death rate *(per 1 000 person-years)*	1970	10.0		2003	11.8	

	Year	Male	Female	Year	Male	Female
Life expectancy *(years)*						
at birth..	1982	66.0	73.9	2000	70.5	77.8
at age 15..	1982	53.0	60.4	2000	56.3	63.5
at age 60..	1982	14.7	18.7	2000	16.2	20.7
Survival probability						
from birth to age 15..................................	1982	0.97	0.98	2000	0.99	0.99
from age 15 to age 60................................	1982	0.75	0.89	2000	0.82	0.93
from age 60 to age 80................................	1982	0.29	0.49	2000	0.33	0.53

Infant and child mortality

	Year	Male	Female	Both sexes	Year	Male	Female	Both sexes
Infant mortality rate *(per 1 000 live births)*	1982	22	15	19	2000	8	7	7
Mortality from age 1 to age 4 *(per 1 000 live births)*	1982	3	3	3	2000	1	1	1
Under-five mortality rate *(per 1 000 live births)*	1982	25	17	21	2000	9	8	9

II. Data and estimates from United Nations sources

United Nations Population Division estimates

	1990-1995	2000-2005
Annual number of deaths *(thousands)*	49	52
Crude death rate *(per 1 000 person-years)*	11	11
Life expectancy at birth *(years)*		
Male..	68.3	71.3
Female...	76.5	78.4
Under-five mortality rate *(per 1 000 live births)*	12	8

Maternal mortality

	2000
Maternal mortality ratio *(deaths per 100 000 births)*	8

HIV/AIDS

	2003	[Low estimate - high estimate]
Number of HIV-infected persons, ...	<200	[<400]
Adult HIV prevalence *(percentage of adults 15-49)*	<0.1	[<0.2]

Policy views

	1976	2003
Life expectancy...	..	Acceptable
Under-five mortality...		Acceptable
Maternal mortality...		Acceptable
Level of concern about AIDS.................................		Minor concern

Life Expectancy at Birth

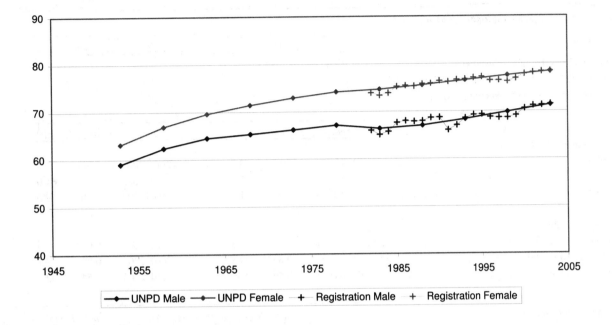

Infant Mortality Rate

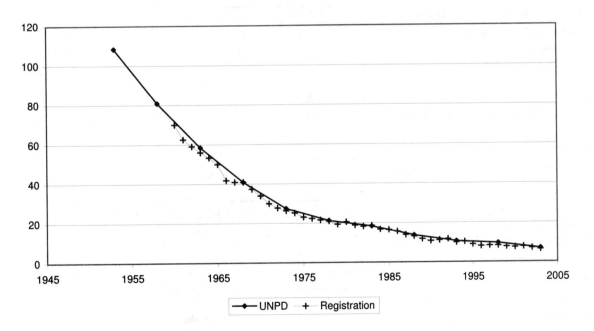

Indicator	Period				
	Earlier year			Later year	

I. Data and estimates from national and other sources

General mortality

	Year	Value		Year	Value	
Annual number of deaths *(thousands)*	1970	53.8		2003	78.4	
Annual number of deaths under age one *(thousands)*	1970	9.2		2003	0.9	
Crude death rate *(per 1 000 person-years)*	1970	6.3		2003	7.0	

	Year	Male	Female	Year	Male	Female
Life expectancy *(years)*						
at birth..	1969-1971	70.3	73.7	2001-2003	75.0	78.0
at age 15..	1969-1971	59.3	62.1	2001-2003	60.0	64.0
at age 60..	1969-1971	19.1	21.3	2001-2003	20.0	22.0
Survival probability						
from birth to age 15...	1969-1971	0.94	0.95	2001-2003	0.99	0.99
from age 15 to age 60...	1969-1971	0.85	0.88	2001-2003	0.87	0.91
from age 60 to age 80...	1969-1971	0.46	0.56	2001-2003	0.54	0.64

Infant and child mortality

	Year	Male	Female	Both sexes	Year	Male	Female	Both sexes
Infant mortality rate *(per 1 000 live births)*	1975	31	25	28	2001-2003	7	6	6
Mortality from age 1 to age 4 *(per 1 000 live births)*	1975	6	6	6	2001-2003	2	2	2
Under-five mortality rate *(per 1 000 live births)*	1975	37	30	34	2001-2003	9	7	8

II. Data and estimates from United Nations sources

United Nations Population Division estimates

	1990-1995	2000-2005
Annual number of deaths *(thousands)*	75	78
Crude death rate *(per 1 000 person-years)*	7	7
Life expectancy at birth *(years)*		
Male...	72.9	75.3
Female..	76.7	79.1
Under-five mortality rate *(per 1 000 live births)*	19	8

Maternal mortality

	2000
Maternal mortality ratio *(deaths per 100 000 births)*	33

HIV/AIDS

	2003	[Low estimate - high estimate]
Number of HIV-infected persons, ...	3 300	[1 100 - 6 600]
Adult HIV prevalence *(percentage of adults 15-49)*	0.1	[<0.2]

Policy views

	1976	2003
Life expectancy..	Acceptable	Acceptable
Under-five mortality..		Acceptable
Maternal mortality...		Acceptable
Level of concern about AIDS...		Major concern

Life Expectancy at Birth

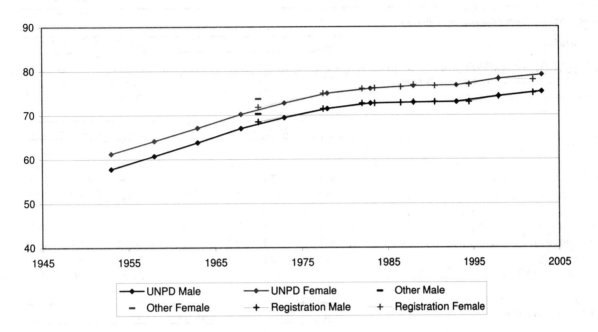

Infant Mortality Rate

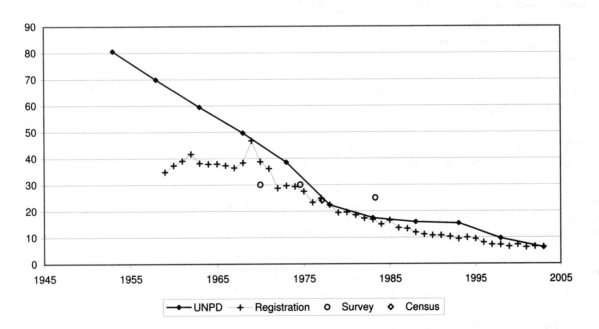

Indicator	Period				
	Earlier year			**Later year**	

I. Data and estimates from national and other sources

General mortality

	Year	Value		Year	Value	
Annual number of deaths *(thousands)*	1970	6.0		2003	5.2	
Annual number of deaths under age one *(thousands)*	1970	0.3		2003	0.0	
Crude death rate *(per 1 000 person-years)*	1970	9.9		2003	6.4	

	Year	Male	Female	Year	Male	Female
Life expectancy *(years)*						
at birth..	1973	70.0	72.9	2002-2003	77.0	81.4
at age 15..	1973	57.2	60.8	2002-2003	62.6	67.0
at age 60..	1973	16.5	18.5	2002-2003	20.7	23.6
Survival probability						
from birth to age 15...	1973	0.97	0.96	2002-2003	0.99	0.99
from age 15 to age 60...	1973	0.85	0.90	2002-2003	0.91	0.95
from age 60 to age 80...	1973	0.33	0.43	2002-2003	0.56	0.69

Infant and child mortality

	Year	Male	Female	Both sexes	Year	Male	Female	Both sexes
Infant mortality rate *(per 1 000 live births)*	1973	25	31	27	2002-2003	4	4	4
Mortality from age 1 to age 4 *(per 1 000 live births)*	1973	3	5	4	2002-2003	1	2	2
Under-five mortality rate *(per 1 000 live births)*	1973	28	36	32	2002-2003	5	6	6

II. Data and estimates from United Nations sources

United Nations Population Division estimates

	1990-1995	2000-2005
Annual number of deaths *(thousands)*	5	6
Crude death rate *(per 1 000 person-years)*	8	7
Life expectancy at birth *(years)*		
Male...	74.7	76.0
Female..	79.2	81.0
Under-five mortality rate *(per 1 000 live births)*	8	7

Maternal mortality

	2000
Maternal mortality ratio *(deaths per 100 000 births)*	47

HIV/AIDS

	2003	[Low estimate - high estimate]
Number of HIV-infected persons, ...	..	..
Adult HIV prevalence *(percentage of adults 15-49)*	..	..

Policy views

	1976	2003
Life expectancy...	Acceptable	Acceptable
Under-five mortality..		Acceptable
Maternal mortality..		Acceptable
Level of concern about AIDS....................................		Major concern

Life Expectancy at Birth

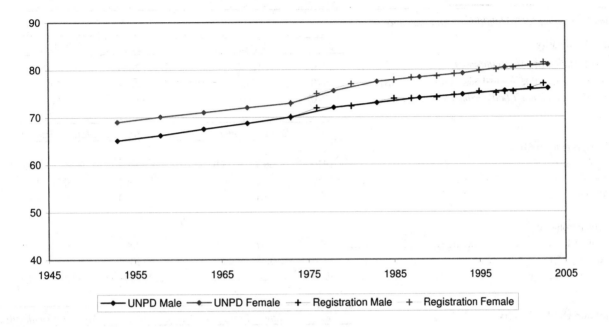

Infant Mortality Rate

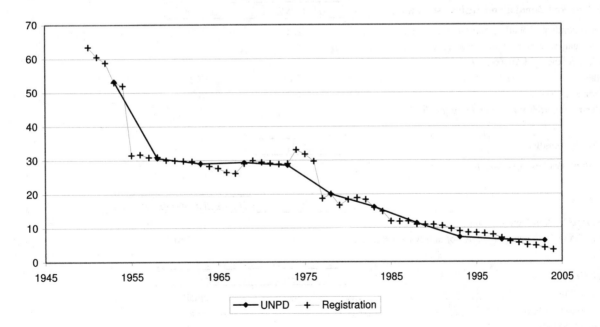

Indicator	Period					
	Earlier year			Later year		

I. Data and estimates from national and other sources

General mortality

	Year	Value		Year	Value	
Annual number of deaths *(thousands)*	1970	123.3		2004	107.2	
Annual number of deaths under age one *(thousands)*	1970	3.0		2004	0.4	
Crude death rate *(per 1 000 person-years)*	1970	12.6		2004	10.5	

	Year	Male	Female	Year	Male	Female
Life expectancy *(years)*						
at birth.........	1970	66.1	73.0	2004	72.5	79.0
at age 15...	1970	53.1	59.7	2004	58.0	64.4
at age 60...	1970	14.1	18.0	2004	17.6	21.6
Survival probability						
from birth to age 15...	1970	0.97	0.98	2004	0.99	0.99
from age 15 to age 60...	1970	0.77	0.89	2004	0.84	0.93
from age 60 to age 80...	1970	0.24	0.42	2004	0.42	0.62

Infant and child mortality

	Year	Male	Female	Both sexes	Year	Male	Female	Both sexes
Infant mortality rate *(per 1 000 live births)*	1970	23	18	21	2004	4	3	4
Mortality from age 1 to age 4 *(per 1 000 live births)*	1970	4	3	3	2004	1	1	1
Under-five mortality rate *(per 1 000 live births)*	1970	27	20	24	2004	5	4	5

II. Data and estimates from United Nations sources

United Nations Population Division estimates

	1990-1995	2000-2005
Annual number of deaths *(thousands)*	121	110
Crude death rate *(per 1 000 person-years)*	12	11
Life expectancy at birth *(years)*		
Male.........	68.8	72.2
Female.........	76.2	78.7
Under-five mortality rate *(per 1 000 live births)*	10	6

Maternal mortality

	2000
Maternal mortality ratio *(deaths per 100 000 births)*	9

HIV/AIDS

	2003	[Low estimate - high estimate]
Number of HIV-infected persons, ...	2 500	[800 - 4 900]
Adult HIV prevalence *(percentage of adults 15-49)*	0.1	[<0.2]

Policy views

	1976	2003
Life expectancy...	..	Acceptable
Under-five mortality..		Acceptable
Maternal mortality...		Acceptable
Level of concern about AIDS.................................		Major concern

Life Expectancy at Birth

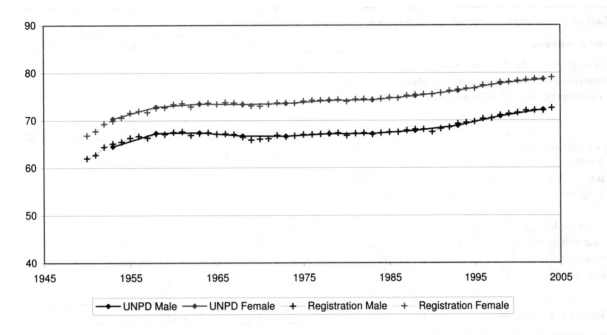

Legend: UNPD Male — UNPD Female — Registration Male + Registration Female +

Infant Mortality Rate

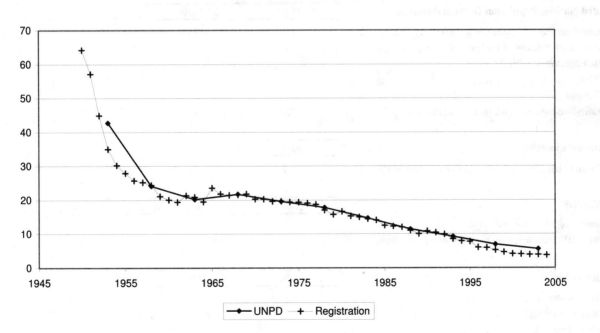

Legend: UNPD — Registration +

Indicator	Period			
	Earlier year		Later year	

I. Data and estimates from national and other sources

General mortality

	Year	Value	Year	Value
Annual number of deaths *(thousands)*	..	..	..	..
Annual number of deaths under age one *(thousands)*	..	..	..	..
Crude death rate *(per 1 000 person-years)*	..	..	..	..

	Year	Male	Female	Year	Male	Female
Life expectancy *(years)*						
at birth...	..	..	..	..	..	..
at age 15...	..	..	..	..	..	..
at age 60...	..	..	..	..	..	..
Survival probability						
from birth to age 15.......................................	..	..	..	..	..	..
from age 15 to age 60.....................................	..	..	..	..	..	..
from age 60 to age 80.....................................	..	..	..	..	..	..

Infant and child mortality

	Year	Male	Female	Both sexes	Year	Male	Female	Both sexes
Infant mortality rate *(per 1 000 live births)*	..	..	..	..	..	..	..	..
Mortality from age 1 to age 4 *(per 1 000 live births)*	..	..	..	..	..	..	..	..
Under-five mortality rate *(per 1 000 live births)*	..	..	..	..	..	..	..	..

II. Data and estimates from United Nations sources

United Nations Population Division estimates

	1990-1995	2000-2005
Annual number of deaths *(thousands)*	180	238
Crude death rate *(per 1 000 person-years)*	9	11
Life expectancy at birth *(years)*		
Male...	62.2	60.1
Female..	67.3	66.1
Under-five mortality rate *(per 1 000 live births)*	52	59

Maternal mortality

	2000
Maternal mortality ratio *(deaths per 100 000 births)*	67

HIV/AIDS

	2003	[Low estimate - high estimate]
Number of HIV-infected persons, ...	..	..
Adult HIV prevalence *(percentage of adults 15-49)*	..	..

Policy views

	1976	2003
Life expectancy...	Unacceptable	Acceptable
Under-five mortality..		..
Maternal mortality..		..
Level of concern about AIDS.................................		Minor concern

Democratic People's Republic of Korea

Life Expectancy at Birth

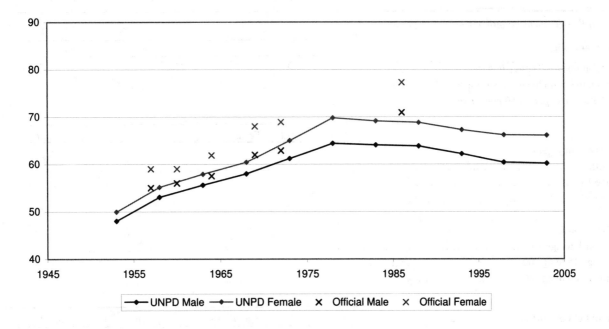

Infant Mortality Rate

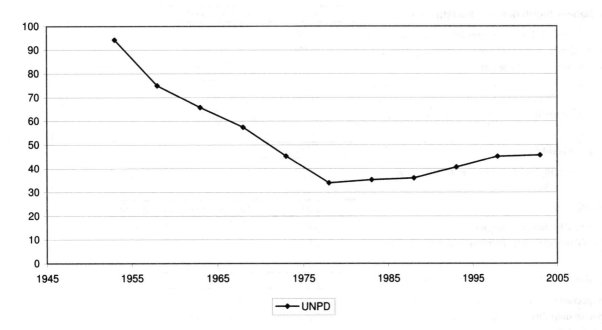

Indicator	Period							
	Earlier year				Later year			

I. Data and estimates from national and other sources

General mortality

	Year	Value			Year	Value		
Annual number of deaths *(thousands)*	..	..			..	..		
Annual number of deaths under age one *(thousands)*	..	..			..	..		
Crude death rate *(per 1 000 person-years)*	..	..			..	..		

	Year	Male	Female		Year	Male	Female	
Life expectancy *(years)*								
at birth...	..	..	..		..	..	..	
at age 15...	..	..	..		..	..	..	
at age 60...	..	..	..		..	..	..	
Survival probability								
from birth to age 15..	..	..	..		..	..	..	
from age 15 to age 60..	..	..	..		..	..	..	
from age 60 to age 80..	..	..	..		..	..	..	

Infant and child mortality

	Year	Male	Female	Both sexes	Year	Male	Female	Both sexes
Infant mortality rate *(per 1 000 live births)*	..	..	..	..	1997	..	..	136
Mortality from age 1 to age 4 *(per 1 000 live births)*	..	..	..	..	..	..	..	..
Under-five mortality rate *(per 1 000 live births)*	..	..	..	..	1997	..	..	220

II. Data and estimates from United Nations sources

United Nations Population Division estimates

	1990-1995	2000-2005
Annual number of deaths *(thousands)*	805	1 097
Crude death rate *(per 1 000 person-years)*	19	20
Life expectancy at birth *(years)*		
Male..	43.1	42.1
Female..	46.3	44.1
Under-five mortality rate *(per 1 000 live births)*	209	212

Maternal mortality

	2000
Maternal mortality ratio *(deaths per 100 000 births)*	990

HIV/AIDS

	2003	*[Low estimate - high estimate]*
Number of HIV-infected persons, ...	1 100 000	[450 000 - 2 600 000]
Adult HIV prevalence *(percentage of adults 15-49)*	4.2	[1.7 - 9.9]

Policy views

	1976	2003
Life expectancy..	Unacceptable	Unacceptable
Under-five mortality..		Unacceptable
Maternal mortality...		Unacceptable
Level of concern about AIDS..		Major concern

Democratic Republic of the Congo

Life Expectancy at Birth

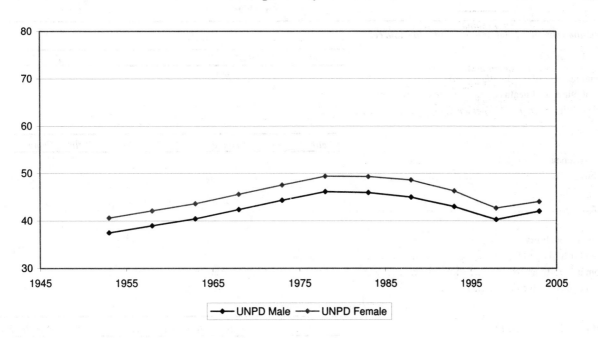

Infant Mortality Rate

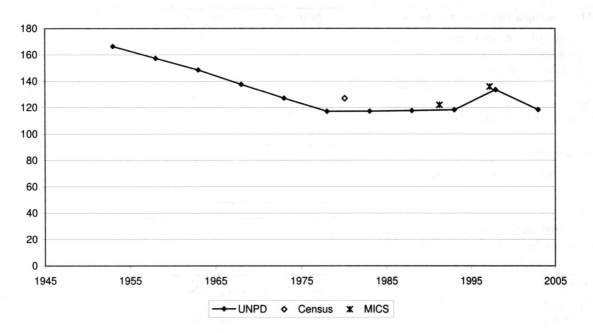

Indicator	Period					
	Earlier year			Later year		

I. Data and estimates from national and other sources

General mortality

	Year	Value			Year	Value	
Annual number of deaths *(thousands)*	..	..			..	..	
Annual number of deaths under age one *(thousands)*	..	..			..	..	
Crude death rate *(per 1 000 person-years)*	..	..			..	..	

	Year	Male	Female		Year	Male	Female
Life expectancy *(years)*							
at birth	..	..	..		..	..	..
at age 15	..	..	..		..	..	..
at age 60	..	..	..		..	..	..
Survival probability							
from birth to age 15	..	..	..		..	..	..
from age 15 to age 60	..	..	..		..	..	..
from age 60 to age 80	..	..	..		..	..	..

Infant and child mortality

	Year	Male	Female	Both sexes	Year	Male	Female	Both sexes
Infant mortality rate *(per 1 000 live births)*	..	..	..	..	1998-2003	..	..	60
Mortality from age 1 to age 4 *(per 1 000 live births)*	..	..	..	..	..	..	..	..
Under-five mortality rate *(per 1 000 live births)*	..	..	..	..	1998-2003	..	..	83

II. Data and estimates from United Nations sources

United Nations Population Division estimates

	1990-1995	2000-2005
Annual number of deaths *(thousands)*	12	11
Crude death rate *(per 1 000 person-years)*	16	13
Life expectancy at birth *(years)*		
Male	47.1	54.1
Female	48.7	56.3
Under-five mortality rate *(per 1 000 live births)*	197	134

Maternal mortality

	2000
Maternal mortality ratio *(deaths per 100 000 births)*	660

HIV/AIDS

	2003	[Low estimate - high estimate]
Number of HIV-infected persons,	..	..
Adult HIV prevalence *(percentage of adults 15-49)*	..	..

Policy views

	1976	2003
Life expectancy	..	Unacceptable
Under-five mortality		Unacceptable
Maternal mortality		Unacceptable
Level of concern about AIDS		Minor concern

Democratic Republic of Timor-Leste

Life Expectancy at Birth

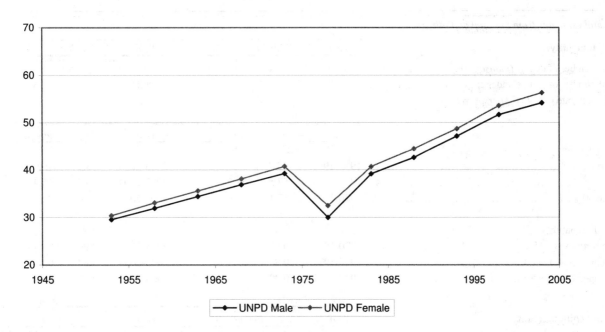

Infant Mortality Rate

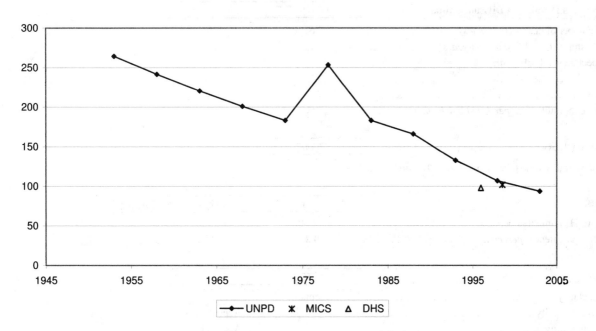

Indicator	Period				
	Earlier year			Later year	

I. Data and estimates from national and other sources

General mortality

	Year	Value		Year	Value
Annual number of deaths *(thousands)*	1970	48.2		2004	55.8
Annual number of deaths under age one *(thousands)*	1970	1.0		2003	0.3
Crude death rate *(per 1 000 person-years)*	1970	9.8		2004	10.3

	Year	Male	Female	Year	Male	Female
Life expectancy *(years)*						
at birth	1970-1971	70.7	75.9	2003-2004	75.2	79.9
at age 15	1970-1971	57.5	62.3	2003-2004	60.7	65.4
at age 60	1970-1971	17.1	20.6	2003-2004	19.4	22.7
Survival probability						
from birth to age 15	1970-1971	0.97	0.98	2003-2004	0.99	0.99
from age 15 to age 60	1970-1971	0.84	0.89	2003-2004	0.88	0.93
from age 60 to age 80	1970-1971	0.39	0.56	2003-2004	0.50	0.64

Infant and child mortality

	Year	Male	Female	Both sexes	Year	Male	Female	Both sexes
Infant mortality rate *(per 1 000 live births)*	1970-1971	17	11	14	2003-2004	5	4	4
Mortality from age 1 to age 4 *(per 1 000 live births)*	1970-1971	3	2	3	2003-2004	1	1	1
Under-five mortality rate *(per 1 000 live births)*	1970-1971	20	14	17	2003-2004	6	5	5

II. Data and estimates from United Nations sources

United Nations Population Division estimates

	1990-1995	2000-2005
Annual number of deaths *(thousands)*	61	58
Crude death rate *(per 1 000 person-years)*	12	11
Life expectancy at birth *(years)*		
Male	72.5	74.8
Female	77.8	79.4
Under-five mortality rate *(per 1 000 live births)*	8	6

Maternal mortality

	2000
Maternal mortality ratio *(deaths per 100 000 births)*	5

HIV/AIDS

	2003	*[Low estimate - high estimate]*
Number of HIV-infected persons,	5 000	[2 500 - 8 200]
Adult HIV prevalence *(percentage of adults 15-49)*	0.2	[0.1 - 0.3]

Policy views

	1976	2003
Life expectancy	Acceptable	Acceptable
Under-five mortality		Acceptable
Maternal mortality		Acceptable
Level of concern about AIDS		Major concern

Life Expectancy at Birth

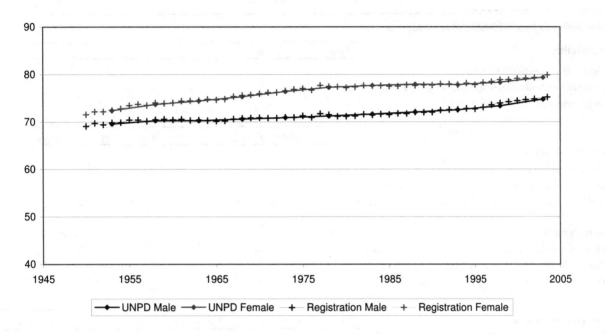

Infant Mortality Rate

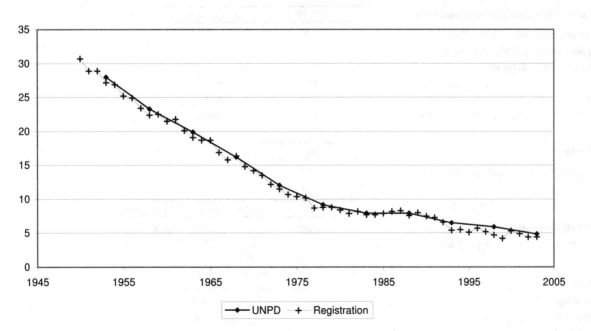

Indicator	Period				
	Earlier year			Later year	

I. Data and estimates from national and other sources

General mortality	Year	Value		Year	Value	
Annual number of deaths *(thousands)*	..	..		..	..	
Annual number of deaths under age one *(thousands)*	..	..		..	..	
Crude death rate *(per 1 000 person-years)*	..	..		..	..	

	Year	Male	Female	Year	Male	Female
Life expectancy *(years)*						
at birth	..	..	..	..	..	..
at age 15	..	..	..	..	..	..
at age 60	..	..	..	..	..	..
Survival probability						
from birth to age 15	..	..	..	..	..	..
from age 15 to age 60	..	..	..	..	..	..
from age 60 to age 80	..	..	..	..	..	..

Infant and child mortality	Year	Male	Female	Both sexes	Year	Male	Female	Both sexes
Infant mortality rate *(per 1 000 live births)*	..	..	..	..	1997-2002	..	..	103
Mortality from age 1 to age 4 *(per 1 000 live births)*	..	..	..	..	..	..	..	..
Under-five mortality rate *(per 1 000 live births)*	..	..	..	..	1997-2002	..	..	124

II. Data and estimates from United Nations sources

United Nations Population Division estimates	1990-1995	2000-2005
Annual number of deaths *(thousands)*	8	10
Crude death rate *(per 1 000 person-years)*	14	13
Life expectancy at birth *(years)*		
Male	49.7	51.4
Female	52.8	53.9
Under-five mortality rate *(per 1 000 live births)*	168	140

Maternal mortality	2000
Maternal mortality ratio *(deaths per 100 000 births)*	730

HIV/AIDS	2003	[Low estimate - high estimate]
Number of HIV-infected persons,	9 100	[2 300 - 24 000]
Adult HIV prevalence *(percentage of adults 15-49)*	2.9	[0.7 - 7.5]

Policy views	1976	2003
Life expectancy	..	Unacceptable
Under-five mortality		Unacceptable
Maternal mortality		Unacceptable
Level of concern about AIDS		Major concern

Life Expectancy at Birth

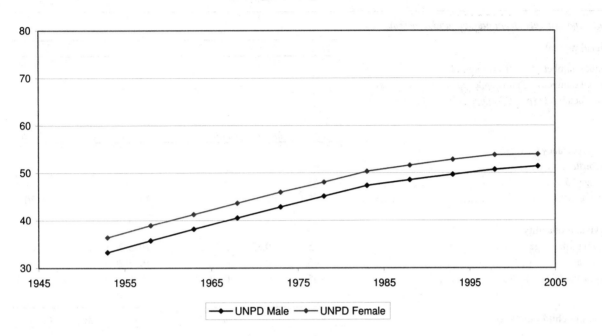

Infant Mortality Rate

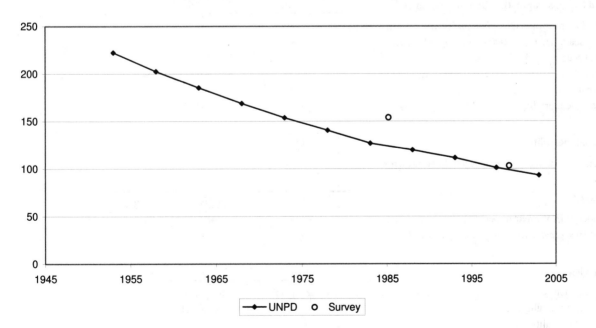

Dominican Republic

Indicator		Period				
		Earlier year			Later year	

I. Data and estimates from national and other sources

General mortality

	Year	Value		Year	Value	
Annual number of deaths *(thousands)*	..	..		..	..	
Annual number of deaths under age one *(thousands)*	..	..		..	..	
Crude death rate *(per 1 000 person-years)*	..	..		..	..	

	Year	Male	Female	Year	Male	Female
Life expectancy *(years)*						
at birth..	1965	52.6	56.0	1995-2000	69.9	73.1
at age 15..	1965	48.6	51.4	1995-2000	58.1	61.6
at age 60..	1965	15.3	17.1	1995-2000	18.5	20.7
Survival probability						
from birth to age 15..	1965	0.82	0.84	1995-2000	0.94	0.95
from age 15 to age 60...	1965	0.63	0.69	1995-2000	0.83	0.88
from age 60 to age 80...	1965	0.31	0.39	1995-2000	0.44	0.54

Infant and child mortality

	Year	Male	Female	Both sexes	Year	Male	Female	Both sexes
Infant mortality rate *(per 1 000 live births)*	1970	100	84	92	1992-2002	38	31	35
Mortality from age 1 to age 4 *(per 1 000 live births)*	1970	46	38	42	1992-2002	9	9	9
Under-five mortality rate *(per 1 000 live births)*	1970	141	119	130	1992-2002	46	40	43

II. Data and estimates from United Nations sources

United Nations Population Division estimates

	1990-1995	2000-2005
Annual number of deaths *(thousands)*	48	56
Crude death rate *(per 1 000 person-years)*	6	7
Life expectancy at birth *(years)*		
Male..	63.8	63.7
Female...	68.6	70.9
Under-five mortality rate *(per 1 000 live births)*	67	51

Maternal mortality

	2000
Maternal mortality ratio *(deaths per 100 000 births)*	150

HIV/AIDS

	2003	[Low estimate - high estimate]
Number of HIV-infected persons, ...	88 000	[48 000 - 160 000]
Adult HIV prevalence *(percentage of adults 15-49)*	1.7	[0.9 - 3.0]

Policy views

	1976	2003
Life expectancy...	Unacceptable	Unacceptable
Under-five mortality...		Unacceptable
Maternal mortality..		Unacceptable
Level of concern about AIDS...............................		Major concern

Life Expectancy at Birth

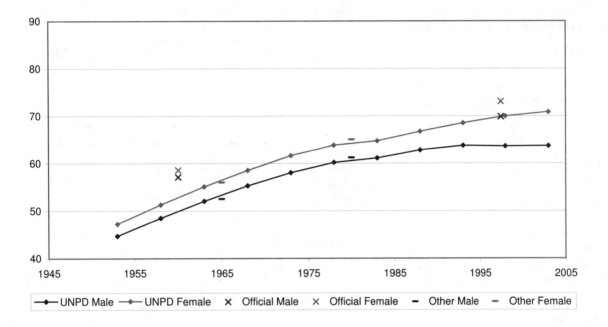

Infant Mortality Rate

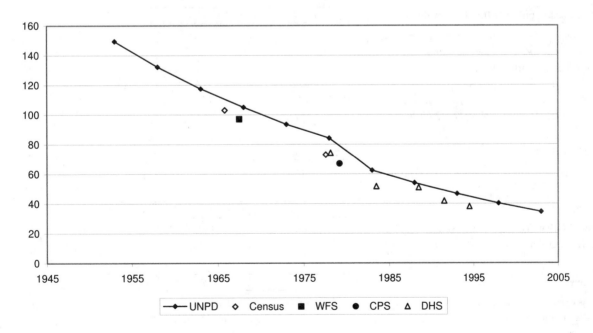

Indicator	Period				
	Earlier year			Later year	

I. Data and estimates from national and other sources

General mortality	Year	Value		Year	Value
Annual number of deaths *(thousands)*	..	..		..	..
Annual number of deaths under age one *(thousands)*	..	..		..	..
Crude death rate *(per 1 000 person-years)*	..	..		..	..

	Year	Male	Female	Year	Male	Female
Life expectancy *(years)*						
at birth	1970-1975	57.4	60.5	2000-2005	71.3	77.2
at age 15	1970-1975	53.2	55.3	2000-2005	59.3	64.5
at age 60	1970-1975	16.4	17.6	2000-2005	21.6	23.7
Survival probability						
from birth to age 15	1970-1975	0.84	0.86	2000-2005	0.96	0.97
from age 15 to age 60	1970-1975	0.74	0.78	2000-2005	0.81	0.89
from age 60 to age 80	1970-1975	0.36	0.41	2000-2005	0.61	0.69

Infant and child mortality	Year	Male	Female	Both sexes	Year	Male	Female	Both sexes
Infant mortality rate *(per 1 000 live births)*	1975	82	70	76	1994-1999	37	24	30
Mortality from age 1 to age 4 *(per 1 000 live births)*	1975	46	50	48	1994-1999	8	9	9
Under-five mortality rate *(per 1 000 live births)*	1975	123	116	120	1994-1999	45	33	39

II. Data and estimates from United Nations sources

United Nations Population Division estimates	1990-1995	2000-2005
Annual number of deaths *(thousands)*	63	63
Crude death rate *(per 1 000 person-years)*	6	5
Life expectancy at birth *(years)*		
Male	67.6	71.3
Female	72.6	77.2
Under-five mortality rate *(per 1 000 live births)*	57	30

Maternal mortality	2000
Maternal mortality ratio *(deaths per 100 000 births)*	130

HIV/AIDS	2003	[Low estimate - high estimate]
Number of HIV-infected persons,	21 000	[10 000 - 38 000]
Adult HIV prevalence *(percentage of adults 15-49)*	0.3	[0.1 - 0.5]

Policy views	1976	2003
Life expectancy	Acceptable	Unacceptable
Under-five mortality		Unacceptable
Maternal mortality		Unacceptable
Level of concern about AIDS		Major concern

Life Expectancy at Birth

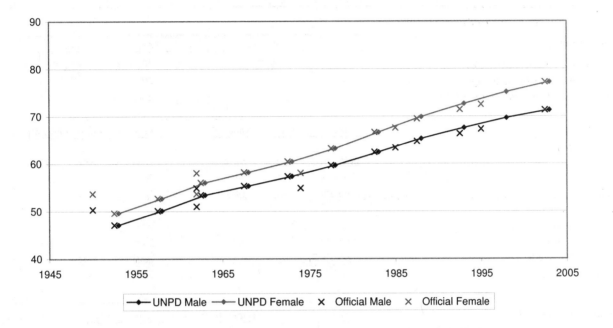

Infant Mortality Rate

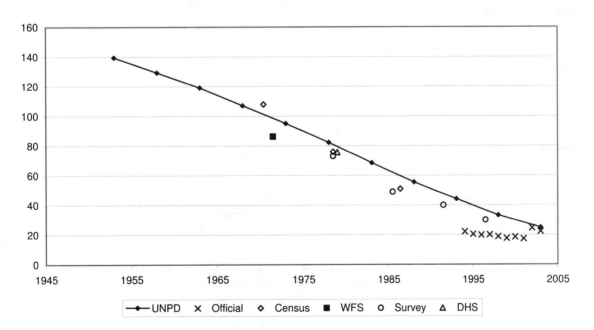

Indicator	Period							
	Earlier year				Later year			

I. Data and estimates from national and other sources

General mortality

	Year	Value			Year	Value		
Annual number of deaths *(thousands)*	1970	500.6			2003	440.0		
Annual number of deaths under age one *(thousands)*	1970	135.1			2001	49.1		
Crude death rate *(per 1 000 person-years)*	1970	15.1			2003	6.5		

	Year	Male	Female		Year	Male	Female	
Life expectancy *(years)*								
at birth..	1965-1967	50.3	51.5		2001	65.6	67.4	
at age 15...	1965-1967	51.6	54.4		2001	55.1	57.2	
at age 60...	1965-1967	14.4	14.9		2001	15.4	15.5	
Survival probability								
from birth to age 15...	1965-1967	0.75	0.74		2001	0.93	0.93	
from age 15 to age 60..	1965-1967	0.73	0.82		2001	0.81	0.87	
from age 60 to age 80..	..	..	..		2001	0.28	0.27	

Infant and child mortality

	Year	Male	Female	Both sexes	Year	Male	Female	Both sexes
Infant mortality rate *(per 1 000 live births)*	1975	139	139	139	1990-2000	55	55	55
Mortality from age 1 to age 4 *(per 1 000 live births)*	1975	70	90	80	1990-2000	15	16	15
Under-five mortality rate *(per 1 000 live births)*	1975	200	217	208	1990-2000	69	70	69

II. Data and estimates from United Nations sources

United Nations Population Division estimates

	1990-1995	2000-2005
Annual number of deaths *(thousands)*	461	421
Crude death rate *(per 1 000 person-years)*	8	6
Life expectancy at birth *(years)*		
Male..	62.4	67.5
Female...	65.6	71.8
Under-five mortality rate *(per 1 000 live births)*	82	43

Maternal mortality

	2000
Maternal mortality ratio *(deaths per 100 000 births)*	84

HIV/AIDS

	2003	*[Low estimate - high estimate]*
Number of HIV-infected persons, ...	12 000	[5 000 - 31 000]
Adult HIV prevalence *(percentage of adults 15-49)*	<0.1	[<0.2]

Policy views

	1976	2003
Life expectancy..	Unacceptable	Unacceptable
Under-five mortality...		Unacceptable
Maternal mortality..		Unacceptable
Level of concern about AIDS...................................		Minor concern

Life Expectancy at Birth

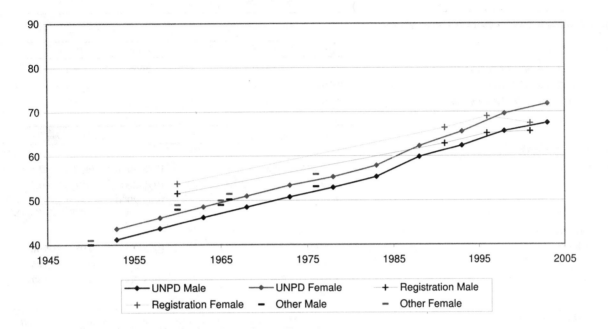

Infant Mortality Rate

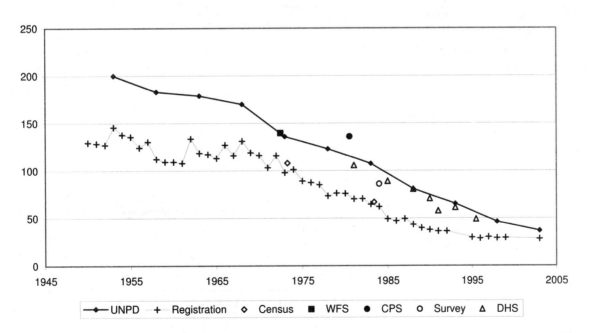

Indicator	Period						
	Earlier year				Later year		

I. Data and estimates from national and other sources

General mortality

	Year	Value			Year	Value	
Annual number of deaths *(thousands)*	1970	35.1			2002	27.5	
Annual number of deaths under age one *(thousands)*	1970	9.4			2002	1.3	
Crude death rate *(per 1 000 person-years)*	1970	9.9			2002	4.2	

	Year	Male	Female		Year	Male	Female
Life expectancy *(years)*							
at birth..	1970-1972	54.8	59.9		1995-2000	66.5	72.5
at age 15...	1970-1972	52.9	57.4		1995-2000	55.1	60.7
at age 60...	1970-1972	17.3	19.0		1995-2000	18.3	21.2
Survival probability							
from birth to age 15..	1970-1972	0.80	0.82		1995-2000	0.95	0.96
from age 15 to age 60..	1970-1972	0.72	0.80		1995-2000	0.76	0.85
from age 60 to age 80..	1970-1972	0.40	0.47		1995-2000	0.45	0.57

Infant and child mortality

	Year	Male	Female	Both sexes	Year	Male	Female	Both sexes
Infant mortality rate *(per 1 000 live births)*	1980	97	82	90	1997-2002	26	22	24
Mortality from age 1 to age 4 *(per 1 000 live births)*	1980	41	44	43	1997-2002	7	5	6
Under-five mortality rate *(per 1 000 live births)*	1980	135	123	129	1997-2002	33	27	30

II. Data and estimates from United Nations sources

United Nations Population Division estimates

	1990-1995	2000-2005
Annual number of deaths *(thousands)*	36	38
Crude death rate *(per 1 000 person-years)*	7	6
Life expectancy at birth *(years)*		
Male..	63.3	67.7
Female...	71.1	73.7
Under-five mortality rate *(per 1 000 live births)*	51	35

Maternal mortality

	2000
Maternal mortality ratio *(deaths per 100 000 births)*	150

HIV/AIDS

	2003	*[Low estimate - high estimate]*
Number of HIV-infected persons, ...	29 000	[14 000 - 50 000]
Adult HIV prevalence *(percentage of adults 15-49)*	0.7	[0.3 - 1.1]

Policy views

	1976	2003
Life expectancy..	Unacceptable	Unacceptable
Under-five mortality...		Unacceptable
Maternal mortality..		Unacceptable
Level of concern about AIDS......................................		Major concern

Life Expectancy at Birth

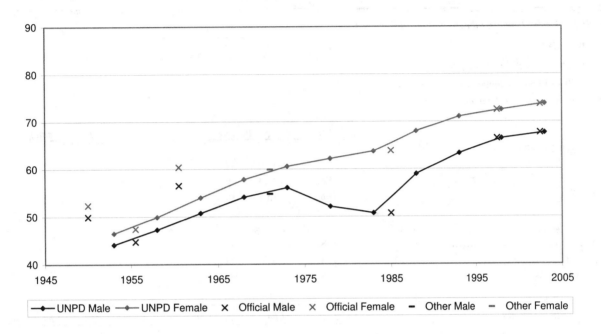

Infant Mortality Rate

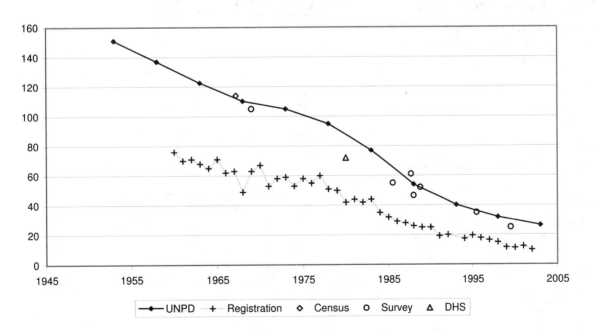

Indicator	Period					
	Earlier year			**Later year**		

I. Data and estimates from national and other sources

General mortality

	Year	Value		Year	Value	
Annual number of deaths *(thousands)*	..	..		..	..	
Annual number of deaths under age one *(thousands)*	..	..		..	..	
Crude death rate *(per 1 000 person-years)*	..	..		..	..	

	Year	Male	Female	Year	Male	Female
Life expectancy *(years)*						
at birth..	1981	44.9	47.8	..	..	..
at age 15..	1981	44.4	46.8	..	..	..
at age 60..	1981	13.1	14.4	..	..	..
Survival probability						
from birth to age 15..	1981	0.75	0.77	..	..	..
from age 15 to age 60..	1981	0.56	0.62	..	..	..
from age 60 to age 80..	1981	0.21	0.27	..	..	..

Infant and child mortality

	Year	Male	Female	Both sexes	Year	Male	Female	Both sexes
Infant mortality rate *(per 1 000 live births)*	..	..	..	..	1996	..	..	110
Mortality from age 1 to age 4 *(per 1 000 live births)*	..	..	..	..	..	..	..	..
Under-five mortality rate *(per 1 000 live births)*	..	..	..	..	1996	..	..	183

II. Data and estimates from United Nations sources

United Nations Population Division estimates

	1990-1995	2000-2005
Annual number of deaths *(thousands)*	7	10
Crude death rate *(per 1 000 person-years)*	19	20
Life expectancy at birth *(years)*		
Male...	44.1	42.8
Female..	47.7	44.2
Under-five mortality rate *(per 1 000 live births)*	207	181

Maternal mortality

	2000
Maternal mortality ratio *(deaths per 100 000 births)*	880

HIV/AIDS

	2003	*[Low estimate - high estimate]*
Number of HIV-infected persons, ...	..	..
Adult HIV prevalence *(percentage of adults 15-49)*	..	..

Policy views

	1976	2003
Life expectancy..	Unacceptable	Unacceptable
Under-five mortality..		Unacceptable
Maternal mortality...		Unacceptable
Level of concern about AIDS....................................		..

Life Expectancy at Birth

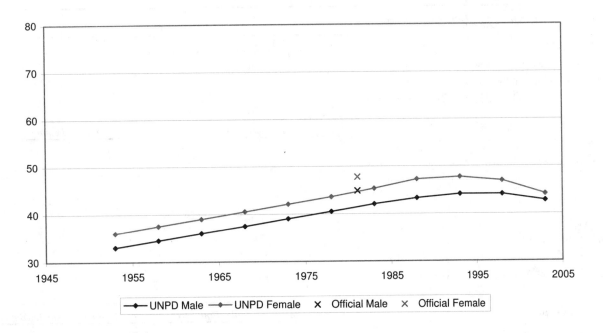

Infant Mortality Rate

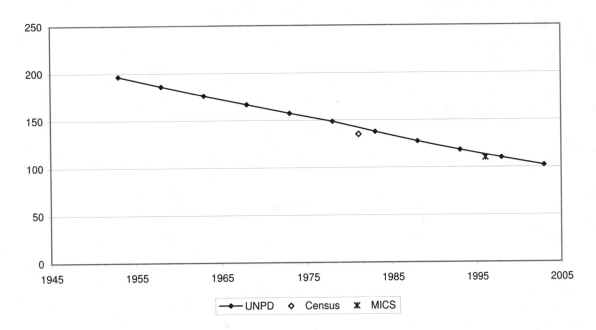

Indicator	Period			
	Earlier year		Later year	

I. Data and estimates from national and other sources

General mortality

	Year	Value	Year	Value
Annual number of deaths *(thousands)*	..	..	..	..
Annual number of deaths under age one *(thousands)*	..	..	..	..
Crude death rate *(per 1 000 person-years)*	..	..	..	..

	Year	Male	Female	Year	Male	Female
Life expectancy *(years)*						
at birth..............	..	..	..	..	..	..
at age 15.............	..	..	..	..	..	..
at age 60.............	..	..	..	..	..	..
Survival probability						
from birth to age 15.............	..	..	..	..	..	..
from age 15 to age 60.............	..	..	..	..	..	..
from age 60 to age 80.............	..	..	..	..	..	..

Infant and child mortality

	Year	Male	Female	Both sexes	Year	Male	Female	Both sexes
Infant mortality rate *(per 1 000 live births)*	..	..	..	..	1992-2002	64	50	58
Mortality from age 1 to age 4 *(per 1 000 live births)*	..	..	..	..	1992-2002	55	50	52
Under-five mortality rate *(per 1 000 live births)*	..	..	..	..	1992-2002	116	98	107

II. Data and estimates from United Nations sources

United Nations Population Division estimates

	1990-1995	2000-2005
Annual number of deaths *(thousands)*	46	46
Crude death rate *(per 1 000 person-years)*	15	12
Life expectancy at birth *(years)*		
Male...	47.1	51.5
Female..	51.8	55.4
Under-five mortality rate *(per 1 000 live births)*	135	94

Maternal mortality

	2000
Maternal mortality ratio *(deaths per 100 000 births)*	630

HIV/AIDS

	2003	*[Low estimate - high estimate]*
Number of HIV-infected persons, ...	60 000	[21 000 - 170 000]
Adult HIV prevalence *(percentage of adults 15-49)*	2.7	[0.9 - 7.3]

Policy views

	1976	2003
Life expectancy..	..	Unacceptable
Under-five mortality..		Unacceptable
Maternal mortality..		Unacceptable
Level of concern about AIDS..................................		Major concern

Life Expectancy at Birth

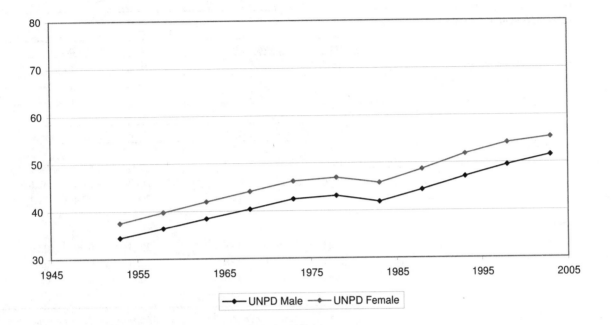

Infant Mortality Rate

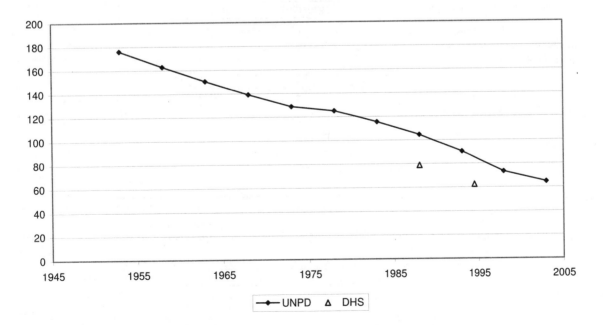

Indicator	Period							
	Earlier year				*Later year*			

I. Data and estimates from national and other sources

General mortality

	Year	Value			Year	Value		
Annual number of deaths *(thousands)*	1970	15.2			2004	17.8		
Annual number of deaths under age one *(thousands)*	1970	0.4			2004	0.1		
Crude death rate *(per 1 000 person-years)*	1970	11.2			2003	13.4		

	Year	Male	Female		Year	Male	Female	
Life expectancy *(years)*								
at birth..	1970	65.5	74.1		2003	66.0	76.9	
at age 15..	1970	52.6	61.1		2003	51.9	62.6	
at age 60..	1970	15.2	19.4		2003	15.4	21.1	
Survival probability								
from birth to age 15...	1981	0.97	0.98		2003	0.99	0.99	
from age 15 to age 60...	1981	0.69	0.88		2003	0.70	0.89	
from age 60 to age 80...	1981	0.28	0.50		2003	0.32	0.58	

Infant and child mortality

	Year	Male	Female	Both sexes	Year	Male	Female	Both sexes
Infant mortality rate *(per 1 000 live births)*	1981	19	15	17	2003	8	5	7
Mortality from age 1 to age 4 *(per 1 000 live births)*	1981	6	4	5	2003	2	2	2
Under-five mortality rate *(per 1 000 live births)*	1981	24	19	22	2003	11	7	9

II. Data and estimates from United Nations sources

United Nations Population Division estimates

	1990-1995	2000-2005
Annual number of deaths *(thousands)*	21	18
Crude death rate *(per 1 000 person-years)*	14	14
Life expectancy at birth *(years)*		
Male..	63.2	65.4
Female...	74.4	76.9
Under-five mortality rate *(per 1 000 live births)*	20	12

Maternal mortality

	2000
Maternal mortality ratio *(deaths per 100 000 births)*	63

HIV/AIDS

	2003	*[Low estimate - high estimate]*
Number of HIV-infected persons, ...	7 800	[2 600 - 15 000]
Adult HIV prevalence *(percentage of adults 15-49)*	1.1	[0.4 - 2.1]

Policy views

	1976	2003
Life expectancy..	..	Acceptable
Under-five mortality..		Acceptable
Maternal mortality..		Acceptable
Level of concern about AIDS..................................		Major concern

Life Expectancy at Birth

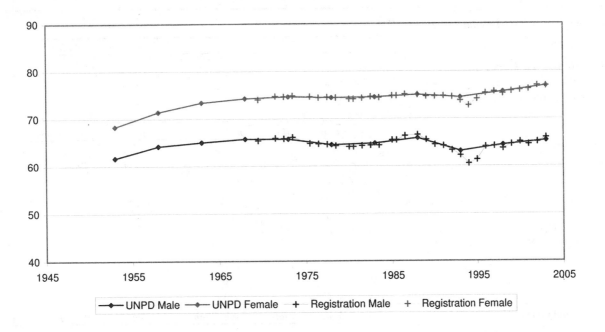

UNPD Male — UNPD Female — + Registration Male + Registration Female

Infant Mortality Rate

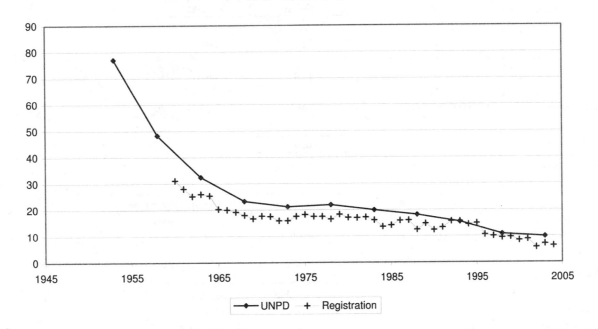

UNPD + Registration

Indicator	Period							
	Earlier year				**Later year**			

I. Data and estimates from national and other sources

General mortality

	Year	Value			Year	Value		
Annual number of deaths *(thousands)*	..	..			..	..		
Annual number of deaths under age one *(thousands)*	..	..			..	..		
Crude death rate *(per 1 000 person-years)*	..	..			..	..		

	Year	Male	Female		Year	Male	Female	
Life expectancy *(years)*								
at birth..	..	..	..		1994	49.8	51.8	
at age 15..	..	..	..		..	..	..	
at age 60..	..	..	..		..	..	..	
Survival probability								
from birth to age 15..	..	..	..		..	..	..	
from age 15 to age 60..	..	..	..		..	..	..	
from age 60 to age 80..	..	..	..		..	..	..	

Infant and child mortality

	Year	Male	Female	Both sexes	Year	Male	Female	Both sexes
Infant mortality rate *(per 1 000 live births)*	..	..	..	..	1990-2000	124	101	113
Mortality from age 1 to age 4 *(per 1 000 live births)*	..	..	..	..	1990-2000	83	86	85
Under-five mortality rate *(per 1 000 live births)*	1974	226	204	215	1990-2000	197	178	188

II. Data and estimates from United Nations sources

United Nations Population Division estimates

	1990-1995	2000-2005
Annual number of deaths *(thousands)*	979	1 191
Crude death rate *(per 1 000 person-years)*	18	16
Life expectancy at birth *(years)*		
Male...	45.6	46.5
Female..	48.9	48.6
Under-five mortality rate *(per 1 000 live births)*	198	172

Maternal mortality

	2000
Maternal mortality ratio *(deaths per 100 000 births)*	850

HIV/AIDS

	2003	[Low estimate - high estimate]
Number of HIV-infected persons, ...	1 500 000	[950 000 - 2 300 000]
Adult HIV prevalence *(percentage of adults 15-49)*	4.4	[2.8 - 6.7]

Policy views

	1976	2003
Life expectancy...	Unacceptable	Unacceptable
Under-five mortality..		Unacceptable
Maternal mortality..		Unacceptable
Level of concern about AIDS...................................		Major concern

Life Expectancy at Birth

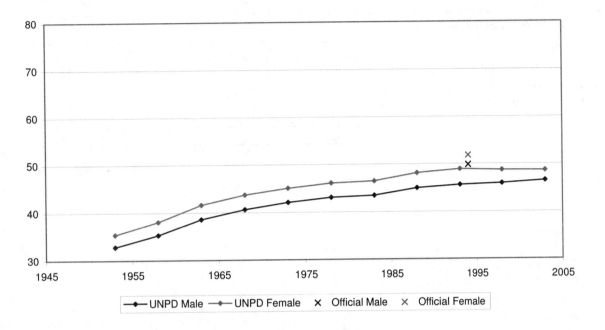

Infant Mortality Rate

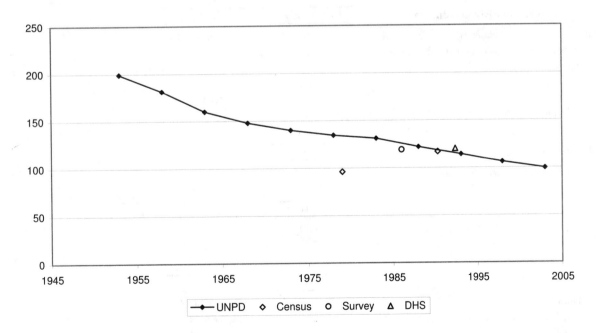

Fiji

Indicator	Period					
	Earlier year			**Later year**		

I. Data and estimates from national and other sources

General mortality

	Year	Value		Year	Value	
Annual number of deaths *(thousands)*	1970	2.4		1999	3.6	
Annual number of deaths under age one *(thousands)*	1970	0.3		1999	0.3	
Crude death rate *(per 1 000 person-years)*	1970	4.7		1999	4.5	

	Year	Male	Female	Year	Male	Female
Life expectancy *(years)*						
at birth	1976	60.7	63.9	1996	64.5	68.7
at age 15	1976	50.9	53.0	..	..	..
at age 60	1976	13.9	14.7	..	..	..
Survival probability						
from birth to age 15	1976	0.92	0.94	..	..	..
from age 15 to age 60	1976	0.73	0.78	..	..	..
from age 60 to age 80	1976	0.22	0.26	..	..	..

Infant and child mortality

	Year	Male	Female	Both sexes	Year	Male	Female	Both sexes
Infant mortality rate *(per 1 000 live births)*	1976	37	28	33	1996	22	23	22
Mortality from age 1 to age 4 *(per 1 000 live births)*	1976	31	24	28	1996	5	5	5
Under-five mortality rate *(per 1 000 live births)*	1976	67	52	60	..	..	..	..

II. Data and estimates from United Nations sources

United Nations Population Division estimates

	1990-1995	2000-2005
Annual number of deaths *(thousands)*	5	5
Crude death rate *(per 1 000 person-years)*	6	6
Life expectancy at birth *(years)*		
Male	64.6	65.7
Female	68.8	70.0
Under-five mortality rate *(per 1 000 live births)*	44	27

Maternal mortality

	2000
Maternal mortality ratio *(deaths per 100 000 births)*	75

HIV/AIDS

	2003	[Low estimate - high estimate]
Number of HIV-infected persons,	600	[200 - 1 300]
Adult HIV prevalence *(percentage of adults 15-49)*	0.1	[0.0 - 0.2]

Policy views

	1976	2003
Life expectancy	Acceptable	Acceptable
Under-five mortality		Unacceptable
Maternal mortality		Unacceptable
Level of concern about AIDS		Major concern

Life Expectancy at Birth

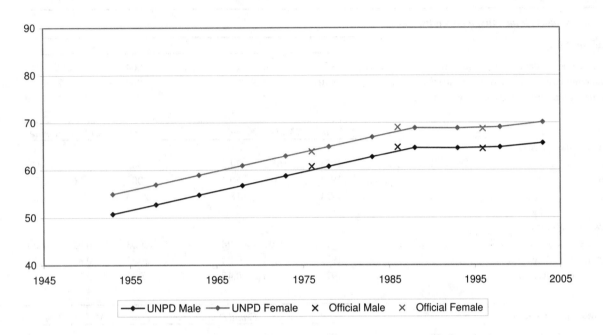

Infant Mortality Rate

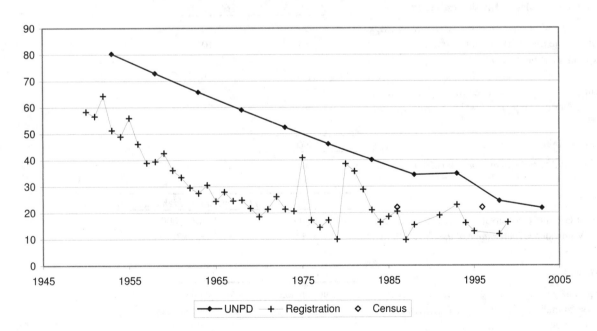

Indicator	Period				
	Earlier year			**Later year**	

I. Data and estimates from national and other sources

General mortality

	Year	Value		Year	Value
Annual number of deaths *(thousands)*	1970	44.1		2004	47.5
Annual number of deaths under age one *(thousands)*	1970	0.9		2003	0.2
Crude death rate *(per 1 000 person-years)*	1970	9.6		2004	9.1

	Year	Male	Female	Year	Male	Female
Life expectancy *(years)*						
at birth..	1971	65.9	74.2	2003	75.1	81.8
at age 15..	1971	56.4	60.4	2003	60.6	67.2
at age 60..	1971	14.3	18.3	2003	19.9	24.2
Survival probability						
from birth to age 15..	1971	0.98	0.98	2003	0.99	1.00
from age 15 to age 60..	1971	0.74	0.90	2003	0.87	0.94
from age 60 to age 80..	1971	0.26	0.45	2003	0.52	0.72

Infant and child mortality

	Year	Male	Female	Both sexes	Year	Male	Female	Both sexes
Infant mortality rate *(per 1 000 live births)*	1971	15	11	13	2002	3	3	3
Mortality from age 1 to age 4 *(per 1 000 live births)*	1971	3	3	3	2002	1	0	1
Under-five mortality rate *(per 1 000 live births)*	1971	17	13	15	2002	4	3	4

II. Data and estimates from United Nations sources

United Nations Population Division estimates

	1990-1995	2000-2005
Annual number of deaths *(thousands)*	50	50
Crude death rate *(per 1 000 person-years)*	10	10
Life expectancy at birth *(years)*		
Male...	72.0	75.0
Female..	79.6	81.7
Under-five mortality rate *(per 1 000 live births)*	6	5

Maternal mortality

	2000
Maternal mortality ratio *(deaths per 100 000 births)*	6

HIV/AIDS

	2003	[Low estimate - high estimate]
Number of HIV-infected persons, ...	1 500	[500 - 3 000]
Adult HIV prevalence *(percentage of adults 15-49)*	0.1	[<0.2]

Policy views

	1976	2003
Life expectancy..	Unacceptable	Acceptable
Under-five mortality...		Acceptable
Maternal mortality...		Acceptable
Level of concern about AIDS.....................................		Minor concern

Life Expectancy at Birth

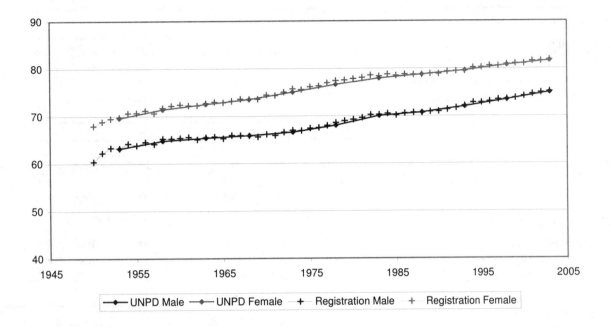

Infant Mortality Rate

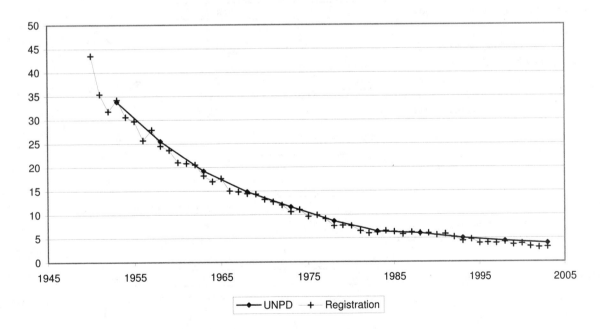

Indicator	Period				
	Earlier year			Later year	

I. Data and estimates from national and other sources

General mortality

	Year	Value		Year	Value	
Annual number of deaths *(thousands)*	1970	542.3		2003	549.6	
Annual number of deaths under age one *(thousands)*	1970	15.4		2002	3.1	
Crude death rate *(per 1 000 person-years)*	1970	10.7		2003	9.2	

	Year	Male	Female	Year	Male	Female
Life expectancy *(years)*						
at birth..	1971	68.5	76.1	2002	75.8	83.0
at age 15...	1971	55.1	62.5	2002	61.3	68.5
at age 60...	1971	16.2	20.9	2002	20.8	25.8
Survival probability						
from birth to age 15...	1971	0.98	0.98	2002	0.99	0.99
from age 15 to age 60.......................................	1971	0.79	0.90	2002	0.86	0.94
from age 60 to age 80.......................................	1971	0.35	0.57	2002	0.56	0.76

Infant and child mortality

	Year	Male	Female	Both sexes	Year	Male	Female	Both sexes
Infant mortality rate *(per 1 000 live births)*	1971	16	12	14	2002	5	4	4
Mortality from age 1 to age 4 *(per 1 000 live births)*	1971	3	3	3	2002	1	1	1
Under-five mortality rate *(per 1 000 live births)*	1971	19	15	17	2002	6	4	5

II. Data and estimates from United Nations sources

United Nations Population Division estimates

	1990-1995	2000-2005
Annual number of deaths *(thousands)*	526	564
Crude death rate *(per 1 000 person-years)*	9	9
Life expectancy at birth *(years)*		
Male...	73.3	75.8
Female..	81.5	83.0
Under-five mortality rate *(per 1 000 live births)*	8	5

Maternal mortality

	2000
Maternal mortality ratio *(deaths per 100 000 births)*	17

HIV/AIDS

	2003	[Low estimate - high estimate]
Number of HIV-infected persons, ...	120 000	[60 000 - 200 000]
Adult HIV prevalence *(percentage of adults 15-49)*	0.4	[0.2 - 0.7]

Policy views

	1976	2003
Life expectancy...	Unacceptable	Acceptable
Under-five mortality...		Acceptable
Maternal mortality...		Unacceptable
Level of concern about AIDS.................................		Major concern

Life Expectancy at Birth

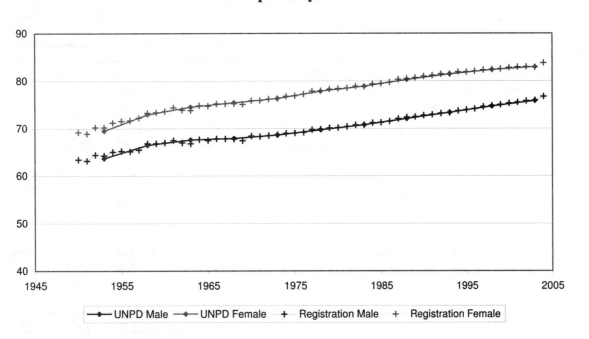

Infant Mortality Rate

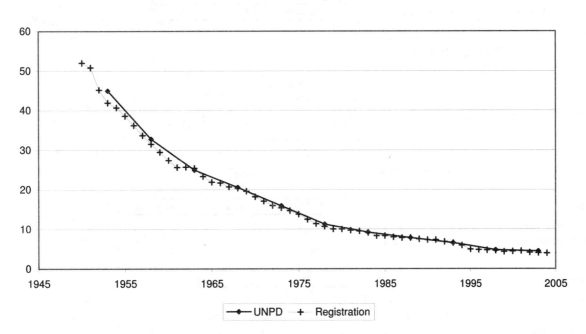

French Guiana

Indicator	Period				
	Earlier year			Later year	

I. Data and estimates from national and other sources

General mortality

	Year	Value		Year	Value
Annual number of deaths *(thousands)*	1970	0.4		2003	0.7
Annual number of deaths under age one *(thousands)*	1970	0.1		2003	0.1
Crude death rate *(per 1 000 person-years)*	1970	7.8		2003	3.8

	Year	Male	Female	Year	Male	Female
Life expectancy *(years)*						
at birth..	..	..	..	2002	72.5	79.2
at age 15..	..	..	..	2002	58.9	65.7
at age 60..	..	..	..	2002	19.8	23.8
Survival probability						
from birth to age 15...............................	..	..	..	2002	0.98	0.98
from age 15 to age 60.............................	..	..	..	2002	0.83	0.92
from age 60 to age 80.............................	..	..	..	2002	0.51	0.72

Infant and child mortality

	Year	Male	Female	Both sexes	Year	Male	Female	Both sexes
Infant mortality rate *(per 1 000 live births)*	..	..	..	..	2002	11	9	10
Mortality from age 1 to age 4 *(per 1 000 live births)*	..	..	..	..	2002	6	6	6
Under-five mortality rate *(per 1 000 live births)*	..	..	..	..	2002	17	15	16

II. Data and estimates from United Nations sources

United Nations Population Division estimates

	1990-1995	2000-2005
Annual number of deaths *(thousands)*	1	1
Crude death rate *(per 1 000 person-years)*	4	4
Life expectancy at birth *(years)*		
Male...	70.0	72.5
Female..	76.0	78.4
Under-five mortality rate *(per 1 000 live births)*	23	16

Maternal mortality

	2000
Maternal mortality ratio *(deaths per 100 000 births)*	..

HIV/AIDS

	2003	[Low estimate - high estimate]
Number of HIV-infected persons, ...	..	..
Adult HIV prevalence *(percentage of adults 15-49)*	..	..

Policy views

	1976	2003
Life expectancy...	..	..
Under-five mortality...		..
Maternal mortality..		..
Level of concern about AIDS..................................		..

Life Expectancy at Birth

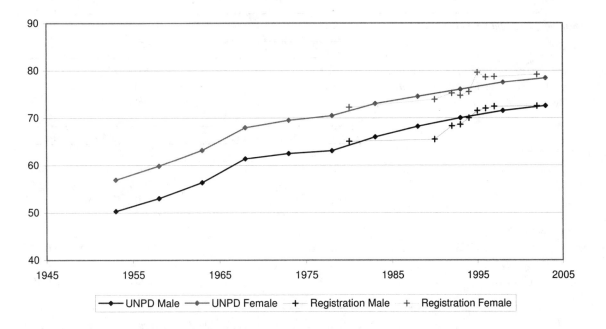

Infant Mortality Rate

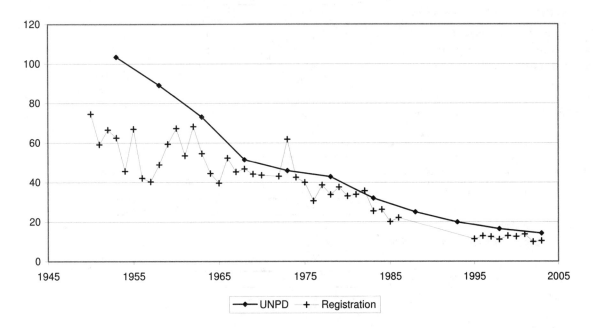

Indicator	Period				
	Earlier year		Later year		

I. Data and estimates from national and other sources

General mortality

	Year	Value		Year	Value	
Annual number of deaths *(thousands)*	1970	1.1		2003	1.1	
Annual number of deaths under age one *(thousands)*	1968	0.2		2003	0.0	
Crude death rate *(per 1 000 person-years)*	1970	9.8		2003	4.5	

	Year	Male	Female	Year	Male	Female
Life expectancy *(years)*						
at birth...	..	..	..	2004	71.5	76.7
at age 15..	..	..	..	2004	57.4	62.6
at age 60..	..	..	..	2004	17.1	20.6
Survival probability						
from birth to age 15...	..	..	..	2004	0.99	0.99
from age 15 to age 60...	..	..	..	2004	0.85	0.91
from age 60 to age 80...	..	..	..	2004	0.40	0.56

Infant and child mortality

	Year	Male	Female	Both sexes	Year	Male	Female	Both sexes
Infant mortality rate *(per 1 000 live births)*	..	..	..	..	2004	4	4	4
Mortality from age 1 to age 4 *(per 1 000 live births)*	..	..	..	..	2004	4	3	3
Under-five mortality rate *(per 1 000 live births)*	..	..	..	..	2004	8	7	7

II. Data and estimates from United Nations sources

United Nations Population Division estimates

	1990-1995	2000-2005
Annual number of deaths *(thousands)*	1	1
Crude death rate *(per 1 000 person-years)*	5	5
Life expectancy at birth *(years)*		
Male...	67.9	70.6
Female..	72.8	75.8
Under-five mortality rate *(per 1 000 live births)*	15	11

Maternal mortality

	2000
Maternal mortality ratio *(deaths per 100 000 births)*	..

HIV/AIDS

	2003	*[Low estimate - high estimate]*
Number of HIV-infected persons, ...	..	..
Adult HIV prevalence *(percentage of adults 15-49)*	..	..

Policy views

	1976	2003
Life expectancy..	..	..
Under-five mortality..		..
Maternal mortality..		..
Level of concern about AIDS....................................		..

Life Expectancy at Birth

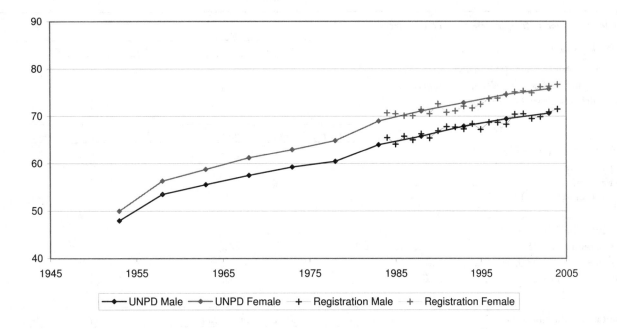

Infant Mortality Rate

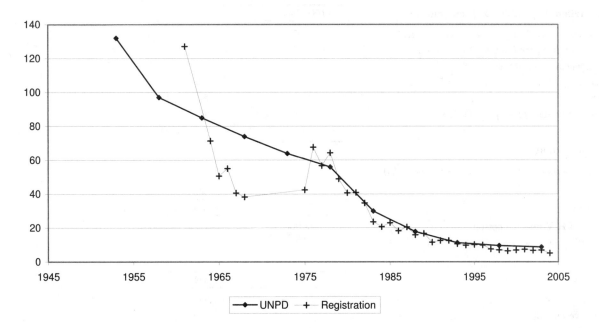

Indicator	Period			
	Earlier year		Later year	

I. Data and estimates from national and other sources

General mortality	Year	Value	Year	Value
Annual number of deaths *(thousands)*	..	..	..	..
Annual number of deaths under age one *(thousands)*	..	..	..	..
Crude death rate *(per 1 000 person-years)*	..	..	..	..

	Year	Male	Female	Year	Male	Female
Life expectancy *(years)*						
at birth...	..	..	..	..	..	..
at age 15..	..	..	..	..	..	..
at age 60..	..	..	..	..	..	..
Survival probability						
from birth to age 15..	..	..	..	..	..	..
from age 15 to age 60..	..	..	..	..	..	..
from age 60 to age 80..	..	..	..	..	..	..

Infant and child mortality	Year	Male	Female	Both sexes	Year	Male	Female	Both sexes
Infant mortality rate *(per 1 000 live births)*	..	..	..	..	1990-2000	74	49	61
Mortality from age 1 to age 4 *(per 1 000 live births)*	..	..	..	..	1990-2000	32	33	32
Under-five mortality rate *(per 1 000 live births)*	..	..	..	..	1990-2000	103	80	91

II. Data and estimates from United Nations sources

United Nations Population Division estimates	1990-1995	2000-2005
Annual number of deaths *(thousands)*	12	17
Crude death rate *(per 1 000 person-years)*	11	12
Life expectancy at birth *(years)*		
Male...	57.9	53.8
Female..	61.6	55.4
Under-five mortality rate *(per 1 000 live births)*	95	95

Maternal mortality	2000
Maternal mortality ratio *(deaths per 100 000 births)*	420

HIV/AIDS	2003	[Low estimate - high estimate]
Number of HIV-infected persons, ...	48 000	[24 000 - 91 000]
Adult HIV prevalence *(percentage of adults 15-49)*	8.1	[4.1 - 15.3]

Policy views	1976	2003
Life expectancy..	Unacceptable	Unacceptable
Under-five mortality..		Unacceptable
Maternal mortality..		Unacceptable
Level of concern about AIDS...................................		Major concern

Life Expectancy at Birth

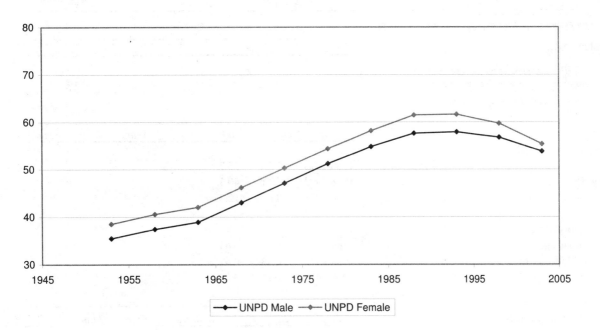

Infant Mortality Rate

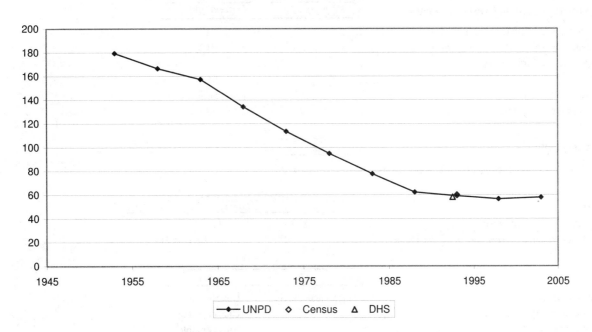

Indicator	Period						
	Earlier year				Later year		

I. Data and estimates from national and other sources

General mortality

	Year	Value			Year	Value	
Annual number of deaths *(thousands)*	..	..			..	..	
Annual number of deaths under age one *(thousands)*	..	..			..	..	
Crude death rate *(per 1 000 person-years)*	..	..			..	..	

	Year	Male	Female		Year	Male	Female
Life expectancy *(years)*							
at birth..	1968-1973	32.3	35.7		..	..	..
at age 15..	1968-1973	39.2	40.3		..	..	..
at age 60..	1968-1973	11.7	12.3		..	..	..
Survival probability							
from birth to age 15......................................	1968-1973	0.58	0.63		..	..	..
from age 15 to age 60....................................	1968-1973	0.43	0.47		..	..	..
from age 60 to age 80....................................	1968-1973	0.16	0.18		..	..	..

Infant and child mortality

	Year	Male	Female	Both sexes	Year	Male	Female	Both sexes
Infant mortality rate *(per 1 000 live births)*	..	..	..	..	1996	..	..	92
Mortality from age 1 to age 4 *(per 1 000 live births)*	..	..	..	..	..	..	..	..
Under-five mortality rate *(per 1 000 live births)*	..	..	..	..	1996	..	..	149

II. Data and estimates from United Nations sources

United Nations Population Division estimates

	1990-1995	2000-2005
Annual number of deaths *(thousands)*	15	17
Crude death rate *(per 1 000 person-years)*	15	12
Life expectancy at birth *(years)*		
Male...	49.9	54.0
Female..	53.0	56.9
Under-five mortality rate *(per 1 000 live births)*	170	129

Maternal mortality

	2000
Maternal mortality ratio *(deaths per 100 000 births)*	540

HIV/AIDS

	2003	[Low estimate - high estimate]
Number of HIV-infected persons, ...	6 800	[1 800 - 24 000]
Adult HIV prevalence *(percentage of adults 15-49)*	1.2	[0.3 - 4.2]

Policy views

	1976	2003
Life expectancy...	Unacceptable	Unacceptable
Under-five mortality...		Unacceptable
Maternal mortality..		Unacceptable
Level of concern about AIDS...................................		Major concern

Life Expectancy at Birth

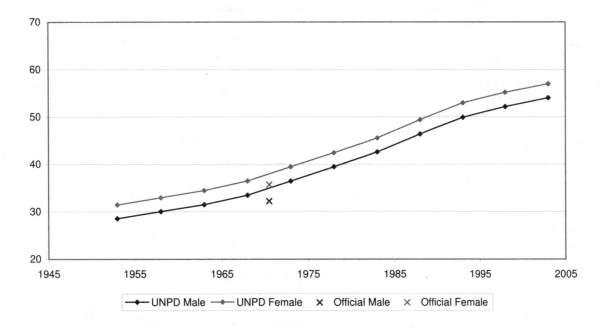

Infant Mortality Rate

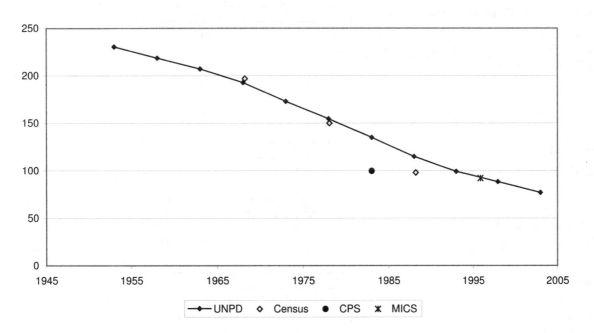

Indicator	Period					
	Earlier year			Later year		

I. Data and estimates from national and other sources

General mortality

	Year	Value		Year	Value	
Annual number of deaths *(thousands)*	1970	34.3		2003	46.1	
Annual number of deaths under age one *(thousands)*	1970	2.3		2003	1.1	
Crude death rate *(per 1 000 person-years)*	1970	7.3		2003	10.6	

	Year	Male	Female	Year	Male	Female
Life expectancy *(years)*						
at birth...	1981	66.8	74.7	2003	69.1	74.7
at age 15...	1981	54.9	62.3	2003	56.3	61.7
at age 60...	1981	16.5	20.4	2003	16.8	19.5
Survival probability						
from birth to age 15..	1981	0.96	0.96	2003	0.97	0.97
from age 15 to age 60..	1981	0.78	0.90	2003	0.80	0.91
from age 60 to age 80..	1981	0.37	0.56	2003	0.35	0.52

Infant and child mortality

	Year	Male	Female	Both sexes	Year	Male	Female	Both sexes
Infant mortality rate *(per 1 000 live births)*	1981	33	26	29	1990-1999	48	32	41
Mortality from age 1 to age 4 *(per 1 000 live births)*	1981	7	7	7	1990-1999	5	4	4
Under-five mortality rate *(per 1 000 live births)*	1981	40	33	36	1990-1999	53	35	45

II. Data and estimates from United Nations sources

United Nations Population Division estimates

	1990-1995	2000-2005
Annual number of deaths *(thousands)*	51	51
Crude death rate *(per 1 000 person-years)*	10	11
Life expectancy at birth *(years)*		
Male..	66.5	66.5
Female..	74.3	74.3
Under-five mortality rate *(per 1 000 live births)*	43	43

Maternal mortality

	2000
Maternal mortality ratio *(deaths per 100 000 births)*	32

HIV/AIDS

	2003	*[Low estimate - high estimate]*
Number of HIV-infected persons, ...	3 000	[2 000 - 12 000]
Adult HIV prevalence *(percentage of adults 15-49)*	0.1	[0.1 - 0.4]

Policy views

	1976	2003
Life expectancy...	..	Unacceptable
Under-five mortality..		Unacceptable
Maternal mortality..		Unacceptable
Level of concern about AIDS...................................		Major concern

Life Expectancy at Birth

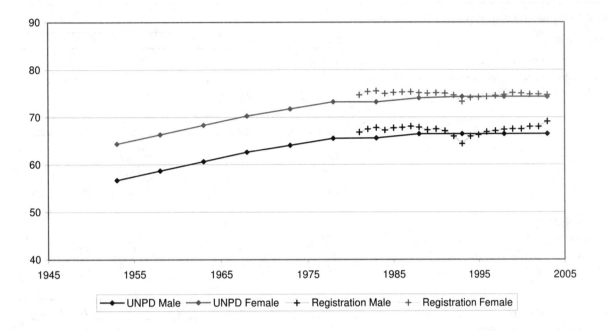

Infant Mortality Rate

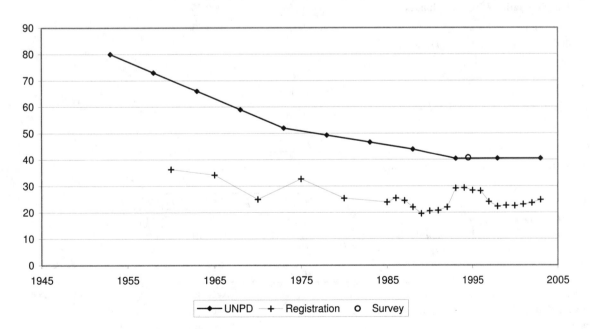

Indicator	Period				
	Earlier year			Later year	

I. Data and estimates from national and other sources

General mortality

	Year	Value		Year	Value
Annual number of deaths *(thousands)*	1970	975.7		2003	853.9
Annual number of deaths under age one *(thousands)*	1970	23.5		2003	3.0
Crude death rate *(per 1 000 person-years)*	1970	12.6		2003	10.3

	Year	Male	Female	Year	Male	Female
Life expectancy *(years)*						
at birth..	1970	67.5	73.6	2002-2004	75.9	81.5
at age 15..	1970	54.8	60.4	2002-2004	61.4	67.0
at age 60..	1970	15.2	18.8	2002-2004	20.0	24.1
Survival probability						
from birth to age 15..	1970	0.97	0.97	2002-2004	0.99	0.99
from age 15 to age 60..	1970	0.81	0.89	2002-2004	0.88	0.94
from age 60 to age 80..	1970	0.29	0.47	2002-2004	0.53	0.71

Infant and child mortality

	Year	Male	Female	Both sexes	Year	Male	Female	Both sexes
Infant mortality rate *(per 1 000 live births)*	1970	24	19	21	2002-2004	5	4	4
Mortality from age 1 to age 4 *(per 1 000 live births)*	1970	4	3	4	2002-2004	1	1	1
Under-five mortality rate *(per 1 000 live births)*	1970	29	22	25	2002-2004	5	5	5

II. Data and estimates from United Nations sources

United Nations Population Division estimates

	1990-1995	2000-2005
Annual number of deaths *(thousands)*	901	853
Crude death rate *(per 1 000 person-years)*	11	10
Life expectancy at birth *(years)*		
Male...	72.6	75.6
Female...	79.1	81.4
Under-five mortality rate *(per 1 000 live births)*	7	6

Maternal mortality

	2000
Maternal mortality ratio *(deaths per 100 000 births)*	8

HIV/AIDS

	2003	[Low estimate - high estimate]
Number of HIV-infected persons, ...	43 000	[21 000 - 71 000]
Adult HIV prevalence *(percentage of adults 15-49)*	0.1	[0.1 - 0.2]

Policy views

	1976	2003
Life expectancy...	..	Acceptable
Under-five mortality...		Acceptable
Maternal mortality...		Acceptable
Level of concern about AIDS...................................		Major concern

Life Expectancy at Birth

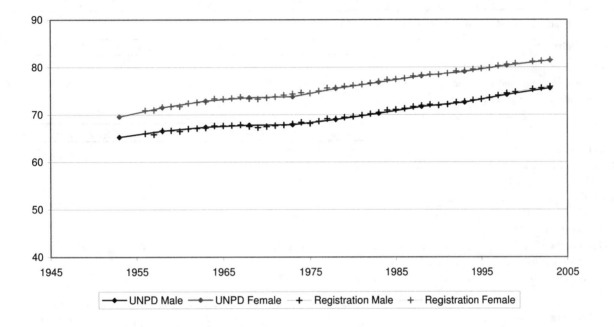

Infant Mortality Rate

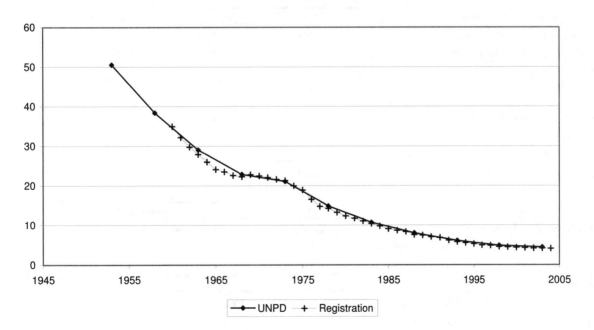

Indicator	Period						
	Earlier year				**Later year**		

I. Data and estimates from national and other sources

General mortality

	Year	Value			Year	Value	
Annual number of deaths *(thousands)*	..	..			..	..	
Annual number of deaths under age one *(thousands)*	..	..			..	..	
Crude death rate *(per 1 000 person-years)*	..	..			..	..	

	Year	Male	Female		Year	Male	Female
Life expectancy *(years)*							
at birth	..	..	..		..	..	..
at age 15	..	..	..		..	..	..
at age 60	..	..	..		..	..	..
Survival probability							
from birth to age 15	..	..	..		..	..	..
from age 15 to age 60	..	..	..		..	..	..
from age 60 to age 80	..	..	..		..	..	..

Infant and child mortality

	Year	Male	Female	Both sexes	Year	Male	Female	Both sexes
Infant mortality rate *(per 1 000 live births)*	1975	113	92	103	1993-2003	70	59	65
Mortality from age 1 to age 4 *(per 1 000 live births)*	1975	75	73	74	1993-2003	44	52	48
Under-five mortality rate *(per 1 000 live births)*	1975	179	158	169	1993-2003	111	108	110

II. Data and estimates from United Nations sources

United Nations Population Division estimates

	1990-1995	2000-2005
Annual number of deaths *(thousands)*	184	227
Crude death rate *(per 1 000 person-years)*	11	11
Life expectancy at birth *(years)*		
Male	55.4	56.2
Female	58.0	57.2
Under-five mortality rate *(per 1 000 live births)*	121	102

Maternal mortality

	2000
Maternal mortality ratio *(deaths per 100 000 births)*	540

HIV/AIDS

	2003	*[Low estimate - high estimate]*
Number of HIV-infected persons,	350 000	[210 000 - 560 000]
Adult HIV prevalence *(percentage of adults 15-49)*	3.1	[1.9 - 5.0]

Policy views

	1976	2003
Life expectancy	Unacceptable	Unacceptable
Under-five mortality		Unacceptable
Maternal mortality		Unacceptable
Level of concern about AIDS		Major concern

Life Expectancy at Birth

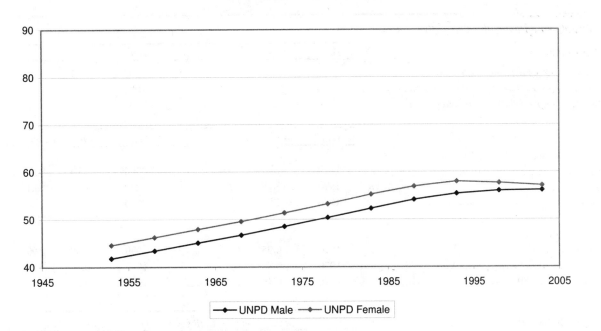

Infant Mortality Rate

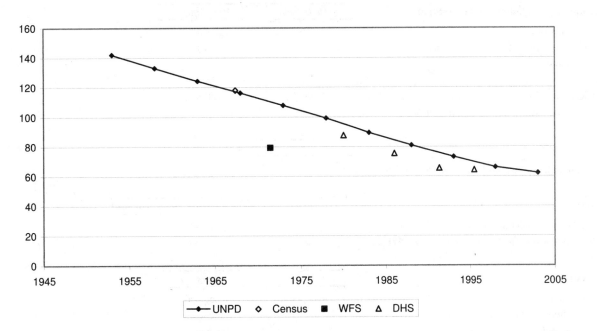

Indicator	Period							
	Earlier year				**Later year**			

I. Data and estimates from national and other sources

General mortality

	Year	Value			Year	Value		
Annual number of deaths *(thousands)*	1970	74.0			2003	105.5		
Annual number of deaths under age one *(thousands)*	1970	4.3			2003	0.4		
Crude death rate *(per 1 000 person-years)*	1970	8.5			2003	9.6		

	Year	Male	Female		Year	Male	Female	
Life expectancy *(years)*								
at birth..	1970	70.1	73.6		2000	75.4	80.5	
at age 15..	1970	58.9	62.0		2000	61.1	66.1	
at age 60..	1970	17.5	19.3		2000	20.0	22.8	
Survival probability								
from birth to age 15..	1970	0.95	0.96		1999	0.99	0.99	
from age 15 to age 60......................................	1970	0.88	0.92		1999	0.88	0.95	
from age 60 to age 80......................................	1970	0.40	0.49		1999	0.53	0.69	

Infant and child mortality

	Year	Male	Female	Both sexes	Year	Male	Female	Both sexes
Infant mortality rate *(per 1 000 live births)*	1970	42	35	39	1999	7	6	6
Mortality from age 1 to age 4 *(per 1 000 live births)*	1970	7	6	6	1999	1	1	1
Under-five mortality rate *(per 1 000 live births)*	1970	48	41	45	1999	8	7	7

II. Data and estimates from United Nations sources

United Nations Population Division estimates

	1990-1995	*2000-2005*
Annual number of deaths *(thousands)*	99	109
Crude death rate *(per 1 000 person-years)*	10	10
Life expectancy at birth *(years)*		
Male...	74.8	75.6
Female..	79.7	80.8
Under-five mortality rate *(per 1 000 live births)*	9	8

Maternal mortality

	2000
Maternal mortality ratio *(deaths per 100 000 births)*	9

HIV/AIDS

	2003	*[Low estimate - high estimate]*
Number of HIV-infected persons, ...	9 100	[4 500 - 15 000]
Adult HIV prevalence *(percentage of adults 15-49)*	0.2	[0.1 - 0.3]

Policy views

	1976	*2003*
Life expectancy...	Acceptable	Acceptable
Under-five mortality...		Acceptable
Maternal mortality...		Acceptable
Level of concern about AIDS....................................		Major concern

Life Expectancy at Birth

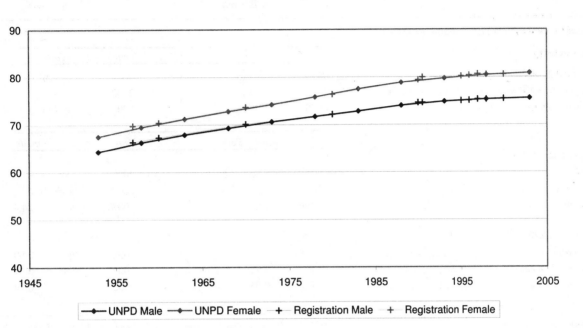

Infant Mortality Rate

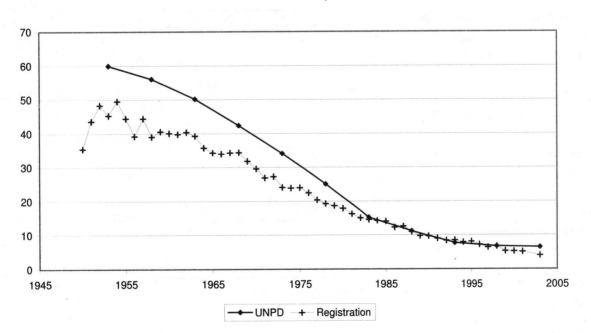

I. Data and estimates from national and other sources

General mortality

Indicator	Year	Value		Year	Value	
Annual number of deaths *(thousands)*	1970	2.5		2003	2.6	
Annual number of deaths under age one *(thousands)*	1970	0.4		2003	0.1	
Crude death rate *(per 1 000 person-years)*	1970	7.8		2003	6.0	

	Year	Male	Female	Year	Male	Female
Life expectancy *(years)*						
at birth	1963-1967	62.5	67.3	2002	74.6	81.5
at age 15	1963-1967	52.9	57.0	2002	60.5	67.1
at age 60	1963-1967	15.3	18.3	2002	20.9	24.4
Survival probability						
from birth to age 15	1963-1967	0.92	0.93	2002	0.99	0.99
from age 15 to age 60	1963-1967	0.72	0.80	2002	0.85	0.94
from age 60 to age 80	1963-1967	0.03	0.47	2002	0.57	0.74

Infant and child mortality

Indicator	Year	Male	Female	Both sexes	Year	Male	Female	Both sexes
Infant mortality rate *(per 1 000 live births)*	1963-1967	53	43	48	2002	8	6	7
Mortality from age 1 to age 4 *(per 1 000 live births)*	1963-1967	18	18	18	2002	1	0	1
Under-five mortality rate *(per 1 000 live births)*	1963-1967	70	61	65	2002	9	6	8

II. Data and estimates from United Nations sources

United Nations Population Division estimates

Indicator	1990-1995	2000-2005
Annual number of deaths *(thousands)*	2	3
Crude death rate *(per 1 000 person-years)*	6	6
Life expectancy at birth *(years)*		
Male	72.4	74.9
Female	80.1	81.7
Under-five mortality rate *(per 1 000 live births)*	12	10

Maternal mortality

Indicator	2000
Maternal mortality ratio *(deaths per 100 000 births)*	..

HIV/AIDS

Indicator	2003	[Low estimate - high estimate]
Number of HIV-infected persons,	..	..
Adult HIV prevalence *(percentage of adults 15-49)*	..	..

Policy views

Indicator	1976	2003
Life expectancy	..	..
Under-five mortality		..
Maternal mortality		..
Level of concern about AIDS		..

Life Expectancy at Birth

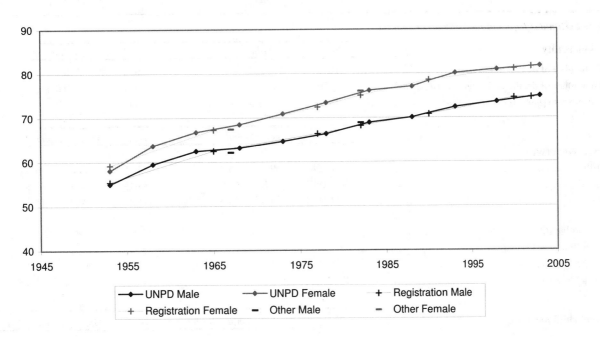

Infant Mortality Rate

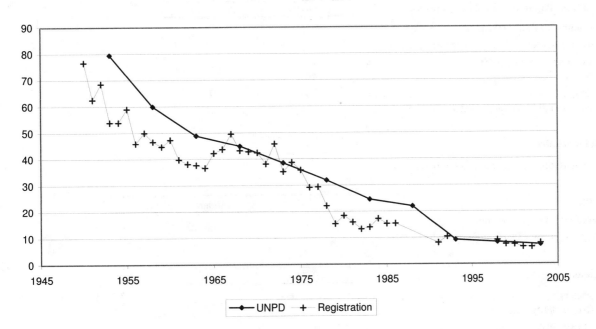

Indicator	Period				
	Earlier year			Later year	

I. Data and estimates from national and other sources

General mortality

	Year	Value		Year	Value
Annual number of deaths *(thousands)*	1970	0.4		2004	0.7
Annual number of deaths under age one *(thousands)*	1970	0.1		2004	0.0
Crude death rate *(per 1 000 person-years)*	1970	4.2		2004	4.2

	Year	Male	Female	Year	Male	Female
Life expectancy *(years)*						
at birth	1979-1981	69.5	75.6	1988-1992	69.8	74.4
at age 15	1979-1981	55.8	61.9	1988-1992	56.4	60.5
at age 60	1979-1981	16.8	20.2	1988-1992	17.3	18.7
Survival probability						
from birth to age 15	..	..	..	..	..	..
from age 15 to age 60	..	..	..	..	..	..
from age 60 to age 80	..	..	..	..	..	..

Infant and child mortality

	Year	Male	Female	Both sexes	Year	Male	Female	Both sexes
Infant mortality rate *(per 1 000 live births)*	1970	26	17	22	2004	..	..	12
Mortality from age 1 to age 4 *(per 1 000 live births)*	..	..	..	..		..	..	..
Under-five mortality rate *(per 1 000 live births)*	..	..	..	..		..	..	..

II. Data and estimates from United Nations sources

United Nations Population Division estimates

	1990-1995	2000-2005
Annual number of deaths *(thousands)*	1	1
Crude death rate *(per 1 000 person-years)*	5	5
Life expectancy at birth *(years)*		
Male	70.4	72.4
Female	75.0	77.0
Under-five mortality rate *(per 1 000 live births)*	14	11

Maternal mortality

	2000
Maternal mortality ratio *(deaths per 100 000 births)*	..

HIV/AIDS

	2003	[Low estimate - high estimate]
Number of HIV-infected persons,	..	..
Adult HIV prevalence *(percentage of adults 15-49)*	..	..

Policy views

	1976	2003
Life expectancy	..	..
Under-five mortality		..
Maternal mortality		..
Level of concern about AIDS		..

Life Expectancy at Birth

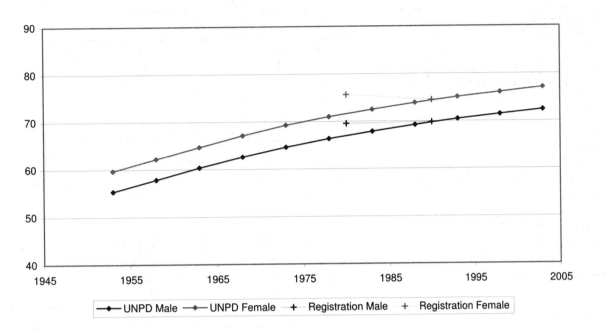

Infant Mortality Rate

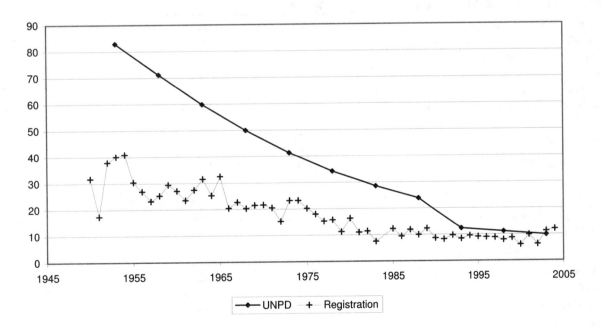

Guatemala

I. Data and estimates from national and other sources

Indicator	Period					
	Earlier year			**Later year**		

General mortality

	Year	Value		Year	Value	
Annual number of deaths *(thousands)*	1970	77.3		2004	65.7	
Annual number of deaths under age one *(thousands)*	1970	18.5		2004	9.9	
Crude death rate *(per 1 000 person-years)*	1970	14.7		2004	5.3	

	Year	Male	Female	Year	Male	Female
Life expectancy *(years)*						
at birth..	1972-1973	53.7	55.5	1995-2000	61.4	67.2
at age 15...	1972-1973	50.9	52.2	1995-2000	51.2	56.9
at age 60...	1972-1973	16.2	16.6	1995-2000	16.8	18.6
Survival probability						
from birth to age 15...	1972-1973	0.81	0.82	1995-2000	0.92	0.93
from age 15 to age 60...	1972-1973	0.68	0.72	1995-2000	0.69	0.80
from age 60 to age 80...	1972-1973	0.35	0.37	1995-2000	0.38	0.46

Infant and child mortality

	Year	Male	Female	Both sexes	Year	Male	Female	Both sexes
Infant mortality rate *(per 1 000 live births)*	1975	113	97	105	1988-1998	50	48	49
Mortality from age 1 to age 4 *(per 1 000 live births)*	1975	49	56	53	1988-1998	15	18	16
Under-five mortality rate *(per 1 000 live births)*	1975	156	148	152	1988-1998	64	65	65

II. Data and estimates from United Nations sources

United Nations Population Division estimates

	1990-1995	2000-2005
Annual number of deaths *(thousands)*	80	79
Crude death rate *(per 1 000 person-years)*	8	7
Life expectancy at birth *(years)*		
Male...	59.4	63.4
Female...	66.1	70.8
Under-five mortality rate *(per 1 000 live births)*	79	52

Maternal mortality

	2000
Maternal mortality ratio *(deaths per 100 000 births)*	240

HIV/AIDS

	2003	*[Low estimate - high estimate]*
Number of HIV-infected persons, ...	78 000	[38 000 - 130 000]
Adult HIV prevalence *(percentage of adults 15-49)*	1.1	[0.6 - 1.8]

Policy views

	1976	2003
Life expectancy...	Unacceptable	Unacceptable
Under-five mortality...		Unacceptable
Maternal mortality..		Unacceptable
Level of concern about AIDS..................................		Major concern

Life Expectancy at Birth

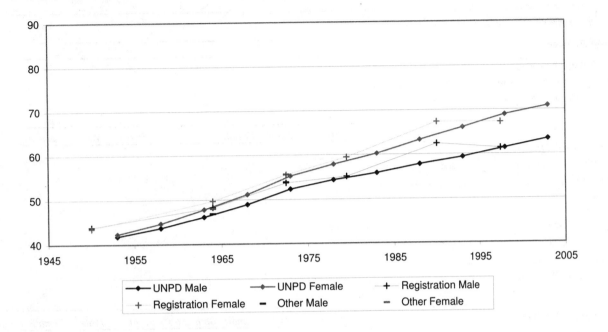

Infant Mortality Rate

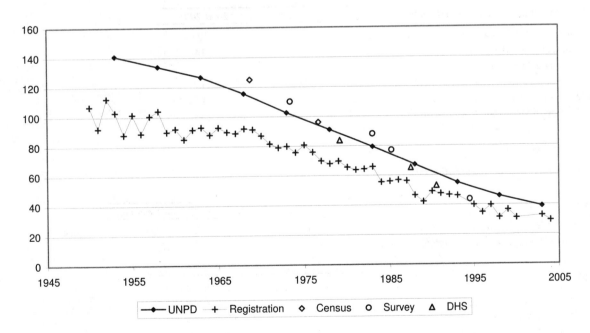

Indicator	Period			
	Earlier year		Later year	

I. Data and estimates from national and other sources

General mortality

	Year	Value	Year	Value
Annual number of deaths *(thousands)*	..	..	..	..
Annual number of deaths under age one *(thousands)*	..	..	..	..
Crude death rate *(per 1 000 person-years)*	..	..	..	..

	Year	Male	Female	Year	Male	Female
Life expectancy *(years)*						
at birth..	..	..	..	..	..	..
at age 15..	..	..	..	..	..	..
at age 60..	..	..	..	..	..	..
Survival probability						
from birth to age 15...	..	..	..	..	..	..
from age 15 to age 60...	..	..	..	..	..	..
from age 60 to age 80...	..	..	..	..	..	..

Infant and child mortality

	Year	Male	Female	Both sexes	Year	Male	Female	Both sexes
Infant mortality rate *(per 1 000 live births)*	..	..	..	..	1989-1999	112	101	107
Mortality from age 1 to age 4 *(per 1 000 live births)*	..	..	..	..	1989-1999	101	98	99
Under-five mortality rate *(per 1 000 live births)*	..	..	..	..	1989-1999	202	188	195

II. Data and estimates from United Nations sources

United Nations Population Division estimates

	1990-1995	2000-2005
Annual number of deaths *(thousands)*	117	123
Crude death rate *(per 1 000 person-years)*	17	14
Life expectancy at birth *(years)*		
Male..	48.2	53.2
Female...	49.4	54.0
Under-five mortality rate *(per 1 000 live births)*	224	166

Maternal mortality

	2000
Maternal mortality ratio *(deaths per 100 000 births)*	740

HIV/AIDS

	2003	*[Low estimate - high estimate]*
Number of HIV-infected persons, ...	140 000	[51 000 - 360 000]
Adult HIV prevalence *(percentage of adults 15-49)*	3.2	[1.2 - 8.2]

Policy views

	1976	2003
Life expectancy..	Unacceptable	Unacceptable
Under-five mortality..		Unacceptable
Maternal mortality..		Unacceptable
Level of concern about AIDS....................................		Major concern

Life Expectancy at Birth

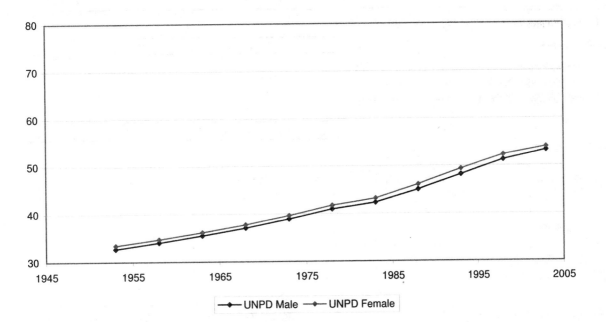

Infant Mortality Rate

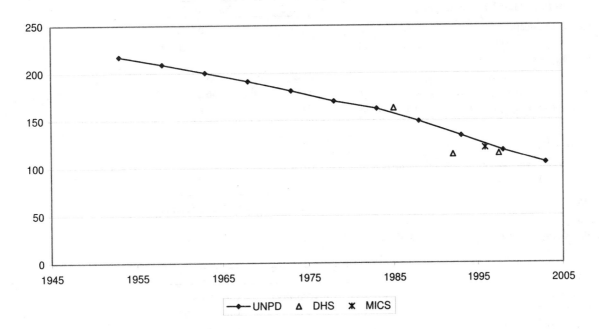

Indicator	Period			
	Earlier year		Later year	

I. Data and estimates from national and other sources

General mortality

	Year	Value	Year	Value
Annual number of deaths *(thousands)*	..	..	..	..
Annual number of deaths under age one *(thousands)*	..	..	..	..
Crude death rate *(per 1 000 person-years)*	..	..	..	..

	Year	Male	Female	Year	Male	Female
Life expectancy *(years)*						
at birth..	..	..	..	..	..	..
at age 15..	..	..	..	..	..	..
at age 60..	..	..	..	..	..	..
Survival probability						
from birth to age 15....................................	..	..	..	..	..	..
from age 15 to age 60.................................	..	..	..	..	..	..
from age 60 to age 80.................................	..	..	..	..	..	..

Infant and child mortality

	Year	Male	Female	Both sexes	Year	Male	Female	Both sexes
Infant mortality rate *(per 1 000 live births)*	..	..	..	..	1996	..	..	142
Mortality from age 1 to age 4 *(per 1 000 live births)*	..	..	..	..	..	..	..	..
Under-five mortality rate *(per 1 000 live births)*	..	..	..	..	1996	..	..	240

II. Data and estimates from United Nations sources

United Nations Population Division estimates

	1990-1995	2000-2005
Annual number of deaths *(thousands)*	24	30
Crude death rate *(per 1 000 person-years)*	22	20
Life expectancy at birth *(years)*		
Male...	41.4	43.1
Female...	44.8	46.2
Under-five mortality rate *(per 1 000 live births)*	246	211

Maternal mortality

	2000
Maternal mortality ratio *(deaths per 100 000 births)*	1 100

HIV/AIDS

	2003	[Low estimate - high estimate]
Number of HIV-infected persons, ...	..	..
Adult HIV prevalence *(percentage of adults 15-49)*	..	..

Policy views

	1976	2003
Life expectancy...	Unacceptable	Unacceptable
Under-five mortality...		Unacceptable
Maternal mortality...		Unacceptable
Level of concern about AIDS.................................		Major concern

Life Expectancy at Birth

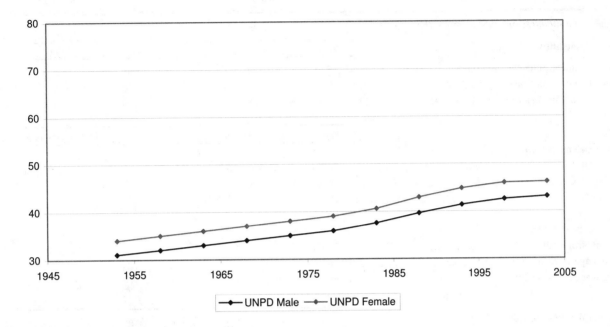

Infant Mortality Rate

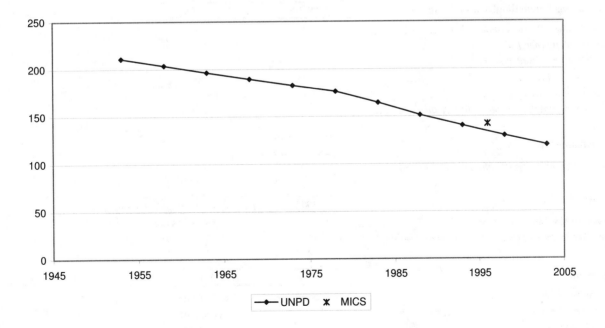

Indicator	Period				
	Earlier year			Later year	

I. Data and estimates from national and other sources

General mortality

	Year	Value		Year	Value
Annual number of deaths *(thousands)*	1970	4.8		1999	4.2
Annual number of deaths under age one *(thousands)*	1970	0.9		1996	0.4
Crude death rate *(per 1 000 person-years)*	1970	6.8		1999	5.4

	Year	Male	Female	Year	Male	Female
Life expectancy *(years)*						
at birth...	1970	61.4	66.2	..	..	..
at age 15...	1970	51.4	55.4	..	..	..
at age 60...	1970	14.5	16.9	..	..	..
Survival probability						
from birth to age 15.................................	1959-1961	0.91	0.92	..	..	..
from age 15 to age 60..............................	1959-1961	0.67	0.73	..	..	..
from age 60 to age 80..............................	1959-1961	0.22	0.34	..	..	..

Infant and child mortality

	Year	Male	Female	Both sexes	Year	Male	Female	Both sexes
Infant mortality rate *(per 1 000 live births)*	1959-1961	59	50	55	1996	..	..	58
Mortality from age 1 to age 4 *(per 1 000 live births)*	1959-1961	22	19	20	..	..	..	..
Under-five mortality rate *(per 1 000 live births)*	1959-1961	79	68	74	1996	..	..	78

II. Data and estimates from United Nations sources

United Nations Population Division estimates

	1990-1995	2000-2005
Annual number of deaths *(thousands)*	7	7
Crude death rate *(per 1 000 person-years)*	10	9
Life expectancy at birth *(years)*		
Male...	56.5	59.8
Female..	63.3	65.9
Under-five mortality rate *(per 1 000 live births)*	89	68

Maternal mortality

	2000
Maternal mortality ratio *(deaths per 100 000 births)*	170

HIV/AIDS

	2003	*[Low estimate - high estimate]*
Number of HIV-infected persons, ...	11 000	[3 500 - 35 000]
Adult HIV prevalence *(percentage of adults 15-49)*	2.5	[0.8 - 7.7]

Policy views

	1976	2003
Life expectancy..	Unacceptable	Unacceptable
Under-five mortality...		Unacceptable
Maternal mortality...		Unacceptable
Level of concern about AIDS.................................		Major concern

Life Expectancy at Birth

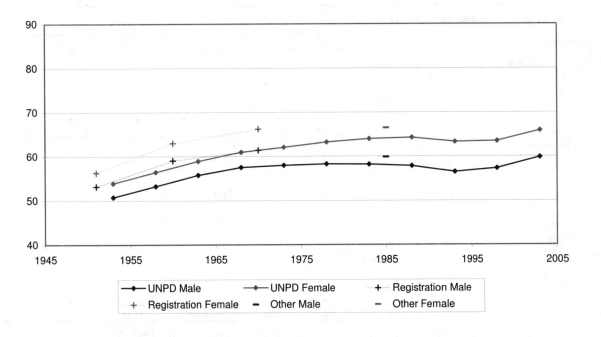

Infant Mortality Rate

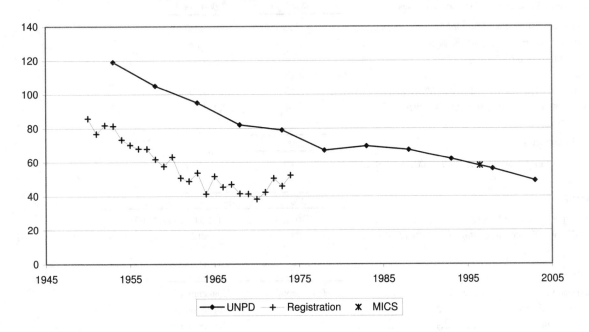

Indicator	Period			
	Earlier year		Later year	

I. Data and estimates from national and other sources

General mortality

	Year	Value	Year	Value
Annual number of deaths *(thousands)*	..	..	..	..
Annual number of deaths under age one *(thousands)*	..	..	..	..
Crude death rate *(per 1 000 person-years)*	..	..	..	..

	Year	Male	Female	Year	Male	Female
Life expectancy *(years)*						
at birth...	1970-1971	47.6	48.3	..	..	..
at age 15...	1970-1971	48.0	48.3	..	..	..
at age 60...	1970-1971	14.8	15.4	..	..	..
Survival probability						
from birth to age 15..	..	..	..	..	..	..
from age 15 to age 60..	..	..	..	..	..	..
from age 60 to age 80..	..	..	..	..	..	..

Infant and child mortality

	Year	Male	Female	Both sexes	Year	Male	Female	Both sexes
Infant mortality rate *(per 1 000 live births)*	1970	158	141	150	1990-2000	97	83	89
Mortality from age 1 to age 4 *(per 1 000 live births)*	1970	80	96	88	1990-2000	52	54	53
Under-five mortality rate *(per 1 000 live births)*	1970	226	224	225	1990-2000	143	132	138

II. Data and estimates from United Nations sources

United Nations Population Division estimates

	1990-1995	2000-2005
Annual number of deaths *(thousands)*	113	112
Crude death rate *(per 1 000 person-years)*	16	14
Life expectancy at birth *(years)*		
Male...	46.3	50.6
Female..	50.3	52.3
Under-five mortality rate *(per 1 000 live births)*	134	110

Maternal mortality

	2000
Maternal mortality ratio *(deaths per 100 000 births)*	680

HIV/AIDS

	2003	[Low estimate - high estimate]
Number of HIV-infected persons, ...	280 000	[120 000 - 600 000]
Adult HIV prevalence *(percentage of adults 15-49)*	5.6	[2.5 - 11.9]

Policy views

	1976	2003
Life expectancy..	Unacceptable	Unacceptable
Under-five mortality..		Unacceptable
Maternal mortality..		Unacceptable
Level of concern about AIDS..................................		Major concern

Life Expectancy at Birth

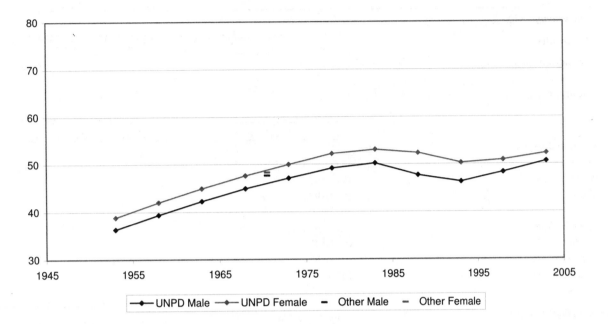

Infant Mortality Rate

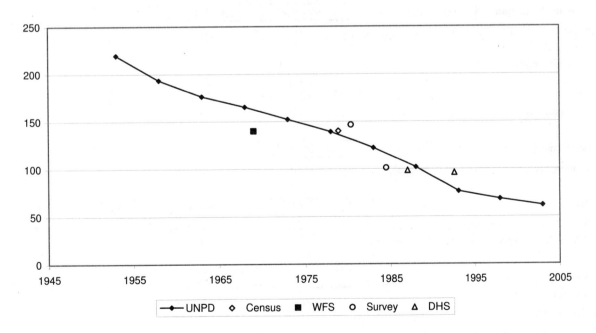

Indicator	Period			
	Earlier year		Later year	

I. Data and estimates from national and other sources

General mortality

	Year	Value	Year	Value
Annual number of deaths *(thousands)*	..	..	..	..
Annual number of deaths under age one *(thousands)*	..	..	..	..
Crude death rate *(per 1 000 person-years)*	..	..	..	..

	Year	Male	Female	Year	Male	Female
Life expectancy *(years)*						
at birth	1973-1975	50.2	54.3	..	..	..
at age 15	1973-1975	48.5	51.8	..	..	..
at age 60	1973-1975	15.8	16.0	..	..	..
Survival probability						
from birth to age 15	1973-1975	0.78	0.81	..	..	..
from age 15 to age 60	1973-1975	0.63	0.71	..	..	..
from age 60 to age 80	1973-1975	0.32	0.33	..	..	..

Infant and child mortality

	Year	Male	Female	Both sexes	Year	Male	Female	Both sexes
Infant mortality rate *(per 1 000 live births)*	1978	92	70	81	1996-2000	..	..	34
Mortality from age 1 to age 4 *(per 1 000 live births)*	1978	34	36	35	..	..	..	..
Under-five mortality rate *(per 1 000 live births)*	1978	123	103	113	1996-2000	..	..	45

II. Data and estimates from United Nations sources

United Nations Population Division estimates

	1990-1995	2000-2005
Annual number of deaths *(thousands)*	35	42
Crude death rate *(per 1 000 person-years)*	7	6
Life expectancy at birth *(years)*		
Male	63.7	65.6
Female	68.4	69.7
Under-five mortality rate *(per 1 000 live births)*	64	48

Maternal mortality

	2000
Maternal mortality ratio *(deaths per 100 000 births)*	110

HIV/AIDS

	2003	[Low estimate - high estimate]
Number of HIV-infected persons,	63 000	[35 000 - 110 000]
Adult HIV prevalence *(percentage of adults 15-49)*	1.8	[1.0 - 3.2]

Policy views

	1976	2003
Life expectancy	Acceptable	Unacceptable
Under-five mortality		Unacceptable
Maternal mortality		Unacceptable
Level of concern about AIDS		Major concern

Life Expectancy at Birth

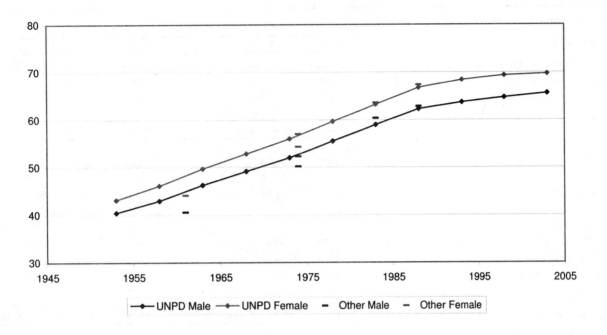

Infant Mortality Rate

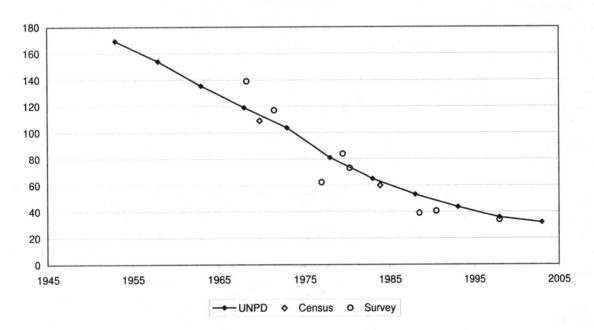

Indicator	Period				
	Earlier year			**Later year**	

I. Data and estimates from national and other sources

General mortality

	Year	Value		Year	Value
Annual number of deaths *(thousands)*	1970	120.2		2003	135.8
Annual number of deaths under age one *(thousands)*	1970	5.4		2003	0.7
Crude death rate *(per 1 000 person-years)*	1970	11.6		2003	13.4

	Year	Male	Female	Year	Male	Female
Life expectancy *(years)*						
at birth..	1972	66.9	72.6	2003	68.3	76.5
at age 15..	1972	54.9	60.2	2003	54.0	62.2
at age 60..	1972	15.6	18.6	2003	15.8	20.6
Survival probability						
from birth to age 15...	1972	0.96	0.96	2002	0.99	0.99
from age 15 to age 60...	1972	0.80	0.88	2002	0.74	0.89
from age 60 to age 80...	1972	0.31	0.46	2002	0.34	0.57

Infant and child mortality

	Year	Male	Female	Both sexes	Year	Male	Female	Both sexes
Infant mortality rate *(per 1 000 live births)*	1972	37	29	33	2002	7	7	7
Mortality from age 1 to age 4 *(per 1 000 live births)*	1972	3	3	3	2002	2	1	1
Under-five mortality rate *(per 1 000 live births)*	1972	40	32	36	2002	9	8	9

II. Data and estimates from United Nations sources

United Nations Population Division estimates

	1990-1995	*2000-2005*
Annual number of deaths *(thousands)*	148	132
Crude death rate *(per 1 000 person-years)*	14	13
Life expectancy at birth *(years)*		
Male...	64.8	68.4
Female..	73.9	76.7
Under-five mortality rate *(per 1 000 live births)*	16	11

Maternal mortality

	2000
Maternal mortality ratio *(deaths per 100 000 births)*	16

HIV/AIDS

	2003	*[Low estimate - high estimate]*
Number of HIV-infected persons, ...	2 800	[900 - 5 500]
Adult HIV prevalence *(percentage of adults 15-49)*	0.1	[0.0 - 0.2]

Policy views

	1976	*2003*
Life expectancy...	Acceptable	Unacceptable
Under-five mortality...		Unacceptable
Maternal mortality...		Unacceptable
Level of concern about AIDS.................................		Major concern

Life Expectancy at Birth

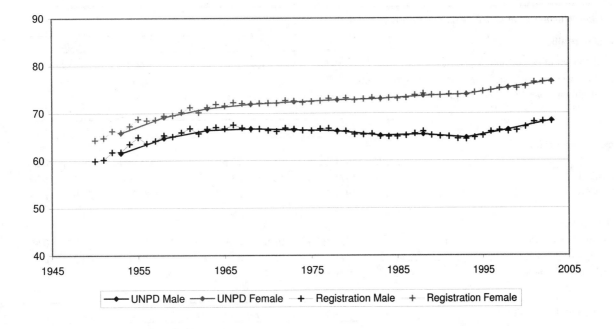

Infant Mortality Rate

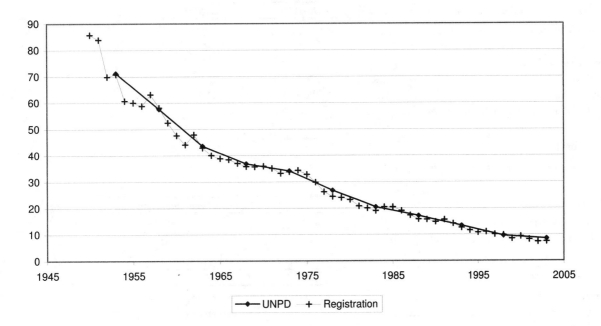

Indicator	Period				
	Earlier year			Later year	

I. Data and estimates from national and other sources

General mortality

	Year	Value		Year	Value
Annual number of deaths *(thousands)*	1970	1.5		2003	1.8
Annual number of deaths under age one *(thousands)*	1970	0.1		2003	0.0
Crude death rate *(per 1 000 person-years)*	1970	7.1		2003	6.3

	Year	Male	Female	Year	Male	Female
Life expectancy *(years)*						
at birth..	1971-1975	71.6	77.5	2002-2003	79.0	82.4
at age 15..	1971-1975	58.0	63.6	2002-2003	64.4	67.7
at age 60..	1971-1975	18.6	21.7	2002-2003	21.9	24.7
Survival probability						
from birth to age 15..	1971-1975	0.98	0.99	2001	0.99	0.99
from age 15 to age 60..	1971-1975	0.82	0.90	2001	0.92	0.95
from age 60 to age 80..	1971-1975	0.47	0.61	2001	0.60	0.74

Infant and child mortality

	Year	Male	Female	Both sexes	Year	Male	Female	Both sexes
Infant mortality rate *(per 1 000 live births)*	1971-1975	14	9	11	2001	3	2	2
Mortality from age 1 to age 4 *(per 1 000 live births)*	1971-1975	3	3	3	2001	1	1	1
Under-five mortality rate *(per 1 000 live births)*	1971-1975	17	12	15	2001	4	3	3

II. Data and estimates from United Nations sources

United Nations Population Division estimates

	1990-1995	2000-2005
Annual number of deaths *(thousands)*	2	2
Crude death rate *(per 1 000 person-years)*	7	6
Life expectancy at birth *(years)*		
Male..	76.3	78.7
Female...	80.8	82.5
Under-five mortality rate *(per 1 000 live births)*	6	4

Maternal mortality

	2000
Maternal mortality ratio *(deaths per 100 000 births)*	0

HIV/AIDS

	2003	[Low estimate - high estimate]
Number of HIV-infected persons, ...	<500	[<1 000]
Adult HIV prevalence *(percentage of adults 15-49)*	0.2	[0.1 - 0.3]

Policy views

	1976	2003
Life expectancy..	Acceptable	Acceptable
Under-five mortality...		Acceptable
Maternal mortality...		Acceptable
Level of concern about AIDS..................................		Major concern

Life Expectancy at Birth

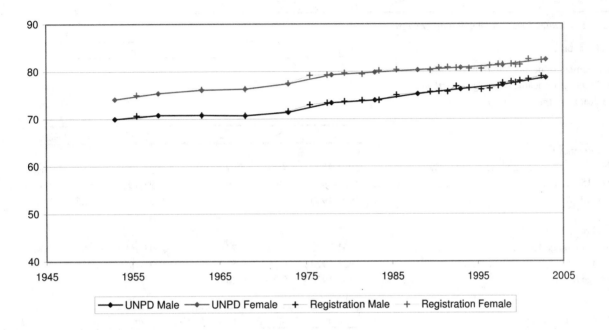

Infant Mortality Rate

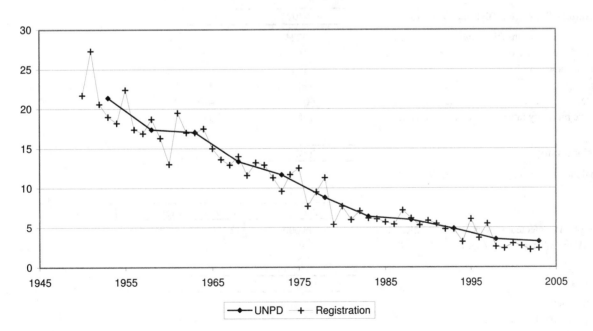

Indicator	Period			
	Earlier year		Later year	

I. Data and estimates from national and other sources

General mortality

	Year	Value	Year	Value
Annual number of deaths *(thousands)*	..	..	..	..
Annual number of deaths under age one *(thousands)*	..	..	..	..
Crude death rate *(per 1 000 person-years)*	..	..	..	..

	Year	Male	Female	Year	Male	Female
Life expectancy *(years)*						
at birth..	1961-1970	46.4	44.7	1993-1997	60.4	61.8
at age 15..	1961-1970	45.0	44.0	1993-1997	53.1	55.8
at age 60..	1961-1970	13.6	13.8	1993-1997	15.5	17.5
Survival probability						
from birth to age 15...	1961-1970	0.76	0.74	1993-1997	0.88	0.87
from age 15 to age 60...	1961-1970	0.55	0.53	1993-1997	0.74	0.77
from age 60 to age 80...	1961-1970	0.25	0.26	..	..	..

Infant and child mortality

	Year	Male	Female	Both sexes	Year	Male	Female	Both sexes
Infant mortality rate *(per 1 000 live births)*	1977	116	124	120	1988-1998	75	71	73
Mortality from age 1 to age 4 *(per 1 000 live births)*	1977	72	81	76	1988-1998	25	37	31
Under-five mortality rate *(per 1 000 live births)*	1977	179	195	187	1988-1998	98	105	101

II. Data and estimates from United Nations sources

United Nations Population Division estimates

	1990-1995	2000-2005
Annual number of deaths *(thousands)*	9 322	9 365
Crude death rate *(per 1 000 person-years)*	10	9
Life expectancy at birth *(years)*		
Male..	59.0	61.7
Female...	60.1	64.7
Under-five mortality rate *(per 1 000 live births)*	128	99

Maternal mortality

	2000
Maternal mortality ratio *(deaths per 100 000 births)*	540

HIV/AIDS

	2003	*[Low estimate - high estimate]*
Number of HIV-infected persons, ...	5 100 000	[2 500 000 - 8 500 000]
Adult HIV prevalence *(percentage of adults 15-49)*	0.9	[0.5 - 1.5]

Policy views

	1976	2003
Life expectancy...	Unacceptable	Unacceptable
Under-five mortality..		Unacceptable
Maternal mortality..		Unacceptable
Level of concern about AIDS....................................		Major concern

Life Expectancy at Birth

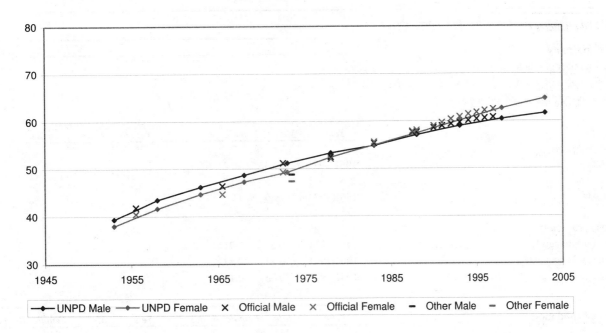

Infant Mortality Rate

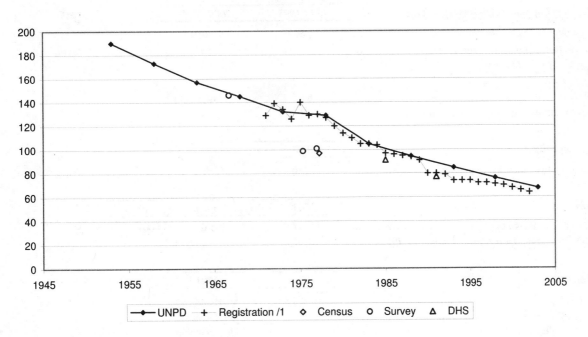

[1] Refers to sample registration

Indonesia

I. Data and estimates from national and other sources

General mortality

Indicator	Year	Value	Year	Value
Annual number of deaths *(thousands)*	..	..	..	..
Annual number of deaths under age one *(thousands)*	..	..	..	..
Crude death rate *(per 1 000 person-years)*	..	..	..	..

	Year	Male	Female	Year	Male	Female
Life expectancy *(years)*						
at birth	1961-1971	37.4	40.0	..	..	..
at age 15	1961-1971	38.5	40.5	..	..	..
at age 60	1961-1971	9.3	11.1	..	..	..
Survival probability						
from birth to age 15	1961-1971	0.68	0.71	..	..	..
from age 15 to age 60	1961-1971	0.43	0.47	..	..	..
from age 60 to age 80	1961-1971	0.06	0.15	..	..	..

Infant and child mortality

	Year	Male	Female	Both sexes	Year	Male	Female	Both sexes
Infant mortality rate *(per 1 000 live births)*	1970	120	91	106	1992-2002	46	40	43
Mortality from age 1 to age 4 *(per 1 000 live births)*	1970	87	68	77	1992-2002	13	11	12
Under-five mortality rate *(per 1 000 live births)*	1970	196	153	175	1992-2002	58	51	54

II. Data and estimates from United Nations sources

United Nations Population Division estimates

	1990-1995	2000-2005
Annual number of deaths *(thousands)*	1 562	1 610
Crude death rate *(per 1 000 person-years)*	8	7
Life expectancy at birth *(years)*		
Male	61.0	64.6
Female	64.5	68.6
Under-five mortality rate *(per 1 000 live births)*	79	54

Maternal mortality

	2000
Maternal mortality ratio *(deaths per 100 000 births)*	230

HIV/AIDS

	2003	[Low estimate - high estimate]
Number of HIV-infected persons,	110 000	[53 000 - 180 000]
Adult HIV prevalence *(percentage of adults 15-49)*	0.1	[0.0 - 0.2]

Policy views

	1976	2003
Life expectancy	Unacceptable	Unacceptable
Under-five mortality		Unacceptable
Maternal mortality		Unacceptable
Level of concern about AIDS		Major concern

Life Expectancy at Birth

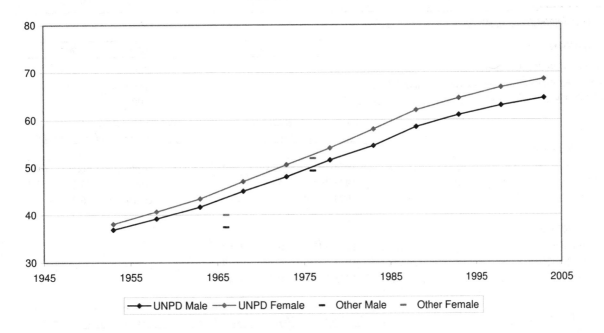

Infant Mortality Rate

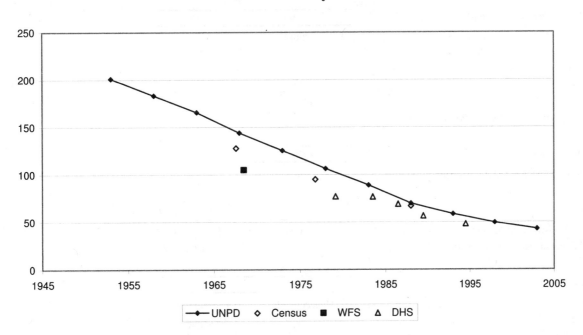

Iran (Islamic Republic of)

Indicator	Period					
	Earlier year			Later year		

I. Data and estimates from national and other sources

General mortality

	Year	Value		Year	Value	
Annual number of deaths *(thousands)*	..	..		2003	368.5	
Annual number of deaths under age one *(thousands)*	..	..		1999	39.2	
Crude death rate *(per 1 000 person-years)*	..	..		2003	5.5	

	Year	Male	Female	Year	Male	Female
Life expectancy *(years)*						
at birth..	1973-1976	57.6	57.4	1996	66.1	68.4
at age 15..	1973-1976	54.4	56.2	1996	55.1	57.3
at age 60..	1973-1976	16.1	17.9	1996	16.2	17.8
Survival probability						
from birth to age 15...	1973-1976	0.83	0.80	..	..	..
from age 15 to age 60...	1973-1976	0.77	0.79	..	..	..
from age 60 to age 80...	1973-1976	0.35	0.44	..	..	..

Infant and child mortality

	Year	Male	Female	Both sexes	Year	Male	Female	Both sexes
Infant mortality rate *(per 1 000 live births)*	..	..	..	..	2000	33	24	29
Mortality from age 1 to age 4 *(per 1 000 live births)*	..	..	..	..	..	..	..	..
Under-five mortality rate *(per 1 000 live births)*	..	..	..	..	2000	38	35	36

II. Data and estimates from United Nations sources

United Nations Population Division estimates

	1990-1995	2000-2005
Annual number of deaths *(thousands)*	389	358
Crude death rate *(per 1 000 person-years)*	7	5
Life expectancy at birth *(years)*		
Male...	65.1	68.8
Female..	67.5	71.7
Under-five mortality rate *(per 1 000 live births)*	64	39

Maternal mortality

	2000
Maternal mortality ratio *(deaths per 100 000 births)*	76

HIV/AIDS

	2003	[Low estimate - high estimate]
Number of HIV-infected persons, ...	31 000	[10 000 - 61 000]
Adult HIV prevalence *(percentage of adults 15-49)*	0.1	[0.0 - 0.2]

Policy views

	1976	2003
Life expectancy...	Unacceptable	Unacceptable
Under-five mortality...		Unacceptable
Maternal mortality..		Unacceptable
Level of concern about AIDS.................................		Major concern

Iran (Islamic Republic of)

Life Expectancy at Birth

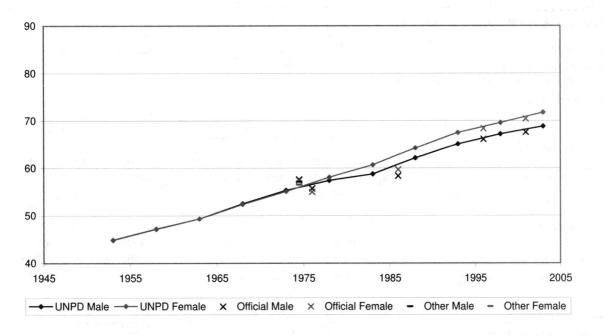

Infant Mortality Rate

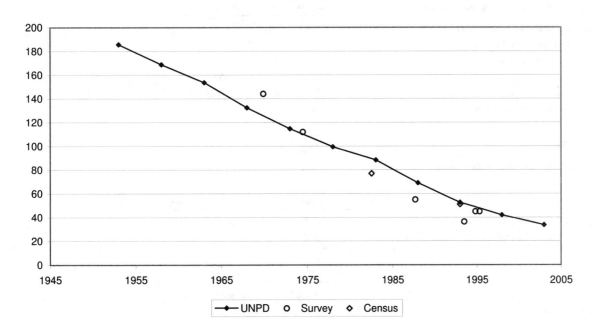

Indicator	Period					
	Earlier year			Later year		

I. Data and estimates from national and other sources

General mortality

	Year	Value		Year	Value	
Annual number of deaths *(thousands)*	..	..		..	..	
Annual number of deaths under age one *(thousands)*	..	..		..	..	
Crude death rate *(per 1 000 person-years)*	..	..		..	..	

	Year	Male	Female	Year	Male	Female
Life expectancy *(years)*						
at birth...	1973-1974	59.9	59.9	1990	77.4	78.2
at age 15..	1973-1974	54.9	53.1	1990	69.4	65.0
at age 60..	1973-1974	16.8	16.4	1990	24.8	22.0
Survival probability						
from birth to age 15..	1973-1974	0.85	0.86	1990	0.97	0.98
from age 15 to age 60...	1973-1974	0.77	0.77	1990	0.86	0.94
from age 60 to age 80...	1973-1974	0.38	0.36	1990	0.62	0.82

Infant and child mortality

	Year	Male	Female	Both sexes	Year	Male	Female	Both sexes
Infant mortality rate *(per 1 000 live births)*	1973	86	77	82	1990	17	15	16
Mortality from age 1 to age 4 *(per 1 000 live births)*	1973	38	34	36	1990	4	5	5
Under-five mortality rate *(per 1 000 live births)*	1973	121	109	115	1990	21	20	21

II. Data and estimates from United Nations sources

United Nations Population Division estimates

	1990-1995	2000-2005
Annual number of deaths *(thousands)*	193	262
Crude death rate *(per 1 000 person-years)*	10	10
Life expectancy at birth *(years)*		
Male..	58.0	57.3
Female...	61.1	60.4
Under-five mortality rate *(per 1 000 live births)*	101	124

Maternal mortality

	2000
Maternal mortality ratio *(deaths per 100 000 births)*	250

HIV/AIDS

	2003	*[Low estimate - high estimate]*
Number of HIV-infected persons, ...	<500	[<1 000]
Adult HIV prevalence *(percentage of adults 15-49)*	<0.1	[<0.2]

Policy views

	1976	2003
Life expectancy..	Acceptable	Unacceptable
Under-five mortality..		Unacceptable
Maternal mortality..		Unacceptable
Level of concern about AIDS.....................................		Major concern

Life Expectancy at Birth

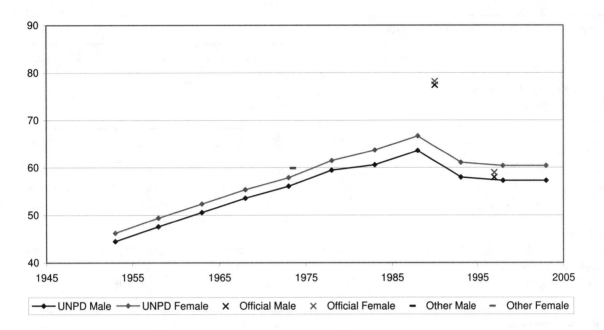

Infant Mortality Rate

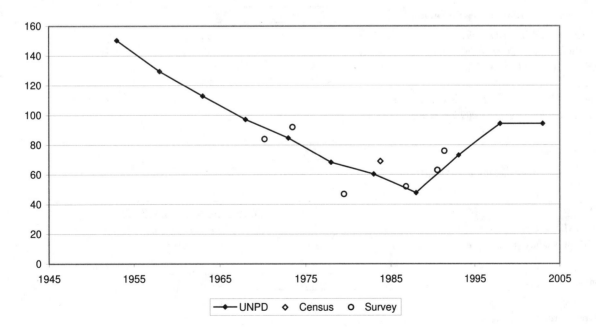

Ireland

Indicator	Period						
	Earlier year				Later year		

I. Data and estimates from national and other sources

General mortality

	Year	Value			Year	Value	
Annual number of deaths *(thousands)*	1970	33.7			2003	28.8	
Annual number of deaths under age one *(thousands)*	1970	1.3			2003	0.3	
Crude death rate *(per 1 000 person-years)*	1970	11.4			2003	7.2	

	Year	Male	Female		Year	Male	Female
Life expectancy *(years)*							
at birth	1970-1972	68.8	73.5		2001-2003	75.1	80.3
at age 15	1970-1972	55.7	60.2		2001-2003	60.8	65.8
at age 60	1970-1972	15.6	18.7		2001-2003	19.2	22.9
Survival probability							
from birth to age 15	1970-1972	0.97	0.98		2001-2003	0.99	0.99
from age 15 to age 60	1970-1972	0.82	0.88		2001-2003	0.89	0.94
from age 60 to age 80	1970-1972	0.32	0.46		2001-2003	0.49	0.66

Infant and child mortality

	Year	Male	Female	Both sexes	Year	Male	Female	Both sexes
Infant mortality rate *(per 1 000 live births)*	1970-1972	21	17	19	2001-2003	7	5	6
Mortality from age 1 to age 4 *(per 1 000 live births)*	1970-1972	3	3	3	2001-2003	1	1	1
Under-five mortality rate *(per 1 000 live births)*	1970-1972	24	20	22	2001-2003	8	6	7

II. Data and estimates from United Nations sources

United Nations Population Division estimates

	1990-1995	2000-2005
Annual number of deaths *(thousands)*	31	30
Crude death rate *(per 1 000 person-years)*	9	8
Life expectancy at birth *(years)*		
Male	72.6	75.1
Female	78.1	80.3
Under-five mortality rate *(per 1 000 live births)*	8	7

Maternal mortality

	2000
Maternal mortality ratio *(deaths per 100 000 births)*	5

HIV/AIDS

	2003	*[Low estimate - high estimate]*
Number of HIV-infected persons,	2 800	[1 100 - 5 300]
Adult HIV prevalence *(percentage of adults 15-49)*	0.1	[0.0 - 0.3]

Policy views

	1976	2003
Life expectancy	Acceptable	Acceptable
Under-five mortality		Acceptable
Maternal mortality		Acceptable
Level of concern about AIDS		Minor concern

Life Expectancy at Birth

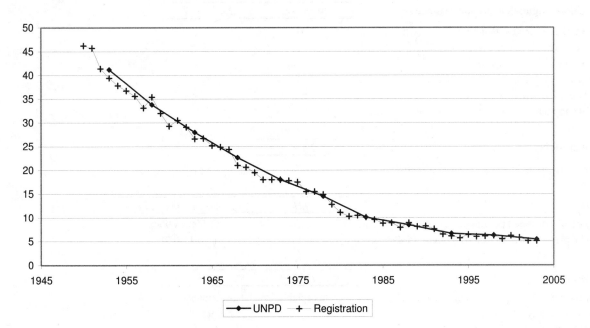

Infant Mortality Rate

Indicator	Period					
	Earlier year			**Later year**		

I. Data and estimates from national and other sources

General mortality	Year	Value		Year	Value	
Annual number of deaths *(thousands)*	1970	20.4		2004	37.7	
Annual number of deaths under age one *(thousands)*	1970	1.8		2004	0.7	
Crude death rate *(per 1 000 person-years)*	1970	6.9		2003	5.7	

	Year	Male	Female	Year	Male	Female
Life expectancy *(years)*						
at birth...	1970	69.6	73.0	2003	77.7	81.9
at age 15...	1970	57.0	60.1	2003	63.3	67.4
at age 60...	1970	17.0	18.4	2003	21.5	24.2
Survival probability						
from birth to age 15..	1972	0.97	0.97	2003	0.99	0.99
from age 15 to age 60......................................	1972	0.84	0.89	2003	0.91	0.95
from age 60 to age 80......................................	1972	0.37	0.44	2003	0.57	0.69

Infant and child mortality	Year	Male	Female	Both sexes	Year	Male	Female	Both sexes
Infant mortality rate *(per 1 000 live births)*	1975	24	20	22	2003	5	5	5
Mortality from age 1 to age 4 *(per 1 000 live births)*	1975	4	4	4	2003	2	1	1
Under-five mortality rate *(per 1 000 live births)*	1975	28	24	26	2003	7	6	6

II. Data and estimates from United Nations sources

United Nations Population Division estimates	*1990-1995*	*2000-2005*
Annual number of deaths *(thousands)*	31	36
Crude death rate *(per 1 000 person-years)*	6	6
Life expectancy at birth *(years)*		
Male..	75.2	77.5
Female..	78.9	81.6
Under-five mortality rate *(per 1 000 live births)*	10	6

Maternal mortality	*2000*
Maternal mortality ratio *(deaths per 100 000 births)*	17

HIV/AIDS	*2003*	*[Low estimate - high estimate]*
Number of HIV-infected persons, ...	3 000	[1 500 - 4 900]
Adult HIV prevalence *(percentage of adults 15-49)*	0.1	[0.1 - 0.2]

Policy views	*1976*	*2003*
Life expectancy..	Acceptable	Acceptable
Under-five mortality...		Acceptable
Maternal mortality...		Acceptable
Level of concern about AIDS.....................................		Minor concern

Life Expectancy at Birth

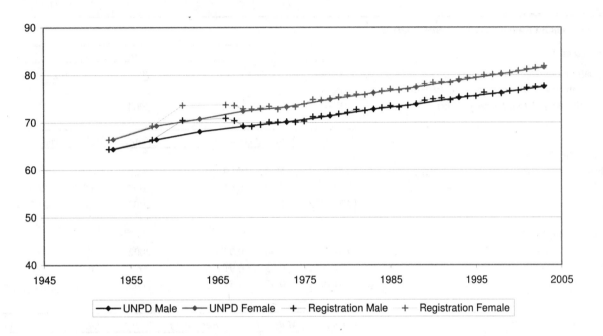

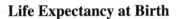

Infant Mortality Rate

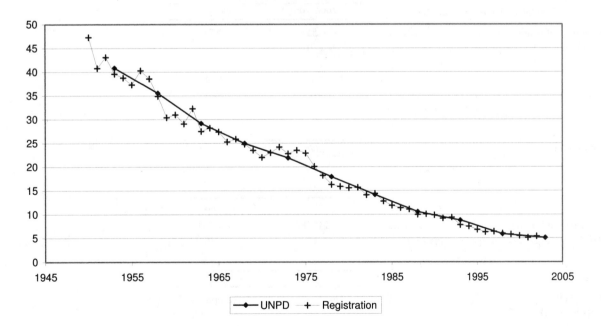

I. Data and estimates from national and other sources

Indicator	Period							
	Earlier year				Later year			

General mortality

	Year	Value			Year	Value		
Annual number of deaths *(thousands)*	1970	521.1			2004	546.7		
Annual number of deaths under age one *(thousands)*	1970	26.6			2004	2.3		
Crude death rate *(per 1 000 person-years)*	1970	9.7			2004	9.4		

	Year	Male	Female		Year	Male	Female	
Life expectancy *(years)*								
at birth	1970-1972	69.0	74.9		2002	77.1	83.0	
at age 15	1970-1972	56.7	62.2		2002	62.6	68.4	
at age 60	1970-1972	16.7	20.2		2002	20.8	25.2	
Survival probability								
from birth to age 15	1970-1972	0.96	0.97		2002	0.99	0.99	
from age 15 to age 60	1970-1972	0.83	0.91		2002	0.91	0.95	
from age 60 to age 80	1970-1972	0.37	0.53		2002	0.56	0.74	

Infant and child mortality

	Year	Male	Female	Both sexes	Year	Male	Female	Both sexes
Infant mortality rate *(per 1 000 live births)*	1970-1972	31	25	28	2002	5	4	4
Mortality from age 1 to age 4 *(per 1 000 live births)*	1970-1972	4	3	4	2002	1	1	1
Under-five mortality rate *(per 1 000 live births)*	1970-1972	34	28	31	2002	6	5	5

II. Data and estimates from United Nations sources

United Nations Population Division estimates

	1990-1995	2000-2005
Annual number of deaths *(thousands)*	551	577
Crude death rate *(per 1 000 person-years)*	10	10
Life expectancy at birth *(years)*		
Male	74.0	76.8
Female	80.5	83.0
Under-five mortality rate *(per 1 000 live births)*	9	6

Maternal mortality

	2000
Maternal mortality ratio *(deaths per 100 000 births)*	5

HIV/AIDS

	2003	[Low estimate - high estimate]
Number of HIV-infected persons,	140 000	[67 000 - 220 000]
Adult HIV prevalence *(percentage of adults 15-49)*	0.5	[0.2 - 0.8]

Policy views

	1976	2003
Life expectancy	Unacceptable	Acceptable
Under-five mortality		Acceptable
Maternal mortality		Acceptable
Level of concern about AIDS		Major concern

Life Expectancy at Birth

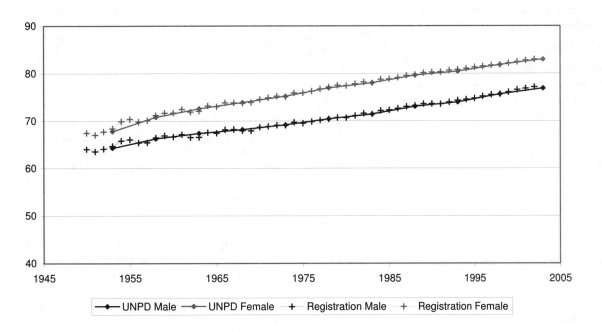

Infant Mortality Rate

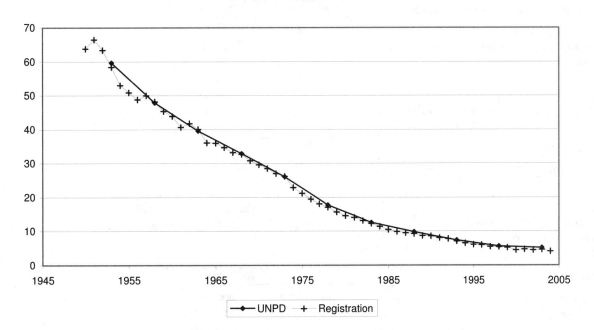

Indicator	Period						
	Earlier year				Later year		

I. Data and estimates from national and other sources

General mortality

	Year	Value			Year	Value	
Annual number of deaths *(thousands)*	..	..			..	..	
Annual number of deaths under age one *(thousands)*	..	..			..	..	
Crude death rate *(per 1 000 person-years)*	..	..			..	..	

	Year	Male	Female		Year	Male	Female
Life expectancy *(years)*							
at birth..................	1969-1971	65.8	70.1		2000-2002	72.8	76.5
at age 15..................	1969-1971	55.6	58.8		2000-2002	59.5	63.1
at age 60..................	1969-1971	17.0	19.4		2000-2002	20.8	22.6
Survival probability							
from birth to age 15..................	1969-1971	0.93	0.95		2000-2002	0.98	0.98
from age 15 to age 60..................	1969-1971	0.78	0.83		2000-2002	0.82	0.87
from age 60 to age 80..................	1969-1971	0.38	0.48		2000-2002	0.52	0.59

Infant and child mortality

	Year	Male	Female	Both sexes	Year	Male	Female	Both sexes
Infant mortality rate *(per 1 000 live births)*	1970	53	43	48	2000-2002	18	18	18
Mortality from age 1 to age 4 *(per 1 000 live births)*	1970	16	15	16	2000-2002	4	2	3
Under-five mortality rate *(per 1 000 live births)*	1970	69	57	63	2000-2002	21	20	21

II. Data and estimates from United Nations sources

United Nations Population Division estimates

	1990-1995	2000-2005
Annual number of deaths *(thousands)*	17	20
Crude death rate *(per 1 000 person-years)*	7	8
Life expectancy at birth *(years)*		
Male.................................	69.9	68.9
Female..............................	73.5	72.5
Under-five mortality rate *(per 1 000 live births)*	23	21

Maternal mortality

	2000
Maternal mortality ratio *(deaths per 100 000 births)*	87

HIV/AIDS

	2003	[Low estimate - high estimate]
Number of HIV-infected persons, ...	22 000	[11 000 - 41 000]
Adult HIV prevalence *(percentage of adults 15-49)*	1.2	[0.6 - 2.2]

Policy views

	1976	2003
Life expectancy.................................	Acceptable	Acceptable
Under-five mortality.............................		Acceptable
Maternal mortality..............................		Acceptable
Level of concern about AIDS....................		Major concern

Life Expectancy at Birth

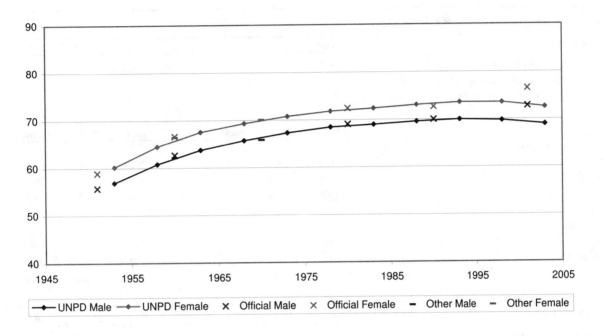

Infant Mortality Rate

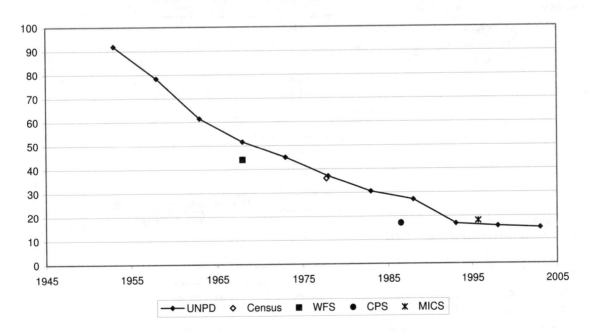

Indicator	Period					
	Earlier year				**Later year**	

I. Data and estimates from national and other sources

General mortality

	Year	Value		Year	Value	
Annual number of deaths *(thousands)*	1970	718.1		2003	1 015.0	
Annual number of deaths under age one *(thousands)*	1970	25.6		2003	3.4	
Crude death rate *(per 1 000 person-years)*	1970	6.9		2003	8.0	

	Year	Male	Female	Year	Male	Female
Life expectancy *(years)*						
at birth	1970	69.3	74.7	2003	78.4	85.3
at age 15	1970	56.0	61.1	2003	63.8	70.7
at age 60	1970	15.9	19.3	2003	22.0	27.5
Survival probability						
from birth to age 15	1970	0.98	0.98	2003	0.99	1.00
from age 15 to age 60	1970	0.83	0.90	2003	0.90	0.96
from age 60 to age 80	1970	0.33	0.49	2003	0.61	0.80

Infant and child mortality

	Year	Male	Female	Both sexes	Year	Male	Female	Both sexes
Infant mortality rate *(per 1 000 live births)*	1970	15	12	13	2003	3	3	3
Mortality from age 1 to age 4 *(per 1 000 live births)*	1970	5	4	4	2003	1	1	1
Under-five mortality rate *(per 1 000 live births)*	1970	20	15	18	2003	4	4	4

II. Data and estimates from United Nations sources

United Nations Population Division estimates

	1990-1995	*2000-2005*
Annual number of deaths *(thousands)*	876	1 019
Crude death rate *(per 1 000 person-years)*	7	8
Life expectancy at birth *(years)*		
Male	76.2	78.3
Female	82.4	85.3
Under-five mortality rate *(per 1 000 live births)*	6	4

Maternal mortality

	2000
Maternal mortality ratio *(deaths per 100 000 births)*	10

HIV/AIDS

	2003	*[Low estimate - high estimate]*
Number of HIV-infected persons,	12 000	[5 700 - 19 000]
Adult HIV prevalence *(percentage of adults 15-49)*	<0.1	[<0.2]

Policy views

	1976	*2003*
Life expectancy	Acceptable	Acceptable
Under-five mortality		Unacceptable
Maternal mortality		Unacceptable
Level of concern about AIDS		Major concern

Life Expectancy at Birth

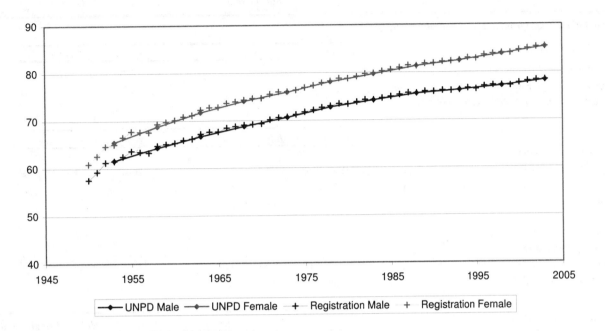

Infant Mortality Rate

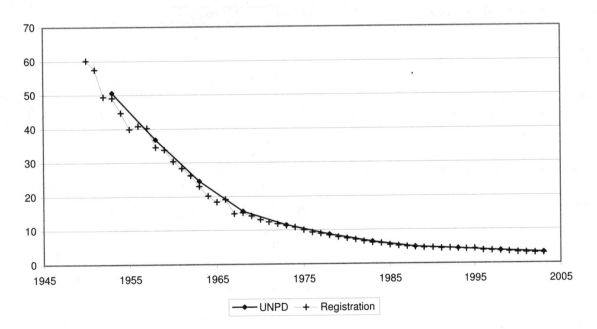

Jordan

Indicator	Period					
	Earlier year				**Later year**	

I. Data and estimates from national and other sources

General mortality

	Year	Value			Year	Value	
Annual number of deaths *(thousands)*	..	..			2003	16.9	
Annual number of deaths under age one *(thousands)*	..	..			..	..	
Crude death rate *(per 1 000 person-years)*	..	..			2003	3.1	

	Year	Male	Female		Year	Male	Female
Life expectancy *(years)*							
at birth..	1959-1963	52.6	52.0		2001	68.8	71.1
at age 15..	1959-1963	48.2	50.1		..	..	..
at age 60..	1959-1963	14.4	15.7		..	..	..
Survival probability							
from birth to age 15...	1959-1963	0.83	0.79		..	..	..
from age 15 to age 60..	1959-1963	0.65	0.69		..	..	..
from age 60 to age 80..	1959-1963	0.26	0.32		..	..	..

Infant and child mortality

	Year	Male	Female	Both sexes	Year	Male	Female	Both sexes
Infant mortality rate *(per 1 000 live births)*	1970	76	81	78	1992-2002	25	23	24
Mortality from age 1 to age 4 *(per 1 000 live births)*	1970	33	34	34	1992-2002	5	5	5
Under-five mortality rate *(per 1 000 live births)*	1970	106	112	109	1992-2002	31	28	29

II. Data and estimates from United Nations sources

United Nations Population Division estimates

	1990-1995	2000-2005
Annual number of deaths *(thousands)*	22	22
Crude death rate *(per 1 000 person-years)*	6	4
Life expectancy at birth *(years)*		
Male...	67.6	69.8
Female...	69.5	72.8
Under-five mortality rate *(per 1 000 live births)*	38	27

Maternal mortality

	2000
Maternal mortality ratio *(deaths per 100 000 births)*	41

HIV/AIDS

	2003	*[Low estimate - high estimate]*
Number of HIV-infected persons, ...	600	[<1 000]
Adult HIV prevalence *(percentage of adults 15-49)*	<0.1	[<0.2]

Policy views

	1976	2003
Life expectancy...	Acceptable	Acceptable
Under-five mortality..		Unacceptable
Maternal mortality..		Unacceptable
Level of concern about AIDS...................................		Major concern

Life Expectancy at Birth

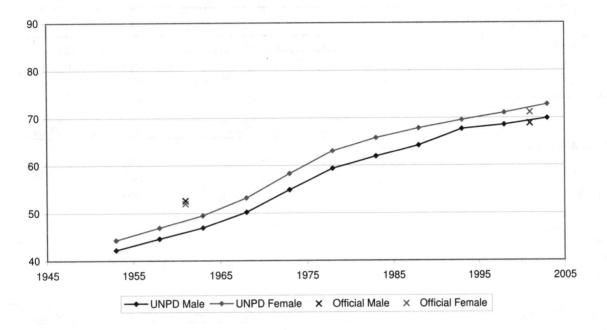

Infant Mortality Rate

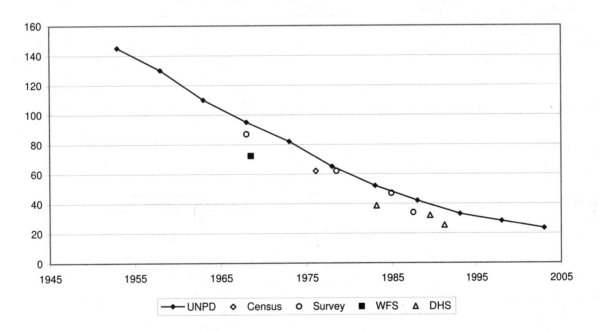

Indicator	Period				
	Earlier year			Later year	

I. Data and estimates from national and other sources

General mortality

	Year	Value		Year	Value	
Annual number of deaths *(thousands)*	..	..		2003	155.3	
Annual number of deaths under age one *(thousands)*	..	..		2003	3.8	
Crude death rate *(per 1 000 person-years)*	..	..		2003	10.4	

	Year	Male	Female	Year	Male	Female
Life expectancy *(years)*						
at birth..........	1981	61.5	72.0	1997	59.0	70.2
at age 15.............	..	..	..	1997	46.6	57.4
at age 60.............	..	..	..	1997	13.0	18.0
Survival probability						
from birth to age 15...............	..	..	..	..	..	..
from age 15 to age 60....................	..	..	..	..	..	..
from age 60 to age 80....................	..	..	..	..	..	..

Infant and child mortality

	Year	Male	Female	Both sexes	Year	Male	Female	Both sexes
Infant mortality rate *(per 1 000 live births)*	..	..	..	..	1989-1999	62	47	55
Mortality from age 1 to age 4 *(per 1 000 live births)*	..	..	..	..	1989-1999	11	6	9
Under-five mortality rate *(per 1 000 live births)*	..	..	..	..	1989-1999	72	53	63

II. Data and estimates from United Nations sources

United Nations Population Division estimates

	1990-1995	2000-2005
Annual number of deaths *(thousands)*	146	162
Crude death rate *(per 1 000 person-years)*	9	11
Life expectancy at birth *(years)*		
Male.........................	60.5	57.8
Female.........................	70.3	68.9
Under-five mortality rate *(per 1 000 live births)*	68	77

Maternal mortality

	2000
Maternal mortality ratio *(deaths per 100 000 births)*	210

HIV/AIDS

	2003	[Low estimate - high estimate]
Number of HIV-infected persons, ...	16 500	[5 800 - 35 000]
Adult HIV prevalence *(percentage of adults 15-49)*	0.2	[0.1 - 0.3]

Policy views

	1976	2003
Life expectancy..	..	Unacceptable
Under-five mortality...		Unacceptable
Maternal mortality..		Unacceptable
Level of concern about AIDS....................................		Major concern

Life Expectancy at Birth

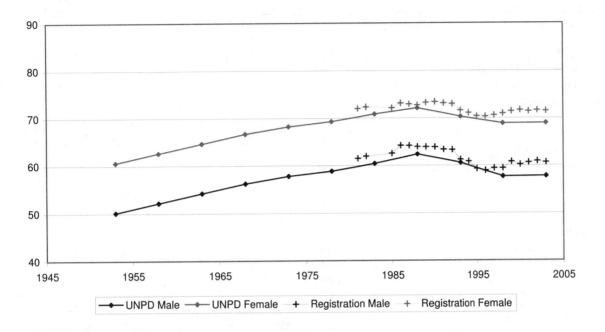

Infant Mortality Rate

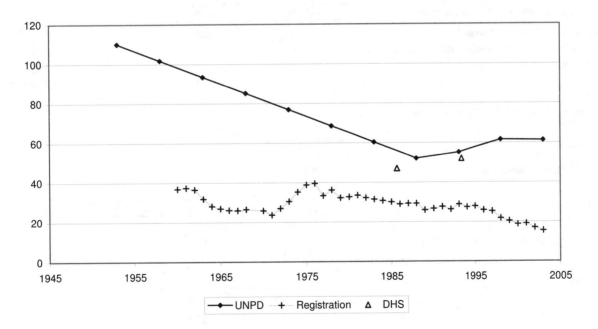

Indicator	Period			
	Earlier year		Later year	

I. Data and estimates from national and other sources

General mortality

	Year	Value	Year	Value
Annual number of deaths *(thousands)*	..	..	..	..
Annual number of deaths under age one *(thousands)*	..	..	..	..
Crude death rate *(per 1 000 person-years)*	..	..	..	..

	Year	Male	Female	Year	Male	Female
Life expectancy *(years)*						
at birth..	1969	46.9	51.2	..	..	..
at age 15...	1969	46.7	49.7	..	..	..
at age 60...	1969	14.5	15.7	..	..	..
Survival probability						
from birth to age 15..	1969	0.75	0.78	..	..	..
from age 15 to age 60..	1969	0.61	0.67	..	..	..
from age 60 to age 80..	1969	0.27	0.33	..	..	..

Infant and child mortality

	Year	Male	Female	Both sexes	Year	Male	Female	Both sexes
Infant mortality rate *(per 1 000 live births)*	1973	96	86	91	1993-2003	84	67	76
Mortality from age 1 to age 4 *(per 1 000 live births)*	1973	66	59	63	1993-2003	42	39	40
Under-five mortality rate *(per 1 000 live births)*	1973	155	140	148	1993-2003	122	103	113

II. Data and estimates from United Nations sources

United Nations Population Division estimates

	1990-1995	2000-2005
Annual number of deaths *(thousands)*	261	503
Crude death rate *(per 1 000 person-years)*	10	16
Life expectancy at birth *(years)*		
Male..	55.0	47.9
Female..	59.4	46.2
Under-five mortality rate *(per 1 000 live births)*	104	118

Maternal mortality

	2000
Maternal mortality ratio *(deaths per 100 000 births)*	1 000

HIV/AIDS

	2003	[Low estimate - high estimate]
Number of HIV-infected persons, ...	1 200 000	[820 000 - 1 700 000]
Adult HIV prevalence *(percentage of adults 15-49)*	6.7	[4.7 - 9.6]

Policy views

	1976	2003
Life expectancy..	Unacceptable	Unacceptable
Under-five mortality..		Unacceptable
Maternal mortality..		Unacceptable
Level of concern about AIDS......................................		Major concern

Life Expectancy at Birth

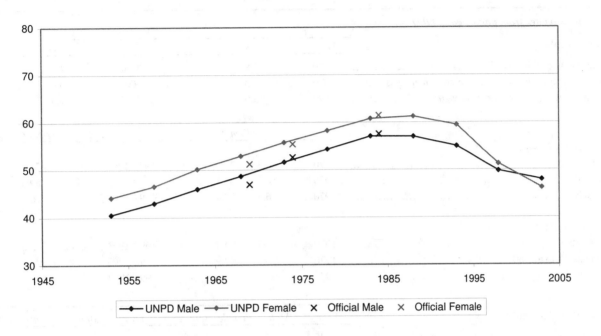

Infant Mortality Rate

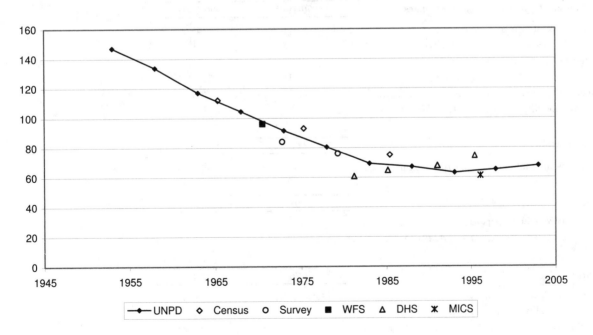

Kuwait

Indicator	Period				
	Earlier year			**Later year**	

I. Data and estimates from national and other sources

General mortality

	Year	Value		Year	Value
Annual number of deaths *(thousands)*	1970	3.8		2002	4.3
Annual number of deaths under age one *(thousands)*	1970	1.3		2002	0.4
Crude death rate *(per 1 000 person-years)*	1970	5.0		2002	1.9

	Year	Male	Female	Year	Male	Female
Life expectancy *(years)*						
at birth	1970	66.4	71.5	1992-1993	71.8	73.3
at age 15	1970	56.0	61.6	1992-1993	58.2	59.4
at age 60	1970	16.8	20.4	1992-1993	17.3	16.8
Survival probability						
from birth to age 15	1970	0.93	0.94	1992-1993	0.98	0.98
from age 15 to age 60	1970	0.80	0.89	1992-1993	0.86	0.91
from age 60 to age 80	1970	0.37	0.51	1992-1993	0.48	0.42

Infant and child mortality

	Year	Male	Female	Both sexes	Year	Male	Female	Both sexes
Infant mortality rate *(per 1 000 live births)*	1975	39	33	36	1992-1993	13	10	11
Mortality from age 1 to age 4 *(per 1 000 live births)*	1975	9	8	8	1992-1993	3	2	2
Under-five mortality rate *(per 1 000 live births)*	1975	47	41	44	1992-1993	15	12	14

II. Data and estimates from United Nations sources

United Nations Population Division estimates

	1990-1995	2000-2005
Annual number of deaths *(thousands)*	4	4
Crude death rate *(per 1 000 person-years)*	2	2
Life expectancy at birth *(years)*		
Male	73.5	75.1
Female	77.3	79.4
Under-five mortality rate *(per 1 000 live births)*	16	12

Maternal mortality

	2000
Maternal mortality ratio *(deaths per 100 000 births)*	5

HIV/AIDS

	2003	*[Low estimate - high estimate]*
Number of HIV-infected persons,	..	..
Adult HIV prevalence *(percentage of adults 15-49)*	..	..

Policy views

	1976	2003
Life expectancy	Acceptable	Acceptable
Under-five mortality		Acceptable
Maternal mortality		Acceptable
Level of concern about AIDS		Major concern

Life Expectancy at Birth

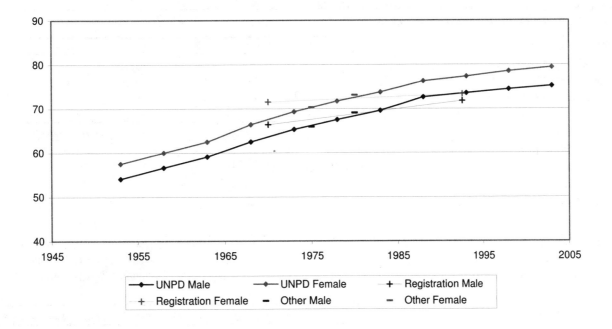

Legend:
- UNPD Male
- UNPD Female
- Registration Male
- Registration Female
- Other Male
- Other Female

Infant Mortality Rate

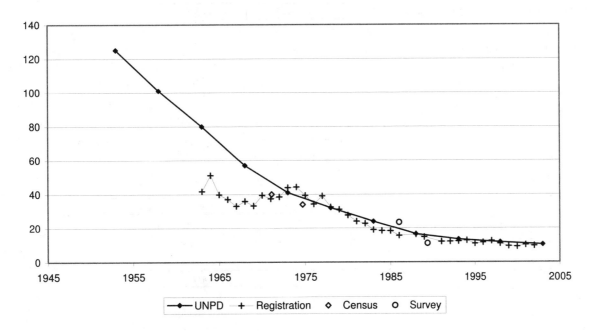

Legend:
- UNPD
- Registration
- Census
- Survey

Indicator	Period				
	Earlier year			Later year	

I. Data and estimates from national and other sources

General mortality

	Year	Value		Year	Value
Annual number of deaths *(thousands)*	..	..		2003	35.9
Annual number of deaths under age one *(thousands)*	..	..		2003	2.2
Crude death rate *(per 1 000 person-years)*	..	..		2003	7.1

	Year	Male	Female	Year	Male	Female
Life expectancy *(years)*						
at birth...	1970	63.6	71.8	2002	64.4	72.1
at age 15...	..	..	..	2002	51.8	59.1
at age 60...	..	..	..	2002	15.0	18.3
Survival probability						
from birth to age 15.................................	..	..	..	2002	0.96	0.97
from age 15 to age 60..............................	..	..	..	2002	0.71	0.86
from age 60 to age 80..............................	..	..	..	2002	0.31	0.46

Infant and child mortality

	Year	Male	Female	Both sexes	Year	Male	Female	Both sexes
Infant mortality rate *(per 1 000 live births)*	..	..	..	..	1987-1997	72	60	66
Mortality from age 1 to age 4 *(per 1 000 live births)*	..	..	..	..	1987-1997	10	11	10
Under-five mortality rate *(per 1 000 live births)*	..	..	..	..	1987-1997	81	70	76

II. Data and estimates from United Nations sources

United Nations Population Division estimates

	1990-1995	2000-2005
Annual number of deaths *(thousands)*	36	38
Crude death rate *(per 1 000 person-years)*	8	7
Life expectancy at birth *(years)*		
Male..	61.5	62.6
Female...	70.0	71.1
Under-five mortality rate *(per 1 000 live births)*	72	66

Maternal mortality

	2000
Maternal mortality ratio *(deaths per 100 000 births)*	110

HIV/AIDS

	2003	[Low estimate - high estimate]
Number of HIV-infected persons, ...	3 900	[1 500 - 8 000]
Adult HIV prevalence *(percentage of adults 15-49)*	0.1	[<0.2]

Policy views

	1976	2003
Life expectancy...	..	Unacceptable
Under-five mortality..		Unacceptable
Maternal mortality..		Unacceptable
Level of concern about AIDS...................................		Minor concern

Life Expectancy at Birth

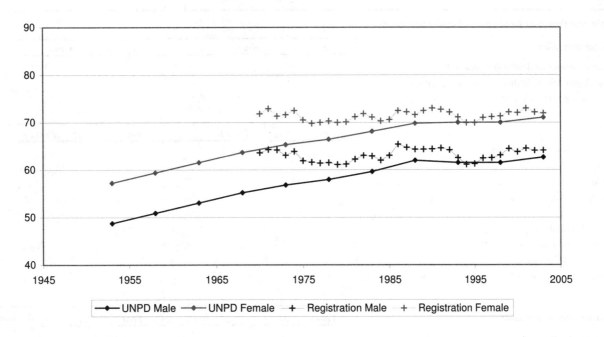

| | UNPD Male | UNPD Female | + Registration Male | + Registration Female |

Infant Mortality Rate

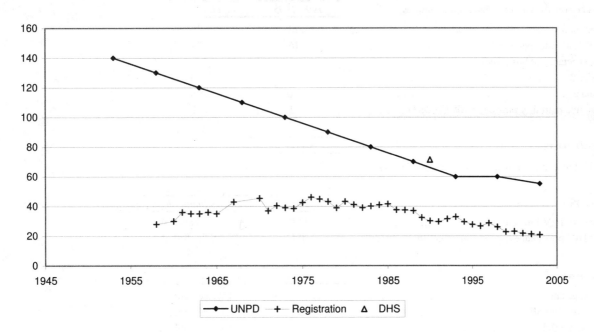

| | UNPD | + Registration | Δ DHS |

Indicator	Period						
	Earlier year				Later year		

I. Data and estimates from national and other sources

General mortality	Year	Value			Year	Value	
Annual number of deaths *(thousands)*	..	..			..	..	
Annual number of deaths under age one *(thousands)*	..	..			..	..	
Crude death rate *(per 1 000 person-years)*	..	..			..	..	

	Year	Male	Female		Year	Male	Female
Life expectancy *(years)*							
at birth	..	..	..		..	..	..
at age 15	..	..	..		..	..	..
at age 60	..	..	..		..	..	..
Survival probability							
from birth to age 15	..	..	..		..	..	..
from age 15 to age 60	..	..	..		..	..	..
from age 60 to age 80	..	..	..		..	..	..

Infant and child mortality	Year	Male	Female	Both sexes	Year	Male	Female	Both sexes
Infant mortality rate *(per 1 000 live births)*	..	..	..	..	1995-1999	..	..	82
Mortality from age 1 to age 4 *(per 1 000 live births)*	..	..	..	..	..	..	..	..
Under-five mortality rate *(per 1 000 live births)*	..	..	..	..	1995-1999	..	..	107

II. Data and estimates from United Nations sources

United Nations Population Division estimates	1990-1995	2000-2005
Annual number of deaths *(thousands)*	70	71
Crude death rate *(per 1 000 person-years)*	16	13
Life expectancy at birth *(years)*		
Male	49.5	53.3
Female	52.0	55.8
Under-five mortality rate *(per 1 000 live births)*	171	141

Maternal mortality	2000
Maternal mortality ratio *(deaths per 100 000 births)*	650

HIV/AIDS	2003	*[Low estimate - high estimate]*
Number of HIV-infected persons,	1 700	[600 - 3 600]
Adult HIV prevalence *(percentage of adults 15-49)*	0.1	[<0.2]

Policy views	1976	2003
Life expectancy	Unacceptable	Unacceptable
Under-five mortality		Unacceptable
Maternal mortality		Unacceptable
Level of concern about AIDS		Minor concern

Lao People's Democratic Republic

Life Expectancy at Birth

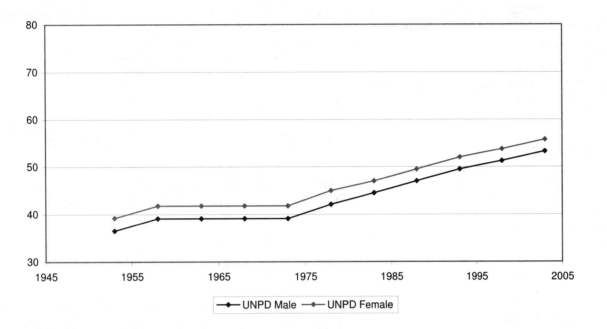

Infant Mortality Rate

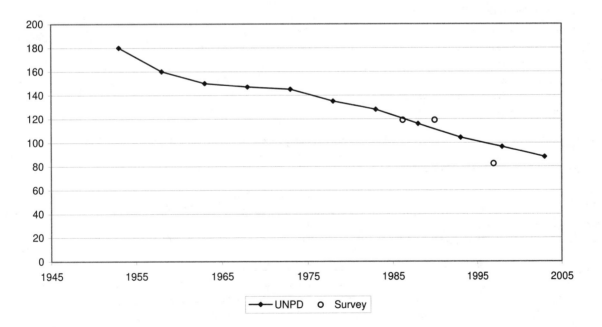

Indicator	Period					
	Earlier year				Later year	

I. Data and estimates from national and other sources

General mortality

	Year	Value			Year	Value	
Annual number of deaths *(thousands)*	1970	26.5			2004	32.0	
Annual number of deaths under age one *(thousands)*	1970	0.6			2004	0.2	
Crude death rate *(per 1 000 person-years)*	1970	11.3			2004	13.9	

	Year	Male	Female	Year	Male	Female
Life expectancy *(years)*						
at birth...	1970	65.7	74.2	2003	65.9	76.1
at age 15..	1970	52.9	60.8	2003	52.0	62.1
at age 60..	1970	15.9	19.7	2003	15.3	20.8
Survival probability						
from birth to age 15...	1970	0.97	0.98	2003	0.98	0.99
from age 15 to age 60...	1970	0.74	0.88	2003	0.70	0.88
from age 60 to age 80...	1970	0.33	0.50	2003	0.32	0.57

Infant and child mortality

	Year	Male	Female	Both sexes	Year	Male	Female	Both sexes
Infant mortality rate *(per 1 000 live births)*	1970	22	14	18	2003	11	8	10
Mortality from age 1 to age 4 *(per 1 000 live births)*	1970	6	4	5	2003	3	3	3
Under-five mortality rate *(per 1 000 live births)*	1970	27	18	23	2003	14	11	12

II. Data and estimates from United Nations sources

United Nations Population Division estimates

	1990-1995	2000-2005
Annual number of deaths *(thousands)*	38	31
Crude death rate *(per 1 000 person-years)*	14	13
Life expectancy at birth *(years)*		
Male...	61.8	65.6
Female...	73.8	76.9
Under-five mortality rate *(per 1 000 live births)*	27	14

Maternal mortality

	2000
Maternal mortality ratio *(deaths per 100 000 births)*	42

HIV/AIDS

	2003	[Low estimate - high estimate]
Number of HIV-infected persons, ...	7 600	[3 700 - 12 000]
Adult HIV prevalence *(percentage of adults 15-49)*	0.6	[0.3 - 1.0]

Policy views

	1976	2003
Life expectancy...	..	Unacceptable
Under-five mortality...		Unacceptable
Maternal mortality..		Unacceptable
Level of concern about AIDS......................................		Major concern

Life Expectancy at Birth

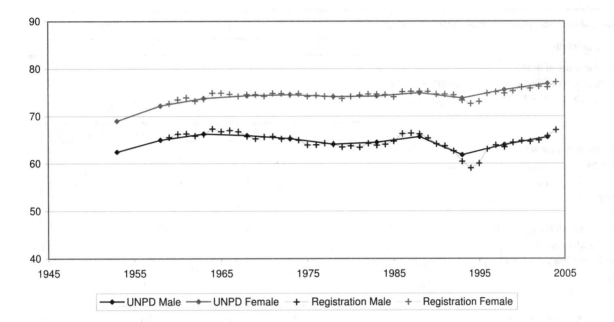

Legend: UNPD Male — UNPD Female — Registration Male + Registration Female +

Infant Mortality Rate

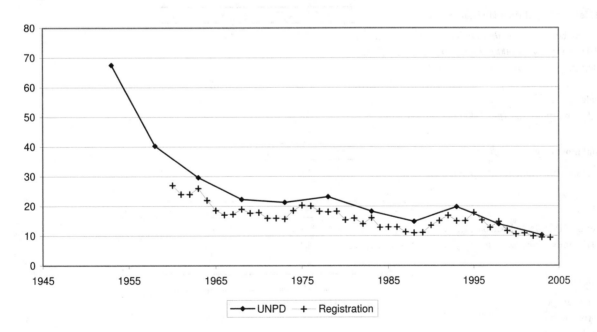

Legend: UNPD — Registration +

Indicator	Period							
	Earlier year				Later year			

I. Data and estimates from national and other sources

General mortality

	Year	Value			Year	Value		
Annual number of deaths *(thousands)*	..	..			..	..		
Annual number of deaths under age one *(thousands)*	..	..			..	..		
Crude death rate *(per 1 000 person-years)*	..	..			..	..		

	Year	Male	Female		Year	Male	Female	
Life expectancy *(years)*								
at birth	..	..	..		..	..	..	
at age 15	..	..	..		..	..	..	
at age 60	..	..	..		..	..	..	
Survival probability								
from birth to age 15	..	..	..		..	..	..	
from age 15 to age 60	..	..	..		..	..	..	
from age 60 to age 80	..	..	..		..	..	..	

Infant and child mortality

	Year	Male	Female	Both sexes	Year	Male	Female	Both sexes
Infant mortality rate *(per 1 000 live births)*	..	..	..	..	1991-1996	28	28	28
Mortality from age 1 to age 4 *(per 1 000 live births)*	..	..	..	..	..	..	..	..
Under-five mortality rate *(per 1 000 live births)*	..	..	..	..	1991-1996	..	..	32

II. Data and estimates from United Nations sources

United Nations Population Division estimates

	1990-1995	2000-2005
Annual number of deaths *(thousands)*	22	23
Crude death rate *(per 1 000 person-years)*	7	7
Life expectancy at birth *(years)*		
Male	67.2	69.7
Female	71.6	74.0
Under-five mortality rate *(per 1 000 live births)*	38	26

Maternal mortality

	2000
Maternal mortality ratio *(deaths per 100 000 births)*	150

HIV/AIDS

	2003	*[Low estimate - high estimate]*
Number of HIV-infected persons,	2 800	[700 - 4 100]
Adult HIV prevalence *(percentage of adults 15-49)*	0.1	[0.0 - 0.2]

Policy views

	1976	2003
Life expectancy	Unacceptable	Acceptable
Under-five mortality		Acceptable
Maternal mortality		Acceptable
Level of concern about AIDS		Minor concern

Life Expectancy at Birth

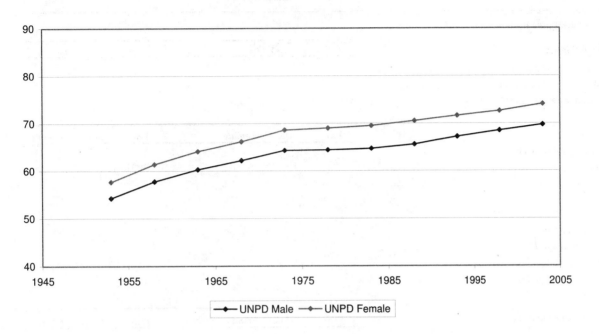

Infant Mortality Rate

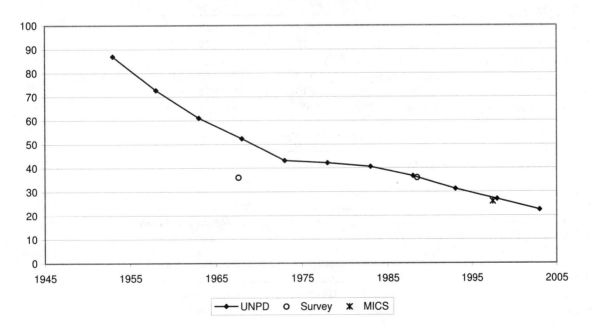

Indicator	Period							
	Earlier year				**Later year**			

I. Data and estimates from national and other sources

General mortality

	Year	Value			Year	Value		
Annual number of deaths *(thousands)*	..	..			..	..		
Annual number of deaths under age one *(thousands)*	..	..			..	..		
Crude death rate *(per 1 000 person-years)*	..	..			..	..		

	Year	Male	Female		Year	Male	Female	
Life expectancy *(years)*								
at birth................	..	..	..		2001	48.7	56.3	
at age 15................	..	..	..		..	..	..	
at age 60................	..	..	..		..	..	..	
Survival probability								
from birth to age 15................	..	..	..		..	..	..	
from age 15 to age 60................	..	..	..		..	..	..	
from age 60 to age 80................	..	..	..		..	..	..	

Infant and child mortality

	Year	Male	Female	Both sexes	Year	Male	Female	Both sexes
Infant mortality rate *(per 1 000 live births)*	1972	129	120	125	1998	..	..	76
Mortality from age 1 to age 4 *(per 1 000 live births)*	1972	75	59	67	..	..	..	..
Under-five mortality rate *(per 1 000 live births)*	1972	195	172	184	1998	..	..	106

II. Data and estimates from United Nations sources

United Nations Population Division estimates

	1990-1995	2000-2005
Annual number of deaths *(thousands)*	18	42
Crude death rate *(per 1 000 person-years)*	11	24
Life expectancy at birth *(years)*		
Male...	55.8	34.9
Female..	60.5	38.1
Under-five mortality rate *(per 1 000 live births)*	107	123

Maternal mortality

	2000
Maternal mortality ratio *(deaths per 100 000 births)*	550

HIV/AIDS

	2003	*[Low estimate - high estimate]*
Number of HIV-infected persons, ...	320 000	[290 000 - 360 000]
Adult HIV prevalence *(percentage of adults 15-49)*	28.9	[26.3 - 31.7]

Policy views

	1976	2003
Life expectancy...	Unacceptable	Unacceptable
Under-five mortality...		Unacceptable
Maternal mortality..		Unacceptable
Level of concern about AIDS..................................		Major concern

Life Expectancy at Birth

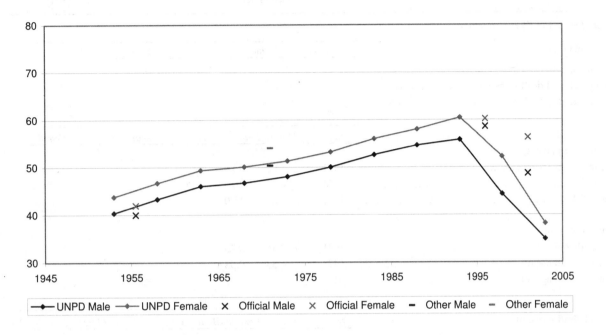

Infant Mortality Rate

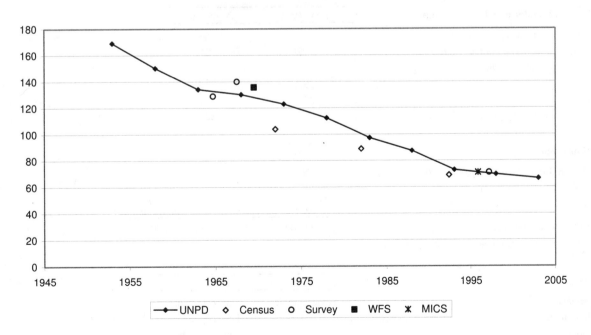

Indicator	Period				
	Earlier year			**Later year**	

I. Data and estimates from national and other sources

General mortality

	Year	Value		Year	Value
Annual number of deaths *(thousands)*	..	..		..	..
Annual number of deaths under age one *(thousands)*	..	..		..	..
Crude death rate *(per 1 000 person-years)*	..	..		..	..

	Year	Male	Female	Year	Male	Female
Life expectancy *(years)*						
at birth..	1971	45.8	44.0	..	..	..
at age 15...	1971	44.3	46.9	..	..	..
at age 60...	1971	14.9	15.0	..	..	..
Survival probability						
from birth to age 15...	1971	0.76	0.70	..	..	..
from age 15 to age 60...	1971	0.53	0.58	..	..	..
from age 60 to age 80...	..	..	..	..	..	..

Infant and child mortality

	Year	Male	Female	Both sexes	Year	Male	Female	Both sexes
Infant mortality rate *(per 1 000 live births)*	1970	187	168	178	..	..	..	..
Mortality from age 1 to age 4 *(per 1 000 live births)*	1970	109	105	107	..	..	..	..
Under-five mortality rate *(per 1 000 live births)*	1970	276	256	266	..	..	..	..

II. Data and estimates from United Nations sources

United Nations Population Division estimates	*1990-1995*	*2000-2005*
Annual number of deaths *(thousands)*	49	66
Crude death rate *(per 1 000 person-years)*	23	21
Life expectancy at birth *(years)*		
Male...	39.1	41.4
Female..	42.0	43.5
Under-five mortality rate *(per 1 000 live births)*	266	224

Maternal mortality	*2000*
Maternal mortality ratio *(deaths per 100 000 births)*	760

HIV/AIDS	*2003*	*[Low estimate - high estimate]*
Number of HIV-infected persons, ...	100 000	[47 000 - 220 000]
Adult HIV prevalence *(percentage of adults 15-49)*	5.9	[2.7 - 12.4]

Policy views	*1976*	*2003*
Life expectancy..	Unacceptable	Unacceptable
Under-five mortality..		Unacceptable
Maternal mortality..		Unacceptable
Level of concern about AIDS...................................		Minor concern

Life Expectancy at Birth

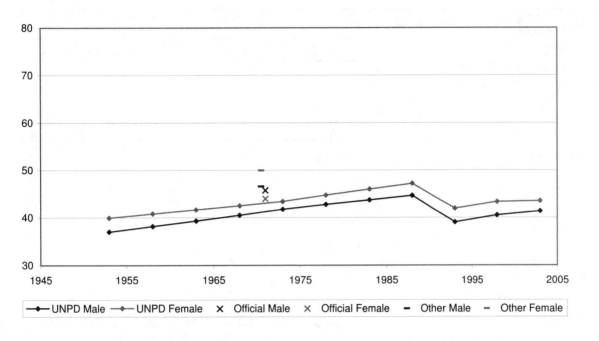

Infant Mortality Rate

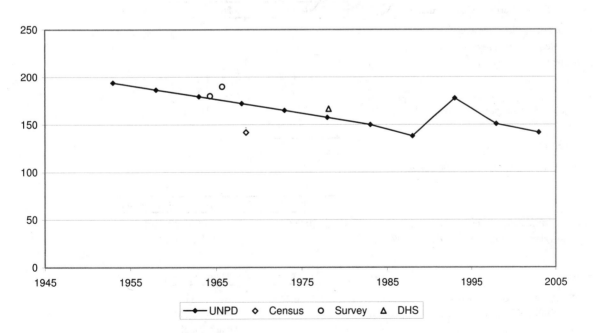

Libyan Arab Jamahiriya

Indicator	Period				
	Earlier year			Later year	

I. Data and estimates from national and other sources

General mortality

	Year	Value		Year	Value
Annual number of deaths *(thousands)*	..	..		..	..
Annual number of deaths under age one *(thousands)*	..	..		..	..
Crude death rate *(per 1 000 person-years)*	..	..		..	..

	Year	Male	Female	Year	Male	Female
Life expectancy *(years)*						
at birth..	..	..	..	..	..	..
at age 15..	..	..	..	..	..	..
at age 60..	..	..	..	..	..	..
Survival probability						
from birth to age 15..	..	..	..	..	..	..
from age 15 to age 60..	..	..	..	..	..	..
from age 60 to age 80..	..	..	..	..	..	..

Infant and child mortality

	Year	Male	Female	Both sexes	Year	Male	Female	Both sexes
Infant mortality rate *(per 1 000 live births)*	1975	101	99	100	..	..	..	..
Mortality from age 1 to age 4 *(per 1 000 live births)*	1975	50	53	51	..	..	..	..
Under-five mortality rate *(per 1 000 live births)*	1975	146	146	146	..	..	..	..

II. Data and estimates from United Nations sources

United Nations Population Division estimates

	1990-1995	2000-2005
Annual number of deaths *(thousands)*	21	22
Crude death rate *(per 1 000 person-years)*	5	4
Life expectancy at birth *(years)*		
Male..	67.4	71.4
Female...	71.9	76.1
Under-five mortality rate *(per 1 000 live births)*	34	21

Maternal mortality

	2000
Maternal mortality ratio *(deaths per 100 000 births)*	97

HIV/AIDS

	2003	[Low estimate - high estimate]
Number of HIV-infected persons, ...	10 000	[3 300 - 20 000]
Adult HIV prevalence *(percentage of adults 15-49)*	0.3	[0.1 - 0.6]

Policy views

	1976	2003
Life expectancy...	Unacceptable	Acceptable
Under-five mortality..		Unacceptable
Maternal mortality..		Unacceptable
Level of concern about AIDS....................................		Not a concern

Life Expectancy at Birth

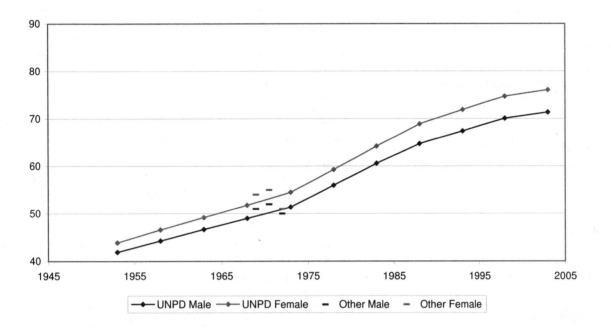

Infant Mortality Rate

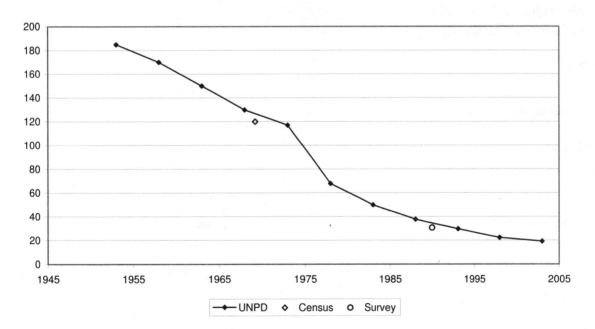

Indicator	Period						
	Earlier year				Later year		

I. Data and estimates from national and other sources

General mortality

	Year	Value			Year	Value	
Annual number of deaths *(thousands)*	1970	28.0			2004	41.3	
Annual number of deaths under age one *(thousands)*	1970	1.1			2004	0.2	
Crude death rate *(per 1 000 person-years)*	1970	9.0			2004	12.0	

	Year	Male	Female		Year	Male	Female
Life expectancy *(years)*							
at birth...	1970	66.8	75.0		2003	66.5	77.8
at age 15...	1970	53.9	61.9		2003	52.3	63.5
at age 60...	1970	17.0	20.5		2003	16.2	22.1
Survival probability							
from birth to age 15..............................	1970	0.97	0.98		2003	0.99	0.99
from age 15 to age 60............................	1970	0.75	0.89		2003	0.70	0.89
from age 60 to age 80............................	1970	0.38	0.53		2003	0.35	0.62

Infant and child mortality

	Year	Male	Female	Both sexes	Year	Male	Female	Both sexes
Infant mortality rate *(per 1 000 live births)*	1970	22	17	20	2003	8	6	7
Mortality from age 1 to age 4 *(per 1 000 live births)*	1970	4	4	4	2003	2	2	2
Under-five mortality rate *(per 1 000 live births)*	1970	26	21	24	2003	10	7	9

II. Data and estimates from United Nations sources

United Nations Population Division estimates

	1990-1995	2000-2005
Annual number of deaths *(thousands)*	43	41
Crude death rate *(per 1 000 person-years)*	12	12
Life expectancy at birth *(years)*		
Male..	64.1	66.5
Female...	75.4	77.8
Under-five mortality rate *(per 1 000 live births)*	22	12

Maternal mortality

	2000
Maternal mortality ratio *(deaths per 100 000 births)*	13

HIV/AIDS

	2003	[Low estimate - high estimate]
Number of HIV-infected persons, ...	1 300	[400 - 2 600]
Adult HIV prevalence *(percentage of adults 15-49)*	0.1	[<0.2]

Policy views

	1976	2003
Life expectancy..	..	Acceptable
Under-five mortality..		Acceptable
Maternal mortality..		Acceptable
Level of concern about AIDS....................................		Major concern

Life Expectancy at Birth

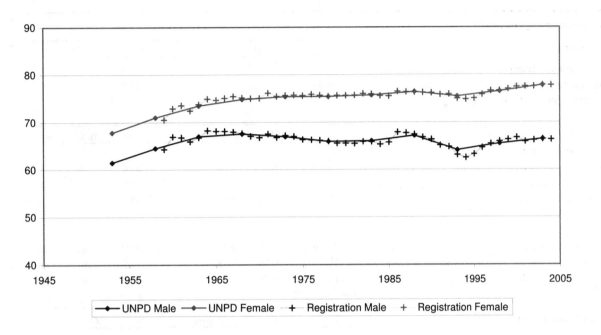

Infant Mortality Rate

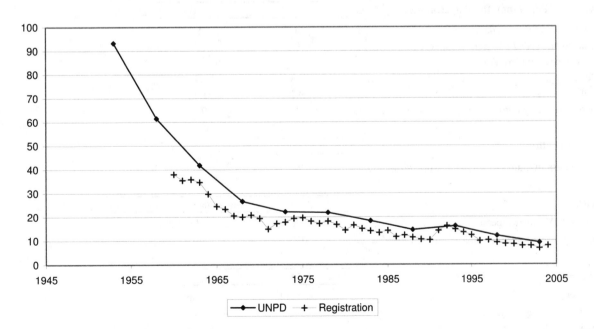

Indicator	Period					
	Earlier year				Later year	

I. Data and estimates from national and other sources

General mortality

	Year	Value			Year	Value	
Annual number of deaths *(thousands)*	1970	4.2			2004	3.4	
Annual number of deaths under age one *(thousands)*	1970	0.1			2004	0.0	
Crude death rate *(per 1 000 person-years)*	1970	12.3			2004	7.6	

	Year	Male	Female	Year	Male	Female
Life expectancy *(years)*						
at birth	1971-1973	67.0	73.9	2002	74.9	81.5
at age 15	..	..	..	2002	60.7	67.1
at age 60	1971-1973	14.7	19.0	2002	19.6	24.2
Survival probability						
from birth to age 15	1971-1973	0.97	0.98	2002	0.99	0.99
from age 15 to age 60	1971-1973	0.78	0.88	2002	0.88	0.94
from age 60 to age 80	1971-1973	0.28	0.48	2002	0.51	0.69

Infant and child mortality

	Year	Male	Female	Both sexes	Year	Male	Female	Both sexes
Infant mortality rate *(per 1 000 live births)*	1971-1973	20	14	17	2002	5	5	5
Mortality from age 1 to age 4 *(per 1 000 live births)*	1971-1973	4	4	4	2002	2	1	2
Under-five mortality rate *(per 1 000 live births)*	1971-1973	24	17	21	2002	7	6	7

II. Data and estimates from United Nations sources

United Nations Population Division estimates

	1990-1995	2000-2005
Annual number of deaths *(thousands)*	4	4
Crude death rate *(per 1 000 person-years)*	9	8
Life expectancy at birth *(years)*		
Male	72.4	75.1
Female	79.2	81.4
Under-five mortality rate *(per 1 000 live births)*	11	7

Maternal mortality

	2000
Maternal mortality ratio *(deaths per 100 000 births)*	28

HIV/AIDS

	2003	*[Low estimate - high estimate]*
Number of HIV-infected persons,	<500	[<1 000]
Adult HIV prevalence *(percentage of adults 15-49)*	0.2	[0.1 - 0.4]

Policy views

	1976	2003
Life expectancy	Acceptable	Acceptable
Under-five mortality		Acceptable
Maternal mortality		Acceptable
Level of concern about AIDS		Minor concern

Life Expectancy at Birth

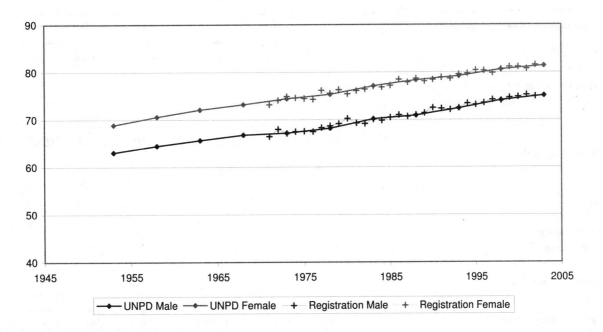

Infant Mortality Rate

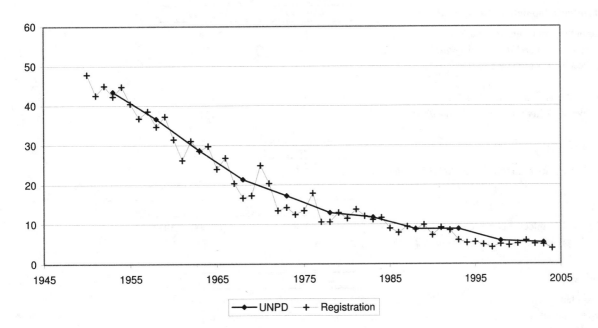

Madagascar

Indicator	Period							
	Earlier year				*Later year*			

I. Data and estimates from national and other sources

General mortality	Year	Value			Year	Value		
Annual number of deaths *(thousands)*	..	..			..	..		
Annual number of deaths under age one *(thousands)*	..	..			..	..		
Crude death rate *(per 1 000 person-years)*	..	..			..	..		

	Year	Male	Female		Year	Male	Female	
Life expectancy *(years)*								
at birth..	1966	37.5	38.3		..	..	..	
at age 15...	..	..	..		..	..	..	
at age 60...	..	..	..		..	..	..	
Survival probability								
from birth to age 15...	1972	0.74	0.77		..	..	..	
from age 15 to age 60...	1972	0.63	0.69		..	..	..	
from age 60 to age 80...	1972	0.22	0.25		..	..	..	

Infant and child mortality	Year	Male	Female	Both sexes	Year	Male	Female	Both sexes
Infant mortality rate *(per 1 000 live births)*	1987	100	100	100	1993-2003	75	64	70
Mortality from age 1 to age 4 *(per 1 000 live births)*	1987	73	69	71	1993-2003	45	45	45
Under-five mortality rate *(per 1 000 live births)*	1987	166	162	164	1993-2003	117	106	111

II. Data and estimates from United Nations sources

United Nations Population Division estimates	1990-1995	2000-2005
Annual number of deaths *(thousands)*	187	209
Crude death rate *(per 1 000 person-years)*	14	12
Life expectancy at birth *(years)*		
Male...	50.8	54.0
Female..	53.4	56.7
Under-five mortality rate *(per 1 000 live births)*	165	131

Maternal mortality	2000
Maternal mortality ratio *(deaths per 100 000 births)*	550

HIV/AIDS	2003	*[Low estimate - high estimate]*
Number of HIV-infected persons, ...	140 000	[68 000 - 250 000]
Adult HIV prevalence *(percentage of adults 15-49)*	1.7	[0.8 - 2.7]

Policy views	1976	2003
Life expectancy...	Unacceptable	Unacceptable
Under-five mortality..		Unacceptable
Maternal mortality..		Unacceptable
Level of concern about AIDS....................................		Major concern

Life Expectancy at Birth

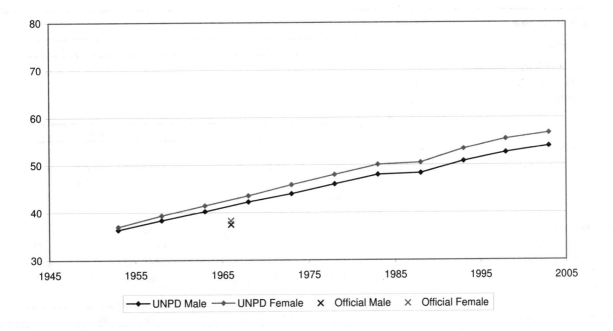

Infant Mortality Rate

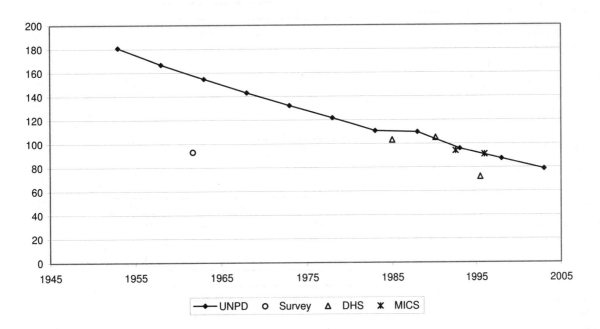

Indicator	Period						
	Earlier year				Later year		

I. Data and estimates from national and other sources

General mortality

	Year	Value			Year	Value	
Annual number of deaths *(thousands)*	..	..			..	..	
Annual number of deaths under age one *(thousands)*	..	..			..	..	
Crude death rate *(per 1 000 person-years)*	..	..			..	..	

	Year	Male	Female		Year	Male	Female
Life expectancy *(years)*							
at birth..	1977	38.1	41.2		1992-1997	43.5	46.8
at age 15..	1977	43.8	46.3		1992-1997	45.7	48.2
at age 60..	1977	13.4	14.4		1992-1997	14.1	15.1
Survival probability							
from birth to age 15....................................	1977	0.63	0.66		1992-1997	0.70	0.73
from age 15 to age 60.................................	1977	0.55	0.61		1992-1997	0.59	0.65
from age 60 to age 80.................................	1977	0.22	0.27		1992-1997	0.25	0.30

Infant and child mortality

	Year	Male	Female	Both sexes	Year	Male	Female	Both sexes
Infant mortality rate *(per 1 000 live births)*	..	..	..	..	1990-2000	117	108	113
Mortality from age 1 to age 4 *(per 1 000 live births)*	..	..	..	..	1990-2000	101	102	102
Under-five mortality rate *(per 1 000 live births)*	1975	317	309	313	1990-2000	207	199	203

II. Data and estimates from United Nations sources

United Nations Population Division estimates

	1990-1995	2000-2005
Annual number of deaths *(thousands)*	192	266
Crude death rate *(per 1 000 person-years)*	20	22
Life expectancy at birth *(years)*		
Male..	43.5	39.7
Female...	47.1	39.6
Under-five mortality rate *(per 1 000 live births)*	227	184

Maternal mortality

	2000
Maternal mortality ratio *(deaths per 100 000 births)*	1 800

HIV/AIDS

	2003	[Low estimate - high estimate]
Number of HIV-infected persons, ...	900 000	[700 000 - 1 100 000]
Adult HIV prevalence *(percentage of adults 15-49)*	14.2	[11.3 - 17.7]

Policy views

	1976	2003
Life expectancy..	Unacceptable	Unacceptable
Under-five mortality..		Unacceptable
Maternal mortality..		Unacceptable
Level of concern about AIDS.....................................		Major concern

Life Expectancy at Birth

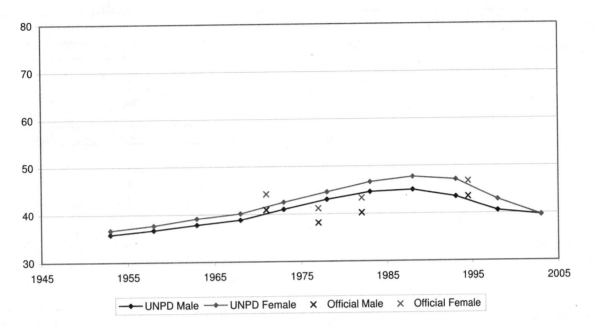

Infant Mortality Rate

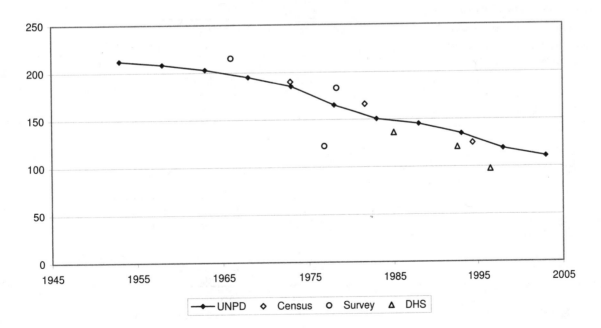

Malaysia

World Mortality Report 2005

Indicator	Period			
	Earlier year		Later year	

I. Data and estimates from national and other sources

General mortality

	Year	Value	Year	Value
Annual number of deaths *(thousands)*	1970	72.6	2003	117.9
Annual number of deaths under age one *(thousands)*	1970	13.8	2000	3.6
Crude death rate *(per 1 000 person-years)*	1970	6.7	2003	4.7

	Year	Male	Female	Year	Male	Female
Life expectancy *(years)*						
at birth	1970	58.6	62.1	2002	70.7	75.3
at age 15	1970	50.4	53.4	2002	56.8	61.2
at age 60	1970	13.7	16.0	2002	17.1	19.1
Survival probability						
from birth to age 15	1970	0.89	0.90	2002	0.98	0.99
from age 15 to age 60	1970	0.69	0.75	2002	0.83	0.91
from age 60 to age 80	1970	0.24	0.36	2002	0.40	0.49

Infant and child mortality

	Year	Male	Female	Both sexes	Year	Male	Female	Both sexes
Infant mortality rate *(per 1 000 live births)*	1975	36	28	32	2002	9	7	8
Mortality from age 1 to age 4 *(per 1 000 live births)*	1975	13	12	12	2002	3	3	3
Under-five mortality rate *(per 1 000 live births)*	1975	48	40	44	2002	12	10	11

II. Data and estimates from United Nations sources

United Nations Population Division estimates

	1990-1995	2000-2005
Annual number of deaths *(thousands)*	98	112
Crude death rate *(per 1 000 person-years)*	5	5
Life expectancy at birth *(years)*		
Male	68.7	70.8
Female	73.1	75.5
Under-five mortality rate *(per 1 000 live births)*	20	13

Maternal mortality

	2000
Maternal mortality ratio *(deaths per 100 000 births)*	41

HIV/AIDS

	2003	[Low estimate - high estimate]
Number of HIV-infected persons,	52 000	[25 000 - 86 000]
Adult HIV prevalence *(percentage of adults 15-49)*	0.4	[0.2 - 0.7]

Policy views

	1976	2003
Life expectancy	Acceptable	Acceptable
Under-five mortality		Acceptable
Maternal mortality		Unacceptable
Level of concern about AIDS		Major concern

Life Expectancy at Birth

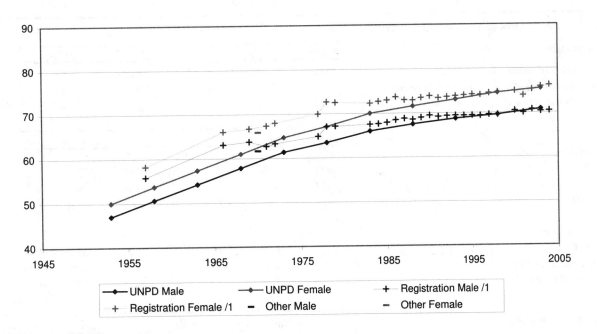

¹ Data until 1990 refer to Peninsular Malaysia only

Infant Mortality Rate

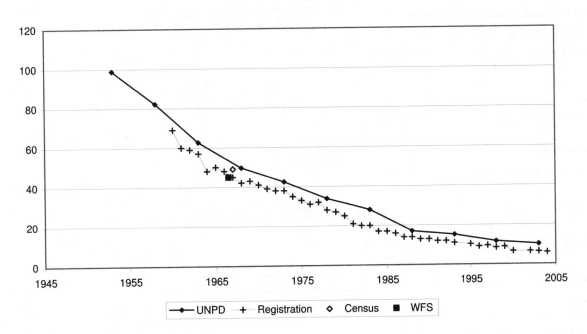

Maldives

Indicator	Period				
	Earlier year			Later year	

I. Data and estimates from national and other sources

General mortality

	Year	Value		Year	Value	
Annual number of deaths *(thousands)*	1974	2.2		2003	1.0	
Annual number of deaths under age one *(thousands)*	1974	0.7		2003	0.1	
Crude death rate *(per 1 000 person-years)*	1974	17.3		2003	3.6	

	Year	Male	Female	Year	Male	Female
Life expectancy *(years)*						
at birth	1982	53.4	49.5	1999	72.1	73.2
at age 15	1982	48.0	43.4	1999	59.2	60.2
at age 60	1982	9.2	8.2	1999	18.8	19.3
Survival probability						
from birth to age 15	1982	0.88	0.84	1992	0.94	0.96
from age 15 to age 60	1982	0.71	0.60	1992	0.81	0.78
from age 60 to age 80	..	..	..	1992	0.39	0.31

Infant and child mortality

	Year	Male	Female	Both sexes	Year	Male	Female	Both sexes
Infant mortality rate *(per 1 000 live births)*	..	..	..	..	1992	32	25	28
Mortality from age 1 to age 4 *(per 1 000 live births)*	..	..	..	..	1992	19	10	15
Under-five mortality rate *(per 1 000 live births)*	1982	128	132	130	1992	51	34	43

II. Data and estimates from United Nations sources

United Nations Population Division estimates

	1990-1995	2000-2005
Annual number of deaths *(thousands)*	2	2
Crude death rate *(per 1 000 person-years)*	9	6
Life expectancy at birth *(years)*		
Male	62.3	66.9
Female	59.8	65.8
Under-five mortality rate *(per 1 000 live births)*	90	55

Maternal mortality

	2000
Maternal mortality ratio *(deaths per 100 000 births)*	110

HIV/AIDS

	2003	[Low estimate - high estimate]
Number of HIV-infected persons,	..	..
Adult HIV prevalence *(percentage of adults 15-49)*	..	..

Policy views

	1976	2003
Life expectancy	Unacceptable	Unacceptable
Under-five mortality		Unacceptable
Maternal mortality		Unacceptable
Level of concern about AIDS		Minor concern

Life Expectancy at Birth

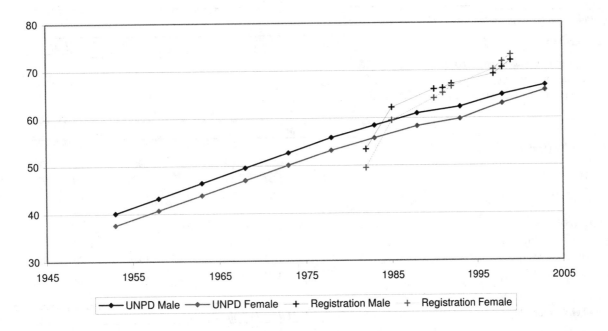

Infant Mortality Rate

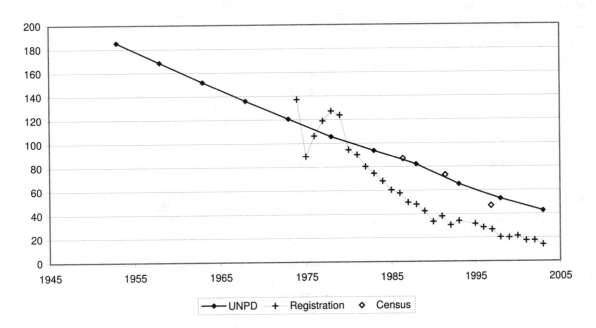

Mali

Indicator	Period					
	Earlier year			*Later year*		

I. Data and estimates from national and other sources

General mortality

	Year	Value		Year	Value	
Annual number of deaths *(thousands)*	..	..		..	..	
Annual number of deaths under age one *(thousands)*	..	..		..	..	
Crude death rate *(per 1 000 person-years)*	..	..		..	..	

	Year	Male	Female	Year	Male	Female
Life expectancy *(years)*						
at birth	1976	46.9	49.7	1987	55.2	58.7
at age 15	1976	52.7	53.6	1987	55.9	57.5
at age 60	1976	17.7	19.4	1987	20.7	22.1
Survival probability						
from birth to age 15	1976	0.68	0.71	1987	0.77	0.80
from age 15 to age 60	1976	0.72	0.72	1987	0.75	0.77
from age 60 to age 80	1976	0.49	0.58	1987	0.53	0.61

Infant and child mortality

	Year	Male	Female	Both sexes	Year	Male	Female	Both sexes
Infant mortality rate *(per 1 000 live births)*	1982	167	148	158	1991-2001	136	116	126
Mortality from age 1 to age 4 *(per 1 000 live births)*	1982	127	130	128	1991-2001	132	125	128
Under-five mortality rate *(per 1 000 live births)*	1982	273	259	266	1991-2001	250	226	238

II. Data and estimates from United Nations sources

United Nations Population Division estimates

	1990-1995	2000-2005
Annual number of deaths *(thousands)*	181	224
Crude death rate *(per 1 000 person-years)*	19	18
Life expectancy at birth *(years)*		
Male	45.8	47.1
Female	47.6	48.4
Under-five mortality rate *(per 1 000 live births)*	241	220

Maternal mortality

	2000
Maternal mortality ratio *(deaths per 100 000 births)*	1 200

HIV/AIDS

	2003	[Low estimate - high estimate]
Number of HIV-infected persons,	140 000	[44 000 - 420 000]
Adult HIV prevalence *(percentage of adults 15-49)*	1.9	[0.6 - 5.9]

Policy views

	1976	2003
Life expectancy	Unacceptable	Unacceptable
Under-five mortality		Unacceptable
Maternal mortality		Unacceptable
Level of concern about AIDS		Major concern

Life Expectancy at Birth

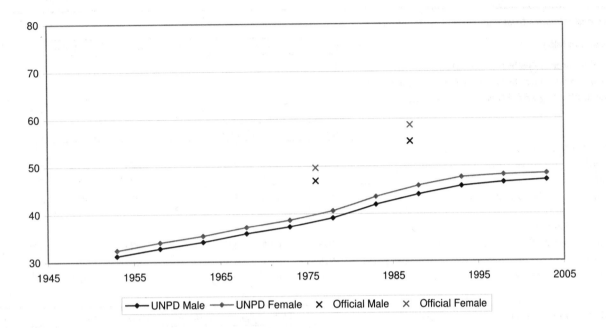

Infant Mortality Rate

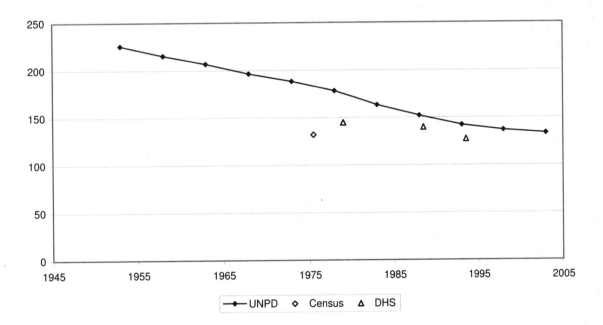

Malta

Indicator	Period					
	Earlier year			*Later year*		

I. Data and estimates from national and other sources

General mortality

	Year	Value		Year	Value	
Annual number of deaths *(thousands)*	1970	3.1		2003	3.1	
Annual number of deaths under age one *(thousands)*	1970	0.1		2003	0.0	
Crude death rate *(per 1 000 person-years)*	1970	10.1		2003	7.7	

	Year	Male	Female	Year	Male	Female
Life expectancy *(years)*						
at birth..	1973	68.1	72.0	2003	76.4	80.4
at age 15..	1973	55.3	58.9	2003	62.1	66.1
at age 60..	1973	14.4	16.5	2003	19.7	22.9
Survival probability						
from birth to age 15..	1973	0.97	0.97	2003	0.99	0.99
from age 15 to age 60..	1973	0.84	0.90	2003	0.92	0.95
from age 60 to age 80..	1973	0.27	0.38	2003	0.51	0.67

Infant and child mortality

	Year	Male	Female	Both sexes	Year	Male	Female	Both sexes
Infant mortality rate *(per 1 000 live births)*	1973	28	19	24	2002	5	3	4
Mortality from age 1 to age 4 *(per 1 000 live births)*	1973	2	4	3	2002	2	3	2
Under-five mortality rate *(per 1 000 live births)*	1973	30	23	26	2002	7	6	6

II. Data and estimates from United Nations sources

United Nations Population Division estimates

	1990-1995	*2000-2005*
Annual number of deaths *(thousands)*	3	3
Crude death rate *(per 1 000 person-years)*	8	8
Life expectancy at birth *(years)*		
Male...	74.0	75.8
Female..	78.4	80.7
Under-five mortality rate *(per 1 000 live births)*	11	8

Maternal mortality

	2000
Maternal mortality ratio *(deaths per 100 000 births)*	0

HIV/AIDS

	2003	*[Low estimate - high estimate]*
Number of HIV-infected persons, ...	<500	[<1 000]
Adult HIV prevalence *(percentage of adults 15-49)*	0.2	[0.1 - 0.3]

Policy views

	1976	*2003*
Life expectancy...	Acceptable	Acceptable
Under-five mortality..		Acceptable
Maternal mortality..		Acceptable
Level of concern about AIDS..................................		Minor concern

Life Expectancy at Birth

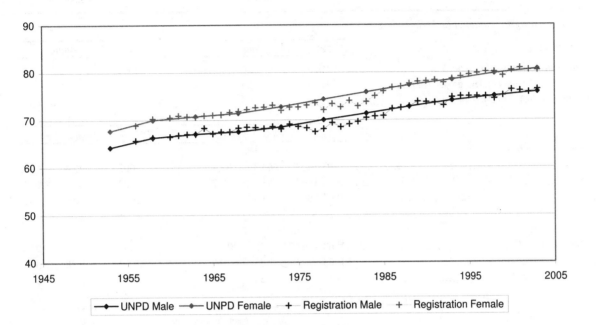

Infant Mortality Rate

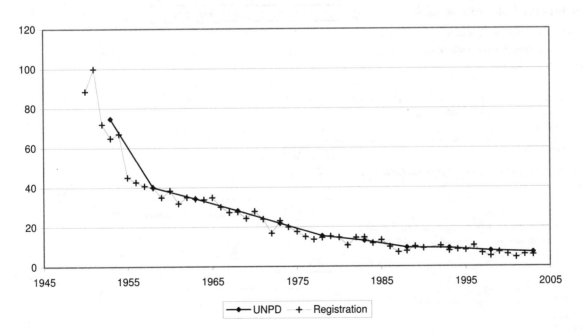

I. Data and estimates from national and other sources

Indicator	Period					
	Earlier year			**Later year**		

General mortality

	Year	Value		Year	Value	
Annual number of deaths *(thousands)*	1970	2.6		2003	2.7	
Annual number of deaths under age one *(thousands)*	1970	0.3		2003	0.0	
Crude death rate *(per 1 000 person-years)*	1970	7.9		2003	7.0	

	Year	Male	Female	Year	Male	Female
Life expectancy *(years)*						
at birth	1963-1967	63.3	67.4	2002	75.4	82.2
at age 15	1963-1967	53.0	56.7	2002	61.1	67.9
at age 60	1963-1967	15.8	18.7	2002	20.4	24.8
Survival probability						
from birth to age 15	1963-1967	0.93	0.93	2002	0.99	0.99
from age 15 to age 60	1963-1967	0.73	0.76	2002	0.88	0.95
from age 60 to age 80	1963-1967	0.34	0.42	2002	0.53	0.74

Infant and child mortality

	Year	Male	Female	Both sexes	Year	Male	Female	Both sexes
Infant mortality rate *(per 1 000 live births)*	1963-1967	48	43	46	2002	7	5	6
Mortality from age 1 to age 4 *(per 1 000 live births)*	1963-1967	18	18	18	2002	1	1	1
Under-five mortality rate *(per 1 000 live births)*	1963-1967	65	61	63	2002	8	6	7

II. Data and estimates from United Nations sources

United Nations Population Division estimates

	1990-1995	*2000-2005*
Annual number of deaths *(thousands)*	3	3
Crude death rate *(per 1 000 person-years)*	7	7
Life expectancy at birth *(years)*		
Male	73.5	75.5
Female	80.0	81.6
Under-five mortality rate *(per 1 000 live births)*	12	9

Maternal mortality

	2000
Maternal mortality ratio *(deaths per 100 000 births)*	..

HIV/AIDS

	2003	*[Low estimate - high estimate]*
Number of HIV-infected persons,	..	..
Adult HIV prevalence *(percentage of adults 15-49)*	..	..

Policy views

	1976	*2003*
Life expectancy	..	..
Under-five mortality		..
Maternal mortality		..
Level of concern about AIDS		..

Life Expectancy at Birth

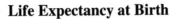

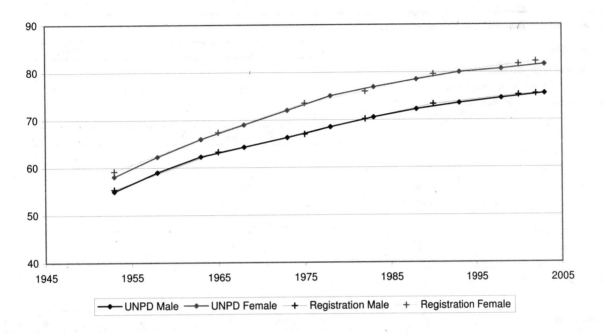

Infant Mortality Rate

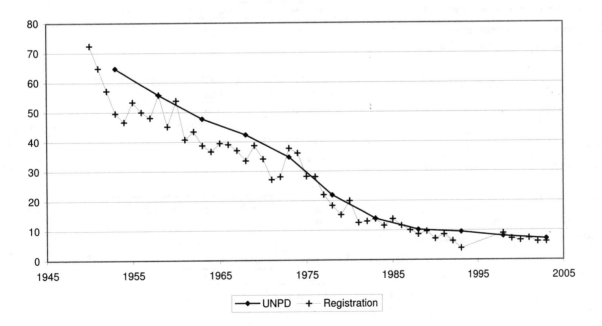

Indicator	Period							
	Earlier year				Later year			

I. Data and estimates from national and other sources

General mortality

	Year	Value			Year	Value		
Annual number of deaths *(thousands)*	..	..			..	..		
Annual number of deaths under age one *(thousands)*	..	..			..	..		
Crude death rate *(per 1 000 person-years)*	..	..			..	..		

	Year	Male	Female		Year	Male	Female	
Life expectancy *(years)*								
at birth...	..	..	..		..	..	..	
at age 15..	..	..	..		..	..	..	
at age 60..	..	..	..		..	..	..	
Survival probability								
from birth to age 15...	..	..	..		..	..	..	
from age 15 to age 60..	..	..	..		..	..	..	
from age 60 to age 80..	..	..	..		..	..	..	

Infant and child mortality

	Year	Male	Female	Both sexes	Year	Male	Female	Both sexes
Infant mortality rate *(per 1 000 live births)*	1975	114	104	109	1990-2000	75	59	67
Mortality from age 1 to age 4 *(per 1 000 live births)*	1975	64	66	65	1990-2000	38	38	38
Under-five mortality rate *(per 1 000 live births)*	1975	170	164	167	1990-2000	110	94	102

II. Data and estimates from United Nations sources

United Nations Population Division estimates

	1990-1995	2000-2005
Annual number of deaths *(thousands)*	35	41
Crude death rate *(per 1 000 person-years)*	16	14
Life expectancy at birth *(years)*		
Male...	47.9	50.9
Female...	51.1	54.1
Under-five mortality rate *(per 1 000 live births)*	181	156

Maternal mortality

	2000
Maternal mortality ratio *(deaths per 100 000 births)*	1 000

HIV/AIDS

	2003	[Low estimate - high estimate]
Number of HIV-infected persons, ...	9 500	[4 500 - 17 000]
Adult HIV prevalence *(percentage of adults 15-49)*	0.6	[0.3 - 1.1]

Policy views

	1976	2003
Life expectancy...	Unacceptable	Unacceptable
Under-five mortality..		Unacceptable
Maternal mortality..		Unacceptable
Level of concern about AIDS.....................................		Major concern

Life Expectancy at Birth

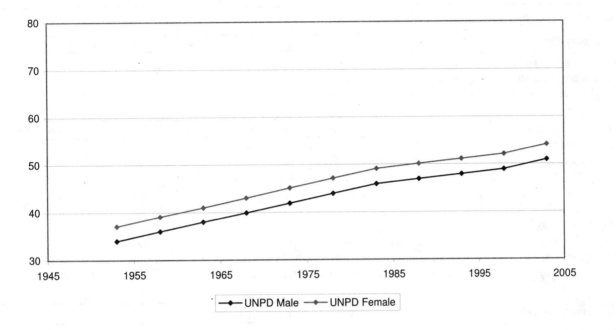

Infant Mortality Rate

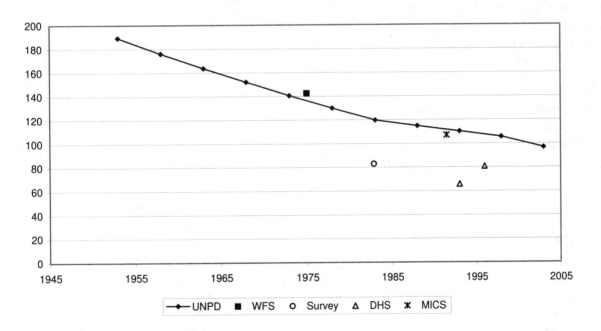

Indicator	Period				
	Earlier year			Later year	

I. Data and estimates from national and other sources

General mortality

	Year	Value		Year	Value
Annual number of deaths (thousands)......................	1970	6.5		2003	8.5
Annual number of deaths under age one (thousands)......	1970	1.2		2003	0.3
Crude death rate (per 1 000 person-years).................	1970	7.8		2003	7.0

	Year	Male	Female	Year	Male	Female
Life expectancy (years)						
at birth..	1971-1973	60.7	65.3	2002-2004	68.4	75.3
at age 15..	1971-1973	51.7	56.3	2002-2004	54.9	61.5
at age 60..	1971-1973	13.3	17.0	2002-2004	16.2	20.1
Survival probability						
from birth to age 15..	1971-1973	0.91	0.91	2002-2004	0.98	0.98
from age 15 to age 60......................................	1971-1973	0.74	0.82	2002-2004	0.77	0.88
from age 60 to age 80......................................	1971-1973	0.21	0.38	2002-2004	0.35	0.52

Infant and child mortality

	Year	Male	Female	Both sexes	Year	Male	Female	Both sexes
Infant mortality rate (per 1 000 live births).................	1975	57	45	51	2002-2004	17	12	15
Mortality from age 1 to age 4 (per 1 000 live births)......	1975	16	17	17	2002-2004	2	3	3
Under-five mortality rate (per 1 000 live births)...........	1975	72	62	67	2002-2004	19	15	17

II. Data and estimates from United Nations sources

United Nations Population Division estimates

	1990-1995	2000-2005
Annual number of deaths (thousands)......................	7	8
Crude death rate (per 1 000 person-years).................	7	7
Life expectancy at birth (years)		
Male..	66.3	68.7
Female..	73.9	75.6
Under-five mortality rate (per 1 000 live births)...........	24	18

Maternal mortality

	2000
Maternal mortality ratio (deaths per 100 000 births)......	24

HIV/AIDS

	2003	[Low estimate - high estimate]
Number of HIV-infected persons...........................	..	..
Adult HIV prevalence (percentage of adults 15-49).......	..	..

Policy views

	1976	2003
Life expectancy..	Acceptable	Acceptable
Under-five mortality..		Unacceptable
Maternal mortality..		Unacceptable
Level of concern about AIDS................................		Major concern

[1] Refers to the Island of Mauritius only

Life Expectancy at Birth

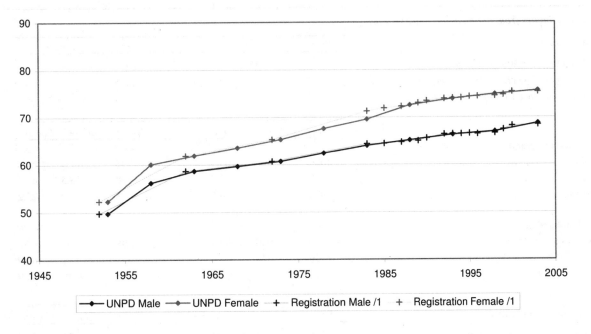

¹ Data until 1989 refer to the Island of Mauritius only

Infant Mortality Rate

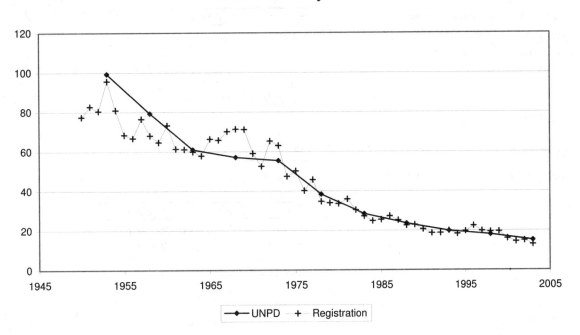

Mexico

Indicator	Period					
	Earlier year				Later year	

I. Data and estimates from national and other sources

General mortality

	Year	Value			Year	Value	
Annual number of deaths *(thousands)*	1970	485.7			2003	472.1	
Annual number of deaths under age one *(thousands)*	..	..			..	..	
Crude death rate *(per 1 000 person-years)*	1970	9.6			2003	4.5	

	Year	Male	Female		Year	Male	Female
Life expectancy *(years)*							
at birth	1970	59.4	63.4		1998	71.4	76.8
at age 15	1970	52.4	56.1		1998	58.5	63.6
at age 60	1970	17.1	18.5		1998	20.0	22.2
Survival probability							
from birth to age 15	1970	0.88	0.89		1998	0.97	0.98
from age 15 to age 60	1970	0.70	0.78		1998	0.81	0.89
from age 60 to age 80	1970	0.39	0.44		1998	0.49	0.59

Infant and child mortality

	Year	Male	Female	Both sexes	Year	Male	Female	Both sexes
Infant mortality rate *(per 1 000 live births)*	1975	76	62	69	1998	21	17	19
Mortality from age 1 to age 4 *(per 1 000 live births)*	1975	27	29	28	1998	4	4	4
Under-five mortality rate *(per 1 000 live births)*	1975	101	89	95	1998	25	21	23

II. Data and estimates from United Nations sources

United Nations Population Division estimates

	1990-1995	2000-2005
Annual number of deaths *(thousands)*	449	462
Crude death rate *(per 1 000 person-years)*	5	4
Life expectancy at birth *(years)*		
Male	69.0	72.4
Female	74.6	77.4
Under-five mortality rate *(per 1 000 live births)*	40	25

Maternal mortality

	2000
Maternal mortality ratio *(deaths per 100 000 births)*	83

HIV/AIDS

	2003	[Low estimate - high estimate]
Number of HIV-infected persons,	160 000	[78 000 - 260 000]
Adult HIV prevalence *(percentage of adults 15-49)*	0.3	[0.1 - 0.4]

Policy views

	1976	2003
Life expectancy	Acceptable	Acceptable
Under-five mortality		Unacceptable
Maternal mortality		Unacceptable
Level of concern about AIDS		Major concern

Life Expectancy at Birth

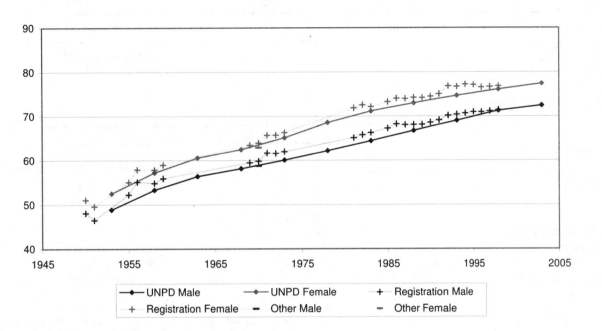

Infant Mortality Rate

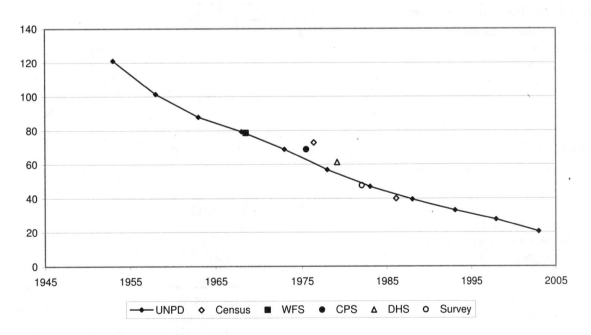

Indicator	Period						
	Earlier year				Later year		

I. Data and estimates from national and other sources

General mortality	Year	Value			Year	Value	
Annual number of deaths *(thousands)*	..	..			..	..	
Annual number of deaths under age one *(thousands)*	..	..			..	..	
Crude death rate *(per 1 000 person-years)*	..	..			..	..	

	Year	Male	Female		Year	Male	Female
Life expectancy *(years)*							
at birth..	..	..	..		1991-1992	64.4	66.8
at age 15...	..	..	..		1991-1992	54.2	56.5
at age 60...	..	..	..		1991-1992	15.9	17.5
Survival probability							
from birth to age 15..	..	..	..		1991-1992	0.93	0.93
from age 15 to age 60..	..	..	..		1991-1992	0.78	0.81
from age 60 to age 80..	..	..	..		1991-1992	0.33	0.40

Infant and child mortality	Year	Male	Female	Both sexes	Year	Male	Female	Both sexes
Infant mortality rate *(per 1 000 live births)*	..	..	..	..	2000	..	..	40
Mortality from age 1 to age 4 *(per 1 000 live births)*	..	..	..	..	2000	..	..	12
Under-five mortality rate *(per 1 000 live births)*	..	..	..	..	..	..	..	..

II. Data and estimates from United Nations sources

United Nations Population Division estimates	1990-1995	2000-2005
Annual number of deaths *(thousands)*	1	1
Crude death rate *(per 1 000 person-years)*	6	6
Life expectancy at birth *(years)*		
Male..	65.9	66.9
Female...	67.0	68.2
Under-five mortality rate *(per 1 000 live births)*	54	48

Maternal mortality	2000
Maternal mortality ratio *(deaths per 100 000 births)*	..

HIV/AIDS	2003	[Low estimate - high estimate]
Number of HIV-infected persons, ...	..	..
Adult HIV prevalence *(percentage of adults 15-49)*	..	..

Policy views	1976	2003
Life expectancy...	..	Unacceptable
Under-five mortality..		Unacceptable
Maternal mortality..		Unacceptable
Level of concern about AIDS...................................		Major concern

Life Expectancy at Birth

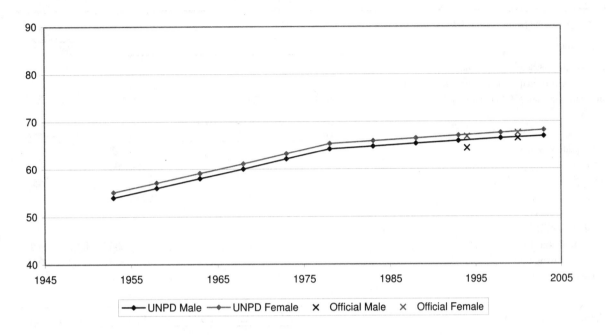

Infant Mortality Rate

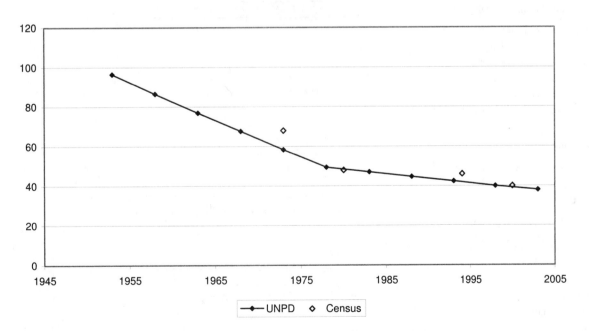

Indicator	Period				
	Earlier year			**Later year**	

I. Data and estimates from national and other sources

General mortality

	Year	Value		Year	Value	
Annual number of deaths *(thousands)*	1965	10.7		2003	16.0	
Annual number of deaths under age one *(thousands)*	..	..		2003	1.1	
Crude death rate *(per 1 000 person-years)*	1965	9.8		2003	6.4	

	Year	Male	Female	Year	Male	Female
Life expectancy *(years)*						
at birth..	..	..	..	1996-2000	61.1	66.6
at age 15...	..	..	..	1996-2000	50.5	55.6
at age 60...	..	..	..	1996-2000	13.6	16.9
Survival probability						
from birth to age 15...	..	..	..	1996-2000	0.93	0.94
from age 15 to age 60...	..	..	..	1996-2000	0.69	0.78
from age 60 to age 80...	..	..	..	..	..	..

Infant and child mortality

	Year	Male	Female	Both sexes	Year	Male	Female	Both sexes
Infant mortality rate *(per 1 000 live births)*	..	..	..	..	1988-1998	81	57	69
Mortality from age 1 to age 4 *(per 1 000 live births)*	..	..	..	..	1988-1998	27	22	25
Under-five mortality rate *(per 1 000 live births)*	..	..	..	..	1988-1998	106	78	92

II. Data and estimates from United Nations sources

United Nations Population Division estimates

	1990-1995	2000-2005
Annual number of deaths *(thousands)*	20	19
Crude death rate *(per 1 000 person-years)*	9	7
Life expectancy at birth *(years)*		
Male..	59.4	61.9
Female..	63.2	65.9
Under-five mortality rate *(per 1 000 live births)*	103	85

Maternal mortality

	2000
Maternal mortality ratio *(deaths per 100 000 births)*	110

HIV/AIDS

	2003	*[Low estimate - high estimate]*
Number of HIV-infected persons, ...	<500	[<1 000]
Adult HIV prevalence *(percentage of adults 15-49)*	<0.1	[<0.2]

Policy views

	1976	2003
Life expectancy..	Unacceptable	Acceptable
Under-five mortality...		Unacceptable
Maternal mortality..		Unacceptable
Level of concern about AIDS...................................		Major concern

Life Expectancy at Birth

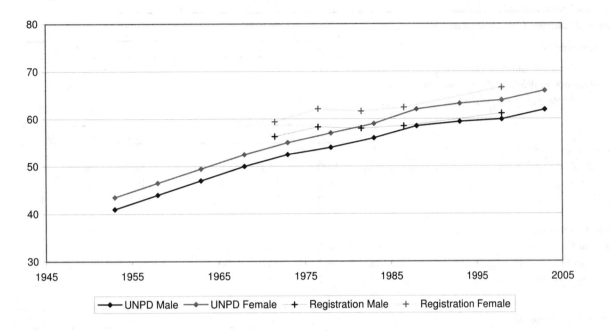

Infant Mortality Rate

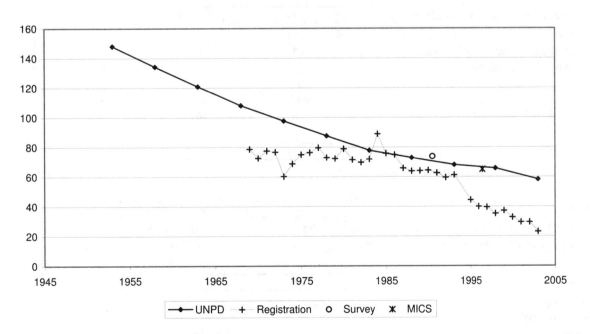

Indicator	Period					
	Earlier year			Later year		

I. Data and estimates from national and other sources

General mortality

	Year	Value		Year	Value	
Annual number of deaths *(thousands)*	..	..		..	..	
Annual number of deaths under age one *(thousands)*	..	..		..	..	
Crude death rate *(per 1 000 person-years)*	..	..		..	..	

	Year	Male	Female	Year	Male	Female
Life expectancy *(years)*						
at birth..	1972	51.7	52.8	1987	63.7	66.4
at age 15...	1972	51.1	51.0	1987	57.1	59.4
at age 60...	1972	15.4	16.2	1987	17.9	19.7
Survival probability						
from birth to age 15...	1972	0.78	0.79	..	..	..
from age 15 to age 60...	1972	0.70	0.70	..	..	..
from age 60 to age 80...	1972	0.31	0.34	..	..	..

Infant and child mortality

	Year	Male	Female	Both sexes	Year	Male	Female	Both sexes
Infant mortality rate *(per 1 000 live births)*	1972	122	111	117	1993-2003	51	37	44
Mortality from age 1 to age 4 *(per 1 000 live births)*	1972	69	77	72	1993-2003	9	11	10
Under-five mortality rate *(per 1 000 live births)*	1972	183	179	181	1993-2003	59	48	54

II. Data and estimates from United Nations sources

United Nations Population Division estimates

	1990-1995	2000-2005
Annual number of deaths *(thousands)*	184	177
Crude death rate *(per 1 000 person-years)*	7	6
Life expectancy at birth *(years)*		
Male..	63.9	67.4
Female...	67.3	71.7
Under-five mortality rate *(per 1 000 live births)*	76	46

Maternal mortality

	2000
Maternal mortality ratio *(deaths per 100 000 births)*	220

HIV/AIDS

	2003	*[Low estimate - high estimate]*
Number of HIV-infected persons, ...	15 000	[5 000 - 30 000]
Adult HIV prevalence *(percentage of adults 15-49)*	0.1	[0.0 - 0.2]

Policy views

	1976	2003
Life expectancy..	Unacceptable	Unacceptable
Under-five mortality...		Unacceptable
Maternal mortality..		Unacceptable
Level of concern about AIDS...................................		Major concern

Life Expectancy at Birth

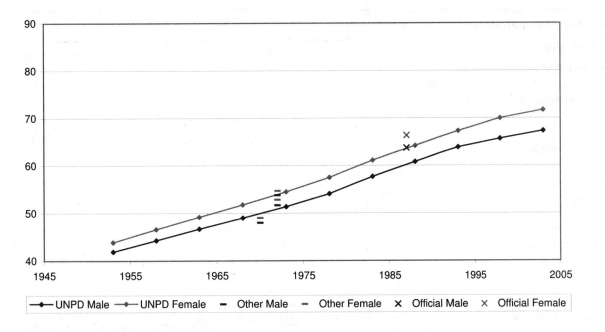

Infant Mortality Rate

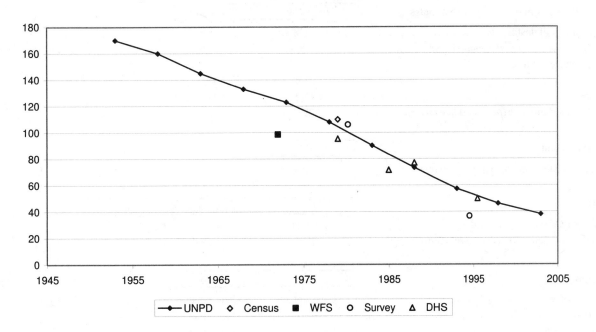

Indicator	Period						
	Earlier year				Later year		

I. Data and estimates from national and other sources

General mortality

	Year	Value			Year	Value	
Annual number of deaths *(thousands)*	..	..			..	..	
Annual number of deaths under age one *(thousands)*	..	..			..	..	
Crude death rate *(per 1 000 person-years)*	..	..			..	..	

	Year	Male	Female		Year	Male	Female
Life expectancy *(years)*							
at birth...	..	..	..		..	..	..
at age 15..	..	..	..		..	..	..
at age 60..	..	..	..		..	..	..
Survival probability							
from birth to age 15..	..	..	..		..	..	..
from age 15 to age 60..	..	..	..		..	..	..
from age 60 to age 80..	..	..	..		..	..	..

Infant and child mortality

	Year	Male	Female	Both sexes	Year	Male	Female	Both sexes
Infant mortality rate *(per 1 000 live births)*	..	..	..	..	1993-2003	128	120	124
Mortality from age 1 to age 4 *(per 1 000 live births)*	..	..	..	..	1993-2003	61	64	62
Under-five mortality rate *(per 1 000 live births)*	1982	284	275	280	1993-2003	181	176	178

II. Data and estimates from United Nations sources

United Nations Population Division estimates

	1990-1995	2000-2005
Annual number of deaths *(thousands)*	298	381
Crude death rate *(per 1 000 person-years)*	20	20
Life expectancy at birth *(years)*		
Male..	41.9	41.0
Female...	45.2	42.8
Under-five mortality rate *(per 1 000 live births)*	233	182

Maternal mortality

	2000
Maternal mortality ratio *(deaths per 100 000 births)*	1 000

HIV/AIDS

	2003	[Low estimate - high estimate]
Number of HIV-infected persons, ...	1 300 000	[980 000 - 1 700 000]
Adult HIV prevalence *(percentage of adults 15-49)*	12.2	[9.4 - 15.7]

Policy views

	1976	2003
Life expectancy..	Unacceptable	Unacceptable
Under-five mortality..		Unacceptable
Maternal mortality..		Unacceptable
Level of concern about AIDS....................................		Major concern

Life Expectancy at Birth

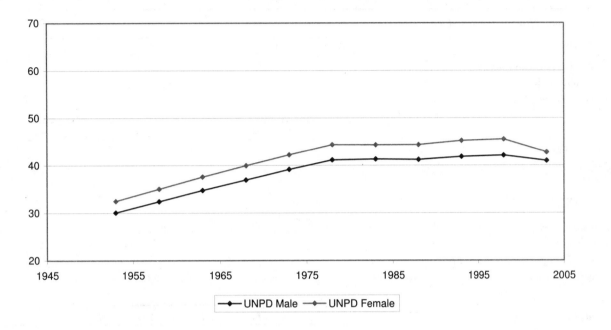

Infant Mortality Rate

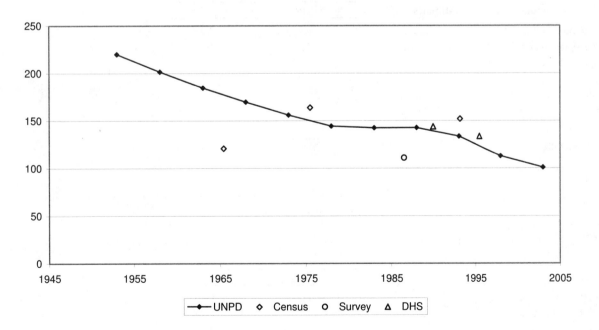

Indicator	Period							
	Earlier year				Later year			

I. Data and estimates from national and other sources

General mortality

	Year	Value			Year	Value		
Annual number of deaths *(thousands)*	..	..			..	..		
Annual number of deaths under age one *(thousands)*	..	..			..	..		
Crude death rate *(per 1 000 person-years)*	..	..			..	..		

	Year	Male	Female		Year	Male	Female	
Life expectancy *(years)*								
at birth..	..	..	..		..	..	..	
at age 15...	..	..	..		..	..	..	
at age 60...	..	..	..		..	..	..	
Survival probability								
from birth to age 15...	..	..	..		..	..	..	
from age 15 to age 60...	..	..	..		..	..	..	
from age 60 to age 80...	..	..	..		..	..	..	

Infant and child mortality

	Year	Male	Female	Both sexes	Year	Male	Female	Both sexes
Infant mortality rate *(per 1 000 live births)*	1982	99	77	88	1999	67	52	60
Mortality from age 1 to age 4 *(per 1 000 live births)*	1982	46	35	41	..	..	..	..
Under-five mortality rate *(per 1 000 live births)*	1982	140	109	125	1999	85	68	78

II. Data and estimates from United Nations sources

United Nations Population Division estimates

	1990-1995	2000-2005
Annual number of deaths *(thousands)*	492	478
Crude death rate *(per 1 000 person-years)*	12	10
Life expectancy at birth *(years)*		
Male...	54.8	57.4
Female..	59.0	62.9
Under-five mortality rate *(per 1 000 live births)*	140	112

Maternal mortality

	2000
Maternal mortality ratio *(deaths per 100 000 births)*	360

HIV/AIDS

	2003	[Low estimate - high estimate]
Number of HIV-infected persons, ...	330 000	[170 000 - 620 000]
Adult HIV prevalence *(percentage of adults 15-49)*	1.2	[0.6 - 2.2]

Policy views

	1976	2003
Life expectancy...	Unacceptable	Acceptable
Under-five mortality..		Unacceptable
Maternal mortality..		Unacceptable
Level of concern about AIDS....................................		Major concern

Life Expectancy at Birth

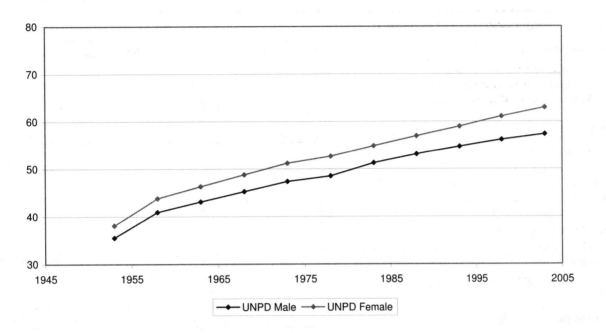

Infant Mortality Rate

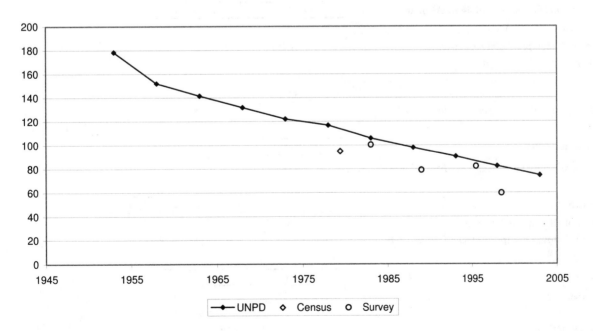

Indicator	Period					
	Earlier year			Later year		

I. Data and estimates from national and other sources

General mortality

	Year	Value		Year	Value	
Annual number of deaths *(thousands)*	..	..		..	..	
Annual number of deaths under age one *(thousands)*	..	..		..	..	
Crude death rate *(per 1 000 person-years)*	..	..		..	..	

	Year	Male	Female	Year	Male	Female
Life expectancy *(years)*						
at birth...	..	..	..	..	..	..
at age 15...	..	..	..	..	..	..
at age 60...	..	..	..	..	..	..
Survival probability						
from birth to age 15...	..	..	..	..	..	..
from age 15 to age 60..	..	..	..	..	..	..
from age 60 to age 80..	..	..	..	..	..	..

Infant and child mortality

	Year	Male	Female	Both sexes	Year	Male	Female	Both sexes
Infant mortality rate *(per 1 000 live births)*	1987	75	64	70	1990-2000	45	34	40
Mortality from age 1 to age 4 *(per 1 000 live births)*	1987	18	25	22	1990-2000	22	20	21
Under-five mortality rate *(per 1 000 live births)*	1987	92	87	90	1990-2000	67	54	60

II. Data and estimates from United Nations sources

United Nations Population Division estimates

	1990-1995	2000-2005
Annual number of deaths *(thousands)*	13	29
Crude death rate *(per 1 000 person-years)*	9	15
Life expectancy at birth *(years)*		
Male..	60.3	47.7
Female..	63.7	49.4
Under-five mortality rate *(per 1 000 live births)*	79	78

Maternal mortality

	2000
Maternal mortality ratio *(deaths per 100 000 births)*	300

HIV/AIDS

	2003	*[Low estimate - high estimate]*
Number of HIV-infected persons, ...	210 000	[180 000 - 250 000]
Adult HIV prevalence *(percentage of adults 15-49)*	21.3	[18.2 - 24.7]

Policy views

	1976	2003
Life expectancy..	..	Unacceptable
Under-five mortality..		Unacceptable
Maternal mortality..		Unacceptable
Level of concern about AIDS.......................................		Major concern

Life Expectancy at Birth

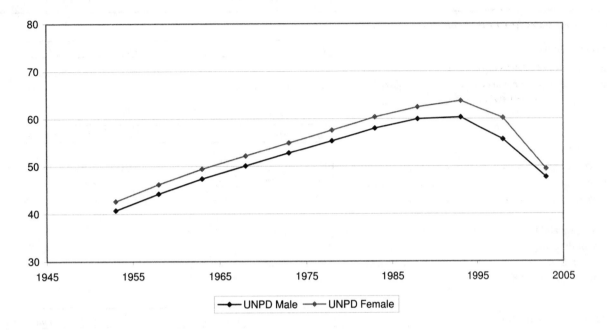

Infant Mortality Rate

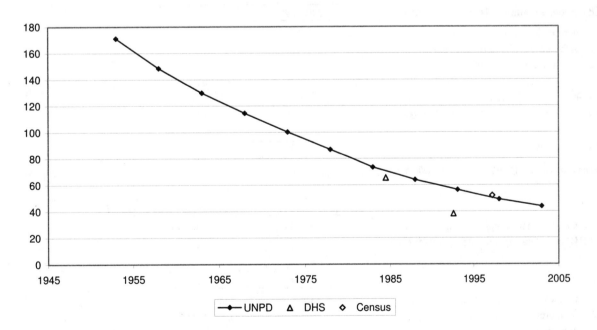

Indicator	Period					
	Earlier year				Later year	

I. Data and estimates from national and other sources

General mortality

	Year	Value			Year	Value	
Annual number of deaths *(thousands)*	..	..			..	..	
Annual number of deaths under age one *(thousands)*	..	..			..	..	
Crude death rate *(per 1 000 person-years)*	..	..			..	..	

	Year	Male	Female		Year	Male	Female
Life expectancy *(years)*							
at birth...	1981	50.9	48.1		2001	60.1	60.7
at age 15...	1981	47.3	46.9		..	..	..
at age 60...	1981	13.8	14.4		..	..	..
Survival probability							
from birth to age 15..	1981	0.81	0.77		..	..	..
from age 15 to age 60..	1981	0.62	0.62		..	..	..
from age 60 to age 80..	1981	0.24	0.27		..	..	..

Infant and child mortality

	Year	Male	Female	Both sexes	Year	Male	Female	Both sexes
Infant mortality rate *(per 1 000 live births)*	1970	157	151	154	1991-2001	79	75	77
Mortality from age 1 to age 4 *(per 1 000 live births)*	1970	87	95	91	1991-2001	28	40	34
Under-five mortality rate *(per 1 000 live births)*	1970	231	231	231	1991-2001	105	112	108

II. Data and estimates from United Nations sources

United Nations Population Division estimates

	1990-1995	2000-2005
Annual number of deaths *(thousands)*	243	225
Crude death rate *(per 1 000 person-years)*	12	9
Life expectancy at birth *(years)*		
Male..	56.0	60.9
Female...	55.8	61.7
Under-five mortality rate *(per 1 000 live births)*	128	88

Maternal mortality

	2000
Maternal mortality ratio *(deaths per 100 000 births)*	740

HIV/AIDS

	2003	*[Low estimate - high estimate]*
Number of HIV-infected persons, ...	61 000	[29 000 - 110 000]
Adult HIV prevalence *(percentage of adults 15-49)*	0.5	[0.3 - 0.9]

Policy views

	1976	2003
Life expectancy..	Unacceptable	Unacceptable
Under-five mortality...		Unacceptable
Maternal mortality..		Unacceptable
Level of concern about AIDS..................................		Major concern

Life Expectancy at Birth

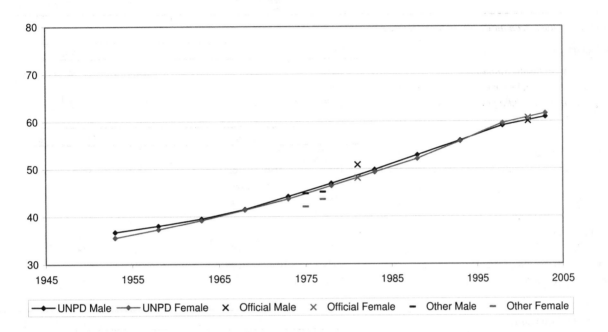

Infant Mortality Rate

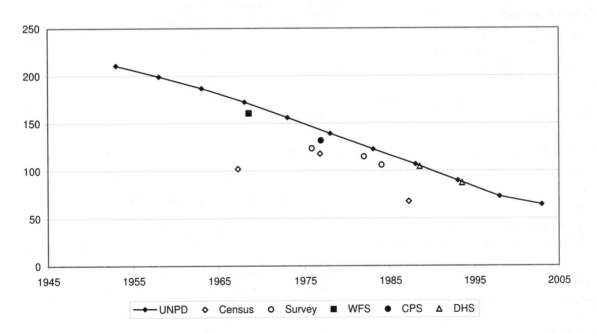

Indicator	Period						
	Earlier year				Later year		

I. Data and estimates from national and other sources

General mortality

	Year	Value			Year	Value	
Annual number of deaths *(thousands)*	1970	109.6			2003	141.9	
Annual number of deaths under age one *(thousands)*	1970	3.0			2003	1.0	
Crude death rate *(per 1 000 person-years)*	1970	8.4			2003	8.7	

	Year	Male	Female		Year	Male	Female
Life expectancy *(years)*							
at birth..	1971	71.0	76.7		2003	76.2	80.9
at age 15..	1971	57.5	63.0		2003	61.9	66.4
at age 60..	1971	16.9	20.6		2003	19.7	23.7
Survival probability							
from birth to age 15....................................	1971	0.98	0.98		2003	0.99	0.99
from age 15 to age 60.................................	1971	0.84	0.92		2003	0.91	0.93
from age 60 to age 80.................................	1971	0.38	0.56		2003	0.51	0.69

Infant and child mortality

	Year	Male	Female	Both sexes	Year	Male	Female	Both sexes
Infant mortality rate *(per 1 000 live births)*	1971	14	11	12	2003	5	4	5
Mortality from age 1 to age 4 *(per 1 000 live births)*	1971	4	3	3	2003	1	1	1
Under-five mortality rate *(per 1 000 live births)*	1971	18	14	16	2003	6	5	6

II. Data and estimates from United Nations sources

United Nations Population Division estimates

	1990-1995	2000-2005
Annual number of deaths *(thousands)*	133	144
Crude death rate *(per 1 000 person-years)*	9	9
Life expectancy at birth *(years)*		
Male..	74.3	75.6
Female...	80.2	81.0
Under-five mortality rate *(per 1 000 live births)*	9	6

Maternal mortality

	2000
Maternal mortality ratio *(deaths per 100 000 births)*	16

HIV/AIDS

	2003	[Low estimate - high estimate]
Number of HIV-infected persons, ...	19 000	[9 500 - 31 000]
Adult HIV prevalence *(percentage of adults 15-49)*	0.2	[0.1 - 0.4]

Policy views

	1976	2003
Life expectancy..	Acceptable	Acceptable
Under-five mortality...		Acceptable
Maternal mortality...		Acceptable
Level of concern about AIDS.....................................		Major concern

Life Expectancy at Birth

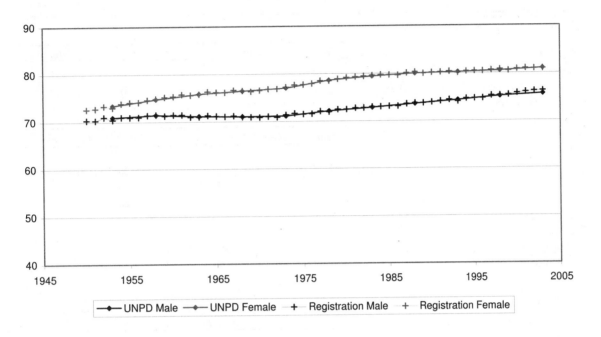

Infant Mortality Rate

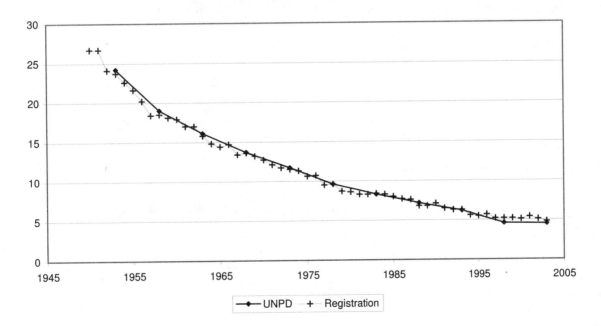

Indicator	Period			
	Earlier year		Later year	

I. Data and estimates from national and other sources

General mortality

	Year	Value	Year	Value
Annual number of deaths *(thousands)*	1970	1.1	2003	1.4
Annual number of deaths under age one *(thousands)*	1971	0.1	1989	0.0
Crude death rate *(per 1 000 person-years)*	1970	6.8	2003	7.7

	Year	Male	Female	Year	Male	Female
Life expectancy *(years)*						
at birth...	1966-1970	58.9	65.7	1998-2002	72.1	78.7
at age 15..	1966-1970	49.8	55.5	1998-2002	58.0	64.6
at age 60..	1966-1970	14.2	16.8	1998-2002	18.5	22.8
Survival probability						
from birth to age 15...	1966-1970	0.91	0.93	..	..	..
from age 15 to age 60...	1966-1970	0.69	0.79	..	..	..
from age 60 to age 80...	1966-1970	0.31	0.35	..	..	..

Infant and child mortality

	Year	Male	Female	Both sexes	Year	Male	Female	Both sexes
Infant mortality rate *(per 1 000 live births)*	1966-1970	64	53	59	2003	..	..	9
Mortality from age 1 to age 4 *(per 1 000 live births)*	1966-1970	13	12	12	..	..	..	..
Under-five mortality rate *(per 1 000 live births)*	1966-1970	76	64	70	..	..	..	..

II. Data and estimates from United Nations sources

United Nations Population Division estimates

	1990-1995	2000-2005
Annual number of deaths *(thousands)*	1	1
Crude death rate *(per 1 000 person-years)*	7	7
Life expectancy at birth *(years)*		
Male..	71.5	72.9
Female..	77.6	79.1
Under-five mortality rate *(per 1 000 live births)*	19	15

Maternal mortality

	2000
Maternal mortality ratio *(deaths per 100 000 births)*	..

HIV/AIDS

	2003	[Low estimate - high estimate]
Number of HIV-infected persons, ...	..	..
Adult HIV prevalence *(percentage of adults 15-49)*	..	..

Policy views

	1976	2003
Life expectancy..	..	..
Under-five mortality..		..
Maternal mortality..		..
Level of concern about AIDS...................................		..

Life Expectancy at Birth

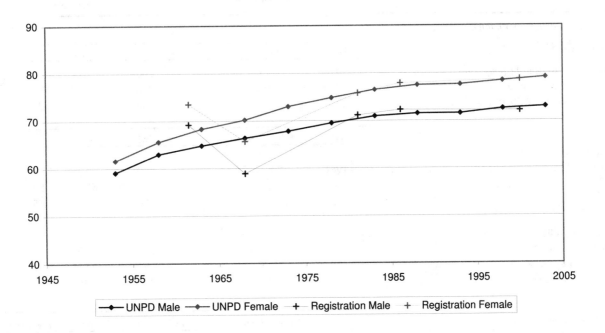

Legend: UNPD Male · UNPD Female · Registration Male · Registration Female

Infant Mortality Rate

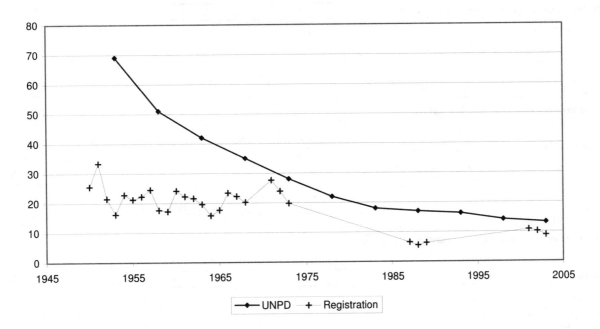

Legend: UNPD · Registration

I. Data and estimates from national and other sources

Indicator	Period							
	Earlier year				Later year			

General mortality

	Year	Value			Year	Value		
Annual number of deaths *(thousands)*	1970	1.0			2003	1.1		
Annual number of deaths under age one *(thousands)*	1970	0.2			2003	0.0		
Crude death rate *(per 1 000 person-years)*	1970	9.3			2003	5.1		

	Year	Male	Female		Year	Male	Female	
Life expectancy *(years)*								
at birth	1981	62.8	70.8		2003	71.3	77.3	
at age 15	..	..	..		2003	57.2	62.9	
at age 60	..	..	..		2003	17.4	21.5	
Survival probability								
from birth to age 15	..	..	..		2003	0.99	0.99	
from age 15 to age 60	..	..	..		2003	0.83	0.89	
from age 60 to age 80	..	..	..		2003	0.38	0.56	

Infant and child mortality

	Year	Male	Female	Both sexes	Year	Male	Female	Both sexes
Infant mortality rate *(per 1 000 live births)*	..	..	..	..	2003	7	4	6
Mortality from age 1 to age 4 *(per 1 000 live births)*	..	..	..	..	2003	4	1	3
Under-five mortality rate *(per 1 000 live births)*	..	..	..	..	2003	10	6	8

II. Data and estimates from United Nations sources

United Nations Population Division estimates

	1990-1995	2000-2005
Annual number of deaths *(thousands)*	1	1
Crude death rate *(per 1 000 person-years)*	5	5
Life expectancy at birth *(years)*		
Male	69.2	72.6
Female	74.5	77.8
Under-five mortality rate *(per 1 000 live births)*	17	9

Maternal mortality

	2000
Maternal mortality ratio *(deaths per 100 000 births)*	..

HIV/AIDS

	2003	[Low estimate - high estimate]
Number of HIV-infected persons,	..	..
Adult HIV prevalence *(percentage of adults 15-49)*	..	..

Policy views

	1976	2003
Life expectancy	..	..
Under-five mortality		..
Maternal mortality		..
Level of concern about AIDS		..

Life Expectancy at Birth

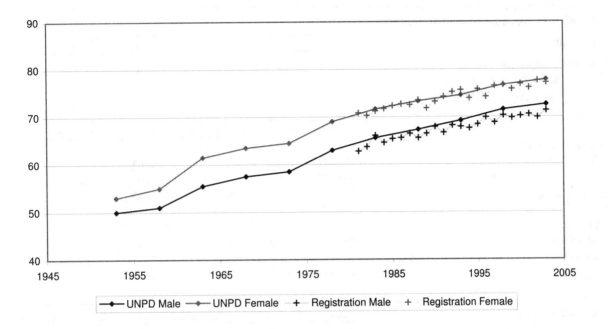

Infant Mortality Rate

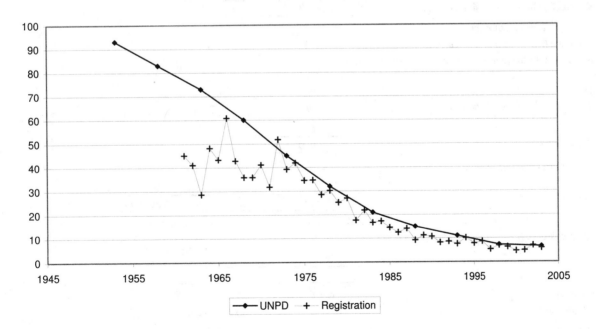

Indicator	Period			
	Earlier year		Later year	

I. Data and estimates from national and other sources

General mortality

	Year	Value	Year	Value
Annual number of deaths *(thousands)*	1970	24.8	2003	28.0
Annual number of deaths under age one *(thousands)*	1970	1.0	2003	0.3
Crude death rate *(per 1 000 person-years)*	1970	8.8	2003	7.0

	Year	Male	Female	Year	Male	Female
Life expectancy *(years)*						
at birth..........	1970-1972	68.6	74.6	2003	77.0	81.4
at age 15..........	1970-1972	55.4	61.2	2003	62.7	67.0
at age 60..........	1970-1972	15.7	19.8	2003	21.1	24.3
Survival probability						
from birth to age 15..........	1970-1972	0.97	0.98	2003	0.99	0.99
from age 15 to age 60..........	1970-1972	0.81	0.89	2003	0.90	0.93
from age 60 to age 80..........	1970-1972	0.32	0.52	2003	0.58	0.70

Infant and child mortality

	Year	Male	Female	Both sexes	Year	Male	Female	Both sexes
Infant mortality rate *(per 1 000 live births)*	1970-1972	18	15	16	2003	6	4	5
Mortality from age 1 to age 4 *(per 1 000 live births)*	1970-1972	4	4	4	2003	1	1	1
Under-five mortality rate *(per 1 000 live births)*	1970-1972	22	18	20	2003	7	6	6

II. Data and estimates from United Nations sources

United Nations Population Division estimates

	1990-1995	2000-2005
Annual number of deaths *(thousands)*	27	29
Crude death rate *(per 1 000 person-years)*	8	7
Life expectancy at birth *(years)*		
Male..........	73.3	76.7
Female..........	78.9	81.3
Under-five mortality rate *(per 1 000 live births)*	9	7

Maternal mortality

	2000
Maternal mortality ratio *(deaths per 100 000 births)*	7

HIV/AIDS

	2003	[Low estimate - high estimate]
Number of HIV-infected persons, ...	1 400	[480 - 2 800]
Adult HIV prevalence *(percentage of adults 15-49)*	0.1	[<0.2]

Policy views

	1976	2003
Life expectancy...	Acceptable	Acceptable
Under-five mortality...		Unacceptable
Maternal mortality...		Acceptable
Level of concern about AIDS...................................		Major concern

Life Expectancy at Birth

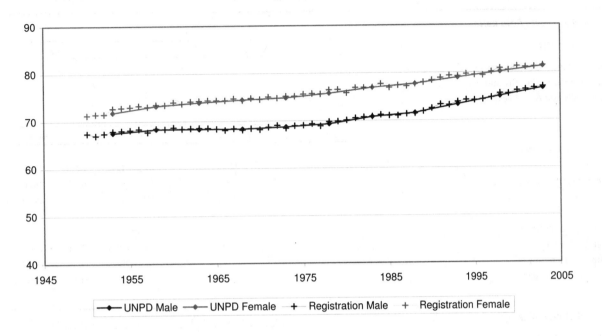

Legend: UNPD Male, UNPD Female, + Registration Male, + Registration Female

Infant Mortality Rate

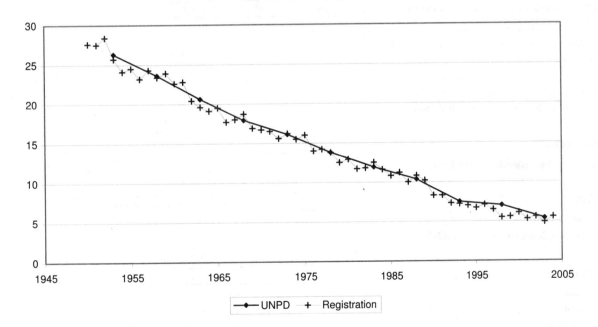

Legend: UNPD, + Registration

Indicator	Period			
	Earlier year		*Later year*	

I. Data and estimates from national and other sources

General mortality

	Year	Value	Year	Value
Annual number of deaths *(thousands)*	..	..	..	..
Annual number of deaths under age one *(thousands)*	..	..	..	..
Crude death rate *(per 1 000 person-years)*	..	..	..	..

	Year	Male	Female	Year	Male	Female
Life expectancy *(years)*						
at birth...	..	..	..	2000-2005	67.2	71.9
at age 15..	..	..	..	2000-2005	55.7	60.0
at age 60..	..	..	..	2000-2005	18.5	20.2
Survival probability						
from birth to age 15...	..	..	..	2000-2005	0.95	0.96
from age 15 to age 60...	..	..	..	2000-2005	0.77	0.85
from age 60 to age 80...	..	..	..	2000-2005	0.47	0.54

Infant and child mortality

	Year	Male	Female	Both sexes	Year	Male	Female	Both sexes
Infant mortality rate *(per 1 000 live births)*	1980	103	83	93	1991-2001	39	32	35
Mortality from age 1 to age 4 *(per 1 000 live births)*	1980	48	40	44	1991-2001	10	9	10
Under-five mortality rate *(per 1 000 live births)*	1980	146	120	133	1991-2001	48	41	45

II. Data and estimates from United Nations sources

United Nations Population Division estimates

	1990-1995	2000-2005
Annual number of deaths *(thousands)*	27	26
Crude death rate *(per 1 000 person-years)*	6	5
Life expectancy at birth *(years)*		
Male...	63.5	67.2
Female..	68.7	71.9
Under-five mortality rate *(per 1 000 live births)*	62	40

Maternal mortality

	2000
Maternal mortality ratio *(deaths per 100 000 births)*	230

HIV/AIDS

	2003	*[Low estimate - high estimate]*
Number of HIV-infected persons, ...	6 400	[3 100 - 12 000]
Adult HIV prevalence *(percentage of adults 15-49)*	0.2	[0.1 - 0.3]

Policy views

	1976	2003
Life expectancy..	Unacceptable	Unacceptable
Under-five mortality..		Unacceptable
Maternal mortality...		Unacceptable
Level of concern about AIDS...		Minor concern

Life Expectancy at Birth

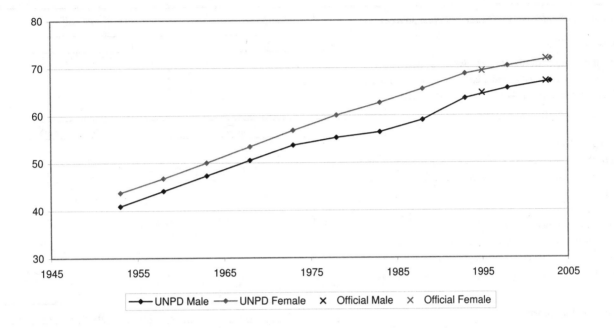

Infant Mortality Rate

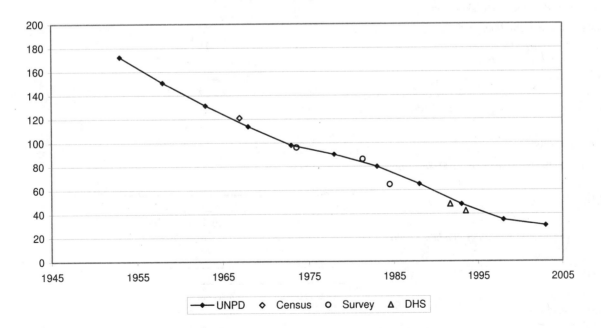

Indicator	Period							
	Earlier year				Later year			

I. Data and estimates from national and other sources

General mortality

	Year	Value			Year	Value		
Annual number of deaths *(thousands)*	..	..			..	..		
Annual number of deaths under age one *(thousands)*	..	..			..	..		
Crude death rate *(per 1 000 person-years)*	..	..			..	..		

	Year	Male	Female		Year	Male	Female	
Life expectancy *(years)*								
at birth	..	..	..		..	..	..	
at age 15	..	..	..		..	..	..	
at age 60	..	..	..		..	..	..	
Survival probability								
from birth to age 15	..	..	..		..	..	..	
from age 15 to age 60	..	..	..		..	..	..	
from age 60 to age 80	..	..	..		..	..	..	

Infant and child mortality

	Year	Male	Female	Both sexes	Year	Male	Female	Both sexes
Infant mortality rate *(per 1 000 live births)*	1987	193	189	191	1988-1998	141	131	136
Mortality from age 1 to age 4 *(per 1 000 live births)*	1987	148	171	159	1988-1998	184	202	193
Under-five mortality rate *(per 1 000 live births)*	1987	313	328	320	1988-1998	299	306	303

II. Data and estimates from United Nations sources

United Nations Population Division estimates

	1990-1995	2000-2005
Annual number of deaths *(thousands)*	229	272
Crude death rate *(per 1 000 person-years)*	25	21
Life expectancy at birth *(years)*		
Male	40.5	44.2
Female	40.6	44.3
Under-five mortality rate *(per 1 000 live births)*	307	264

Maternal mortality

	2000
Maternal mortality ratio *(deaths per 100 000 births)*	1 600

HIV/AIDS

	2003	*[Low estimate - high estimate]*
Number of HIV-infected persons,	70 000	[36 000 - 130 000]
Adult HIV prevalence *(percentage of adults 15-49)*	1.2	[0.7 - 2.3]

Policy views

	1976	2003
Life expectancy	Unacceptable	Unacceptable
Under-five mortality		Unacceptable
Maternal mortality		Unacceptable
Level of concern about AIDS		Major concern

Life Expectancy at Birth

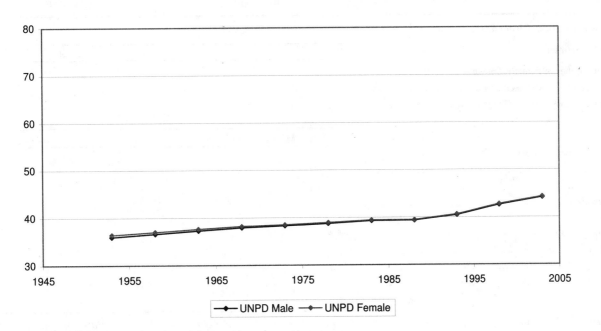

Infant Mortality Rate

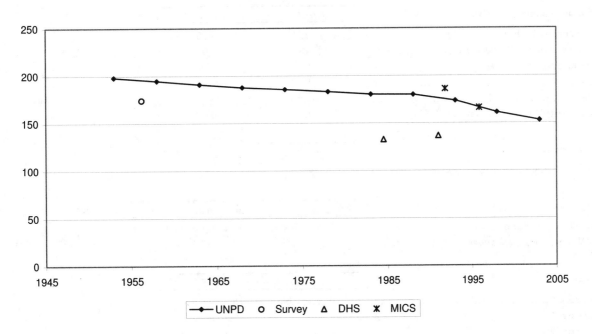

Indicator	Period			
	Earlier year		Later year	

I. Data and estimates from national and other sources

General mortality

	Year	Value	Year	Value
Annual number of deaths *(thousands)*	..	..	..	..
Annual number of deaths under age one *(thousands)*	..	..	..	..
Crude death rate *(per 1 000 person-years)*	..	..	..	..

	Year	Male	Female	Year	Male	Female
Life expectancy *(years)*						
at birth...	..	..	..	..	..	..
at age 15...	..	..	..	..	..	..
at age 60...	..	..	..	..	..	..
Survival probability						
from birth to age 15..............................	..	..	..	..	..	..
from age 15 to age 60............................	..	..	..	..	..	..
from age 60 to age 80............................	..	..	..	..	..	..

Infant and child mortality

	Year	Male	Female	Both sexes	Year	Male	Female	Both sexes
Infant mortality rate *(per 1 000 live births)*	1975	128	108	118	1993-2003	116	102	109
Mortality from age 1 to age 4 *(per 1 000 live births)*	1975	91	90	91	1993-2003	120	123	121
Under-five mortality rate *(per 1 000 live births)*	1975	207	188	198	1993-2003	222	212	217

II. Data and estimates from United Nations sources

United Nations Population Division estimates

	1990-1995	2000-2005
Annual number of deaths *(thousands)*	1 793	2 416
Crude death rate *(per 1 000 person-years)*	18	19
Life expectancy at birth *(years)*		
Male...	45.0	43.1
Female..	47.5	43.5
Under-five mortality rate *(per 1 000 live births)*	206	200

Maternal mortality

	2000
Maternal mortality ratio *(deaths per 100 000 births)*	800

HIV/AIDS

	2003	*[Low estimate - high estimate]*
Number of HIV-infected persons, ...	3 600 000	[2 400 000 - 5 400 000]
Adult HIV prevalence *(percentage of adults 15-49)*	5.4	[3.6 - 8.0]

Policy views

	1976	2003
Life expectancy...	Unacceptable	Unacceptable
Under-five mortality..		Unacceptable
Maternal mortality..		Unacceptable
Level of concern about AIDS.................................		Major concern

Life Expectancy at Birth

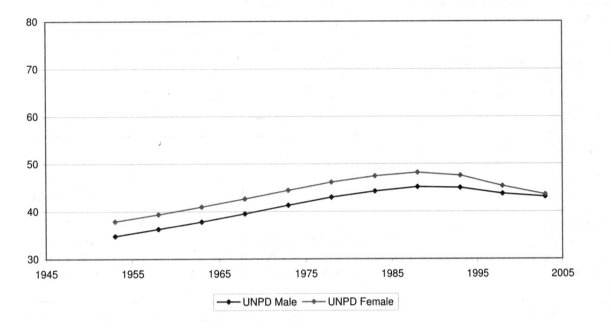

Infant Mortality Rate

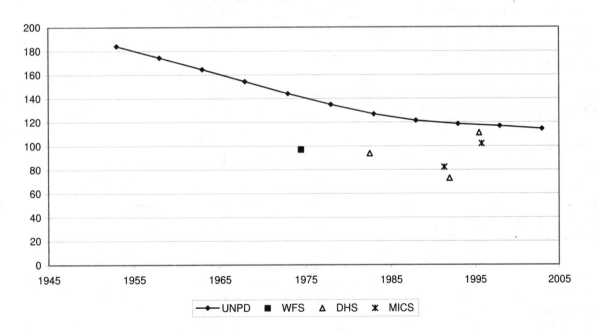

Indicator	Period				
	Earlier year			Later year	

I. Data and estimates from national and other sources

General mortality

	Year	Value		Year	Value
Annual number of deaths *(thousands)*	1970	38.7		2004	41.2
Annual number of deaths under age one *(thousands)*	1970	0.8		2004	0.2
Crude death rate *(per 1 000 person-years)*	1970	10.0		2004	9.0

	Year	Male	Female	Year	Male	Female
Life expectancy *(years)*						
at birth	1971-1972	71.2	77.4	2004	77.5	82.3
at age 15	1971-1972	57.8	63.6	2004	62.9	67.7
at age 60	1971-1972	17.4	21.0	2004	21.1	24.8
Survival probability						
from birth to age 15	1971-1972	0.98	0.98	2004	0.99	0.99
from age 15 to age 60	1971-1972	0.85	0.93	2004	0.91	0.94
from age 60 to age 80	1971-1972	0.40	0.57	2004	0.58	0.73

Infant and child mortality

	Year	Male	Female	Both sexes	Year	Male	Female	Both sexes
Infant mortality rate *(per 1 000 live births)*	1971-1972	14	10	12	2004	3	3	3
Mortality from age 1 to age 4 *(per 1 000 live births)*	1971-1972	4	2	3	2004	1	1	1
Under-five mortality rate *(per 1 000 live births)*	1971-1972	18	12	15	2004	4	4	4

II. Data and estimates from United Nations sources

United Nations Population Division estimates

	1990-1995	2000-2005
Annual number of deaths *(thousands)*	45	44
Crude death rate *(per 1 000 person-years)*	11	10
Life expectancy at birth *(years)*		
Male	74.3	76.7
Female	80.3	81.8
Under-five mortality rate *(per 1 000 live births)*	7	5

Maternal mortality

	2000
Maternal mortality ratio *(deaths per 100 000 births)*	16

HIV/AIDS

	2003	[Low estimate - high estimate]
Number of HIV-infected persons,	2 100	[700 - 4 000]
Adult HIV prevalence *(percentage of adults 15-49)*	0.1	[0.0 - 0.2]

Policy views

	1976	2003
Life expectancy	Acceptable	Acceptable
Under-five mortality		Acceptable
Maternal mortality		Acceptable
Level of concern about AIDS		Minor concern

Life Expectancy at Birth

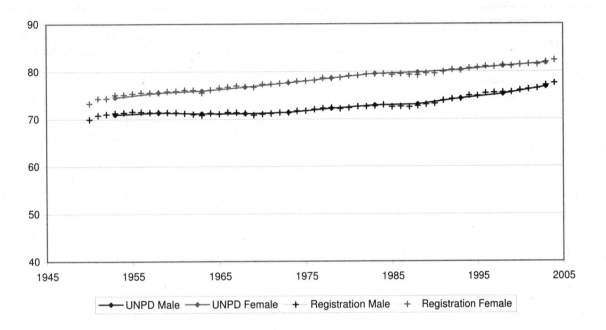

Infant Mortality Rate

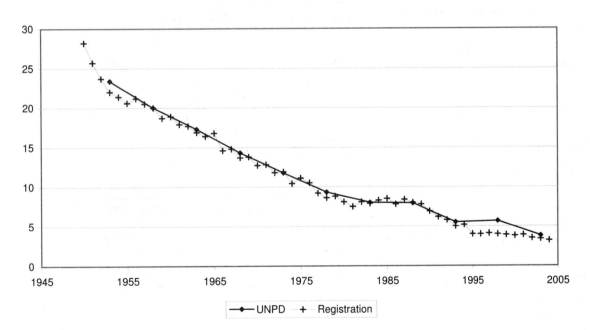

Indicator

	Period			
	Earlier year		Later year	

I. Data and estimates from national and other sources

General mortality

	Year	Value	Year	Value
Annual number of deaths *(thousands)*	..	..	..	..
Annual number of deaths under age one *(thousands)*	..	..	..	..
Crude death rate *(per 1 000 person-years)*	..	..	..	..

	Year	Male	Female	Year	Male	Female
Life expectancy *(years)*						
at birth	..	..	..	2001	70.5	73.6
at age 15	..	..	..	2001	57.8	60.5
at age 60	..	..	..	2001	17.2	19.0
Survival probability						
from birth to age 15	..	..	..	..	..	..
from age 15 to age 60	..	..	..	..	..	..
from age 60 to age 80	..	..	..	..	..	..

Infant and child mortality

	Year	Male	Female	Both sexes	Year	Male	Female	Both sexes
Infant mortality rate *(per 1 000 live births)*	..	..	..	..	1999-2003	27	22	24
Mortality from age 1 to age 4 *(per 1 000 live births)*	..	..	..	..	..	..	..	..
Under-five mortality rate *(per 1 000 live births)*	..	..	..	..	1999-2003	32	25	28

II. Data and estimates from United Nations sources

United Nations Population Division estimates

	1990-1995	2000-2005
Annual number of deaths *(thousands)*	16	15
Crude death rate *(per 1 000 person-years)*	7	4
Life expectancy at birth *(years)*		
Male	68.1	70.8
Female	71.4	73.9
Under-five mortality rate *(per 1 000 live births)*	32	24

Maternal mortality

	2000
Maternal mortality ratio *(deaths per 100 000 births)*	..

HIV/AIDS

	2003	*[Low estimate - high estimate]*
Number of HIV-infected persons,	..	..
Adult HIV prevalence *(percentage of adults 15-49)*	..	..

Policy views

	1976	2003
Life expectancy	..	..
Under-five mortality		..
Maternal mortality		..
Level of concern about AIDS		..

Life Expectancy at Birth

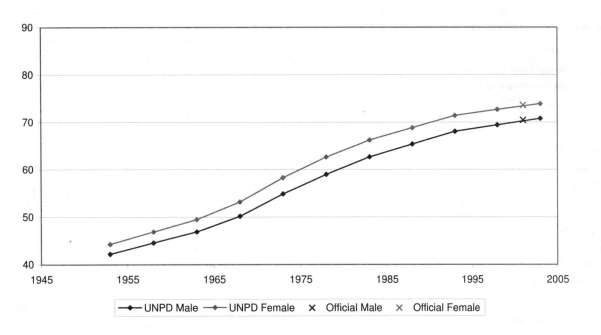

Infant Mortality Rate

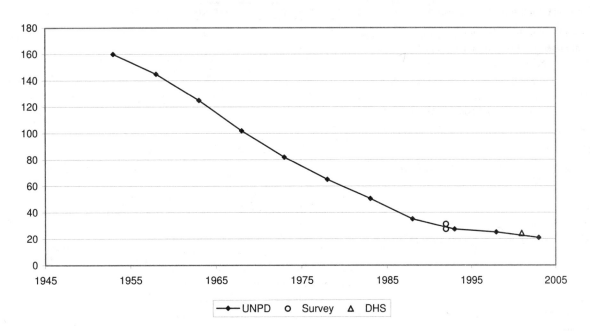

Indicator	Period				
	Earlier year			Later year	

I. Data and estimates from national and other sources

General mortality	Year	Value		Year	Value
Annual number of deaths *(thousands)*	..	..		..	..
Annual number of deaths under age one *(thousands)*	..	..		..	..
Crude death rate *(per 1 000 person-years)*	..	..		..	..

	Year	Male	Female	Year	Male	Female
Life expectancy *(years)*						
at birth	..	..	..	2002	72.2	75.4
at age 15	..	..	..	..	..	..
at age 60	..	..	..	..	..	..
Survival probability						
from birth to age 15	..	..	..	..	..	..
from age 15 to age 60	..	..	..	..	..	..
from age 60 to age 80	..	..	..	..	..	..

Infant and child mortality	Year	Male	Female	Both sexes	Year	Male	Female	Both sexes
Infant mortality rate *(per 1 000 live births)*	1978	78	66	72	1985-1995	21	19	20
Mortality from age 1 to age 4 *(per 1 000 live births)*	1978	29	40	34	1985-1995	6	6	6
Under-five mortality rate *(per 1 000 live births)*	1978	105	103	104	1985-1995	27	25	26

II. Data and estimates from United Nations sources

United Nations Population Division estimates	1990-1995	2000-2005
Annual number of deaths *(thousands)*	7	7
Crude death rate *(per 1 000 person-years)*	4	3
Life expectancy at birth *(years)*		
Male	69.9	72.7
Female	72.9	75.6
Under-five mortality rate *(per 1 000 live births)*	28	18

Maternal mortality	2000
Maternal mortality ratio *(deaths per 100 000 births)*	87

HIV/AIDS	2003	*[Low estimate - high estimate]*
Number of HIV-infected persons,	1 300	[500 - 3 000]
Adult HIV prevalence *(percentage of adults 15-49)*	0.1	[0.0 - 0.2]

Policy views	1976	2003
Life expectancy	Unacceptable	Unacceptable
Under-five mortality		Unacceptable
Maternal mortality		Unacceptable
Level of concern about AIDS		Major concern

Life Expectancy at Birth

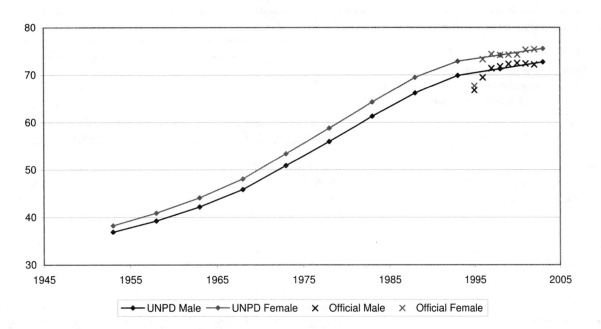

Infant Mortality Rate

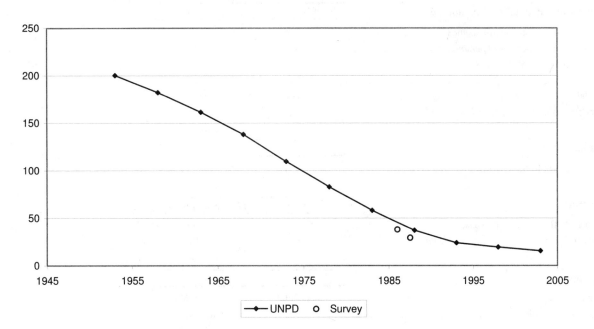

Indicator	Period			
	Earlier year		Later year	

I. Data and estimates from national and other sources

General mortality

	Year	Value		Year	Value	
Annual number of deaths *(thousands)*	..	..		..	..	
Annual number of deaths under age one *(thousands)*	..	..		..	..	
Crude death rate *(per 1 000 person-years)*	..	..		..	..	

	Year	Male	Female	Year	Male	Female
Life expectancy *(years)*						
at birth..	1976-1978	59.0	59.2	2001	64.5	66.1
at age 15..	1976-1978	56.8	56.3	2001	56.9	58.8
at age 60..	1976-1978	19.3	19.3	2001	18.8	20.1
Survival probability						
from birth to age 15..	1976-1978	0.82	0.83	..	..	..
from age 15 to age 60..	1976-1978	0.78	0.78	..	..	..
from age 60 to age 80..	1976-1978	0.51	0.50	..	..	..

Infant and child mortality

	Year	Male	Female	Both sexes	Year	Male	Female	Both sexes
Infant mortality rate *(per 1 000 live births)*	1975	114	101	108	2003	81	71	76
Mortality from age 1 to age 4 *(per 1 000 live births)*	1975	54	67	61	..	..	..	..
Under-five mortality rate *(per 1 000 live births)*	1975	162	162	162	..	..	..	..

II. Data and estimates from United Nations sources

United Nations Population Division estimates

	1990-1995	2000-2005
Annual number of deaths *(thousands)*	1 161	1 248
Crude death rate *(per 1 000 person-years)*	10	8
Life expectancy at birth *(years)*		
Male..	60.6	62.7
Female...	61.4	63.1
Under-five mortality rate *(per 1 000 live births)*	128	114

Maternal mortality

	2000
Maternal mortality ratio *(deaths per 100 000 births)*	500

HIV/AIDS

	2003	[Low estimate - high estimate]
Number of HIV-infected persons, ...	74 000	[24 000 - 150 000]
Adult HIV prevalence *(percentage of adults 15-49)*	0.1	[0.0 - 0.2]

Policy views

	1976	2003
Life expectancy..	Unacceptable	Unacceptable
Under-five mortality..		Unacceptable
Maternal mortality...		Unacceptable
Level of concern about AIDS....................................		Major concern

Life Expectancy at Birth

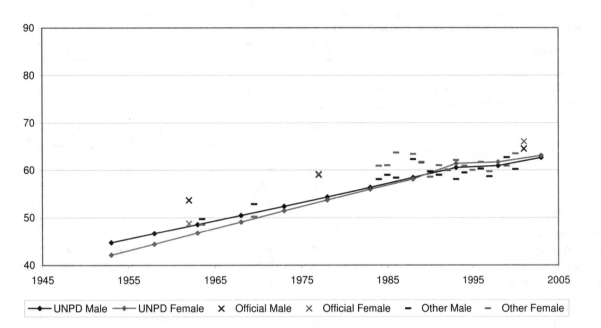

Infant Mortality Rate

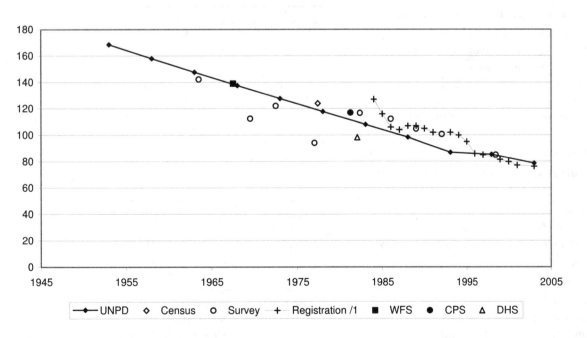

[1] Refers to the annual Pakistan Demographic Survey

Indicator	Period					
	Earlier year			Later year		

I. Data and estimates from national and other sources

General mortality

	Year	Value		Year	Value	
Annual number of deaths *(thousands)*	..	..		..	..	
Annual number of deaths under age one *(thousands)*	..	..		..	..	
Crude death rate *(per 1 000 person-years)*	..	..		..	..	

	Year	Male	Female	Year	Male	Female
Life expectancy *(years)*						
at birth	1970	64.3	67.5	2000	72.2	76.8
at age 15	1970	55.3	58.0	2000	59.5	64.0
at age 60	1970	17.0	19.9	2000	19.3	22.2
Survival probability						
from birth to age 15	1970	0.91	0.92	2000	0.97	0.97
from age 15 to age 60	1970	0.80	0.81	2000	0.86	0.91
from age 60 to age 80	1970	0.38	0.53	2000	0.49	0.63

Infant and child mortality

	Year	Male	Female	Both sexes	Year	Male	Female	Both sexes
Infant mortality rate *(per 1 000 live births)*	1975	44	34	39	2000	22	19	21
Mortality from age 1 to age 4 *(per 1 000 live births)*	1975	16	15	16	2000	6	6	6
Under-five mortality rate *(per 1 000 live births)*	1975	59	48	54	2000	28	25	27

II. Data and estimates from United Nations sources

United Nations Population Division estimates

	1990-1995	2000-2005
Annual number of deaths *(thousands)*	13	15
Crude death rate *(per 1 000 person-years)*	5	5
Life expectancy at birth *(years)*		
Male	70.2	72.3
Female	75.7	77.4
Under-five mortality rate *(per 1 000 live births)*	34	27

Maternal mortality

	2000
Maternal mortality ratio *(deaths per 100 000 births)*	160

HIV/AIDS

	2003	[Low estimate - high estimate]
Number of HIV-infected persons,	16 000	[7 700 - 26 000]
Adult HIV prevalence *(percentage of adults 15-49)*	0.9	[0.5 - 1.5]

Policy views

	1976	2003
Life expectancy	Acceptable	Acceptable
Under-five mortality		Unacceptable
Maternal mortality		Unacceptable
Level of concern about AIDS		Major concern

Life Expectancy at Birth

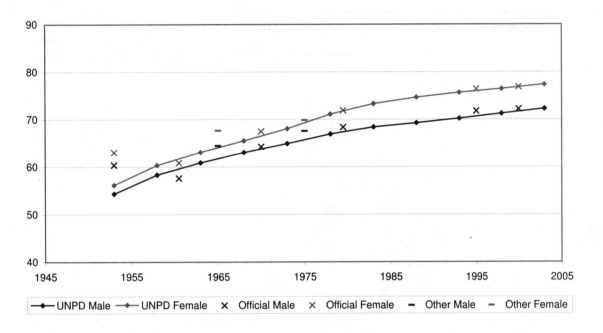

Infant Mortality Rate

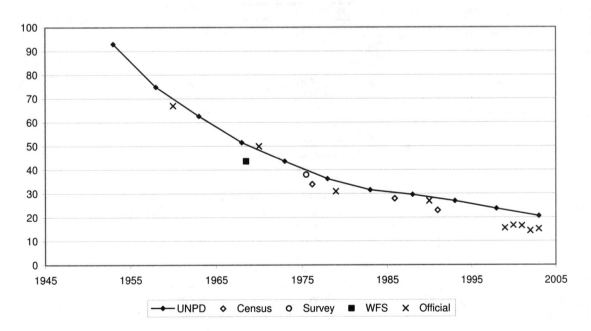

Indicator	Period			
	Earlier year		Later year	

I. Data and estimates from national and other sources

General mortality	Year	Value	Year	Value
Annual number of deaths *(thousands)*	..	..	..	..
Annual number of deaths under age one *(thousands)*	..	..	..	..
Crude death rate *(per 1 000 person-years)*	..	..	..	..

	Year	Male	Female	Year	Male	Female
Life expectancy *(years)*						
at birth...	..	..	..	2000	53.7	54.8
at age 15..	..	..	..	..	..	..
at age 60..	..	..	..	..	..	..
Survival probability						
from birth to age 15..	..	..	..	..	..	..
from age 15 to age 60..	..	..	..	..	..	..
from age 60 to age 80..	..	..	..	..	..	..

Infant and child mortality	Year	Male	Female	Both sexes	Year	Male	Female	Both sexes
Infant mortality rate *(per 1 000 live births)*	..	..	..	..	2000	67	61	64
Mortality from age 1 to age 4 *(per 1 000 live births)*	..	..	..	..	2000	27	23	..
Under-five mortality rate *(per 1 000 live births)*	..	..	..	..	..	..	..	..

II. Data and estimates from United Nations sources

United Nations Population Division estimates	1990-1995	2000-2005
Annual number of deaths *(thousands)*	56	60
Crude death rate *(per 1 000 person-years)*	13	11
Life expectancy at birth *(years)*		
Male...	51.9	54.7
Female..	53.6	55.8
Under-five mortality rate *(per 1 000 live births)*	113	98

Maternal mortality	2000	
Maternal mortality ratio *(deaths per 100 000 births)*	300	

HIV/AIDS	2003	*[Low estimate - high estimate]*
Number of HIV-infected persons, ...	16 000	[7 800 - 28 000]
Adult HIV prevalence *(percentage of adults 15-49)*	0.6	[0.3 - 1.0]

Policy views	1976	2003
Life expectancy..	Unacceptable	Unacceptable
Under-five mortality..		Unacceptable
Maternal mortality..		Unacceptable
Level of concern about AIDS...................................		Major concern

Life Expectancy at Birth

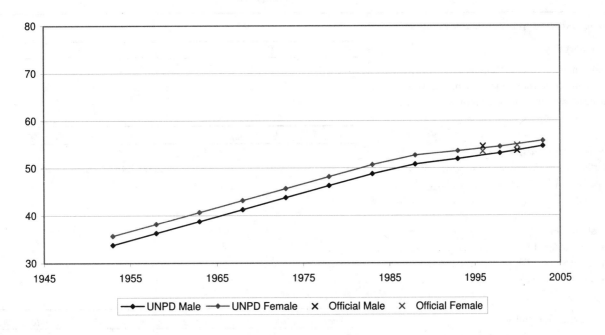

Infant Mortality Rate

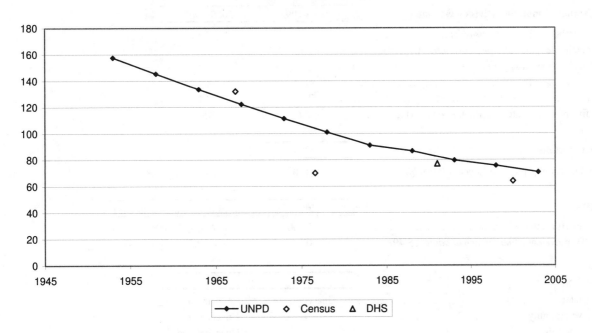

Indicator	Period			
	Earlier year		Later year	

I. Data and estimates from national and other sources

General mortality

	Year	Value	Year	Value
Annual number of deaths *(thousands)*	..	..	..	..
Annual number of deaths under age one *(thousands)*	..	..	..	..
Crude death rate *(per 1 000 person-years)*	..	..	..	..

	Year	Male	Female	Year	Male	Female
Life expectancy *(years)*						
at birth..	..	..	..	2000-2005	68.6	73.1
at age 15..	..	..	..	..	..	..
at age 60..	..	..	..	..	..	..
Survival probability						
from birth to age 15................................	..	..	..	..	..	..
from age 15 to age 60.............................	..	..	..	..	..	..
from age 60 to age 80.............................	..	..	..	..	..	..

Infant and child mortality

	Year	Male	Female	Both sexes	Year	Male	Female	Both sexes
Infant mortality rate *(per 1 000 live births)*	1975	54	52	53	..	..	..	..
Mortality from age 1 to age 4 *(per 1 000 live births)*	1975	21	15	18	..	..	..	..
Under-five mortality rate *(per 1 000 live births)*	1975	73	66	70	..	..	..	..

II. Data and estimates from United Nations sources

United Nations Population Division estimates

	1990-1995	2000-2005
Annual number of deaths *(thousands)*	27	29
Crude death rate *(per 1 000 person-years)*	6	5
Life expectancy at birth *(years)*		
Male...	66.3	68.6
Female..	70.8	73.1
Under-five mortality rate *(per 1 000 live births)*	54	45

Maternal mortality

	2000
Maternal mortality ratio *(deaths per 100 000 births)*	170

HIV/AIDS

	2003	*[Low estimate - high estimate]*
Number of HIV-infected persons, ...	15 000	[7 300 - 25 000]
Adult HIV prevalence *(percentage of adults 15-49)*	0.5	[0.2 - 0.8]

Policy views

	1976	2003
Life expectancy...	Unacceptable	Acceptable
Under-five mortality...		Unacceptable
Maternal mortality...		Unacceptable
Level of concern about AIDS..................................		Minor concern

Life Expectancy at Birth

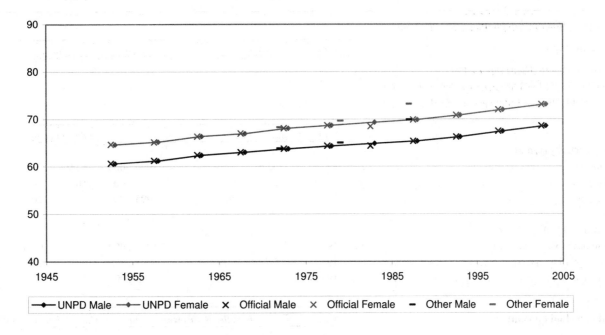

Legend: UNPD Male — UNPD Female — Official Male × Official Female × Other Male − Other Female −

Infant Mortality Rate

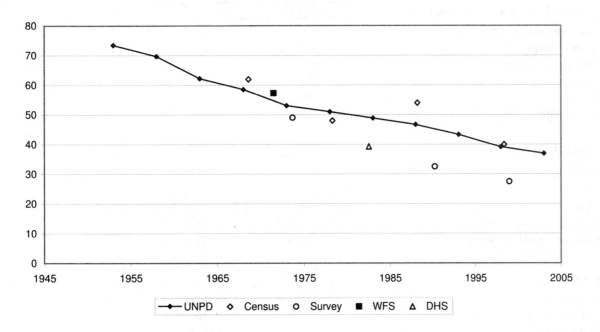

Legend: UNPD ◆ Census ◇ Survey ○ WFS ■ DHS △

Indicator	Period					
	Earlier year				Later year	

I. Data and estimates from national and other sources

General mortality

	Year	Value			Year	Value
Annual number of deaths *(thousands)*	..	..			..	..
Annual number of deaths under age one *(thousands)*	..	..			..	..
Crude death rate *(per 1 000 person-years)*	..	..			..	..

	Year	Male	Female		Year	Male	Female
Life expectancy *(years)*							
at birth	1970	53.6	57.6		1995-2000	65.9	70.9
at age 15	1970	54.1	57.8		1995-2000	56.6	60.7
at age 60	1970	17.8	20.7		1995-2000	18.1	20.3
Survival probability							
from birth to age 15	1970	0.77	0.78		1995-2000	0.92	0.93
from age 15 to age 60	1970	0.74	0.79		1995-2000	0.80	0.87
from age 60 to age 80	1970	0.41	0.52		1995-2000	0.43	0.53

Infant and child mortality

	Year	Male	Female	Both sexes	Year	Male	Female	Both sexes
Infant mortality rate *(per 1 000 live births)*	1973	118	104	111	1990-2000	46	40	43
Mortality from age 1 to age 4 *(per 1 000 live births)*	1973	67	63	65	1990-2000	19	17	18
Under-five mortality rate *(per 1 000 live births)*	1973	177	160	169	1990-2000	64	57	60

II. Data and estimates from United Nations sources

United Nations Population Division estimates

	1990-1995	2000-2005
Annual number of deaths *(thousands)*	159	164
Crude death rate *(per 1 000 person-years)*	7	6
Life expectancy at birth *(years)*		
Male	64.4	67.3
Female	69.2	72.4
Under-five mortality rate *(per 1 000 live births)*	77	52

Maternal mortality

	2000
Maternal mortality ratio *(deaths per 100 000 births)*	410

HIV/AIDS

	2003	[Low estimate - high estimate]
Number of HIV-infected persons,	82 000	[40 000 - 140 000]
Adult HIV prevalence *(percentage of adults 15-49)*	0.5	[0.3 - 0.9]

Policy views

	1976	2003
Life expectancy	Unacceptable	Unacceptable
Under-five mortality		Unacceptable
Maternal mortality		Unacceptable
Level of concern about AIDS		Major concern

Life Expectancy at Birth

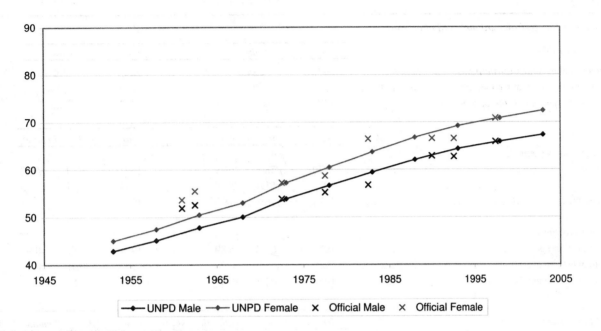

Infant Mortality Rate

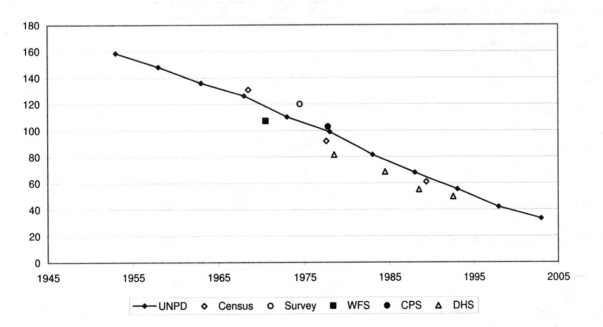

Indicator	Period				
	Earlier year			Later year	

I. Data and estimates from national and other sources

General mortality

	Year	Value		Year	Value
Annual number of deaths *(thousands)*	1970	234.0		2002	396.3
Annual number of deaths under age one *(thousands)*	1970	58.0		2002	23.8
Crude death rate *(per 1 000 person-years)*	1970	6.4		2002	5.0

	Year	Male	Female	Year	Male	Female
Life expectancy *(years)*						
at birth........................	1970	58.6	63.9	1991	63.1	66.7
at age 15........................	1970	51.7	56.2	1991	53.5	56.3
at age 60........................	1970	16.8	18.3	1991	15.5	17.3
Survival probability						
from birth to age 15........................	1970	0.87	0.89	1991	0.92	0.93
from age 15 to age 60........................	1970	0.70	0.79	1991	0.76	0.81
from age 60 to age 80........................	1970	0.38	0.44	1991	0.32	0.40

Infant and child mortality

	Year	Male	Female	Both sexes	Year	Male	Female	Both sexes
Infant mortality rate *(per 1 000 live births)*	1973	63	54	59	1993-2003	35	25	30
Mortality from age 1 to age 4 *(per 1 000 live births)*	1973	19	22	20	1993-2003	14	9	12
Under-five mortality rate *(per 1 000 live births)*	1973	81	75	78	1993-2003	48	34	42

II. Data and estimates from United Nations sources

United Nations Population Division estimates

	1990-1995	2000-2005
Annual number of deaths *(thousands)*	406	401
Crude death rate *(per 1 000 person-years)*	6	5
Life expectancy at birth *(years)*		
Male........................	64.5	68.1
Female........................	68.7	72.4
Under-five mortality rate *(per 1 000 live births)*	54	34

Maternal mortality

	2000
Maternal mortality ratio *(deaths per 100 000 births)*	200

HIV/AIDS

	2003	[Low estimate - high estimate]
Number of HIV-infected persons, ...	9 000	[3 000 - 18 000]
Adult HIV prevalence *(percentage of adults 15-49)*	<0.1	[<0.2]

Policy views

	1976	2003
Life expectancy..	Acceptable	Acceptable
Under-five mortality...		Unacceptable
Maternal mortality...		Unacceptable
Level of concern about AIDS.................................		Major concern

Life Expectancy at Birth

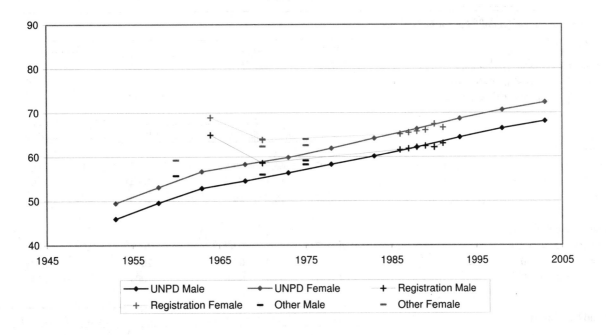

Infant Mortality Rate

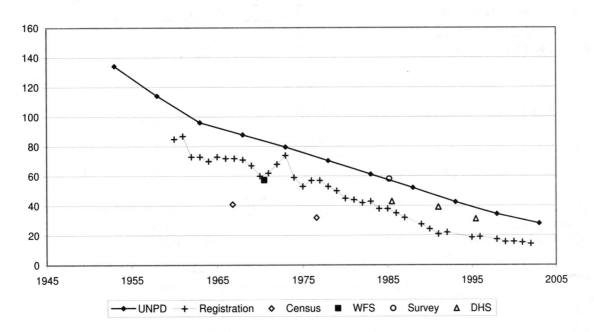

Indicator	Period					
	Earlier year			Later year		

I. Data and estimates from national and other sources

General mortality

	Year	Value		Year	Value	
Annual number of deaths *(thousands)*	1970	266.8		2003	365.2	
Annual number of deaths under age one *(thousands)*	1970	18.1		2003	2.5	
Crude death rate *(per 1 000 person-years)*	1970	8.2		2003	9.6	

	Year	Male	Female	Year	Male	Female
Life expectancy *(years)*						
at birth...	1970-1971	66.8	73.8	2004	70.7	79.2
at age 15..	1970-1971	54.6	61.1	2004	56.4	64.9
at age 60..	1970-1971	15.5	19.3	2004	17.4	22.5
Survival probability						
from birth to age 15...	1970-1971	0.96	0.97	2004	0.99	0.99
from age 15 to age 60...	1970-1971	0.79	0.90	2004	0.79	0.92
from age 60 to age 80...	1970-1971	0.30	0.48	2004	0.40	0.64

Infant and child mortality

	Year	Male	Female	Both sexes	Year	Male	Female	Both sexes
Infant mortality rate *(per 1 000 live births)*	1970-1971	31	24	28	2004	7	6	7
Mortality from age 1 to age 4 *(per 1 000 live births)*	1970-1971	4	3	4	2004	1	1	1
Under-five mortality rate *(per 1 000 live births)*	1970-1971	35	28	32	2004	9	7	8

II. Data and estimates from United Nations sources

United Nations Population Division estimates

	1990-1995	2000-2005
Annual number of deaths *(thousands)*	394	374
Crude death rate *(per 1 000 person-years)*	10	10
Life expectancy at birth *(years)*		
Male..	67.0	70.2
Female..	75.9	78.4
Under-five mortality rate *(per 1 000 live births)*	17	10

Maternal mortality

	2000
Maternal mortality ratio *(deaths per 100 000 births)*	13

HIV/AIDS

	2003	[Low estimate - high estimate]
Number of HIV-infected persons, ...	14 000	[6 900 - 23 000]
Adult HIV prevalence *(percentage of adults 15-49)*	0.1	[0.1 - 0.2]

Policy views

	1976	2003
Life expectancy..	Acceptable	Unacceptable
Under-five mortality..		Unacceptable
Maternal mortality...		Acceptable
Level of concern about AIDS......................................		Minor concern

Life Expectancy at Birth

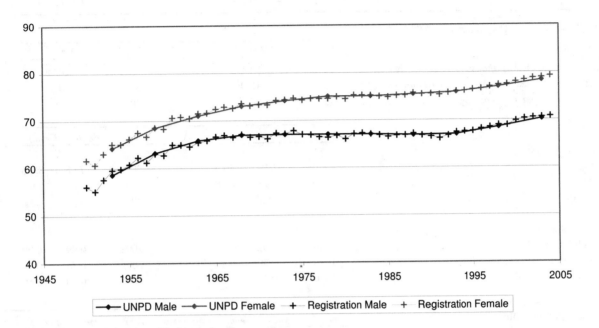

Infant Mortality Rate

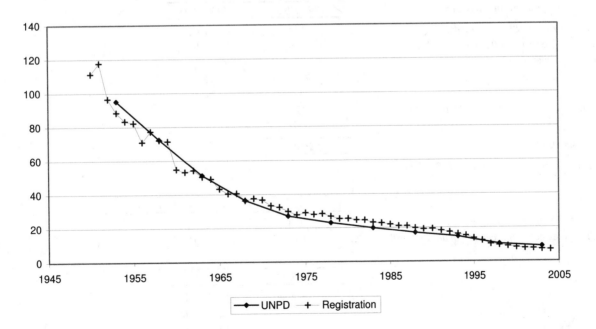

Indicator	Period				
	Earlier year			Later year	

I. Data and estimates from national and other sources

General mortality

	Year	Value		Year	Value
Annual number of deaths *(thousands)*	1970	93.1		2003	108.8
Annual number of deaths under age one *(thousands)*	1970	10.0		2003	0.5
Crude death rate *(per 1 000 person-years)*	1970	10.3		2003	10.5

	Year	Male	Female	Year	Male	Female
Life expectancy *(years)*						
at birth...	1970	64.2	70.5	2002	73.8	80.5
at age 15...	1970	54.9	60.8	2002	59.5	66.1
at age 60...	1970	15.8	19.2	2002	19.4	23.3
Survival probability						
from birth to age 15................................	1970	0.92	0.93	2002	0.99	0.99
from age 15 to age 60.............................	1970	0.80	0.89	2002	0.85	0.94
from age 60 to age 80.............................	1970	0.31	0.45	2002	0.50	0.69

Infant and child mortality

	Year	Male	Female	Both sexes	Year	Male	Female	Both sexes
Infant mortality rate *(per 1 000 live births)*	1970	63	53	58	2002	5	5	5
Mortality from age 1 to age 4 *(per 1 000 live births)*	1970	15	13	14	2002	2	1	2
Under-five mortality rate *(per 1 000 live births)*	1970	76	66	71	2002	7	6	7

II. Data and estimates from United Nations sources

United Nations Population Division estimates

	1990-1995	2000-2005
Annual number of deaths *(thousands)*	102	109
Crude death rate *(per 1 000 person-years)*	10	11
Life expectancy at birth *(years)*		
Male...	70.9	73.8
Female..	78.1	80.5
Under-five mortality rate *(per 1 000 live births)*	12	7

Maternal mortality

	2000
Maternal mortality ratio *(deaths per 100 000 births)*	5

HIV/AIDS

	2003	*[Low estimate - high estimate]*
Number of HIV-infected persons, ...	22 000	[11 000 - 36 000]
Adult HIV prevalence *(percentage of adults 15-49)*	0.4	[0.2 - 0.7]

Policy views

	1976	2003
Life expectancy...	Acceptable	Acceptable
Under-five mortality...		Acceptable
Maternal mortality...		Acceptable
Level of concern about AIDS.................................		Major concern

Life Expectancy at Birth

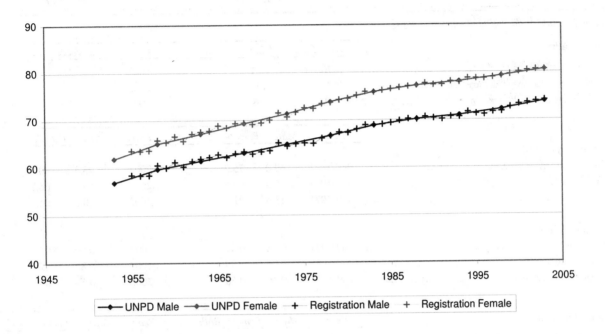

Infant Mortality Rate

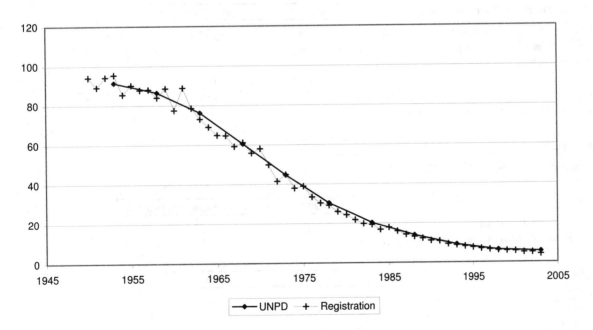

Indicator	Period							
	Earlier year				Later year			

I. Data and estimates from national and other sources

General mortality

	Year	Value			Year	Value		
Annual number of deaths *(thousands)*	1970	18.1			2003	28.4		
Annual number of deaths under age one *(thousands)*	1970	1.9			2003	0.5		
Crude death rate *(per 1 000 person-years)*	1970	6.6			2003	7.3		

	Year	Male	Female		Year	Male	Female	
Life expectancy *(years)*								
at birth...	1969-1971	69.0	75.2		2002	73.2	80.9	
at age 15...	1969-1971	56.9	62.5		2002	59.2	66.7	
at age 60...	1969-1971	18.9	21.3		2002	20.8	24.4	
Survival probability								
from birth to age 15...	1969-1971	0.96	0.97		2002	0.99	0.99	
from age 15 to age 60..	1969-1971	0.79	0.89		2002	0.82	0.92	
from age 60 to age 80..	1969-1971	0.46	0.58		2002	0.54	0.69	

Infant and child mortality

	Year	Male	Female	Both sexes	Year	Male	Female	Both sexes
Infant mortality rate *(per 1 000 live births)*	1972	30	22	26	2002	10	8	9
Mortality from age 1 to age 4 *(per 1 000 live births)*	1972	6	5	5	2002	1	1	1
Under-five mortality rate *(per 1 000 live births)*	1972	35	26	31	2002	11	9	10

II. Data and estimates from United Nations sources

United Nations Population Division estimates

	1990-1995	2000-2005
Annual number of deaths *(thousands)*	29	31
Crude death rate *(per 1 000 person-years)*	8	8
Life expectancy at birth *(years)*		
Male...	69.6	71.6
Female..	79.1	80.5
Under-five mortality rate *(per 1 000 live births)*	14	12

Maternal mortality

	2000
Maternal mortality ratio *(deaths per 100 000 births)*	..

HIV/AIDS

	2003	*[Low estimate - high estimate]*
Number of HIV-infected persons, ...	..	..
Adult HIV prevalence *(percentage of adults 15-49)*	..	..

Policy views

	1976	2003
Life expectancy..	..	..
Under-five mortality..		..
Maternal mortality...		..
Level of concern about AIDS.......................................		..

Life Expectancy at Birth

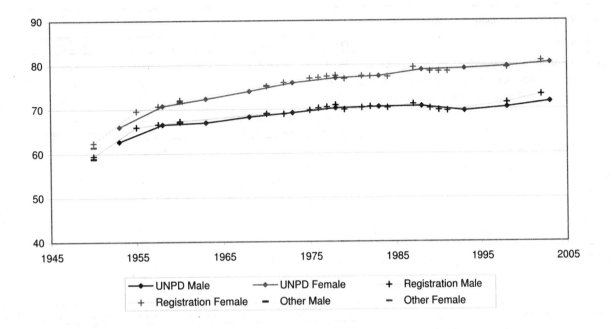

Infant Mortality Rate

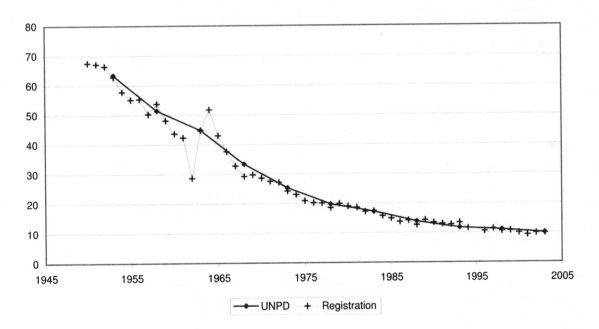

Indicator	Period				
	Earlier year			Later year	

I. Data and estimates from national and other sources

General mortality

	Year	Value		Year	Value
Annual number of deaths *(thousands)*	1970	0.5		2003	1.3
Annual number of deaths under age one *(thousands)*	1980	0.1		2003	0.1
Crude death rate *(per 1 000 person-years)*	1970	4.2		2003	1.8

	Year	Male	Female	Year	Male	Female
Life expectancy *(years)*						
at birth	..	..	..	..	..	..
at age 15	..	..	..	..	..	..
at age 60	..	..	..	..	..	..
Survival probability						
from birth to age 15	..	..	..	..	..	..
from age 15 to age 60	..	..	..	..	..	..
from age 60 to age 80	..	..	..	..	..	..

Infant and child mortality

	Year	Male	Female	Both sexes	Year	Male	Female	Both sexes
Infant mortality rate *(per 1 000 live births)*	..	..	..	..	1993-1998	..	..	10
Mortality from age 1 to age 4 *(per 1 000 live births)*	..	..	..	..	1993-1998	..	..	5
Under-five mortality rate *(per 1 000 live births)*	..	..	..	..	1993-1998	..	..	15

II. Data and estimates from United Nations sources

United Nations Population Division estimates

	1990-1995	2000-2005
Annual number of deaths *(thousands)*	2	2
Crude death rate *(per 1 000 person-years)*	3	3
Life expectancy at birth *(years)*		
Male	68.4	71.1
Female	73.0	75.9
Under-five mortality rate *(per 1 000 live births)*	20	14

Maternal mortality

	2000
Maternal mortality ratio *(deaths per 100 000 births)*	7

HIV/AIDS

	2003	[Low estimate - high estimate]
Number of HIV-infected persons,	..	..
Adult HIV prevalence *(percentage of adults 15-49)*	..	..

Policy views

	1976	2003
Life expectancy	Acceptable	Acceptable
Under-five mortality		Acceptable
Maternal mortality		Acceptable
Level of concern about AIDS		Major concern

Life Expectancy at Birth

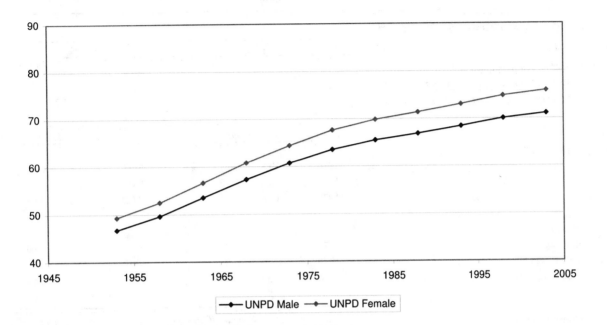

Infant Mortality Rate

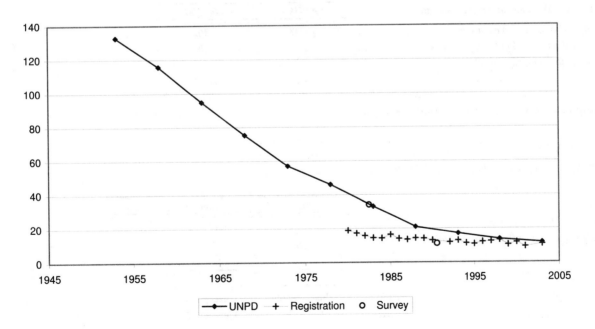

Indicator	Period					
	Earlier year			Later year		

I. Data and estimates from national and other sources

General mortality

	Year	Value		Year	Value	
Annual number of deaths *(thousands)*	..	..		2002	246.5	
Annual number of deaths under age one *(thousands)*	..	..		2002	2.5	
Crude death rate *(per 1 000 person-years)*	..	..		2002	5.2	

	Year	Male	Female	Year	Male	Female
Life expectancy *(years)*						
at birth...	1970	59.8	66.7	2002	73.4	80.4
at age 15...	1970	50.0	56.3	2002	59.1	66.1
at age 60...	1970	12.4	17.3	2002	18.5	23.1
Survival probability						
from birth to age 15...	1970	0.92	0.93	2001	0.99	0.99
from age 15 to age 60...	1970	0.76	0.81	2001	0.85	0.94
from age 60 to age 80...	1970	0.32	0.40	2001	0.43	0.65

Infant and child mortality

	Year	Male	Female	Both sexes	Year	Male	Female	Both sexes
Infant mortality rate *(per 1 000 live births)*	1973	38	32	35	2001	6	6	6
Mortality from age 1 to age 4 *(per 1 000 live births)*	1973	9	9	9	2001	2	2	2
Under-five mortality rate *(per 1 000 live births)*	1973	47	41	44	2001	8	7	7

II. Data and estimates from United Nations sources

United Nations Population Division estimates

	1990-1995	2000-2005
Annual number of deaths *(thousands)*	248	262
Crude death rate *(per 1 000 person-years)*	6	6
Life expectancy at birth *(years)*		
Male...	68.5	73.2
Female..	76.5	80.5
Under-five mortality rate *(per 1 000 live births)*	18	5

Maternal mortality

	2000
Maternal mortality ratio *(deaths per 100 000 births)*	20

HIV/AIDS

	2003	[Low estimate - high estimate]
Number of HIV-infected persons, ...	8 300	[2 700 - 16 000]
Adult HIV prevalence *(percentage of adults 15-49)*	<0.1	[<0.2]

Policy views

	1976	2003
Life expectancy...	Unacceptable	Unacceptable
Under-five mortality..		Unacceptable
Maternal mortality..		Unacceptable
Level of concern about AIDS....................................		Major concern

Life Expectancy at Birth

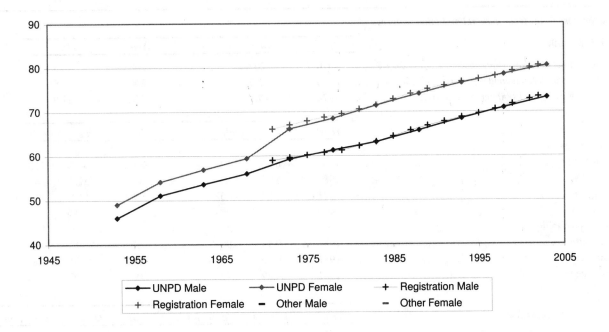

	UNPD Male		UNPD Female		Registration Male
	Registration Female		Other Male		Other Female

Infant Mortality Rate

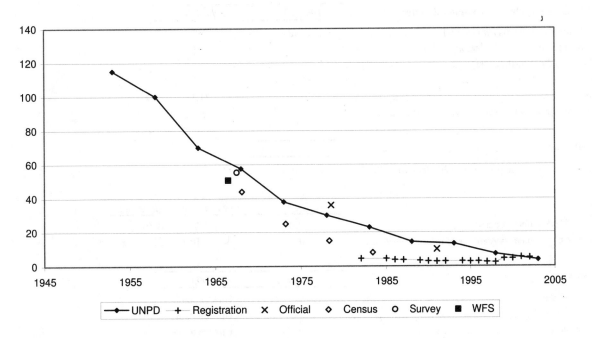

	UNPD		Registration		Official		Census		Survey		WFS

Indicator	Period					
	Earlier year			Later year		

I. Data and estimates from national and other sources

General mortality

	Year	Value		Year	Value	
Annual number of deaths *(thousands)*	1970	26.6		2003	43.1	
Annual number of deaths under age one *(thousands)*	1970	1.7		2003	0.5	
Crude death rate *(per 1 000 person-years)*	1970	7.4		2003	11.9	

	Year	Male	Female	Year	Male	Female
Life expectancy *(years)*						
at birth...	1981	62.5	69.4	2002	64.4	71.7
at age 15...	1981	51.2	57.4	2002	51.1	58.1
at age 60...	1981	14.7	17.5	2002	14.1	17.3
Survival probability						
from birth to age 15...	1981	0.94	0.96	2002	0.97	0.98
from age 15 to age 60..	1981	0.70	0.83	2002	0.70	0.85
from age 60 to age 80..	1981	0.29	0.42	2002	0.26	0.41

Infant and child mortality

	Year	Male	Female	Both sexes	Year	Male	Female	Both sexes
Infant mortality rate *(per 1 000 live births)*	1981	40	29	35	2002	17	14	16
Mortality from age 1 to age 4 *(per 1 000 live births)*	1981	10	8	9	2002	4	3	4
Under-five mortality rate *(per 1 000 live births)*	1981	49	37	43	2002	21	17	19

II. Data and estimates from United Nations sources

United Nations Population Division estimates

	1990-1995	2000-2005
Annual number of deaths *(thousands)*	48	49
Crude death rate *(per 1 000 person-years)*	11	11
Life expectancy at birth *(years)*		
Male...	63.6	63.7
Female..	70.9	71.1
Under-five mortality rate *(per 1 000 live births)*	35	31

Maternal mortality

	2000
Maternal mortality ratio *(deaths per 100 000 births)*	36

HIV/AIDS

	2003	[Low estimate - high estimate]
Number of HIV-infected persons, ...	5 500	[2 700 - 9 000]
Adult HIV prevalence *(percentage of adults 15-49)*	0.2	[0.1 - 0.3]

Policy views

	1976	2003
Life expectancy...	..	Unacceptable
Under-five mortality..		Unacceptable
Maternal mortality..		Unacceptable
Level of concern about AIDS....................................		..

Life Expectancy at Birth

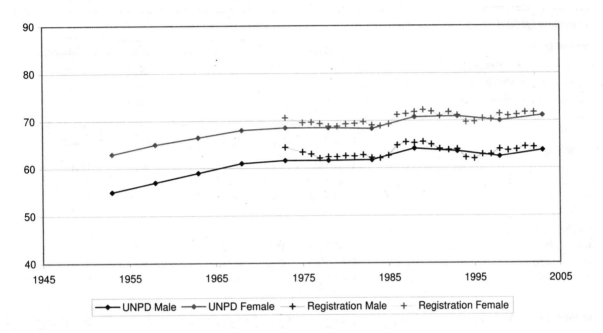

Infant Mortality Rate

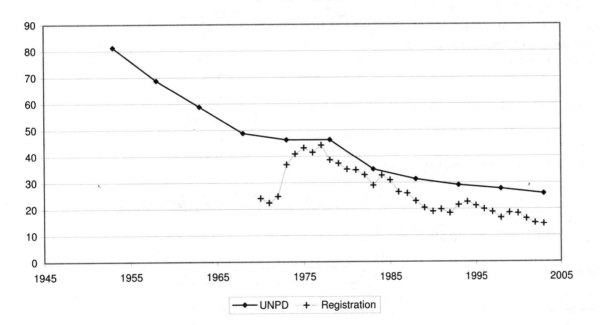

Indicator	Period							
	Earlier year				Later year			

I. Data and estimates from national and other sources

General mortality

	Year	Value			Year	Value		
Annual number of deaths *(thousands)*	1970	3.7			2003	4.0		
Annual number of deaths under age one *(thousands)*	1970	0.7			2003	0.1		
Crude death rate *(per 1 000 person-years)*	1970	8.2			2003	5.3		

	Year	Male	Female		Year	Male	Female	
Life expectancy *(years)*								
at birth	1963-1967	55.8	62.4		2001	71.0	79.4	
at age 15	1963-1967	47.9	54.6		..	..	..	
at age 60	1963-1967	12.9	16.6		..	..	..	
Survival probability								
from birth to age 15	1963-1967	0.88	0.90		..	..	..	
from age 15 to age 60	1963-1967	0.62	0.78		..	..	..	
from age 60 to age 80	1963-1967	0.20	0.37		..	..	..	

Infant and child mortality

	Year	Male	Female	Both sexes	Year	Male	Female	Both sexes
Infant mortality rate *(per 1 000 live births)*	1972-1976	48	36	42	2003	..	..	7
Mortality from age 1 to age 4 *(per 1 000 live births)*	1972-1976	9	8	9	..	..	..	..
Under-five mortality rate *(per 1 000 live births)*	1972-1976	57	44	51	..	..	..	..

II. Data and estimates from United Nations sources

United Nations Population Division estimates

	1990-1995	2000-2005
Annual number of deaths *(thousands)*	3	4
Crude death rate *(per 1 000 person-years)*	5	5
Life expectancy at birth *(years)*		
Male	69.4	71.3
Female	78.3	79.6
Under-five mortality rate *(per 1 000 live births)*	12	10

Maternal mortality

	2000
Maternal mortality ratio *(deaths per 100 000 births)*	..

HIV/AIDS

	2003	*[Low estimate - high estimate]*
Number of HIV-infected persons,	..	..
Adult HIV prevalence *(percentage of adults 15-49)*	..	..

Policy views

	1976	2003
Life expectancy	..	..
Under-five mortality		..
Maternal mortality		..
Level of concern about AIDS		..

Life Expectancy at Birth

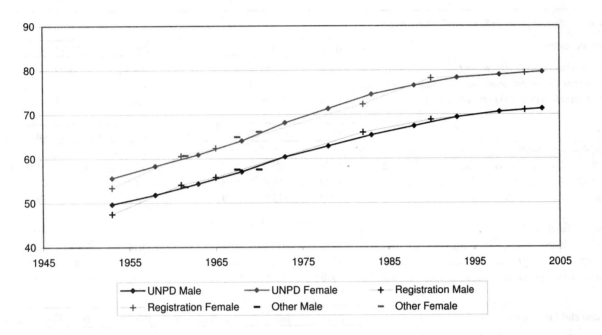

Infant Mortality Rate

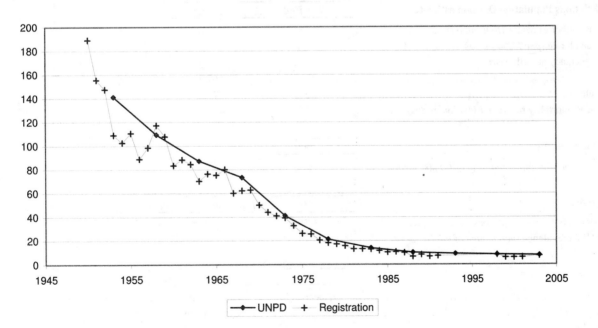

Indicator	Period						
	Earlier year				Later year		

I. Data and estimates from national and other sources

General mortality	Year	Value			Year	Value		
Annual number of deaths *(thousands)*	1970	193.3			2003	266.6		
Annual number of deaths under age one *(thousands)*	1970	21.1			2003	3.5		
Crude death rate *(per 1 000 person-years)*	1970	9.5			2003	12.3		

	Year	Male	Female		Year	Male	Female	
Life expectancy *(years)*								
at birth..	1970	65.7	70.2		2002	67.6	74.9	
at age 15...	1970	55.4	59.3		2002	54.6	61.6	
at age 60...	1970	15.8	17.9		2002	16.3	19.9	
Survival probability								
from birth to age 15..	1970	0.93	0.94		2002	0.97	0.98	
from age 15 to age 60..	1970	0.81	0.88		2002	0.76	0.89	
from age 60 to age 80..	1970	0.33	0.43		2002	0.36	0.52	

Infant and child mortality	Year	Male	Female	Both sexes	Year	Male	Female	Both sexes
Infant mortality rate *(per 1 000 live births)*	1970	51	42	47	2002	20	16	18
Mortality from age 1 to age 4 *(per 1 000 live births)*	1970	10	9	10	2002	4	3	3
Under-five mortality rate *(per 1 000 live births)*	1970	60	51	56	2002	24	19	22

II. Data and estimates from United Nations sources

United Nations Population Division estimates	1990-1995	2000-2005
Annual number of deaths *(thousands)*	261	267
Crude death rate *(per 1 000 person-years)*	11	12
Life expectancy at birth *(years)*		
Male..	65.8	67.7
Female...	73.2	75.0
Under-five mortality rate *(per 1 000 live births)*	29	22

Maternal mortality	2000
Maternal mortality ratio *(deaths per 100 000 births)*	49

HIV/AIDS	2003	*[Low estimate - high estimate]*
Number of HIV-infected persons, ...	6 500	[4 800 - 8 900]
Adult HIV prevalence *(percentage of adults 15-49)*	<0.1	[<0.2]

Policy views	1976	2003
Life expectancy..	Acceptable	Unacceptable
Under-five mortality..		Unacceptable
Maternal mortality...		Unacceptable
Level of concern about AIDS.....................................		Major concern

Life Expectancy at Birth

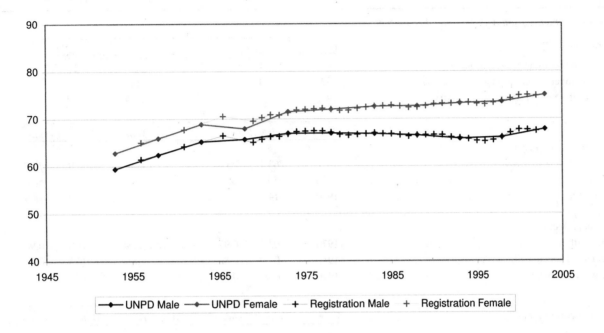

UNPD Male ◆ UNPD Female ◆ Registration Male + Registration Female +

Infant Mortality Rate

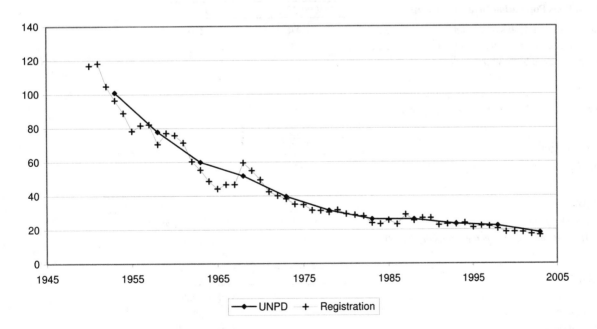

UNPD ◆ Registration +

I. Data and estimates from national and other sources

Indicator	Period				
	Earlier year			Later year	

General mortality

Indicator	Year	Value		Year	Value	
Annual number of deaths *(thousands)*	1970	1 131.2		2004	2 295.4	
Annual number of deaths under age one *(thousands)*	1970	43.5		2004	17.3	
Crude death rate *(per 1 000 person-years)*	1970	8.7		2004	16.0	

	Year	Male	Female	Year	Male	Female
Life expectancy *(years)*						
at birth	1970	63.1	73.4	2004	58.9	72.3
at age 15	1970	50.6	60.5	2004	45.1	58.4
at age 60	1970	14.8	19.5	2004	13.2	18.9
Survival probability						
from birth to age 15	1970	0.96	0.97	2004	0.98	0.98
from age 15 to age 60	1970	0.69	0.88	2004	0.53	0.83
from age 60 to age 80	1970	0.28	0.49	2004	0.23	0.48

Infant and child mortality

Indicator	Year	Male	Female	Both sexes	Year	Male	Female	Both sexes
Infant mortality rate *(per 1 000 live births)*	1970	26	19	22	2004	13	10	12
Mortality from age 1 to age 4 *(per 1 000 live births)*	1970	6	5	6	2004	3	3	3
Under-five mortality rate *(per 1 000 live births)*	1970	32	24	28	2004	16	13	15

II. Data and estimates from United Nations sources

United Nations Population Division estimates

Indicator	1990-1995	2000-2005
Annual number of deaths *(thousands)*	1 978	2 220
Crude death rate *(per 1 000 person-years)*	13	15
Life expectancy at birth *(years)*		
Male	60.6	59.1
Female	72.8	72.2
Under-five mortality rate *(per 1 000 live births)*	26	22

Maternal mortality

Indicator	2000
Maternal mortality ratio *(deaths per 100 000 births)*	67

HIV/AIDS

Indicator	2003	[Low estimate - high estimate]
Number of HIV-infected persons,	860 000	[420 000 - 1 400 000]
Adult HIV prevalence *(percentage of adults 15-49)*	1.1	[0.6 - 1.9]

Policy views

Indicator	1976	2003
Life expectancy	..	Unacceptable
Under-five mortality		Unacceptable
Maternal mortality		Unacceptable
Level of concern about AIDS		Major concern

Life Expectancy at Birth

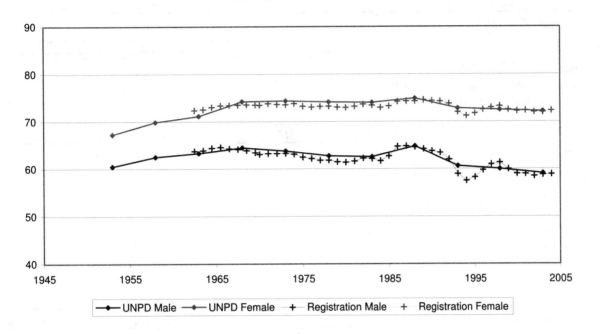

Infant Mortality Rate

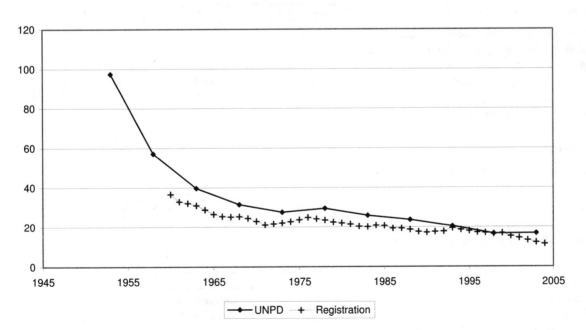

Indicator	Period			
	Earlier year		Later year	

I. Data and estimates from national and other sources

General mortality

	Year	Value	Year	Value
Annual number of deaths *(thousands)*	..	..	..	..
Annual number of deaths under age one *(thousands)*	..	..	..	..
Crude death rate *(per 1 000 person-years)*	..	..	..	..

	Year	Male	Female	Year	Male	Female
Life expectancy *(years)*						
at birth...	..	..	..	..	..	..
at age 15...	..	..	..	..	..	..
at age 60...	..	..	..	..	..	..
Survival probability						
from birth to age 15..	..	..	..	..	..	..
from age 15 to age 60..	..	..	..	..	..	..
from age 60 to age 80..	..	..	..	..	..	..

Infant and child mortality

	Year	Male	Female	Both sexes	Year	Male	Female	Both sexes
Infant mortality rate *(per 1 000 live births)*	1973	140	123	132	1990-2000	123	112	117
Mortality from age 1 to age 4 *(per 1 000 live births)*	1973	108	102	105	1990-2000	105	97	101
Under-five mortality rate *(per 1 000 live births)*	1973	233	213	223	1990-2000	215	198	207

II. Data and estimates from United Nations sources

United Nations Population Division estimates

	1990-1995	2000-2005
Annual number of deaths *(thousands)*	263	156
Crude death rate *(per 1 000 person-years)*	42	18
Life expectancy at birth *(years)*		
Male...	21.9	41.9
Female..	25.6	45.3
Under-five mortality rate *(per 1 000 live births)*	223	190

Maternal mortality

	2000
Maternal mortality ratio *(deaths per 100 000 births)*	1 400

HIV/AIDS

	2003	[Low estimate - high estimate]
Number of HIV-infected persons, ...	250 000	[170 000 - 380 000]
Adult HIV prevalence *(percentage of adults 15-49)*	5.1	[3.4 - 7.6]

Policy views

	1976	2003
Life expectancy...	Acceptable	Unacceptable
Under-five mortality...		Unacceptable
Maternal mortality...		Unacceptable
Level of concern about AIDS..................................		Major concern

Life Expectancy at Birth

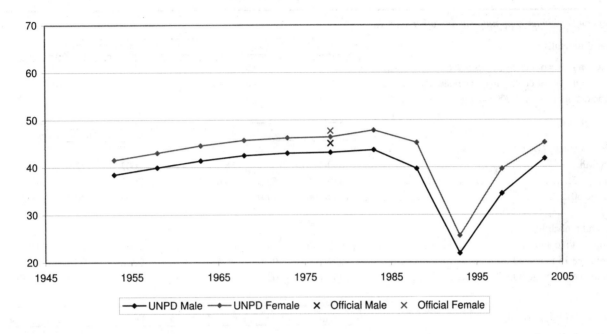

Infant Mortality Rate

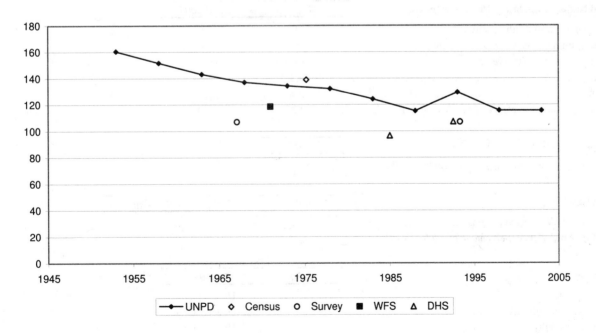

Indicator	Period					
	Earlier year			Later year		

I. Data and estimates from national and other sources

General mortality

	Year	Value			Year	Value	
Annual number of deaths *(thousands)*	1970	0.9			2002	1.0	
Annual number of deaths under age one *(thousands)*	1970	0.2			2002	0.0	
Crude death rate *(per 1 000 person-years)*	1970	8.4			2002	6.0	

	Year	Male	Female		Year	Male	Female
Life expectancy *(years)*							
at birth	1959-1961	55.1	58.5		2002	72.0	76.7
at age 15	1959-1961	52.5	55.4		2002	58.3	63.2
at age 60	1959-1961	17.0	18.9		2002	20.4	21.9
Survival probability							
from birth to age 15	1959-1961	0.81	0.83		2002	0.98	0.98
from age 15 to age 60	1959-1961	0.70	0.76		2002	0.79	0.89
from age 60 to age 80	1959-1961	0.38	0.46		2002	0.49	0.56

Infant and child mortality

	Year	Male	Female	Both sexes	Year	Male	Female	Both sexes
Infant mortality rate *(per 1 000 live births)*	1959-1961	110	104	107	2002	13	15	14
Mortality from age 1 to age 4 *(per 1 000 live births)*	1959-1961	71	64	68	2002	2	1	2
Under-five mortality rate *(per 1 000 live births)*	1959-1961	173	161	167	2002	15	16	15

II. Data and estimates from United Nations sources

United Nations Population Division estimates

	1990-1995	2000-2005
Annual number of deaths *(thousands)*	1	1
Crude death rate *(per 1 000 person-years)*	7	7
Life expectancy at birth *(years)*		
Male	69.3	70.8
Female	73.6	73.9
Under-five mortality rate *(per 1 000 live births)*	22	20

Maternal mortality

	2000
Maternal mortality ratio *(deaths per 100 000 births)*	..

HIV/AIDS

	2003	[Low estimate - high estimate]
Number of HIV-infected persons,	..	..
Adult HIV prevalence *(percentage of adults 15-49)*	..	..

Policy views

	1976	2003
Life expectancy	..	Unacceptable
Under-five mortality		Unacceptable
Maternal mortality		Unacceptable
Level of concern about AIDS		Major concern

Life Expectancy at Birth

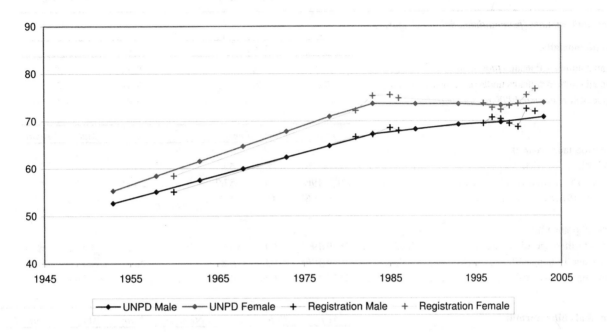

Infant Mortality Rate

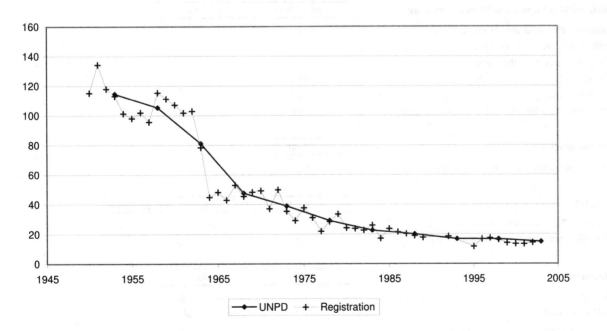

Indicator	Period				
	Earlier year			Later year	

I. Data and estimates from national and other sources

General mortality

	Year	Value		Year	Value
Annual number of deaths *(thousands)*	1970	0.7		2002	0.8
Annual number of deaths under age one *(thousands)*	1970	0.2		2002	0.0
Crude death rate *(per 1 000 person-years)*	1970	7.9		2002	7.1

	Year	Male	Female	Year	Male	Female
Life expectancy *(years)*						
at birth..	1959-1961	58.5	59.7	..	..	..
at age 15..	1959-1961	55.6	57.7	..	..	..
at age 60..	1959-1961	16.5	18.5	..	..	..
Survival probability						
from birth to age 15..............................	1959-1961	0.83	0.82	..	..	..
from age 15 to age 60...........................	1959-1961	0.80	0.82	..	..	..
from age 60 to age 80...........................	1959-1961	0.36	0.47	..	..	..

Infant and child mortality

	Year	Male	Female	Both sexes	Year	Male	Female	Both sexes
Infant mortality rate *(per 1 000 live births)*	1959-1961	118	113	115	2002	..	..	18
Mortality from age 1 to age 4 *(per 1 000 live births)*	1959-1961	57	72	64	..	..	..	..
Under-five mortality rate *(per 1 000 live births)*	1959-1961	168	176	172	..	..	..	..

II. Data and estimates from United Nations sources

United Nations Population Division estimates

	1990-1995	2000-2005
Annual number of deaths *(thousands)*	1	1
Crude death rate *(per 1 000 person-years)*	7	7
Life expectancy at birth *(years)*		
Male...	67.1	68.2
Female..	72.5	73.8
Under-five mortality rate *(per 1 000 live births)*	36	31

Maternal mortality

	2000
Maternal mortality ratio *(deaths per 100 000 births)*	..

HIV/AIDS

	2003	[Low estimate - high estimate]
Number of HIV-infected persons, ...	..	..
Adult HIV prevalence *(percentage of adults 15-49)*	..	..

Policy views

	1976	2003
Life expectancy..	..	Acceptable
Under-five mortality..		Unacceptable
Maternal mortality..		..
Level of concern about AIDS..................................		Major concern

Life Expectancy at Birth

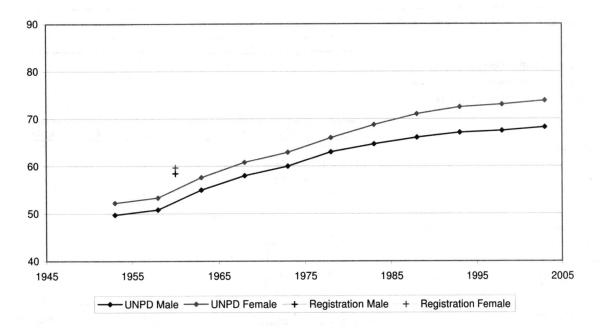

Infant Mortality Rate

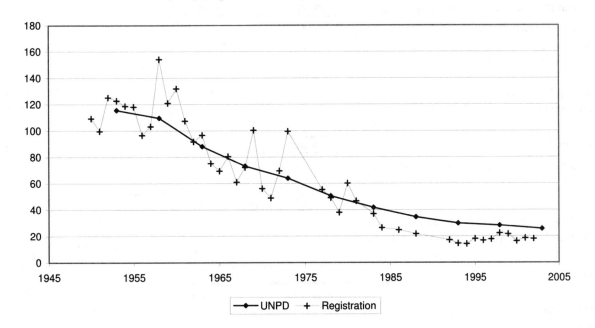

Indicator	Period				
	Earlier year			Later year	

I. Data and estimates from national and other sources

General mortality	Year	Value		Year	Value
Annual number of deaths *(thousands)*	..	..		..	..
Annual number of deaths under age one *(thousands)*	..	..		..	..
Crude death rate *(per 1 000 person-years)*	..	..		..	..

	Year	Male	Female	Year	Male	Female
Life expectancy *(years)*						
at birth..	1971	59.6	63.4	2001	71.8	73.8
at age 15...	1971	51.7	54.2	..	..	..
at age 60...	1971	16.2	17.1	..	..	..
Survival probability						
from birth to age 15.......................................	1971	0.89	0.91	..	..	..
from age 15 to age 60.....................................	1971	0.71	0.77	..	..	..
from age 60 to age 80.....................................	1971	0.38	0.42	..	..	..

Infant and child mortality	Year	Male	Female	Both sexes	Year	Male	Female	Both sexes
Infant mortality rate *(per 1 000 live births)*	1971	71	55	64	2000	..	..	18
Mortality from age 1 to age 4 *(per 1 000 live births)*	1971	26	23	24	..	..	..	..
Under-five mortality rate *(per 1 000 live births)*	1971	95	76	86	..	..	..	..

II. Data and estimates from United Nations sources

United Nations Population Division estimates	1990-1995	2000-2005
Annual number of deaths *(thousands)*	1	1
Crude death rate *(per 1 000 person-years)*	7	6
Life expectancy at birth *(years)*		
Male...	63.1	67.1
Female..	69.7	73.5
Under-five mortality rate *(per 1 000 live births)*	45	31

Maternal mortality	2000
Maternal mortality ratio *(deaths per 100 000 births)*	130

HIV/AIDS	2003	*[Low estimate - high estimate]*
Number of HIV-infected persons, ...	..	..
Adult HIV prevalence *(percentage of adults 15-49)*	..	..

Policy views	1976	2003
Life expectancy...	Acceptable	Unacceptable
Under-five mortality..		..
Maternal mortality..		..
Level of concern about AIDS....................................		Major concern

Life Expectancy at Birth

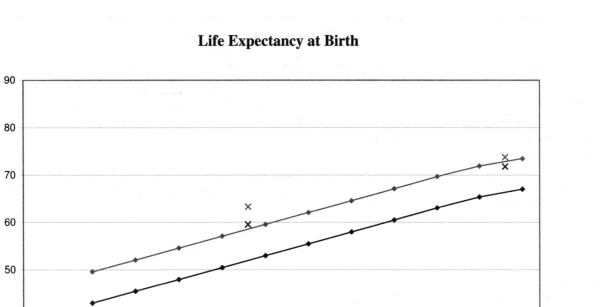

Infant Mortality Rate

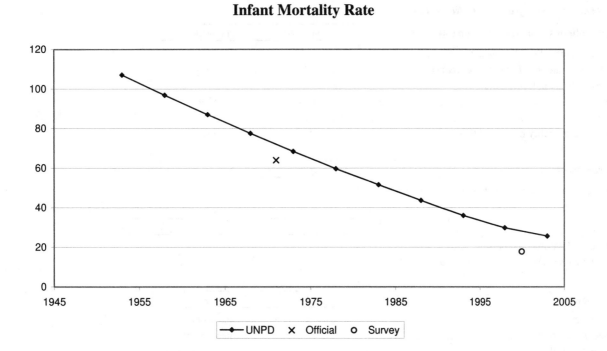

Indicator	Period				
	Earlier year			Later year	

I. Data and estimates from national and other sources

General mortality

	Year	Value		Year	Value
Annual number of deaths *(thousands)*	1970	0.9		1993	1.1
Annual number of deaths under age one *(thousands)*	1970	0.2		1993	0.3
Crude death rate *(per 1 000 person-years)*	1970	12.5		1993	9.0

	Year	Male	Female	Year	Male	Female
Life expectancy *(years)*						
at birth..	..	..	..	..	..	..
at age 15...	..	..	..	..	..	..
at age 60...	..	..	..	..	..	..
Survival probability						
from birth to age 15...	..	..	..	..	..	..
from age 15 to age 60......................................	..	..	..	..	..	..
from age 60 to age 80......................................	..	..	..	..	..	..

Infant and child mortality

	Year	Male	Female	Both sexes	Year	Male	Female	Both sexes
Infant mortality rate *(per 1 000 live births)*	..	..	..	..	1996	..	..	75
Mortality from age 1 to age 4 *(per 1 000 live births)*	..	..	..	..	..	..	..	..
Under-five mortality rate *(per 1 000 live births)*	..	..	..	..	1996	..	..	119

II. Data and estimates from United Nations sources

United Nations Population Division estimates

	1990-1995	2000-2005
Annual number of deaths *(thousands)*	1	1
Crude death rate *(per 1 000 person-years)*	10	9
Life expectancy at birth *(years)*		
Male...	61.0	61.9
Female..	62.7	63.8
Under-five mortality rate *(per 1 000 live births)*	119	112

Maternal mortality

	2000
Maternal mortality ratio *(deaths per 100 000 births)*	..

HIV/AIDS

	2003	[Low estimate - high estimate]
Number of HIV-infected persons, ...	..	..
Adult HIV prevalence *(percentage of adults 15-49)*	..	..

Policy views

	1976	2003
Life expectancy..	Unacceptable	Unacceptable
Under-five mortality..		Unacceptable
Maternal mortality..		Unacceptable
Level of concern about AIDS...................................		Major concern

Life Expectancy at Birth

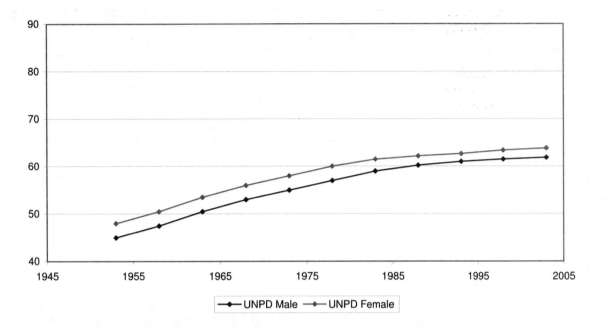

Infant Mortality Rate

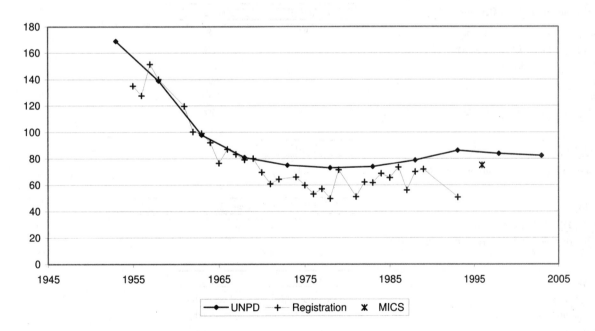

Indicator	Period							
	Earlier year				*Later year*			

I. Data and estimates from national and other sources

General mortality

	Year	Value			Year	Value		
Annual number of deaths *(thousands)*	..	..			..	..		
Annual number of deaths under age one *(thousands)*	..	..			..	..		
Crude death rate *(per 1 000 person-years)*	..	..			..	..		

	Year	Male	Female		Year	Male	Female	
Life expectancy *(years)*								
at birth..	..	..	..		..	..	..	
at age 15..	..	..	..		..	..	..	
at age 60..	..	..	..		..	..	..	
Survival probability								
from birth to age 15.......................................	..	..	..		..	..	..	
from age 15 to age 60.....................................	..	..	..		..	..	..	
from age 60 to age 80.....................................	..	..	..		..	..	..	

Infant and child mortality

	Year	Male	Female	Both sexes	Year	Male	Female	Both sexes
Infant mortality rate *(per 1 000 live births)*	..	..	..	..	1992-1996	21	22	21
Mortality from age 1 to age 4 *(per 1 000 live births)*	..	..	..	..	1992-1996	9	5	8
Under-five mortality rate *(per 1 000 live births)*	1980	89	76	83	1992-1996	30	27	29

II. Data and estimates from United Nations sources

United Nations Population Division estimates

	1990-1995	2000-2005
Annual number of deaths *(thousands)*	81	89
Crude death rate *(per 1 000 person-years)*	5	4
Life expectancy at birth *(years)*		
Male..	67.4	69.9
Female...	70.8	73.8
Under-five mortality rate *(per 1 000 live births)*	39	27

Maternal mortality

	2000
Maternal mortality ratio *(deaths per 100 000 births)*	23

HIV/AIDS

	2003	*[Low estimate - high estimate]*
Number of HIV-infected persons, ...	..	..
Adult HIV prevalence *(percentage of adults 15-49)*	..	..

Policy views

	1976	2003
Life expectancy...	Unacceptable	Acceptable
Under-five mortality..		Acceptable
Maternal mortality..		Acceptable
Level of concern about AIDS.................................		Major concern

Life Expectancy at Birth

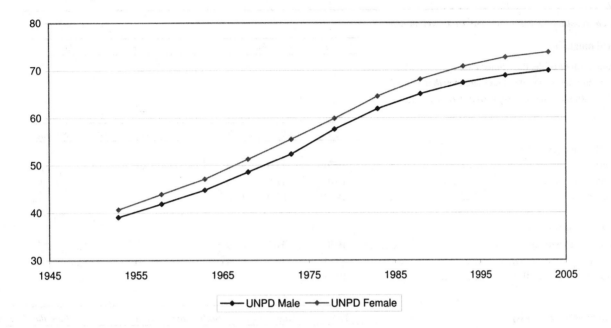

— UNPD Male — UNPD Female

Infant Mortality Rate

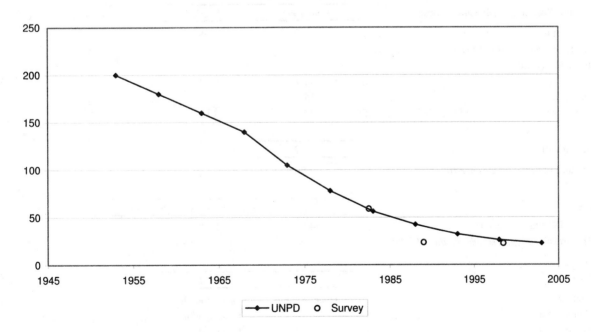

— UNPD ○ Survey

Indicator	Period					
	Earlier year				Later year	

I. Data and estimates from national and other sources

General mortality

	Year	Value			Year	Value
Annual number of deaths *(thousands)*	..	..			..	..
Annual number of deaths under age one *(thousands)*	..	..			..	..
Crude death rate *(per 1 000 person-years)*	..	..			..	..

	Year	Male	Female	Year	Male	Female
Life expectancy *(years)*						
at birth....................	1970	43.0	44.2	..	..	..
at age 15....................	1970	47.8	48.0	..	..	..
at age 60....................	1970	14.0	15.0	..	..	..
Survival probability						
from birth to age 15....................	1970	0.67	0.69	..	..	..
from age 15 to age 60....................	1970	0.64	0.64	..	..	..
from age 60 to age 80....................	1970	0.24	0.27	..	..	..

Infant and child mortality

	Year	Male	Female	Both sexes	Year	Male	Female	Both sexes
Infant mortality rate *(per 1 000 live births)*	1973	171	148	160	1989-1999	74	66	70
Mortality from age 1 to age 4 *(per 1 000 live births)*	1973	127	137	132	1989-1999	82	80	81
Under-five mortality rate *(per 1 000 live births)*	1973	277	265	271	1989-1999	150	141	145

II. Data and estimates from United Nations sources

United Nations Population Division estimates

	1990-1995	2000-2005
Annual number of deaths *(thousands)*	112	129
Crude death rate *(per 1 000 person-years)*	13	12
Life expectancy at birth *(years)*		
Male....................	52.9	54.4
Female....................	55.3	56.8
Under-five mortality rate *(per 1 000 live births)*	144	133

Maternal mortality

	2000
Maternal mortality ratio *(deaths per 100 000 births)*	690

HIV/AIDS

	2003	[Low estimate - high estimate]
Number of HIV-infected persons, ...	44 000	[22 000 - 89 000]
Adult HIV prevalence *(percentage of adults 15-49)*	0.8	[0.4 - 1.7]

Policy views

	1976	2003
Life expectancy....................	Unacceptable	Unacceptable
Under-five mortality....................		Unacceptable
Maternal mortality....................		Unacceptable
Level of concern about AIDS....................		Major concern

Life Expectancy at Birth

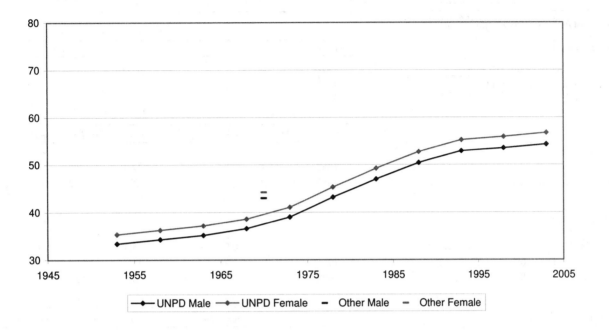

Infant Mortality Rate

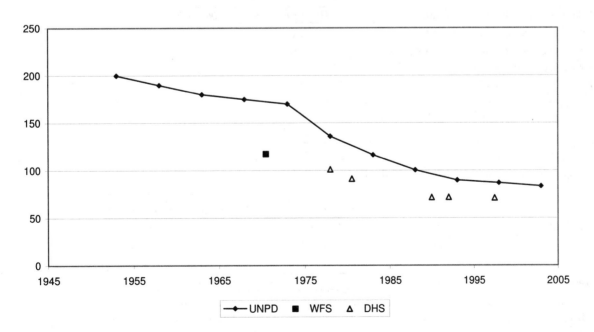

Indicator	Period			
	Earlier year		Later year	

I. Data and estimates from national and other sources

General mortality

	Year	Value	Year	Value
Annual number of deaths *(thousands)*	1970	81.6	2003	111.1
Annual number of deaths under age one *(thousands)*	1970	8.6	2003	0.8
Crude death rate *(per 1 000 person-years)*	1970	9.2	2003	13.7

	Year	Male	Female	Year	Male	Female
Life expectancy *(years)*						
at birth...	1982	67.8	72.6	2001	70.7	75.6
at age 15...	1982	56.1	60.8	2001	57.2	61.7
at age 60...	1982	16.4	18.8	2001	17.2	19.6
Survival probability						
from birth to age 15..	1982	0.95	0.96	2001	0.98	0.99
from age 15 to age 60..	1982	0.81	0.90	2001	0.82	0.90
from age 60 to age 80..	1982	0.36	0.48	2001	0.38	0.49

Infant and child mortality	Year	Male	Female	Both sexes	Year	Male	Female	Both sexes
Infant mortality rate *(per 1 000 live births)*	1982	38	35	36	2001	15	11	13
Mortality from age 1 to age 4 *(per 1 000 live births)*	1982	5	5	5	2001	3	2	2
Under-five mortality rate *(per 1 000 live births)*	1982	43	39	41	2001	18	13	16

II. Data and estimates from United Nations sources

United Nations Population Division estimates	1990-1995	2000-2005
Annual number of deaths *(thousands)*	104	112
Crude death rate *(per 1 000 person-years)*	10	11
Life expectancy at birth *(years)*		
Male...	69.2	70.9
Female..	74.5	75.6
Under-five mortality rate *(per 1 000 live births)*	20	15

Maternal mortality	2000
Maternal mortality ratio *(deaths per 100 000 births)*	11

HIV/AIDS	2003	[Low estimate - high estimate]
Number of HIV-infected persons, ...	10 000	[3 400 - 20 000]
Adult HIV prevalence *(percentage of adults 15-49)*	0.2	[0.1 - 0.4]

Policy views	1976	2003
Life expectancy..	..	Unacceptable
Under-five mortality...		Unacceptable
Maternal mortality..		Acceptable
Level of concern about AIDS..................................		Major concern

Life Expectancy at Birth

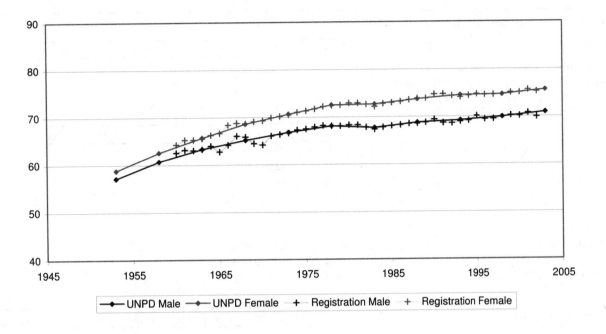

Infant Mortality Rate

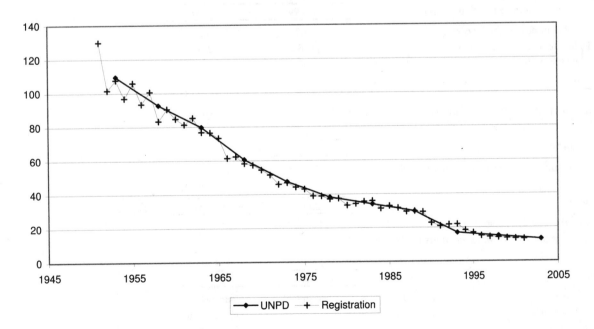

Indicator	Period					
	Earlier year				Later year	

I. Data and estimates from national and other sources

General mortality

	Year	Value			Year	Value	
Annual number of deaths *(thousands)*	..	..			..	..	
Annual number of deaths under age one *(thousands)*	..	..			..	..	
Crude death rate *(per 1 000 person-years)*	..	..			..	..	

	Year	Male	Female		Year	Male	Female
Life expectancy *(years)*							
at birth..	1974	32.9	35.8		..	..	..
at age 15...	1974	40.4	41.6		..	..	..
at age 60...	1974	12.8	13.0		..	..	..
Survival probability							
from birth to age 15...............................	1974	0.58	0.62		..	..	..
from age 15 to age 60.............................	1974	0.48	0.50		..	..	..
from age 60 to age 80.............................	1974	0.21	0.22		..	..	..

Infant and child mortality

	Year	Male	Female	Both sexes	Year	Male	Female	Both sexes
Infant mortality rate *(per 1 000 live births)*	..	..	..	..	1995	..	..	185
Mortality from age 1 to age 4 *(per 1 000 live births)*	..	..	..	..	..	..	..	..
Under-five mortality rate *(per 1 000 live births)*	..	..	..	..	1996	..	..	310

II. Data and estimates from United Nations sources

United Nations Population Division estimates

	1990-1995	2000-2005
Annual number of deaths *(thousands)*	107	119
Crude death rate *(per 1 000 person-years)*	26	24
Life expectancy at birth *(years)*		
Male...	37.0	39.3
Female..	39.7	42.0
Under-five mortality rate *(per 1 000 live births)*	331	290

Maternal mortality

	2000
Maternal mortality ratio *(deaths per 100 000 births)*	2 000

HIV/AIDS

	2003	[Low estimate - high estimate]
Number of HIV-infected persons, ...	..	..
Adult HIV prevalence *(percentage of adults 15-49)*	..	..

Policy views

	1976	2003
Life expectancy...	Unacceptable	Unacceptable
Under-five mortality..		Unacceptable
Maternal mortality...		Unacceptable
Level of concern about AIDS..................................		Major concern

Life Expectancy at Birth

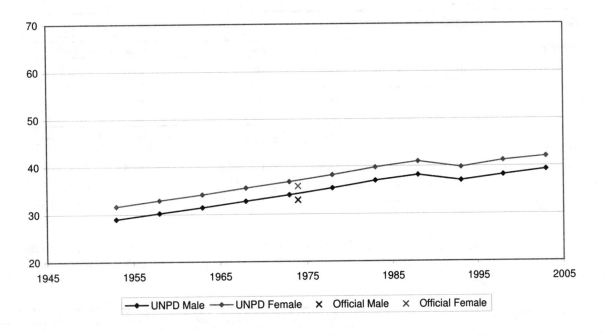

Infant Mortality Rate

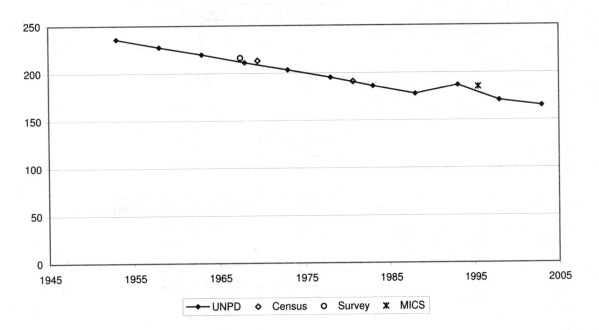

Indicator	Period							
	Earlier year				**Later year**			

I. Data and estimates from national and other sources

General mortality

	Year	Value			Year	Value		
Annual number of deaths *(thousands)*	1970	10.7			2004	15.9		
Annual number of deaths under age one *(thousands)*	1970	1.0			2004	0.1		
Crude death rate *(per 1 000 person-years)*	1970	5.2			2004	3.7		

	Year	Male	Female		Year	Male	Female	
Life expectancy *(years)*								
at birth...	1970	65.1	70.0		2003	76.9	80.9	
at age 15...	1970	52.3	56.9		2003	62.3	66.2	
at age 60...	1970	12.9	15.6		2003	20.2	22.9	
Survival probability								
from birth to age 15...	1970	0.97	0.97		2003	0.99	1.00	
from age 15 to age 60...	1970	0.77	0.86		2003	0.91	0.95	
from age 60 to age 80...	..	..	..		2003	0.55	0.68	

Infant and child mortality

	Year	Male	Female	Both sexes	Year	Male	Female	Both sexes
Infant mortality rate *(per 1 000 live births)*	1975	17	12	15	2003	3	2	3
Mortality from age 1 to age 4 *(per 1 000 live births)*	1975	2	2	2	2003	1	1	1
Under-five mortality rate *(per 1 000 live births)*	1975	19	15	17	2003	4	3	3

II. Data and estimates from United Nations sources

United Nations Population Division estimates

	1990-1995	2000-2005
Annual number of deaths *(thousands)*	16	21
Crude death rate *(per 1 000 person-years)*	5	5
Life expectancy at birth *(years)*		
Male..	73.9	76.7
Female...	78.3	80.5
Under-five mortality rate *(per 1 000 live births)*	7	4

Maternal mortality

	2000
Maternal mortality ratio *(deaths per 100 000 births)*	30

HIV/AIDS

	2003	*[Low estimate - high estimate]*
Number of HIV-infected persons, ...	4 100	[1 300 - 8 000]
Adult HIV prevalence *(percentage of adults 15-49)*	0.2	[0.1 - 0.5]

Policy views

	1976	2003
Life expectancy..	Acceptable	Acceptable
Under-five mortality..		Acceptable
Maternal mortality..		Acceptable
Level of concern about AIDS....................................		Major concern

Life Expectancy at Birth

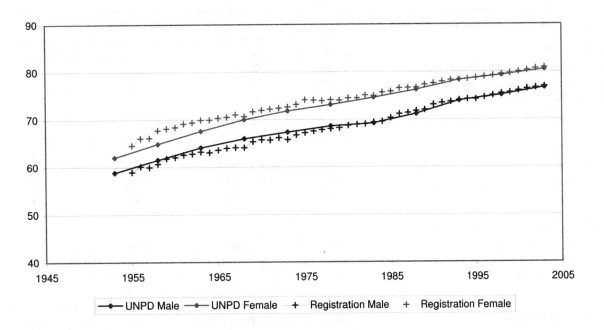

Infant Mortality Rate

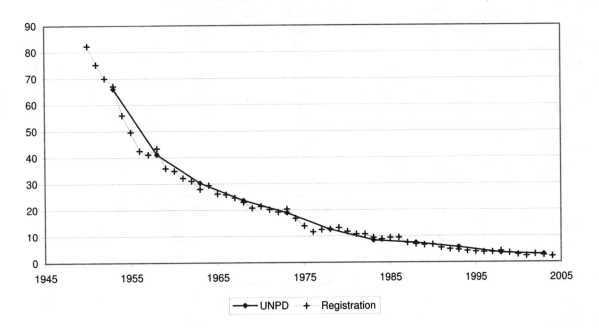

Indicator	Period							
	Earlier year				Later year			

I. Data and estimates from national and other sources

General mortality

	Year	Value			Year	Value		
Annual number of deaths *(thousands)*	1970	42.2			2003	52.2		
Annual number of deaths under age one *(thousands)*	1970	2.1			2003	0.4		
Crude death rate *(per 1 000 person-years)*	1970	9.3			2003	9.7		

	Year	Male	Female		Year	Male	Female	
Life expectancy *(years)*								
at birth...	1970	66.7	72.9		2002	69.9	77.6	
at age 15..	1970	54.5	60.4		2002	55.6	63.5	
at age 60..	1970	15.7	18.7		2002	16.4	20.9	
Survival probability								
from birth to age 15.......................................	1982	0.97	0.98		2002	0.99	0.99	
from age 15 to age 60.....................................	1982	0.76	0.90		2002	0.79	0.92	
from age 60 to age 80.....................................	1982	0.31	0.49		2002	0.36	0.58	

Infant and child mortality

	Year	Male	Female	Both sexes	Year	Male	Female	Both sexes
Infant mortality rate *(per 1 000 live births)*	1982	20	15	18	2002	7	8	8
Mortality from age 1 to age 4 *(per 1 000 live births)*	1982	3	2	3	2002	1	1	1
Under-five mortality rate *(per 1 000 live births)*	1982	23	18	20	2002	9	9	9

II. Data and estimates from United Nations sources

United Nations Population Division estimates

	1990-1995	2000-2005
Annual number of deaths *(thousands)*	53	52
Crude death rate *(per 1 000 person-years)*	10	10
Life expectancy at birth *(years)*		
Male..	67.8	70.0
Female...	76.2	77.9
Under-five mortality rate *(per 1 000 live births)*	15	10

Maternal mortality

	2000
Maternal mortality ratio *(deaths per 100 000 births)*	3

HIV/AIDS

	2003	[Low estimate - high estimate]
Number of HIV-infected persons, ...	<200	[<400]
Adult HIV prevalence *(percentage of adults 15-49)*	<0.1	[<0.2]

Policy views

	1976	2003
Life expectancy...	..	Unacceptable
Under-five mortality..		Acceptable
Maternal mortality..		Acceptable
Level of concern about AIDS.................................		Major concern

Life Expectancy at Birth

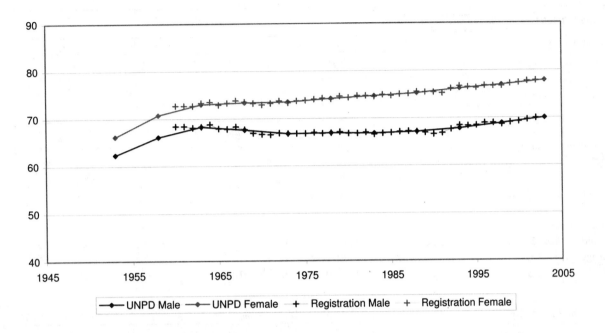

Infant Mortality Rate

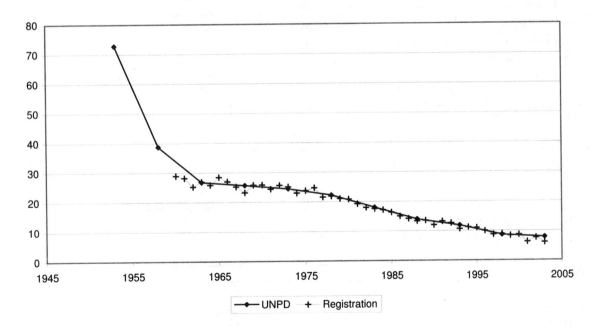

Indicator	Period							
	Earlier year				Later year			

I. Data and estimates from national and other sources

General mortality

	Year	Value			Year	Value		
Annual number of deaths *(thousands)*	1970	17.4			2004	18.5		
Annual number of deaths under age one *(thousands)*	1970	0.7			2004	0.1		
Crude death rate *(per 1 000 person-years)*	1970	10.1			2004	9.3		

	Year	Male	Female		Year	Male	Female	
Life expectancy *(years)*								
at birth...	1970-1972	65.9	73.4		2000-2002	72.3	80.2	
at age 15..	1970-1972	53.2	60.6		2000-2002	57.8	65.6	
at age 60..	1970-1972	15.2	18.9		2000-2002	17.8	23.1	
Survival probability								
from birth to age 15..	1970-1972	0.96	0.97		2000-2002	0.99	0.99	
from age 15 to age 60...	1970-1972	0.75	0.89		2000-2002	0.83	0.93	
from age 60 to age 80...	1970-1972	0.27	0.45		2000-2002	0.42	0.67	

Infant and child mortality

	Year	Male	Female	Both sexes	Year	Male	Female	Both sexes
Infant mortality rate *(per 1 000 live births)*	1970-1972	26	22	24	2000-2002	6	4	5
Mortality from age 1 to age 4 *(per 1 000 live births)*	1970-1972	4	4	4	2000-2002	1	1	1
Under-five mortality rate *(per 1 000 live births)*	1970-1972	30	26	28	2000-2002	6	5	5

II. Data and estimates from United Nations sources

United Nations Population Division estimates

	1990-1995	2000-2005
Annual number of deaths *(thousands)*	20	19
Crude death rate *(per 1 000 person-years)*	10	10
Life expectancy at birth *(years)*		
Male..	69.7	72.6
Female...	77.4	79.9
Under-five mortality rate *(per 1 000 live births)*	9	7

Maternal mortality

	2000
Maternal mortality ratio *(deaths per 100 000 births)*	17

HIV/AIDS

	2003	*[Low estimate - high estimate]*
Number of HIV-infected persons, ...	<500	[<1 000]
Adult HIV prevalence *(percentage of adults 15-49)*	<0.1	[<0.2]

Policy views

	1976	2003
Life expectancy..	..	Acceptable
Under-five mortality...		Acceptable
Maternal mortality..		Acceptable
Level of concern about AIDS......................................		Minor concern

Life Expectancy at Birth

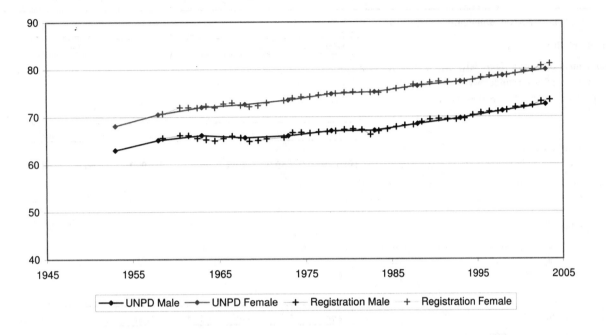

UNPD Male ◆ UNPD Female + Registration Male + Registration Female

Infant Mortality Rate

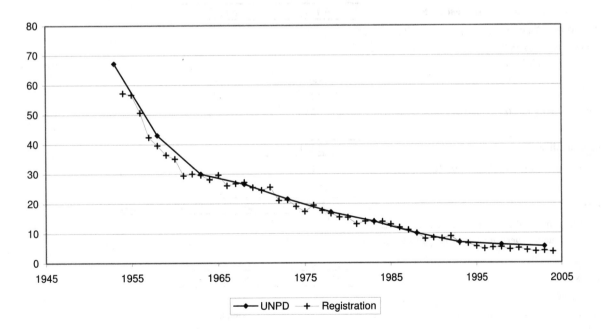

◆ UNPD + Registration

Indicator	Period			
	Earlier year		Later year	

I. Data and estimates from national and other sources

General mortality	Year	Value	Year	Value
Annual number of deaths *(thousands)*	..	..	..	..
Annual number of deaths under age one *(thousands)*	..	..	..	..
Crude death rate *(per 1 000 person-years)*	..	..	..	..

	Year	Male	Female	Year	Male	Female
Life expectancy *(years)*						
at birth...	1980-1984	59.9	61.4	1999	60.6	61.6
at age 15...	..	..	..	..	..	..
at age 60...	..	..	..	..	..	..
Survival probability						
from birth to age 15...	..	..	..	..	..	..
from age 15 to age 60...	..	..	..	..	..	..
from age 60 to age 80...	..	..	..	..	..	..

Infant and child mortality	Year	Male	Female	Both sexes	Year	Male	Female	Both sexes
Infant mortality rate *(per 1 000 live births)*	..	..	..	..	1999	..	..	66
Mortality from age 1 to age 4 *(per 1 000 live births)*	..	..	..	..	..	..	..	..
Under-five mortality rate *(per 1 000 live births)*	..	..	..	..	..	..	..	..

II. Data and estimates from United Nations sources

United Nations Population Division estimates	1990-1995	2000-2005
Annual number of deaths *(thousands)*	3	3
Crude death rate *(per 1 000 person-years)*	8	7
Life expectancy at birth *(years)*		
Male..	60.4	61.6
Female...	61.5	62.9
Under-five mortality rate *(per 1 000 live births)*	63	58

Maternal mortality	2000
Maternal mortality ratio *(deaths per 100 000 births)*	130

HIV/AIDS	2003	[Low estimate - high estimate]
Number of HIV-infected persons, ...	..	..
Adult HIV prevalence *(percentage of adults 15-49)*	..	..

Policy views	1976	2003
Life expectancy..	..	Unacceptable
Under-five mortality..		Unacceptable
Maternal mortality..		Unacceptable
Level of concern about AIDS....................................		Major concern

Life Expectancy at Birth

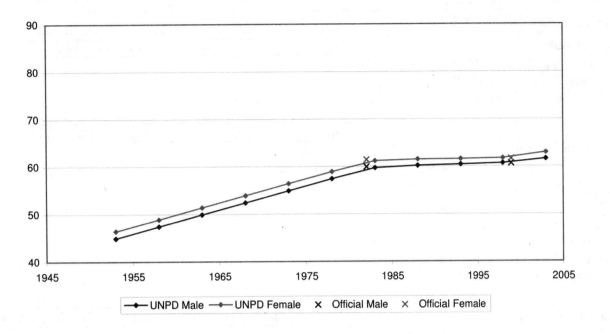

Infant Mortality Rate

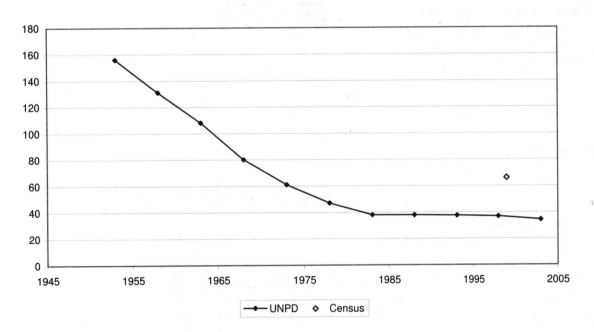

Indicator	Period				
	Earlier year			Later year	

I. Data and estimates from national and other sources

General mortality

	Year	Value		Year	Value	
Annual number of deaths *(thousands)*	..	..		..	..	
Annual number of deaths under age one *(thousands)*	..	..		..	..	
Crude death rate *(per 1 000 person-years)*	..	..		..	..	

	Year	Male	Female	Year	Male	Female
Life expectancy *(years)*						
at birth..	..	..	..	..	..	..
at age 15..	..	..	..	..	..	..
at age 60..	..	..	..	..	..	..
Survival probability						
from birth to age 15..	..	..	..	..	..	..
from age 15 to age 60..	..	..	..	..	..	..
from age 60 to age 80..	..	..	..	..	..	..

Infant and child mortality

	Year	Male	Female	Both sexes	Year	Male	Female	Both sexes
Infant mortality rate *(per 1 000 live births)*	..	..	..	..	1996	..	..	140
Mortality from age 1 to age 4 *(per 1 000 live births)*	..	..	..	..	..	..	..	..
Under-five mortality rate *(per 1 000 live births)*	..	..	..	..	1996	..	..	237

II. Data and estimates from United Nations sources

United Nations Population Division estimates	1990-1995	2000-2005
Annual number of deaths *(thousands)*	153	140
Crude death rate *(per 1 000 person-years)*	24	18
Life expectancy at birth *(years)*		
Male...	38.0	45.0
Female..	41.4	47.3
Under-five mortality rate *(per 1 000 live births)*	270	211

Maternal mortality	2000
Maternal mortality ratio *(deaths per 100 000 births)*	1 100

HIV/AIDS	2003	[Low estimate - high estimate]
Number of HIV-infected persons, ...	..	..
Adult HIV prevalence *(percentage of adults 15-49)*	..	..

Policy views	1976	2003
Life expectancy..	Unacceptable	Unacceptable
Under-five mortality...		Unacceptable
Maternal mortality...		Unacceptable
Level of concern about AIDS......................................		..

Life Expectancy at Birth

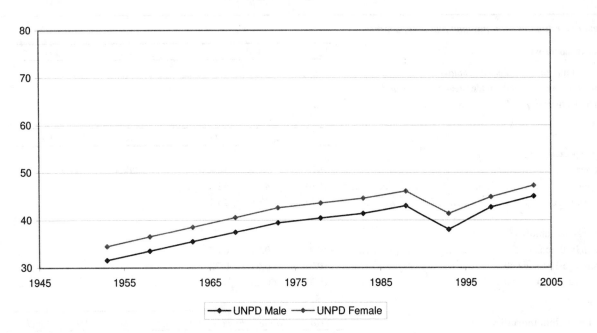

Infant Mortality Rate

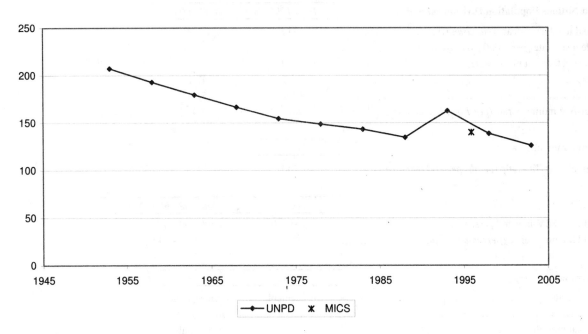

Indicator	Period						
	Earlier year				Later year		

I. Data and estimates from national and other sources

General mortality

	Year	Value			Year	Value	
Annual number of deaths *(thousands)*	..	..			..	..	
Annual number of deaths under age one *(thousands)*	..	..			..	..	
Crude death rate *(per 1 000 person-years)*	..	..			..	..	

	Year	Male	Female		Year	Male	Female
Life expectancy *(years)*							
at birth	1970	51.1	56.4		2004	49.9	52.9
at age 15	1970	47.2	52.7		..	..	..
at age 60	1970	13.8	16.5		..	..	..
Survival probability							
from birth to age 15	1970	0.82	0.83		..	..	..
from age 15 to age 60	1970	0.61	0.72		..	..	..
from age 60 to age 80	1970	0.25	0.39		..	..	..

Infant and child mortality

	Year	Male	Female	Both sexes	Year	Male	Female	Both sexes
Infant mortality rate *(per 1 000 live births)*	1987	50	40	45	1988-1998	49	35	42
Mortality from age 1 to age 4 *(per 1 000 live births)*	1987	24	22	23	1988-1998	18	13	15
Under-five mortality rate *(per 1 000 live births)*	1987	72	61	67	1988-1998	66	48	57

II. Data and estimates from United Nations sources

United Nations Population Division estimates

	1990-1995	2000-2005
Annual number of deaths *(thousands)*	317	754
Crude death rate *(per 1 000 person-years)*	8	16
Life expectancy at birth *(years)*		
Male	58.5	47.1
Female	65.9	51.0
Under-five mortality rate *(per 1 000 live births)*	61	74

Maternal mortality

	2000
Maternal mortality ratio *(deaths per 100 000 births)*	230

HIV/AIDS

	2003	[Low estimate - high estimate]
Number of HIV-infected persons,	5 300 000	[4 500 000 - 6 200 000]
Adult HIV prevalence *(percentage of adults 15-49)*	21.5	[18.5 - 24.9]

Policy views

	1976	2003
Life expectancy	Unacceptable	Unacceptable
Under-five mortality		Unacceptable
Maternal mortality		Unacceptable
Level of concern about AIDS		Major concern

Life Expectancy at Birth

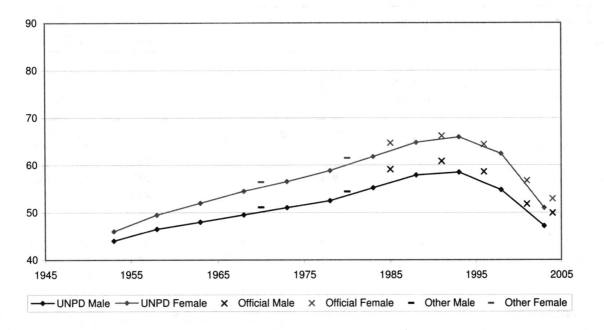

Infant Mortality Rate

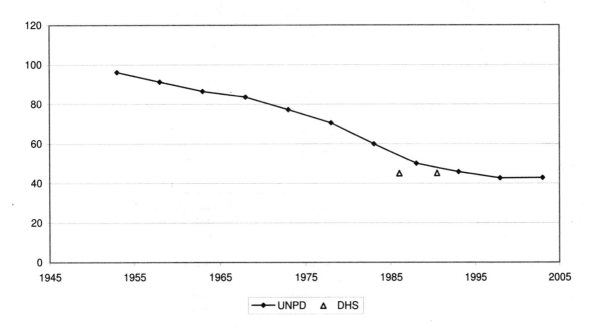

Indicator	Period				
	Earlier year			*Later year*	

I. Data and estimates from national and other sources

General mortality

	Year	Value		Year	Value	
Annual number of deaths *(thousands)*	1970	280.2		2003	383.7	
Annual number of deaths under age one *(thousands)*	1970	17.4		2003	1.6	
Crude death rate *(per 1 000 person-years)*	1970	8.3		2003	9.2	

	Year	Male	Female	Year	Male	Female
Life expectancy *(years)*						
at birth..	1970	69.7	75.0	2002	76.2	83.1
at age 15..	1970	57.1	62.0	2002	61.8	68.5
at age 60..	1970	17.0	20.1	2002	20.7	25.3
Survival probability						
from birth to age 15...	1970	0.96	0.97	2002	0.99	0.99
from age 15 to age 60..	1970	0.84	0.90	2002	0.88	0.95
from age 60 to age 80..	1970	0.38	0.53	2002	0.55	0.76

Infant and child mortality

	Year	Male	Female	Both sexes	Year	Male	Female	Both sexes
Infant mortality rate *(per 1 000 live births)*	1970	31	25	28	2002	5	4	4
Mortality from age 1 to age 4 *(per 1 000 live births)*	1970	4	3	4	2002	1	1	1
Under-five mortality rate *(per 1 000 live births)*	1970	35	28	32	2002	6	5	5

II. Data and estimates from United Nations sources

United Nations Population Division estimates

	1990-1995	*2000-2005*
Annual number of deaths *(thousands)*	364	369
Crude death rate *(per 1 000 person-years)*	9	9
Life expectancy at birth *(years)*		
Male..	73.8	75.8
Female...	81.0	83.1
Under-five mortality rate *(per 1 000 live births)*	8	6

Maternal mortality

	2000
Maternal mortality ratio *(deaths per 100 000 births)*	4

HIV/AIDS

	2003	*[Low estimate - high estimate]*
Number of HIV-infected persons, ...	140 000	[67 000 - 220 000]
Adult HIV prevalence *(percentage of adults 15-49)*	0.7	[0.3 - 1.1]

Policy views

	1976	*2003*
Life expectancy...	Acceptable	Acceptable
Under-five mortality..		Acceptable
Maternal mortality..		Acceptable
Level of concern about AIDS...................................		Major concern

Life Expectancy at Birth

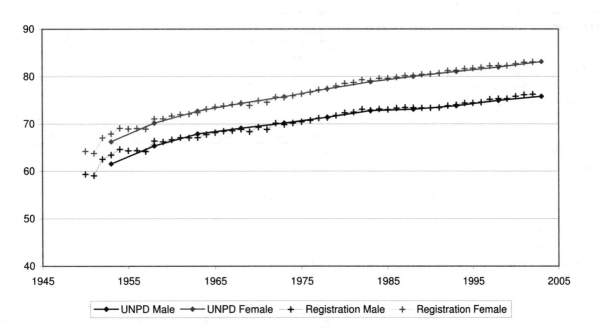

Infant Mortality Rate

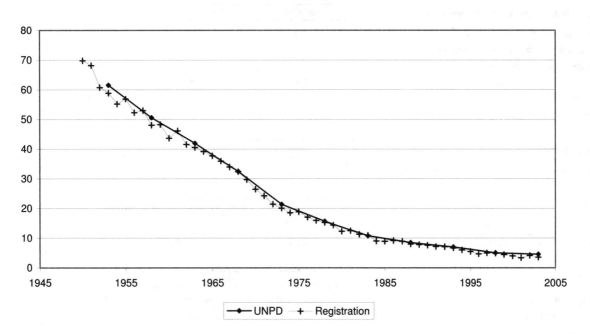

Indicator	Period					
	Earlier year				Later year	

I. Data and estimates from national and other sources

General mortality

	Year	Value			Year	Value	
Annual number of deaths *(thousands)*	1970	94.1			2002	110.6	
Annual number of deaths under age one *(thousands)*	1972	17.6			2001	4.3	
Crude death rate *(per 1 000 person-years)*	1970	7.5			2002	5.8	

	Year	Male	Female		Year	Male	Female
Life expectancy *(years)*							
at birth...	1967	64.8	66.9		1991	68.9	73.6
at age 15...	1967	55.8	57.7		..	..	..
at age 60...	1967	17.0	17.8		..	..	..
Survival probability							
from birth to age 15..	1967	0.91	0.92		..	..	..
from age 15 to age 60..	1967	0.80	0.85		..	..	..
from age 60 to age 80..	..	..	..		..	..	..

Infant and child mortality

	Year	Male	Female	Both sexes	Year	Male	Female	Both sexes
Infant mortality rate *(per 1 000 live births)*	1975	51	41	46	1983-1993	31	20	25
Mortality from age 1 to age 4 *(per 1 000 live births)*	1975	21	23	22	1983-1993	8	7	7
Under-five mortality rate *(per 1 000 live births)*	1975	71	63	67	1983-1993	38	27	32

II. Data and estimates from United Nations sources

United Nations Population Division estimates	1990-1995	2000-2005
Annual number of deaths *(thousands)*	108	122
Crude death rate *(per 1 000 person-years)*	6	6
Life expectancy at birth *(years)*		
Male...	69.1	71.3
Female...	74.3	76.7
Under-five mortality rate *(per 1 000 live births)*	28	20

Maternal mortality

	2000
Maternal mortality ratio *(deaths per 100 000 births)*	92

HIV/AIDS

	2003	[Low estimate - high estimate]
Number of HIV-infected persons, ...	3 500	[1 200 - 6 900]
Adult HIV prevalence *(percentage of adults 15-49)*	<0.1	[<0.2]

Policy views

	1976	2003
Life expectancy...	Acceptable	Acceptable
Under-five mortality...		Unacceptable
Maternal mortality...		Unacceptable
Level of concern about AIDS..................................		Major concern

Life Expectancy at Birth

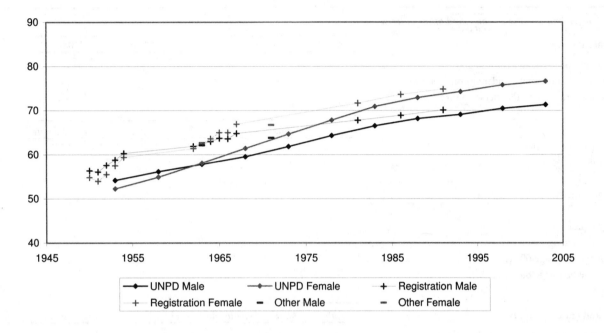

Infant Mortality Rate

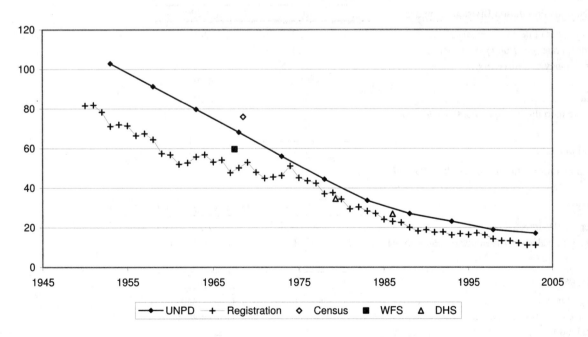

Indicator	Period			
	Earlier year		Later year	

I. Data and estimates from national and other sources

General mortality	Year	Value	Year	Value
Annual number of deaths *(thousands)*	..	..	..	..
Annual number of deaths under age one *(thousands)*	..	..	..	..
Crude death rate *(per 1 000 person-years)*	..	..	..	..

	Year	Male	Female	Year	Male	Female
Life expectancy *(years)*						
at birth	..	..	..	..	..	..
at age 15	..	..	..	..	..	..
at age 60	..	..	..	..	..	..
Survival probability						
from birth to age 15	..	..	..	..	..	..
from age 15 to age 60	..	..	..	..	..	..
from age 60 to age 80	..	..	..	..	..	..

Infant and child mortality	Year	Male	Female	Both sexes	Year	Male	Female	Both sexes
Infant mortality rate *(per 1 000 live births)*	1973	109	91	100	..	..	..	..
Mortality from age 1 to age 4 *(per 1 000 live births)*	1973	69	71	70	..	..	..	..
Under-five mortality rate *(per 1 000 live births)*	1973	170	156	163	..	..	..	..

II. Data and estimates from United Nations sources

United Nations Population Division estimates	1990-1995	2000-2005
Annual number of deaths *(thousands)*	360	388
Crude death rate *(per 1 000 person-years)*	13	11
Life expectancy at birth *(years)*		
Male	51.9	54.9
Female	55.0	57.9
Under-five mortality rate *(per 1 000 live births)*	151	119

Maternal mortality	2000
Maternal mortality ratio *(deaths per 100 000 births)*	590

HIV/AIDS	2003	[Low estimate - high estimate]
Number of HIV-infected persons,	400 000	[120 000 - 1 300 000]
Adult HIV prevalence *(percentage of adults 15-49)*	2.3	[0.7 - 7.2]

Policy views	1976	2003
Life expectancy	Unacceptable	Unacceptable
Under-five mortality		Unacceptable
Maternal mortality		Unacceptable
Level of concern about AIDS		Minor concern

Life Expectancy at Birth

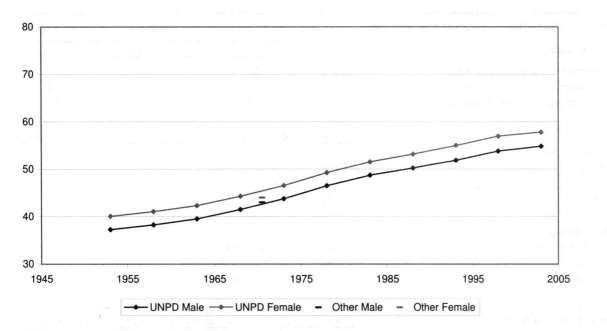

Infant Mortality Rate

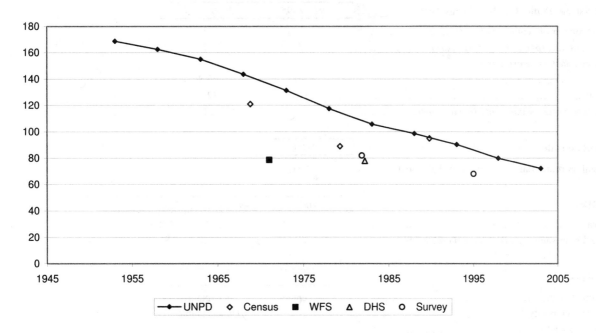

Indicator	Period							
	Earlier year				Later year			

I. Data and estimates from national and other sources

General mortality

	Year	Value			Year	Value		
Annual number of deaths *(thousands)*	1971	2.5			2002	3.1		
Annual number of deaths under age one *(thousands)*	1970	0.5			2002	0.1		
Crude death rate *(per 1 000 person-years)*	1971	6.8			2002	6.6		

	Year	Male	Female		Year	Male	Female	
Life expectancy *(years)*								
at birth	1980	64.7	71.0		..	..	..	
at age 15	1980	54.1	59.5		..	..	..	
at age 60	1980	16.6	19.4		..	..	..	
Survival probability								
from birth to age 15	1980	0.94	0.95		..	..	..	
from age 15 to age 60	1980	0.75	0.85		..	..	..	
from age 60 to age 80	1980	0.35	0.47		..	..	..	

Infant and child mortality

	Year	Male	Female	Both sexes	Year	Male	Female	Both sexes
Infant mortality rate *(per 1 000 live births)*	1980	50	36	43	2002	..	..	15
Mortality from age 1 to age 4 *(per 1 000 live births)*	1980	9	8	8	..	..	..	..
Under-five mortality rate *(per 1 000 live births)*	1980	58	44	51	..	..	..	..

II. Data and estimates from United Nations sources

United Nations Population Division estimates

	1990-1995	2000-2005
Annual number of deaths *(thousands)*	3	3
Crude death rate *(per 1 000 person-years)*	7	7
Life expectancy at birth *(years)*		
Male	65.0	65.8
Female	71.4	72.5
Under-five mortality rate *(per 1 000 live births)*	40	31

Maternal mortality

	2000
Maternal mortality ratio *(deaths per 100 000 births)*	110

HIV/AIDS

	2003	*[Low estimate - high estimate]*
Number of HIV-infected persons,	5 200	[1 400 - 18 000]
Adult HIV prevalence *(percentage of adults 15-49)*	1.7	[0.5 - 5.8]

Policy views

	1976	2003
Life expectancy	Unacceptable	Acceptable
Under-five mortality		Unacceptable
Maternal mortality		Unacceptable
Level of concern about AIDS		Major concern

Life Expectancy at Birth

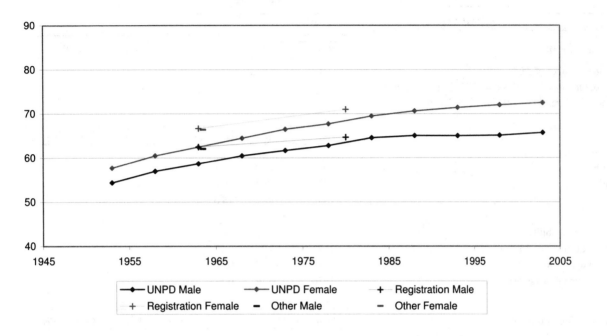

Infant Mortality Rate

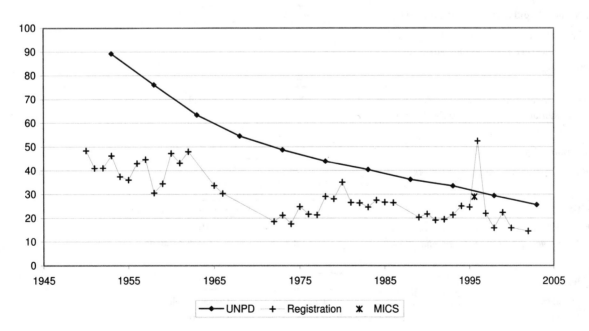

I. Data and estimates from national and other sources

Indicator	Period				
	Earlier year			Later year	

General mortality

	Year	Value		Year	Value	
Annual number of deaths *(thousands)*	..	..		..	..	
Annual number of deaths under age one *(thousands)*	..	..		..	..	
Crude death rate *(per 1 000 person-years)*	..	..		..	..	

	Year	Male	Female	Year	Male	Female
Life expectancy *(years)*						
at birth..	1976	42.9	49.5	1997	58.0	63.0
at age 15...	1976	43.1	49.0	..	..	..
at age 60...	1976	12.6	15.6	..	..	..
Survival probability						
from birth to age 15..	1976	0.73	0.77	..	..	..
from age 15 to age 60..	1976	0.53	0.66	..	..	..
from age 60 to age 80..	1976	0.19	0.32	..	..	..

Infant and child mortality

	Year	Male	Female	Both sexes	Year	Male	Female	Both sexes
Infant mortality rate *(per 1 000 live births)*	1976	165	146	156	1996	..	..	86
Mortality from age 1 to age 4 *(per 1 000 live births)*	1976	90	74	82	..	..	..	..
Under-five mortality rate *(per 1 000 live births)*	1976	240	209	225	1996	..	..	122

II. Data and estimates from United Nations sources

United Nations Population Division estimates	1990-1995	2000-2005
Annual number of deaths *(thousands)*	10	27
Crude death rate *(per 1 000 person-years)*	11	27
Life expectancy at birth *(years)*		
Male...	52.3	32.5
Female..	58.8	33.4
Under-five mortality rate *(per 1 000 live births)*	109	143

Maternal mortality	2000
Maternal mortality ratio *(deaths per 100 000 births)*	370

HIV/AIDS	2003	[Low estimate - high estimate]
Number of HIV-infected persons, ...	220 000	[210 000 - 230 000]
Adult HIV prevalence *(percentage of adults 15-49)*	38.8	[37.2 - 40.4]

Policy views	1976	2003
Life expectancy...	Unacceptable	Unacceptable
Under-five mortality...		Unacceptable
Maternal mortality...		Unacceptable
Level of concern about AIDS..................................		Major concern

Life Expectancy at Birth

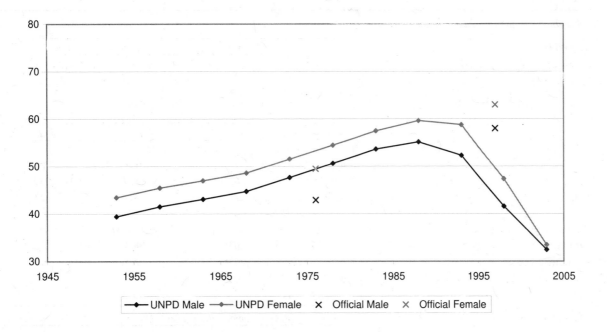

Infant Mortality Rate

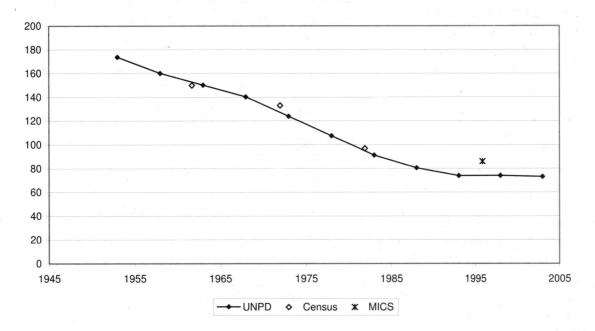

Indicator	Period					
	Earlier year			Later year		

I. Data and estimates from national and other sources

General mortality

	Year	Value		Year	Value	
Annual number of deaths *(thousands)*	1970	80.0		2004	90.5	
Annual number of deaths under age one *(thousands)*	1970	1.2		2004	0.3	
Crude death rate *(per 1 000 person-years)*	1970	10.0		2004	10.1	

	Year	Male	Female	Year	Male	Female
Life expectancy *(years)*						
at birth...	1969-1973	72.0	77.3	2003	77.9	82.4
at age 15..	1969-1973	58.3	63.3	2003	63.3	67.7
at age 60..	1969-1973	17.6	21.0	2003	21.1	24.6
Survival probability						
from birth to age 15...	1969-1973	0.98	0.99	2003	0.99	1.00
from age 15 to age 60...	1969-1973	0.86	0.92	2003	0.92	0.95
from age 60 to age 80...	1969-1973	0.41	0.57	2003	0.58	0.73

Infant and child mortality

	Year	Male	Female	Both sexes	Year	Male	Female	Both sexes
Infant mortality rate *(per 1 000 live births)*	1969-1973	13	9	11	2003	4	3	3
Mortality from age 1 to age 4 *(per 1 000 live births)*	1969-1973	2	2	2	2003	1	1	1
Under-five mortality rate *(per 1 000 live births)*	1969-1973	15	11	13	2003	5	3	4

II. Data and estimates from United Nations sources

United Nations Population Division estimates

	1990-1995	2000-2005
Annual number of deaths *(thousands)*	95	93
Crude death rate *(per 1 000 person-years)*	11	10
Life expectancy at birth *(years)*		
Male..	75.5	77.8
Female..	80.9	82.3
Under-five mortality rate *(per 1 000 live births)*	6	4

Maternal mortality

	2000
Maternal mortality ratio *(deaths per 100 000 births)*	2

HIV/AIDS

	2003	*[Low estimate - high estimate]*
Number of HIV-infected persons, ...	3 600	[1 200 - 6 900]
Adult HIV prevalence *(percentage of adults 15-49)*	0.1	[0.0 - 0.2]

Policy views

	1976	2003
Life expectancy...	Acceptable	Acceptable
Under-five mortality...		Acceptable
Maternal mortality...		Acceptable
Level of concern about AIDS..................................		Major concern

Life Expectancy at Birth

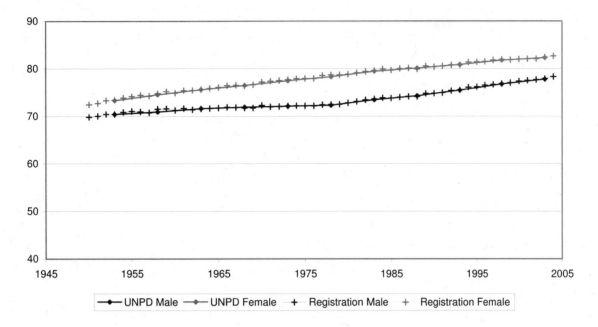

Infant Mortality Rate

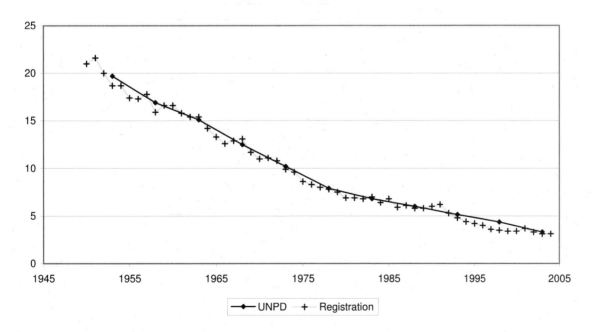

Indicator	Period				
	Earlier year			**Later year**	

I. Data and estimates from national and other sources

General mortality

	Year	Value		Year	Value	
Annual number of deaths *(thousands)*	1970	57.1		2004	60.2	
Annual number of deaths under age one *(thousands)*	1970	1.5		2004	0.3	
Crude death rate *(per 1 000 person-years)*	1970	9.1		2004	8.1	

	Year	Male	Female	Year	Male	Female
Life expectancy *(years)*						
at birth..	1970	70.0	76.2	2003	77.9	83.1
at age 15..	1970	56.9	62.6	2003	63.4	68.5
at age 60..	1970	16.7	20.3	2003	21.5	25.4
Survival probability						
from birth to age 15...	1970	0.97	0.98	2003	0.99	0.99
from age 15 to age 60...	1970	0.83	0.91	2003	0.91	0.95
from age 60 to age 80...	1970	0.37	0.54	2003	0.60	0.76

Infant and child mortality

	Year	Male	Female	Both sexes	Year	Male	Female	Both sexes
Infant mortality rate *(per 1 000 live births)*	1970	17	13	15	2003	4	4	4
Mortality from age 1 to age 4 *(per 1 000 live births)*	1970	4	3	3	2003	1	1	1
Under-five mortality rate *(per 1 000 live births)*	1970	21	16	18	2003	5	5	5

II. Data and estimates from United Nations sources

United Nations Population Division estimates

	1990-1995	2000-2005
Annual number of deaths *(thousands)*	66	61
Crude death rate *(per 1 000 person-years)*	10	8
Life expectancy at birth *(years)*		
Male..	74.7	77.6
Female...	81.4	83.1
Under-five mortality rate *(per 1 000 live births)*	7	6

Maternal mortality

	2000
Maternal mortality ratio *(deaths per 100 000 births)*	7

HIV/AIDS

	2003	[Low estimate - high estimate]
Number of HIV-infected persons, ...	13 000	[6 500 - 21 000]
Adult HIV prevalence *(percentage of adults 15-49)*	0.4	[0.2 - 0.6]

Policy views

	1976	2003
Life expectancy..	Acceptable	Acceptable
Under-five mortality..		Acceptable
Maternal mortality..		Acceptable
Level of concern about AIDS..................................		Major concern

Life Expectancy at Birth

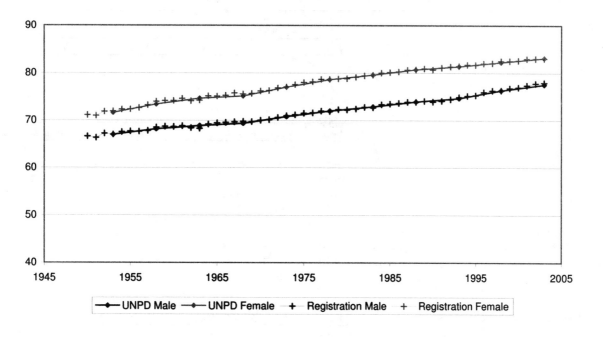

Legend: UNPD Male — UNPD Female — + Registration Male + Registration Female

Infant Mortality Rate

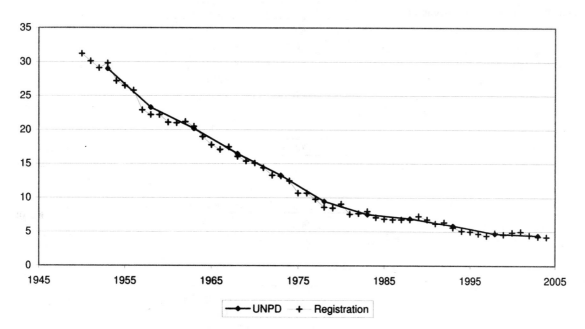

Legend: UNPD + Registration

Indicator	Period				
	Earlier year			Later year	

I. Data and estimates from national and other sources

General mortality

	Year	Value		Year	Value
Annual number of deaths *(thousands)*	..	..		..	..
Annual number of deaths under age one *(thousands)*	..	..		..	..
Crude death rate *(per 1 000 person-years)*	..	..		..	..

	Year	Male	Female	Year	Male	Female
Life expectancy *(years)*						
at birth..	1970	54.5	58.7	..	..	..
at age 15..	1970	51.9	55.0	..	..	..
at age 60..	1970	15.2	17.3	..	..	..
Survival probability						
from birth to age 15..	1970	0.82	0.84	..	..	..
from age 15 to age 60......................................	1970	0.73	0.80	..	..	..
from age 60 to age 80......................................	1970	0.29	0.36	..	..	..

Infant and child mortality

	Year	Male	Female	Both sexes	Year	Male	Female	Both sexes
Infant mortality rate *(per 1 000 live births)*	1972	80	80	80	1996-2001	..	..	18
Mortality from age 1 to age 4 *(per 1 000 live births)*	1972	33	39	36	..	..	..	..
Under-five mortality rate *(per 1 000 live births)*	1972	111	116	113	1996-2001	..	..	20

II. Data and estimates from United Nations sources

United Nations Population Division estimates

	1990-1995	2000-2005
Annual number of deaths *(thousands)*	63	63
Crude death rate *(per 1 000 person-years)*	5	4
Life expectancy at birth *(years)*		
Male..	67.9	71.4
Female..	71.0	74.9
Under-five mortality rate *(per 1 000 live births)*	37	21

Maternal mortality

	2000
Maternal mortality ratio *(deaths per 100 000 births)*	160

HIV/AIDS

	2003	*[Low estimate - high estimate]*
Number of HIV-infected persons, ...	<500	[300 - 2 100]
Adult HIV prevalence *(percentage of adults 15-49)*	<0.1	[<0.2]

Policy views

	1976	2003
Life expectancy...	Unacceptable	Acceptable
Under-five mortality..		Acceptable
Maternal mortality..		Acceptable
Level of concern about AIDS..................................		Minor concern

Life Expectancy at Birth

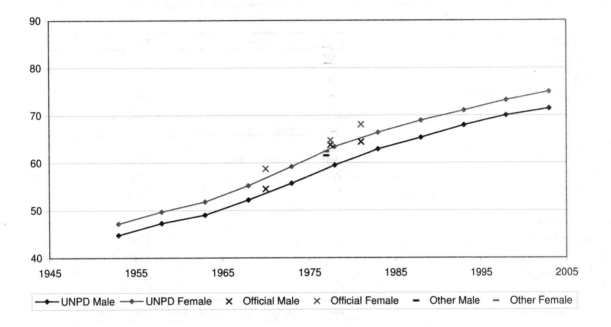

Legend: UNPD Male · UNPD Female · X Official Male · X Official Female · — Other Male · — Other Female

Infant Mortality Rate

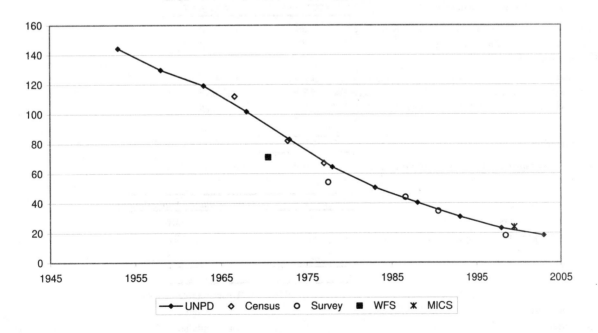

Legend: UNPD · ◇ Census · ○ Survey · ■ WFS · ✖ MICS

Indicator	Period					
	Earlier year			**Later year**		

I. Data and estimates from national and other sources

General mortality

	Year	Value		Year	Value	
Annual number of deaths *(thousands)*	..	..		2003	33.2	
Annual number of deaths under age one *(thousands)*	..	..		2000	2.1	
Crude death rate *(per 1 000 person-years)*	..	..		2003	5.0	

	Year	Male	Female	Year	Male	Female
Life expectancy *(years)*						
at birth...	1981	64.5	69.4	1991	67.6	73.2
at age 15...	..	..	..	1991	57.4	62.5
at age 60...	..	..	..	1991	18.2	22.1
Survival probability						
from birth to age 15...	..	..	..	1991	0.93	0.94
from age 15 to age 60...	..	..	..	1991	0.81	0.87
from age 60 to age 80...	..	..	..	1991	0.39	0.54

Infant and child mortality

	Year	Male	Female	Both sexes	Year	Male	Female	Both sexes
Infant mortality rate *(per 1 000 live births)*	..	..	..	..	1997	..	..	95
Mortality from age 1 to age 4 *(per 1 000 live births)*	..	..	..	..	..	..	..	..
Under-five mortality rate *(per 1 000 live births)*	..	..	..	..	1997	..	..	122

II. Data and estimates from United Nations sources

United Nations Population Division estimates

	1990-1995	2000-2005
Annual number of deaths *(thousands)*	50	48
Crude death rate *(per 1 000 person-years)*	9	8
Life expectancy at birth *(years)*		
Male...	60.5	61.0
Female..	65.7	66.3
Under-five mortality rate *(per 1 000 live births)*	119	116

Maternal mortality

	2000
Maternal mortality ratio *(deaths per 100 000 births)*	100

HIV/AIDS

	2003	*[Low estimate - high estimate]*
Number of HIV-infected persons, ...	<200	[<400]
Adult HIV prevalence *(percentage of adults 15-49)*	<0.1	[<0.2]

Policy views

	1976	2003
Life expectancy..	..	Unacceptable
Under-five mortality..		Unacceptable
Maternal mortality..		Unacceptable
Level of concern about AIDS.................................		Major concern

Life Expectancy at Birth

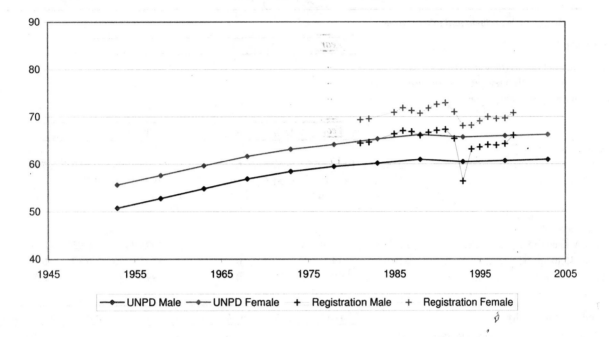

UNPD Male　　UNPD Female　　+ Registration Male　　+ Registration Female

Infant Mortality Rate

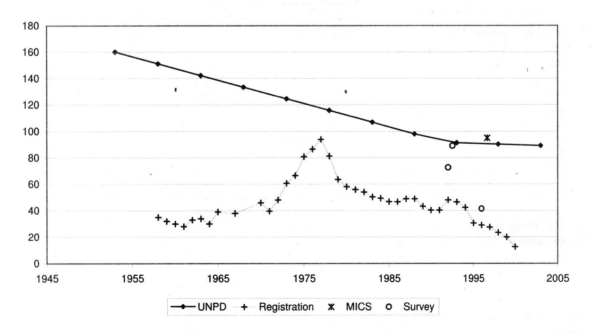

UNPD　　+ Registration　　✖ MICS　　○ Survey

Indicator	Period							
	Earlier year				Later year			

I. Data and estimates from national and other sources

General mortality

	Year	Value			Year	Value		
Annual number of deaths *(thousands)*	..	..			..	..		
Annual number of deaths under age one *(thousands)*	..	..			..	..		
Crude death rate *(per 1 000 person-years)*	..	..			..	..		

	Year	Male	Female		Year	Male	Female	
Life expectancy *(years)*								
at birth	1974-1975	57.6	63.6		1995-1996	70.0	75.0	
at age 15	1974-1975	51.6	56.2		1995-1996	58.2	62.9	
at age 60	1974-1975	15.9	18.9		1995-1996	20.3	23.9	
Survival probability								
from birth to age 15	1970	0.87	0.88		1995-1996	0.95	0.96	
from age 15 to age 60	1970	0.67	0.74		1995-1996	0.80	0.85	
from age 60 to age 80	1970	0.29	0.39		1995-1996	0.45	0.54	

Infant and child mortality

	Year	Male	Female	Both sexes	Year	Male	Female	Both sexes
Infant mortality rate *(per 1 000 live births)*	1972	110	90	100	1995-1996	27	25	26
Mortality from age 1 to age 4 *(per 1 000 live births)*	1972	68	72	70	..	..	..	..
Under-five mortality rate *(per 1 000 live births)*	1972	170	155	163	1995-1996	33	30	31

II. Data and estimates from United Nations sources

United Nations Population Division estimates

	1990-1995	2000-2005
Annual number of deaths *(thousands)*	338	456
Crude death rate *(per 1 000 person-years)*	6	7
Life expectancy at birth *(years)*		
Male	65.9	66.0
Female	71.8	73.7
Under-five mortality rate *(per 1 000 live births)*	37	25

Maternal mortality

	2000
Maternal mortality ratio *(deaths per 100 000 births)*	44

HIV/AIDS

	2003	[Low estimate - high estimate]
Number of HIV-infected persons,	570 000	[310 000 - 1 000 000]
Adult HIV prevalence *(percentage of adults 15-49)*	1.5	[0.8 - 2.8]

Policy views

	1976	2003
Life expectancy	Acceptable	Unacceptable
Under-five mortality		Unacceptable
Maternal mortality		Unacceptable
Level of concern about AIDS		Major concern

Life Expectancy at Birth

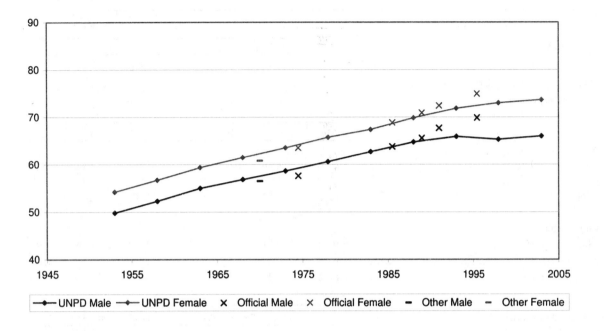

Infant Mortality Rate

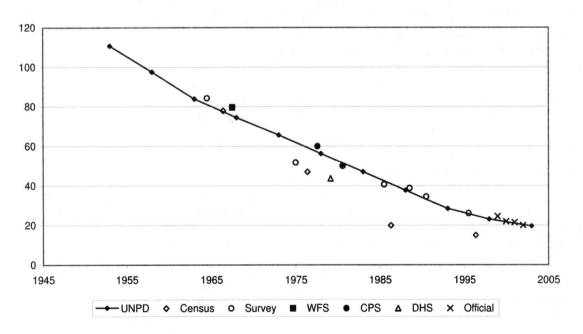

The Former Yugoslav Republic of Macedonia

Indicator	Period							
	Earlier year				Later year			

I. Data and estimates from national and other sources

General mortality

	Year	Value			Year	Value		
Annual number of deaths *(thousands)*	1970	12.4			2003	18.0		
Annual number of deaths under age one *(thousands)*	1970	3.3			2003	0.3		
Crude death rate *(per 1 000 person-years)*	1970	7.7			2003	8.9		

	Year	Male	Female		Year	Male	Female	
Life expectancy *(years)*								
at birth..	1970	65.6	67.6		2001	71.0	76.0	
at age 15..	1970	57.6	60.2		2001	57.3	62.0	
at age 60..	1970	17.3	18.6		2001	16.8	19.4	
Survival probability								
from birth to age 15...	1982	0.94	0.94		2001	0.98	0.99	
from age 15 to age 60...	1982	0.85	0.91		2001	0.84	0.92	
from age 60 to age 80...	1982	0.39	0.49		2001	0.37	0.50	

Infant and child mortality

	Year	Male	Female	Both sexes	Year	Male	Female	Both sexes
Infant mortality rate *(per 1 000 live births)*	1982	51	49	50	2001	14	10	12
Mortality from age 1 to age 4 *(per 1 000 live births)*	1982	5	5	5	2001	2	2	2
Under-five mortality rate *(per 1 000 live births)*	1982	55	54	54	2001	16	12	14

II. Data and estimates from United Nations sources

United Nations Population Division estimates

	1990-1995	2000-2005
Annual number of deaths *(thousands)*	15	17
Crude death rate *(per 1 000 person-years)*	8	8
Life expectancy at birth *(years)*		
Male..	69.4	71.2
Female..	74.0	76.2
Under-five mortality rate *(per 1 000 live births)*	30	18

Maternal mortality

	2000
Maternal mortality ratio *(deaths per 100 000 births)*	23

HIV/AIDS

	2003	[Low estimate - high estimate]
Number of HIV-infected persons, ...	<200	[<400]
Adult HIV prevalence *(percentage of adults 15-49)*	<0.1	[<0.2]

Policy views

	1976	2003
Life expectancy..	..	Unacceptable
Under-five mortality..		Unacceptable
Maternal mortality..		Unacceptable
Level of concern about AIDS...................................		Major concern

The Former Yugoslav Republic of Macedonia

Life Expectancy at Birth

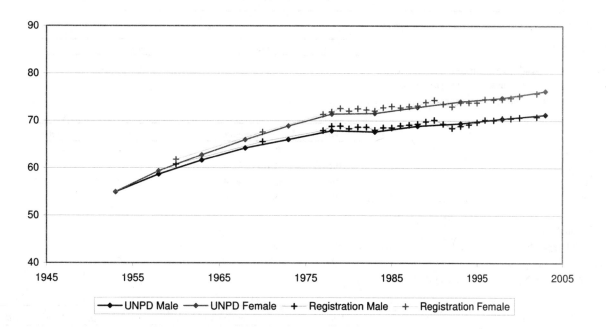

Infant Mortality Rate

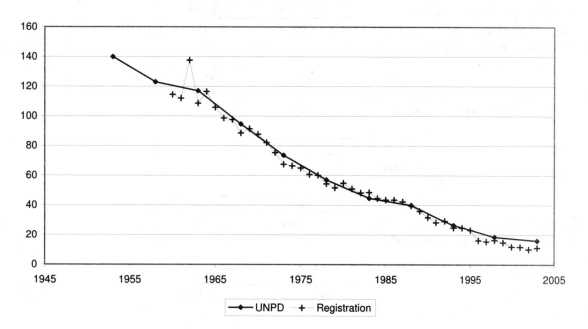

Indicator	Period				
	Earlier year			Later year		

I. Data and estimates from national and other sources

General mortality

	Year	Value		Year	Value	
Annual number of deaths *(thousands)*	..	..		..	..	
Annual number of deaths under age one *(thousands)*	..	..		..	..	
Crude death rate *(per 1 000 person-years)*	..	..		..	..	

	Year	Male	Female	Year	Male	Female
Life expectancy *(years)*						
at birth..	1961	31.6	38.5	..	..	..
at age 15..	1961	33.8	40.4	..	..	..
at age 60..	1961	8.5	11.9	..	..	..
Survival probability						
from birth to age 15...	1961	0.63	0.68	..	..	..
from age 15 to age 60...	1961	0.35	0.50	..	..	..
from age 60 to age 80...	..	..	..	..	..	..

Infant and child mortality

	Year	Male	Female	Both sexes	Year	Male	Female	Both sexes
Infant mortality rate *(per 1 000 live births)*	1983	109	94	102	1988-1998	89	71	80
Mortality from age 1 to age 4 *(per 1 000 live births)*	1983	65	80	72	1988-1998	73	65	69
Under-five mortality rate *(per 1 000 live births)*	1983	167	167	167	1988-1998	156	132	144

II. Data and estimates from United Nations sources

United Nations Population Division estimates

	1990-1995	2000-2005
Annual number of deaths *(thousands)*	48	71
Crude death rate *(per 1 000 person-years)*	11	12
Life expectancy at birth *(years)*		
Male..	55.5	52.3
Female...	60.0	56.2
Under-five mortality rate *(per 1 000 live births)*	148	137

Maternal mortality

	2000
Maternal mortality ratio *(deaths per 100 000 births)*	570

HIV/AIDS

	2003	[Low estimate - high estimate]
Number of HIV-infected persons, ...	110 000	[67 000 - 170 000]
Adult HIV prevalence *(percentage of adults 15-49)*	4.1	[2.7 - 6.4]

Policy views

	1976	2003
Life expectancy...	Unacceptable	Unacceptable
Under-five mortality..		Unacceptable
Maternal mortality...		Unacceptable
Level of concern about AIDS...................................		Major concern

Life Expectancy at Birth

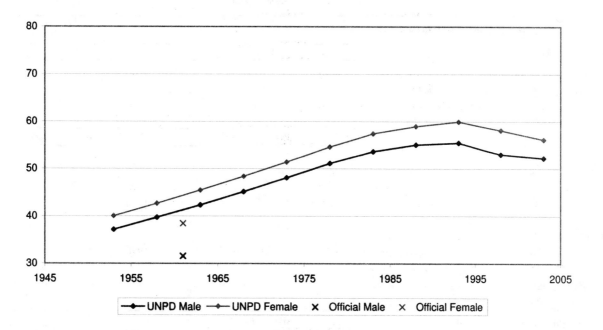

Infant Mortality Rate

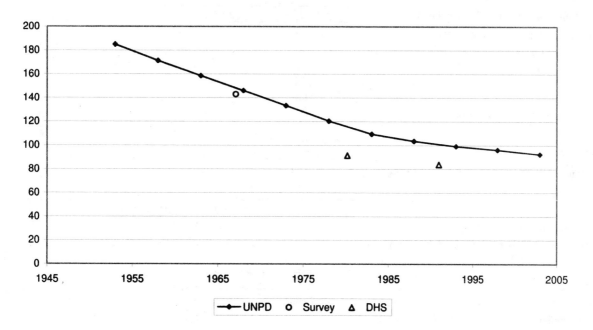

Indicator	Period				
	Earlier year			Later year	

I. Data and estimates from national and other sources

General mortality

	Year	Value		Year	Value	
Annual number of deaths *(thousands)*	1970	0.2		2000	0.7	
Annual number of deaths under age one *(thousands)*	1970	0.0		2000	0.0	
Crude death rate *(per 1 000 person-years)*	1970	2.6		2000	6.5	

	Year	Male	Female	Year	Male	Female
Life expectancy *(years)*						
at birth	..	..	..	1996	69.8	71.8
at age 15	..	..	..	1996	56.7	58.6
at age 60	..	..	..	1996	16.3	17.7
Survival probability						
from birth to age 15	..	..	..	1996	0.97	0.95
from age 15 to age 60	..	..	..	1996	0.84	0.89
from age 60 to age 80	..	..	..	1996	0.34	0.41

Infant and child mortality

	Year	Male	Female	Both sexes	Year	Male	Female	Both sexes
Infant mortality rate *(per 1 000 live births)*	..	..	..	..	1996	19	17	18
Mortality from age 1 to age 4 *(per 1 000 live births)*	..	..	..	..	1996	4	4	4
Under-five mortality rate *(per 1 000 live births)*	..	..	..	..	1996	23	21	22

II. Data and estimates from United Nations sources

United Nations Population Division estimates

	1990-1995	2000-2005
Annual number of deaths *(thousands)*	1	1
Crude death rate *(per 1 000 person-years)*	6	6
Life expectancy at birth *(years)*		
Male	69.0	70.9
Female	71.4	73.4
Under-five mortality rate *(per 1 000 live births)*	31	25

Maternal mortality

	2000
Maternal mortality ratio *(deaths per 100 000 births)*	..

HIV/AIDS

	2003	[Low estimate - high estimate]
Number of HIV-infected persons,	..	..
Adult HIV prevalence *(percentage of adults 15-49)*	..	..

Policy views

	1976	2003
Life expectancy	Unacceptable	Unacceptable
Under-five mortality		Unacceptable
Maternal mortality		Unacceptable
Level of concern about AIDS		Major concern

Life Expectancy at Birth

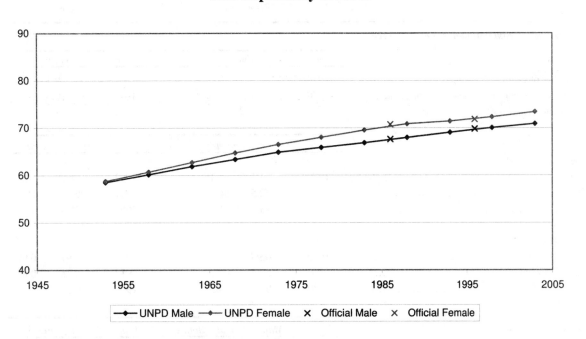

Infant Mortality Rate

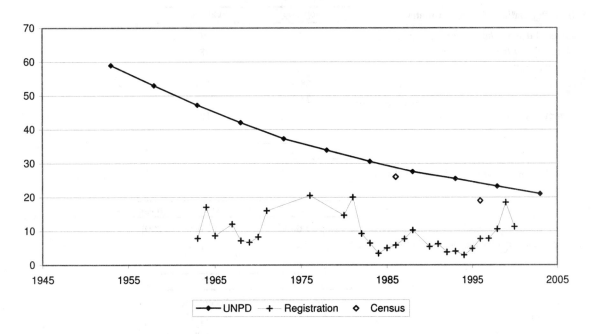

Indicator	Period					
	Earlier year			Later year		

I. Data and estimates from national and other sources

General mortality

	Year	Value		Year	Value	
Annual number of deaths *(thousands)*	1970	6.9		2002	9.7	
Annual number of deaths under age one *(thousands)*	1970	0.9		1999	0.3	
Crude death rate *(per 1 000 person-years)*	1970	7.2		2002	7.6	

	Year	Male	Female	Year	Male	Female
Life expectancy *(years)*						
at birth..	1970	64.1	68.1	1997	68.0	73.0
at age 15...	1970	52.5	56.1	1997	54.8	59.7
at age 60...	1970	13.6	16.3	1997	16.4	19.4
Survival probability						
from birth to age 15...	1970	0.95	0.96	1997	0.97	0.98
from age 15 to age 60..	1970	0.77	0.82	1997	0.78	0.85
from age 60 to age 80..	1970	0.27	0.43	1997	0.36	0.52

Infant and child mortality

	Year	Male	Female	Both sexes	Year	Male	Female	Both sexes
Infant mortality rate *(per 1 000 live births)*	1972	51	41	46	1997	21	18	20
Mortality from age 1 to age 4 *(per 1 000 live births)*	1972	9	8	8	1997	3	3	3
Under-five mortality rate *(per 1 000 live births)*	1972	59	49	54	1997	24	21	23

II. Data and estimates from United Nations sources

United Nations Population Division estimates

	1990-1995	2000-2005
Annual number of deaths *(thousands)*	8	10
Crude death rate *(per 1 000 person-years)*	7	8
Life expectancy at birth *(years)*		
Male..	68.6	66.9
Female...	74.5	73.0
Under-five mortality rate *(per 1 000 live births)*	19	19

Maternal mortality

	2000
Maternal mortality ratio *(deaths per 100 000 births)*	160

HIV/AIDS

	2003	[Low estimate - high estimate]
Number of HIV-infected persons, ...	29 000	[11 000 - 74 000]
Adult HIV prevalence *(percentage of adults 15-49)*	3.2	[1.2 - 8.3]

Policy views

	1976	2003
Life expectancy..	Acceptable	Acceptable
Under-five mortality...		Unacceptable
Maternal mortality..		Unacceptable
Level of concern about AIDS...................................		Major concern

Life Expectancy at Birth

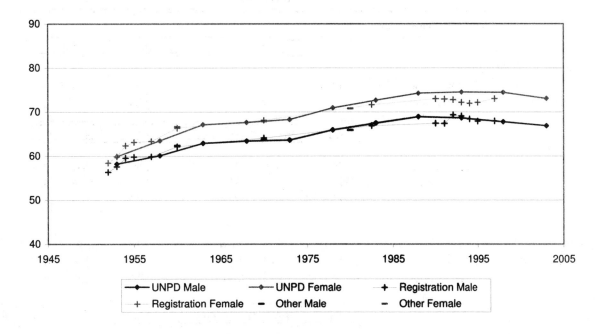

Legend: UNPD Male, UNPD Female, Registration Male, Registration Female, Other Male, Other Female

Infant Mortality Rate

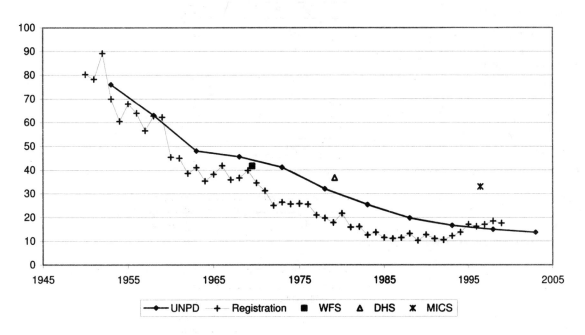

Legend: UNPD, Registration, WFS, DHS, MICS

Indicator	Period			
	Earlier year		Later year	

I. Data and estimates from national and other sources

General mortality

	Year	Value	Year	Value
Annual number of deaths *(thousands)*	..	..	..	..
Annual number of deaths under age one *(thousands)*	..	..	..	..
Crude death rate *(per 1 000 person-years)*	..	..	..	..

	Year	Male	Female	Year	Male	Female
Life expectancy *(years)*						
at birth...	1968-1969	52.7	52.5	1995	69.6	73.1
at age 15..	1968-1969	51.9	52.1	1995	57.9	61.0
at age 60..	1968-1969	14.7	14.9	1995	17.7	19.1
Survival probability						
from birth to age 15..	1968-1969	0.78	0.78	1995	0.95	0.96
from age 15 to age 60......................................	1968-1969	0.73	0.75	1995	0.84	0.90
from age 60 to age 80......................................	1968-1969	0.27	0.27	1995	0.44	0.52

Infant and child mortality

	Year	Male	Female	Both sexes	Year	Male	Female	Both sexes
Infant mortality rate *(per 1 000 live births)*	1975	101	95	98	1995	34	27	31
Mortality from age 1 to age 4 *(per 1 000 live births)*	1975	45	48	47	1995	7	7	7
Under-five mortality rate *(per 1 000 live births)*	1975	141	139	140	1995	40	34	37

II. Data and estimates from United Nations sources

United Nations Population Division estimates

	1990-1995	2000-2005
Annual number of deaths *(thousands)*	52	53
Crude death rate *(per 1 000 person-years)*	6	5
Life expectancy at birth *(years)*		
Male..	68.3	71.1
Female...	72.1	75.3
Under-five mortality rate *(per 1 000 live births)*	40	25

Maternal mortality

	2000
Maternal mortality ratio *(deaths per 100 000 births)*	120

HIV/AIDS

	2003	*[Low estimate - high estimate]*
Number of HIV-infected persons, ...	1 000	[400 - 2 400]
Adult HIV prevalence *(percentage of adults 15-49)*	<0.1	[<0.2]

Policy views

	1976	2003
Life expectancy...	Unacceptable	Acceptable
Under-five mortality..		Unacceptable
Maternal mortality..		Unacceptable
Level of concern about AIDS...................................		Minor concern

Life Expectancy at Birth

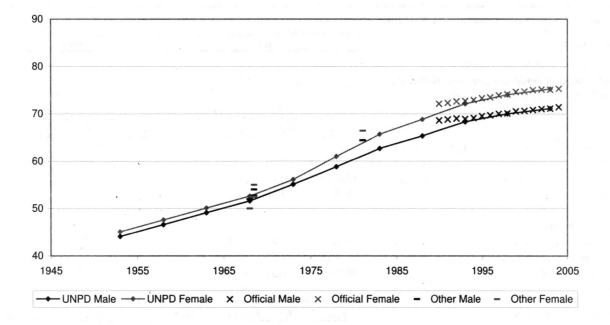

Infant Mortality Rate

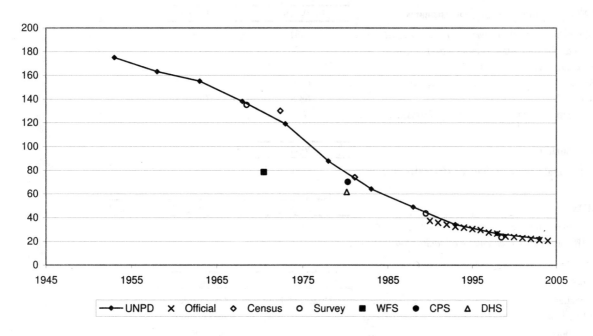

Indicator	Period							
	Earlier year				Later year			

I. Data and estimates from national and other sources

General mortality	Year	Value			Year	Value		
Annual number of deaths *(thousands)*	..	..			..	..		
Annual number of deaths under age one *(thousands)*	..	..			..	..		
Crude death rate *(per 1 000 person-years)*	..	..			..	..		

	Year	Male	Female		Year	Male	Female	
Life expectancy *(years)*								
at birth	1974-1975	55.2	58.3		2003	66.4	71.0	
at age 15	1974-1975	53.2	55.4		..	..	..	
at age 60	1974-1975	15.8	17.2		..	..	..	
Survival probability								
from birth to age 15	1974-1975	0.81	0.82		..	..	..	
from age 15 to age 60	1974-1975	0.75	0.79		..	..	..	
from age 60 to age 80	1974-1975	0.33	0.41		..	..	..	

Infant and child mortality	Year	Male	Female	Both sexes	Year	Male	Female	Both sexes
Infant mortality rate *(per 1 000 live births)*	1973	147	135	141	1988-1998	51	46	48
Mortality from age 1 to age 4 *(per 1 000 live births)*	1973	47	60	54	1988-1998	10	13	12
Under-five mortality rate *(per 1 000 live births)*	1973	187	187	187	1988-1998	61	58	60

II. Data and estimates from United Nations sources

United Nations Population Division estimates	1990-1995	2000-2005
Annual number of deaths *(thousands)*	431	469
Crude death rate *(per 1 000 person-years)*	7	7
Life expectancy at birth *(years)*		
Male	64.0	66.3
Female	68.5	70.9
Under-five mortality rate *(per 1 000 live births)*	65	49

Maternal mortality	2000
Maternal mortality ratio *(deaths per 100 000 births)*	70

HIV/AIDS	2003	*[Low estimate - high estimate]*
Number of HIV-infected persons,	..	..
Adult HIV prevalence *(percentage of adults 15-49)*	..	..

Policy views	1976	2003
Life expectancy	Unacceptable	Acceptable
Under-five mortality		Unacceptable
Maternal mortality		Unacceptable
Level of concern about AIDS		Minor concern

Life Expectancy at Birth

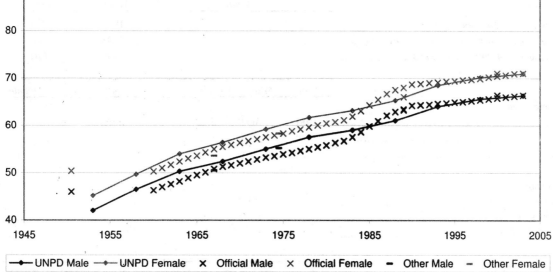

Infant Mortality Rate

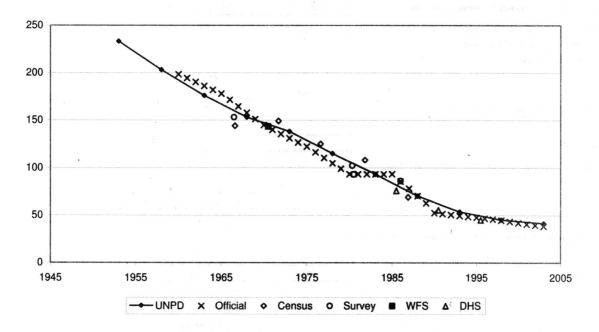

Indicator	Period					
	Earlier year			Later year		

I. Data and estimates from national and other sources

General mortality

	Year	Value		Year	Value	
Annual number of deaths *(thousands)*	..	..		1998	29.6	
Annual number of deaths under age one *(thousands)*	..	..		1998	3.3	
Crude death rate *(per 1 000 person-years)*	..	..		1998	6.1	

	Year	Male	Female	Year	Male	Female
Life expectancy *(years)*						
at birth..	1981	60.0	67.2	2002	64.9	71.8
at age 15...	..	..	..	..	..	..
at age 60...	..	..	..	..	..	..
Survival probability						
from birth to age 15.................................	..	..	..	..	..	..
from age 15 to age 60..............................	..	..	..	..	..	..
from age 60 to age 80..............................	..	..	..	..	..	..

Infant and child mortality

	Year	Male	Female	Both sexes	Year	Male	Female	Both sexes
Infant mortality rate *(per 1 000 live births)*	..	..	..	..	1990-2000	83	60	72
Mortality from age 1 to age 4 *(per 1 000 live births)*	..	..	..	..	1990-2000	19	17	18
Under-five mortality rate *(per 1 000 live births)*	..	..	..	..	1990-2000	101	76	88

II. Data and estimates from United Nations sources

United Nations Population Division estimates

	1990-1995	2000-2005
Annual number of deaths *(thousands)*	33	39
Crude death rate *(per 1 000 person-years)*	8	8
Life expectancy at birth *(years)*		
Male..	59.2	58.2
Female...	67.6	66.7
Under-five mortality rate *(per 1 000 live births)*	94	99

Maternal mortality

	2000
Maternal mortality ratio *(deaths per 100 000 births)*	31

HIV/AIDS

	2003	[Low estimate - high estimate]
Number of HIV-infected persons, ...	<200	[<400]
Adult HIV prevalence *(percentage of adults 15-49)*	<0.1	[<0.2]

Policy views

	1976	2003
Life expectancy..	..	Unacceptable
Under-five mortality..		Unacceptable
Maternal mortality..		Unacceptable
Level of concern about AIDS..................................		Major concern

Life Expectancy at Birth

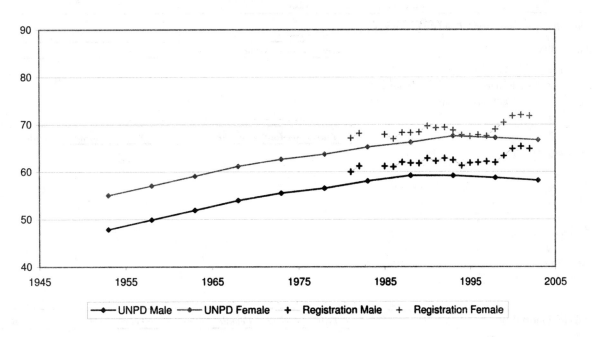

Infant Mortality Rate

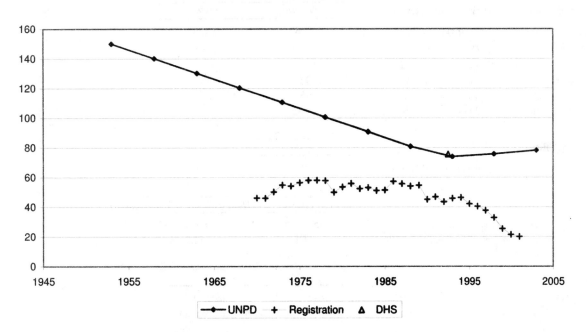

Indicator	Period			
	Earlier year		Later year	

I. Data and estimates from national and other sources

General mortality	Year	Value	Year	Value
Annual number of deaths *(thousands)*	..	..	..	..
Annual number of deaths under age one *(thousands)*	..	..	..	..
Crude death rate *(per 1 000 person-years)*	..	..	..	..

	Year	Male	Female	Year	Male	Female
Life expectancy *(years)*						
at birth	..	..	..	..	..	..
at age 15	..	..	..	..	..	..
at age 60	..	..	..	..	..	..
Survival probability						
from birth to age 15	..	..	..	..	..	..
from age 15 to age 60	..	..	..	..	..	..
from age 60 to age 80	..	..	..	..	..	..

Infant and child mortality	Year	Male	Female	Both sexes	Year	Male	Female	Both sexes
Infant mortality rate *(per 1 000 live births)*	1983	113	104	109	1990-2000	93	86	89
Mortality from age 1 to age 4 *(per 1 000 live births)*	1983	86	75	81	1990-2000	78	70	74
Under-five mortality rate *(per 1 000 live births)*	1983	190	172	181	1990-2000	164	150	157

II. Data and estimates from United Nations sources

United Nations Population Division estimates	1990-1995	2000-2005
Annual number of deaths *(thousands)*	362	428
Crude death rate *(per 1 000 person-years)*	19	16
Life expectancy at birth *(years)*		
Male	42.0	46.5
Female	45.4	47.1
Under-five mortality rate *(per 1 000 live births)*	162	139

Maternal mortality	2000
Maternal mortality ratio *(deaths per 100 000 births)*	880

HIV/AIDS	2003	*[Low estimate - high estimate]*
Number of HIV-infected persons,	530 000	[350 000 - 880 000]
Adult HIV prevalence *(percentage of adults 15-49)*	4.1	[2.8 - 6.6]

Policy views	1976	2003
Life expectancy	Unacceptable	Unacceptable
Under-five mortality		Unacceptable
Maternal mortality		Unacceptable
Level of concern about AIDS		Major concern

Life Expectancy at Birth

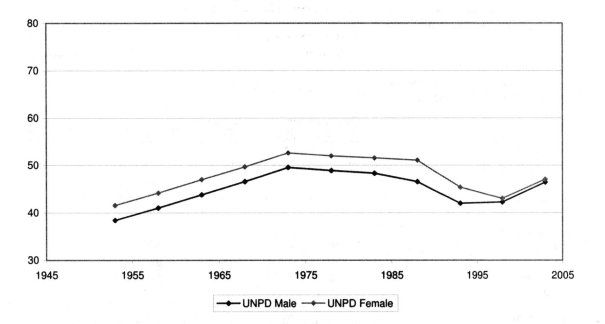

Infant Mortality Rate

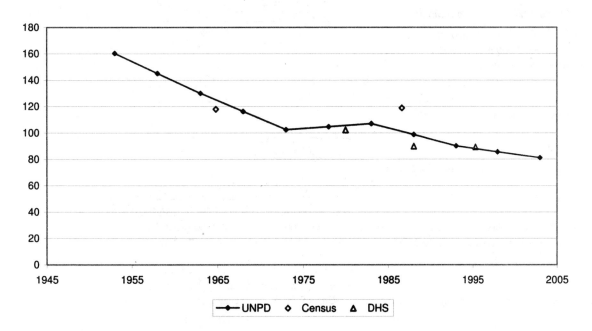

Indicator	Period				
	Earlier year			**Later year**	

I. Data and estimates from national and other sources

General mortality

	Year	Value		Year	Value
Annual number of deaths *(thousands)*	1970	418.7		2004	761.3
Annual number of deaths under age one *(thousands)*	1970	12.2		2004	4.0
Crude death rate *(per 1 000 person-years)*	1970	8.9		2004	16.0

	Year	Male	Female	Year	Male	Female
Life expectancy *(years)*						
at birth..	1970-1971	67.0	74.0	2002-2003	62.6	74.1
at age 15..	..	..	..	2002-2003	48.9	60.1
at age 60..	..	..	..	2002-2003	14.3	19.4
Survival probability						
from birth to age 15..	1981	0.97	0.98	2002-2003	0.98	0.99
from age 15 to age 60..	1981	0.70	0.88	2002-2003	0.63	0.86
from age 60 to age 80..	1981	0.31	0.51	2002-2003	0.27	0.50

Infant and child mortality

	Year	Male	Female	Both sexes	Year	Male	Female	Both sexes
Infant mortality rate *(per 1 000 live births)*	1981	18	14	16	2002-2003	13	9	11
Mortality from age 1 to age 4 *(per 1 000 live births)*	1981	6	5	6	2002-2003	3	3	3
Under-five mortality rate *(per 1 000 live births)*	1981	24	19	22	2002-2003	16	12	14

II. Data and estimates from United Nations sources

United Nations Population Division estimates

	1990-1995	*2000-2005*
Annual number of deaths *(thousands)*	768	780
Crude death rate *(per 1 000 person-years)*	15	16
Life expectancy at birth *(years)*		
Male..	61.9	60.1
Female...	72.0	72.5
Under-five mortality rate *(per 1 000 live births)*	20	18

Maternal mortality

	2000
Maternal mortality ratio *(deaths per 100 000 births)*	35

HIV/AIDS

	2003	*[Low estimate - high estimate]*
Number of HIV-infected persons, ...	360 000	[180 000 - 590 000]
Adult HIV prevalence *(percentage of adults 15-49)*	1.4	[0.7 - 2.3]

Policy views

	1976	*2003*
Life expectancy..	Unacceptable	Unacceptable
Under-five mortality...		Unacceptable
Maternal mortality...		Unacceptable
Level of concern about AIDS..................................		Major concern

Life Expectancy at Birth

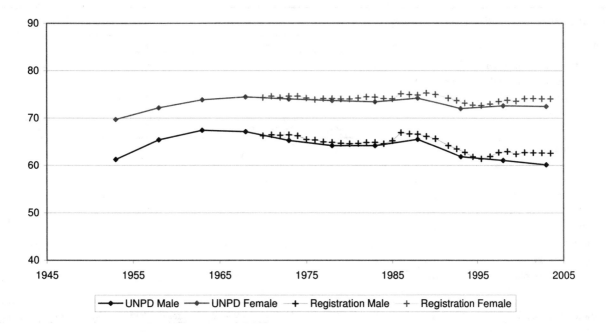

Infant Mortality Rate

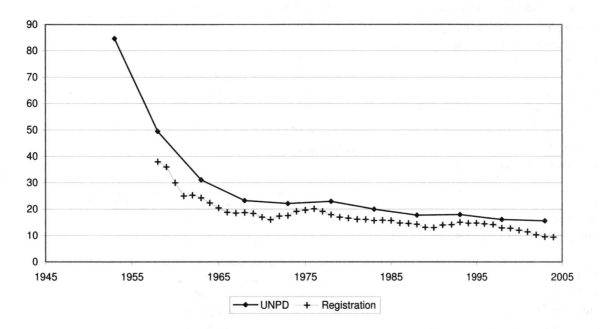

Indicator	Period							
	Earlier year				Later year			

I. Data and estimates from national and other sources

General mortality

	Year	Value			Year	Value		
Annual number of deaths *(thousands)*	..	..			..	..		
Annual number of deaths under age one *(thousands)*	..	..			..	..		
Crude death rate *(per 1 000 person-years)*	..	..			..	..		

	Year	Male	Female		Year	Male	Female	
Life expectancy *(years)*								
at birth..	..	..	..		..	..	..	
at age 15..	..	..	..		..	..	..	
at age 60..	..	..	..		..	..	..	
Survival probability								
from birth to age 15...	..	..	..		..	..	..	
from age 15 to age 60...	..	..	..		..	..	..	
from age 60 to age 80...	..	..	..		..	..	..	

Infant and child mortality

	Year	Male	Female	Both sexes	Year	Male	Female	Both sexes
Infant mortality rate *(per 1 000 live births)*	..	..	..	..	2003	..	..	8
Mortality from age 1 to age 4 *(per 1 000 live births)*	..	..	..	..	..	..	..	..
Under-five mortality rate *(per 1 000 live births)*	1980	33	26	30	2003	..	..	10

II. Data and estimates from United Nations sources

United Nations Population Division estimates

	1990-1995	2000-2005
Annual number of deaths *(thousands)*	5	5
Crude death rate *(per 1 000 person-years)*	2	1
Life expectancy at birth *(years)*		
Male...	72.3	76.3
Female..	76.4	80.6
Under-five mortality rate *(per 1 000 live births)*	18	10

Maternal mortality

	2000
Maternal mortality ratio *(deaths per 100 000 births)*	54

HIV/AIDS

	2003	*[Low estimate - high estimate]*
Number of HIV-infected persons, ...	..	..
Adult HIV prevalence *(percentage of adults 15-49)*	..	..

Policy views

	1976	2003
Life expectancy...	Acceptable	Acceptable
Under-five mortality...		Acceptable
Maternal mortality...		Acceptable
Level of concern about AIDS...................................		Minor concern

Life Expectancy at Birth

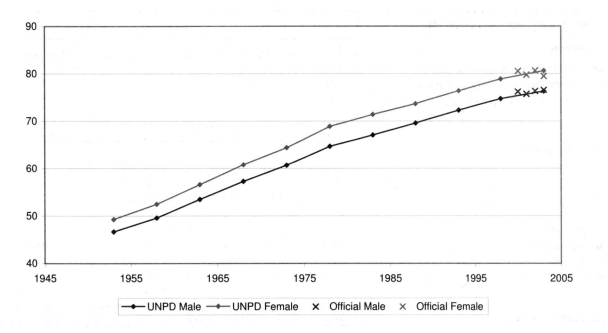

Legend: ◆ UNPD Male ◆ UNPD Female × Official Male × Official Female

Infant Mortality Rate

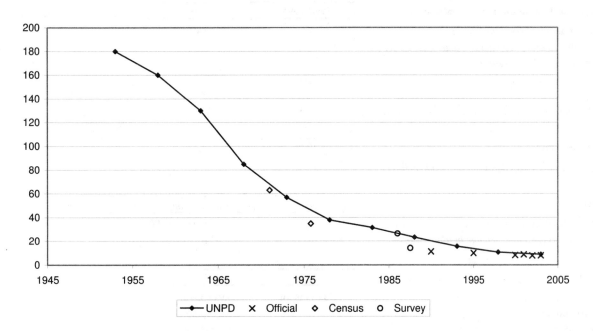

Legend: ◆ UNPD × Official ◇ Census ○ Survey

Indicator	Period				
	Earlier year			Later year	

I. Data and estimates from national and other sources

General mortality

	Year	Value		Year	Value
Annual number of deaths *(thousands)*	1970	652.8		2003	611.2
Annual number of deaths under age one *(thousands)*	1970	16.6		2003	3.7
Crude death rate *(per 1 000 person-years)*	1970	11.7		2003	10.3

	Year	Male	Female	Year	Male	Female
Life expectancy *(years)*						
at birth..	1970	68.5	74.9	2001-2003	75.9	80.5
at age 15..	1970	55.4	61.5	2001-2003	61.6	66.0
at age 60..	1970	15.0	19.7	2001-2003	20.0	23.3
Survival probability						
from birth to age 15..	1970	0.97	0.98	2001-2003	0.99	0.99
from age 15 to age 60..	1970	0.82	0.89	2001-2003	0.89	0.93
from age 60 to age 80..	1970	0.29	0.51	2001-2003	0.52	0.66

Infant and child mortality

	Year	Male	Female	Both sexes	Year	Male	Female	Both sexes
Infant mortality rate *(per 1 000 live births)*	1970	21	16	19	2001-2003	6	5	5
Mortality from age 1 to age 4 *(per 1 000 live births)*	1970	3	3	3	2001-2003	1	1	1
Under-five mortality rate *(per 1 000 live births)*	1970	24	19	22	2001-2003	7	6	6

II. Data and estimates from United Nations sources

United Nations Population Division estimates

	1990-1995	2000-2005
Annual number of deaths *(thousands)*	652	610
Crude death rate *(per 1 000 person-years)*	11	10
Life expectancy at birth *(years)*		
Male..	73.6	75.9
Female..	79.0	80.6
Under-five mortality rate *(per 1 000 live births)*	10	6

Maternal mortality

	2000
Maternal mortality ratio *(deaths per 100 000 births)*	13

HIV/AIDS

	2003	[Low estimate - high estimate]
Number of HIV-infected persons, ...	51 000	[25 000 - 82 000]
Adult HIV prevalence *(percentage of adults 15-49)*	0.2	[0.1 - 0.3]

Policy views

	1976	2003
Life expectancy...	Unacceptable	Unacceptable
Under-five mortality..		Unacceptable
Maternal mortality..		Acceptable
Level of concern about AIDS...................................		Major concern

Life Expectancy at Birth

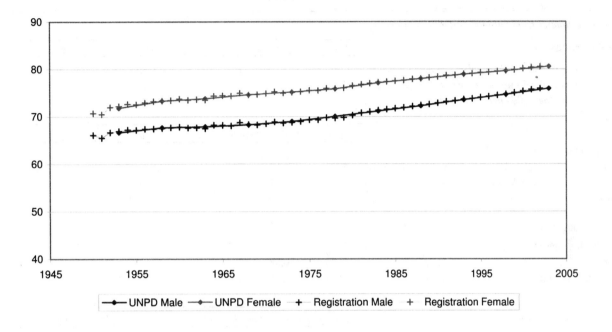

Infant Mortality Rate

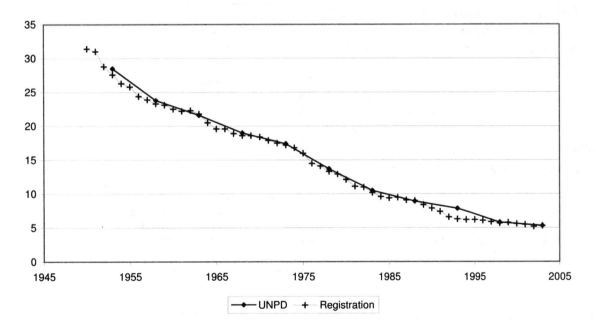

Indicator	Period							
	Earlier year				Later year			

I. Data and estimates from national and other sources

General mortality

	Year	Value			Year	Value		
Annual number of deaths *(thousands)*	..	..			..	..		
Annual number of deaths under age one *(thousands)*	..	..			..	..		
Crude death rate *(per 1 000 person-years)*	..	..			..	..		

	Year	Male	Female		Year	Male	Female	
Life expectancy *(years)*								
at birth	1974	42.8	46.1		..	..	..	
at age 15	1974	45.1	47.5		..	..	..	
at age 60	1974	14.0	14.9		..	..	..	
Survival probability								
from birth to age 15	1974	0.70	0.73		..	..	..	
from age 15 to age 60	1974	0.58	0.64		..	..	..	
from age 60 to age 80	1974	0.25	0.30		..	..	..	

Infant and child mortality

	Year	Male	Female	Both sexes	Year	Male	Female	Both sexes
Infant mortality rate *(per 1 000 live births)*	1978	124	109	117	1989-1999	118	97	108
Mortality from age 1 to age 4 *(per 1 000 live births)*	1978	92	87	89	1989-1999	61	58	60
Under-five mortality rate *(per 1 000 live births)*	1978	205	186	196	1989-1999	172	150	161

II. Data and estimates from United Nations sources

United Nations Population Division estimates

	1990-1995	2000-2005
Annual number of deaths *(thousands)*	390	610
Crude death rate *(per 1 000 person-years)*	14	17
Life expectancy at birth *(years)*		
Male	50.3	45.6
Female	54.8	46.4
Under-five mortality rate *(per 1 000 live births)*	165	164

Maternal mortality

	2000
Maternal mortality ratio *(deaths per 100 000 births)*	1 500

HIV/AIDS

	2003	[Low estimate - high estimate]
Number of HIV-infected persons,	1 600 000	[1 200 000 - 2 300 000]
Adult HIV prevalence *(percentage of adults 15-49)*	8.8	[6.4 - 11.9]

Policy views

	1976	2003
Life expectancy	Unacceptable	Unacceptable
Under-five mortality		Unacceptable
Maternal mortality		Unacceptable
Level of concern about AIDS		Major concern

Life Expectancy at Birth

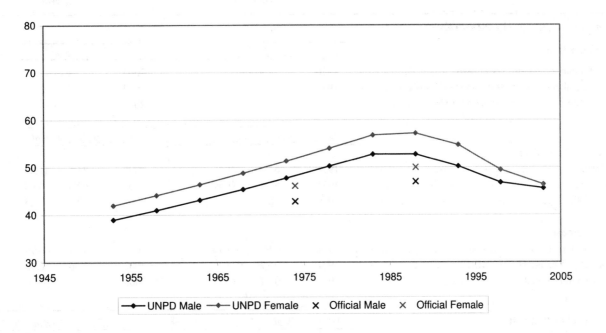

Infant Mortality Rate

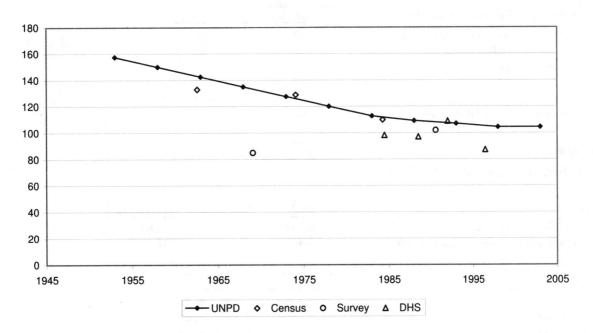

Indicator	Period					
	Earlier year			Later year		

I. Data and estimates from national and other sources

General mortality

	Year	Value		Year	Value	
Annual number of deaths *(thousands)*	1970	1 921.0		2003	2 443.9	
Annual number of deaths under age one *(thousands)*	1970	74.7		2003	28.4	
Crude death rate *(per 1 000 person-years)*	1970	9.4		2003	8.4	

	Year	Male	Female	Year	Male	Female
Life expectancy *(years)*						
at birth..	1971	67.4	74.8	2002	74.5	79.9
at age 15..	1971	54.4	61.5	2002	60.3	65.5
at age 60..	1971	16.1	20.6	2002	20.2	23.5
Survival probability						
from birth to age 15..	1971	0.97	0.98	2002	0.99	0.99
from age 15 to age 60..	1971	0.77	0.87	2002	0.86	0.92
from age 60 to age 80..	1971	0.34	0.55	2002	0.52	0.66

Infant and child mortality

	Year	Male	Female	Both sexes	Year	Male	Female	Both sexes
Infant mortality rate *(per 1 000 live births)*	1971	21	17	19	2002	8	6	7
Mortality from age 1 to age 4 *(per 1 000 live births)*	1971	3	3	3	2002	1	1	1
Under-five mortality rate *(per 1 000 live births)*	1971	25	19	22	2002	9	8	8

II. Data and estimates from United Nations sources

United Nations Population Division estimates

	1990-1995	2000-2005
Annual number of deaths *(thousands)*	2 335	2 438
Crude death rate *(per 1 000 person-years)*	9	8
Life expectancy at birth *(years)*		
Male..	72.2	74.6
Female...	78.9	80.0
Under-five mortality rate *(per 1 000 live births)*	10	8

Maternal mortality

	2000
Maternal mortality ratio *(deaths per 100 000 births)*	17

HIV/AIDS

	2003	[Low estimate - high estimate]
Number of HIV-infected persons, ...	950 000	[470 000 - 1 600 000]
Adult HIV prevalence *(percentage of adults 15-49)*	0.6	[0.3 - 1.1]

Policy views

	1976	2003
Life expectancy...	Acceptable	Unacceptable
Under-five mortality..		Unacceptable
Maternal mortality..		Unacceptable
Level of concern about AIDS....................................		Major concern

Life Expectancy at Birth

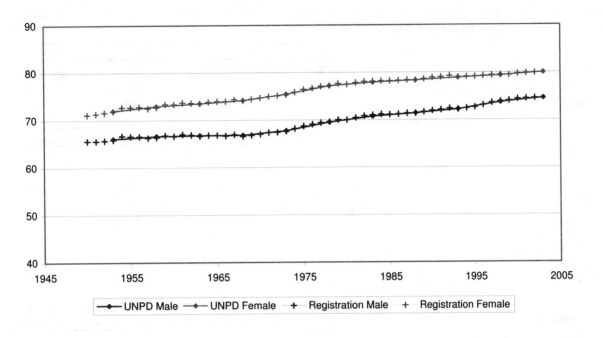

Infant Mortality Rate

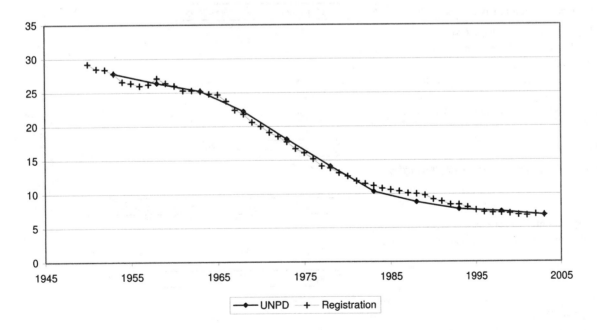

Indicator	Period			
	Earlier year		Later year	

I. Data and estimates from national and other sources

General mortality

	Year	Value	Year	Value
Annual number of deaths *(thousands)*	1970	0.5	2002	0.6
Annual number of deaths under age one *(thousands)*	1970	0.1	2002	0.0
Crude death rate *(per 1 000 person-years)*	1970	6.2	2002	5.7

	Year	Male	Female	Year	Male	Female
Life expectancy *(years)*						
at birth..	..	..	..	..	..	..
at age 15...	..	..	..	..	..	..
at age 60...	..	..	..	..	..	..
Survival probability						
from birth to age 15...	..	..	..	..	..	..
from age 15 to age 60...	..	..	..	..	..	..
from age 60 to age 80...	..	..	..	..	..	..

Infant and child mortality

	Year	Male	Female	Both sexes	Year	Male	Female	Both sexes
Infant mortality rate *(per 1 000 live births)*	..	..	..	..	1993	..	..	12
Mortality from age 1 to age 4 *(per 1 000 live births)*	..	..	..	..	..	..	..	..
Under-five mortality rate *(per 1 000 live births)*	..	..	..	..	..	..	..	..

II. Data and estimates from United Nations sources

United Nations Population Division estimates

	1990-1995	2000-2005
Annual number of deaths *(thousands)*	1	1
Crude death rate *(per 1 000 person-years)*	5	6
Life expectancy at birth *(years)*		
Male...	71.8	74.6
Female..	80.0	82.6
Under-five mortality rate *(per 1 000 live births)*	16	11

Maternal mortality

	2000
Maternal mortality ratio *(deaths per 100 000 births)*	..

HIV/AIDS

	2003	[Low estimate - high estimate]
Number of HIV-infected persons, ...	..	..
Adult HIV prevalence *(percentage of adults 15-49)*	..	..

Policy views

	1976	2003
Life expectancy...	..	..
Under-five mortality..		..
Maternal mortality..		..
Level of concern about AIDS....................................		..

Life Expectancy at Birth

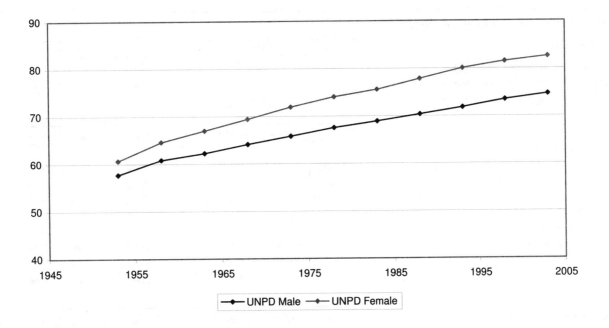

Infant Mortality Rate

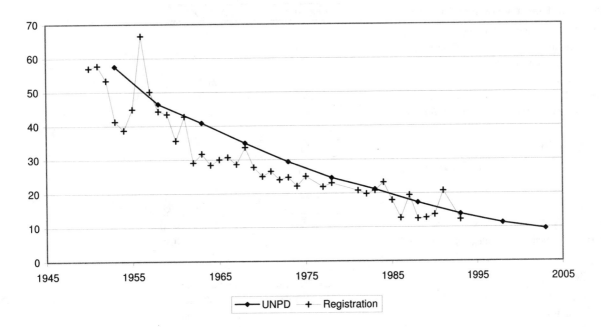

Indicator	Period			
	Earlier year		Later year	

I. Data and estimates from national and other sources

General mortality

	Year	Value	Year	Value
Annual number of deaths *(thousands)*	1970	26.4	2004	30.0
Annual number of deaths under age one *(thousands)*	1970	2.8	2004	0.7
Crude death rate *(per 1 000 person-years)*	1970	9.4	2004	9.1

	Year	Male	Female	Year	Male	Female
Life expectancy *(years)*						
at birth..	1974-1976	65.7	72.5	2003	71.3	79.2
at age 15..	1974-1976	55.0	61.3	2003	57.9	65.5
at age 60..	1974-1976	16.1	20.1	2003	18.0	23.3
Survival probability						
from birth to age 15..	1974-1976	0.94	0.95	2003	0.98	0.98
from age 15 to age 60......................................	1974-1976	0.78	0.88	2003	0.83	0.92
from age 60 to age 80......................................	1974-1976	0.34	0.54	2003	0.43	0.66

Infant and child mortality

	Year	Male	Female	Both sexes	Year	Male	Female	Both sexes
Infant mortality rate *(per 1 000 live births)*	1975	52	42	47	2003	17	12	14
Mortality from age 1 to age 4 *(per 1 000 live births)*	1975	8	7	7	2003	2	2	2
Under-five mortality rate *(per 1 000 live births)*	1975	59	49	54	2003	19	14	17

II. Data and estimates from United Nations sources

United Nations Population Division estimates

	1990-1995	2000-2005
Annual number of deaths *(thousands)*	31	31
Crude death rate *(per 1 000 person-years)*	10	9
Life expectancy at birth *(years)*		
Male..	69.2	71.6
Female...	76.9	78.9
Under-five mortality rate *(per 1 000 live births)*	23	15

Maternal mortality

	2000
Maternal mortality ratio *(deaths per 100 000 births)*	27

HIV/AIDS

	2003	[Low estimate - high estimate]
Number of HIV-infected persons, ...	6 000	[2 800 - 9 700]
Adult HIV prevalence *(percentage of adults 15-49)*	0.3	[0.2 - 0.5]

Policy views

	1976	2003
Life expectancy..	Acceptable	Acceptable
Under-five mortality..		Unacceptable
Maternal mortality...		Unacceptable
Level of concern about AIDS....................................		Major concern

Life Expectancy at Birth

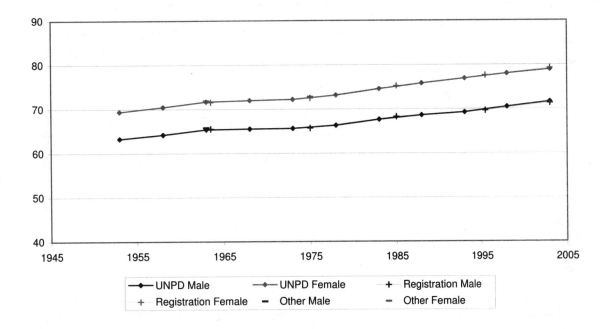

Infant Mortality Rate

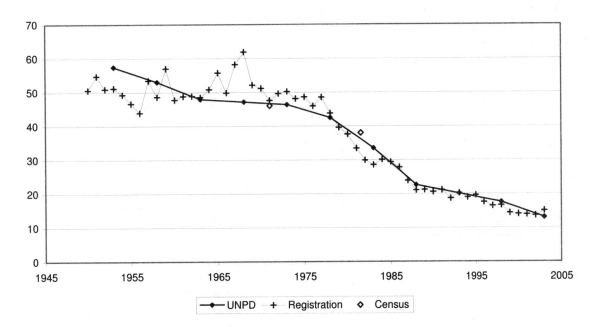

Indicator	Period			
	Earlier year		*Later year*	

I. Data and estimates from national and other sources

General mortality

	Year	Value	Year	Value
Annual number of deaths *(thousands)*	..	..	2001	132.5
Annual number of deaths under age one *(thousands)*	..	..	2001	9.4
Crude death rate *(per 1 000 person-years)*	..	..	2001	5.3

	Year	Male	Female	Year	Male	Female
Life expectancy *(years)*						
at birth...	1970	69.4	76.0	2002	67.6	72.5
at age 15...	..	..	..	..	..	..
at age 60...	..	..	..	..	..	..
Survival probability						
from birth to age 15..............................	..	..	..	..	..	..
from age 15 to age 60...........................	..	..	..	..	..	..
from age 60 to age 80...........................	..	..	..	..	..	..

Infant and child mortality

	Year	Male	Female	Both sexes	Year	Male	Female	Both sexes
Infant mortality rate *(per 1 000 live births)*	..	..	..	..	1992-2002	67	59	63
Mortality from age 1 to age 4 *(per 1 000 live births)*	..	..	..	..	1992-2002	12	14	13
Under-five mortality rate *(per 1 000 live births)*	..	..	..	..	1992-2002	78	72	75

II. Data and estimates from United Nations sources

United Nations Population Division estimates

	1990-1995	*2000-2005*
Annual number of deaths *(thousands)*	160	173
Crude death rate *(per 1 000 person-years)*	7	7
Life expectancy at birth *(years)*		
Male...	63.0	63.3
Female..	69.4	69.7
Under-five mortality rate *(per 1 000 live births)*	71	70

Maternal mortality

	2000
Maternal mortality ratio *(deaths per 100 000 births)*	24

HIV/AIDS

	2003	*[Low estimate - high estimate]*
Number of HIV-infected persons, ...	11 000	[4 900 - 30 000]
Adult HIV prevalence *(percentage of adults 15-49)*	0.1	[0.0 - 0.2]

Policy views

	1976	*2003*
Life expectancy...	..	Unacceptable
Under-five mortality..		Unacceptable
Maternal mortality..		Unacceptable
Level of concern about AIDS..................................		Major concern

Life Expectancy at Birth

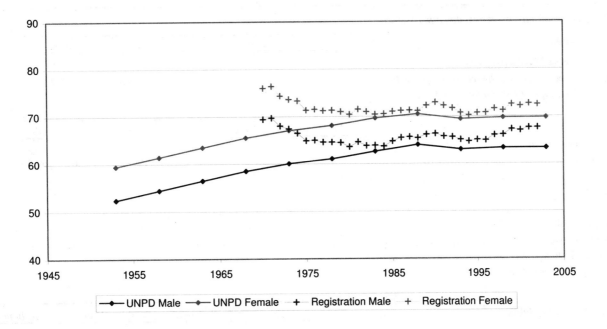

Infant Mortality Rate

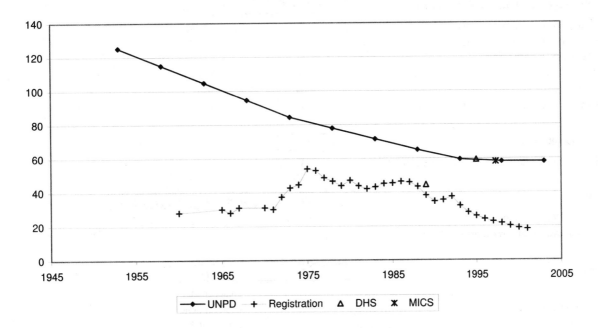

Indicator	Period			
	Earlier year		Later year	

I. Data and estimates from national and other sources

General mortality

	Year	Value	Year	Value
Annual number of deaths *(thousands)*	..	..	..	..
Annual number of deaths under age one *(thousands)*	..	..	..	..
Crude death rate *(per 1 000 person-years)*	..	..	..	..

	Year	Male	Female	Year	Male	Female
Life expectancy *(years)*						
at birth..........	..	..	..	1999	65.6	69.0
at age 15.........	..	..	..	..	..	..
at age 60.........	..	..	..	..	..	..
Survival probability						
from birth to age 15.........	..	..	..	..	..	..
from age 15 to age 60.........	..	..	..	..	..	..
from age 60 to age 80.........	..	..	..	..	..	..

Infant and child mortality

	Year	Male	Female	Both sexes	Year	Male	Female	Both sexes
Infant mortality rate *(per 1 000 live births)*	..	..	..	..	1999	27	26	27
Mortality from age 1 to age 4 *(per 1 000 live births)*	..	..	..	..	1999	6	5	6
Under-five mortality rate *(per 1 000 live births)*	..	..	..	..	1999	..	..	33

II. Data and estimates from United Nations sources

United Nations Population Division estimates

	1990-1995	2000-2005
Annual number of deaths *(thousands)*	1	1
Crude death rate *(per 1 000 person-years)*	7	6
Life expectancy at birth *(years)*		
Male..	62.9	66.8
Female..	65.9	70.4
Under-five mortality rate *(per 1 000 live births)*	47	42

Maternal mortality

	2000
Maternal mortality ratio *(deaths per 100 000 births)*	130

HIV/AIDS

	2003	[Low estimate - high estimate]
Number of HIV-infected persons, ...	..	..
Adult HIV prevalence *(percentage of adults 15-49)*	..	..

Policy views

	1976	2003
Life expectancy..	..	Unacceptable
Under-five mortality...		Unacceptable
Maternal mortality...		Unacceptable
Level of concern about AIDS.....................................		Major concern

Life Expectancy at Birth

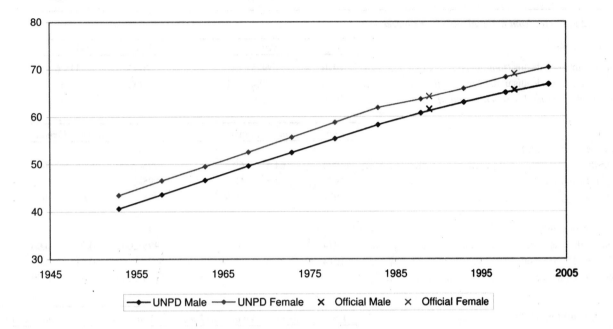

Infant Mortality Rate

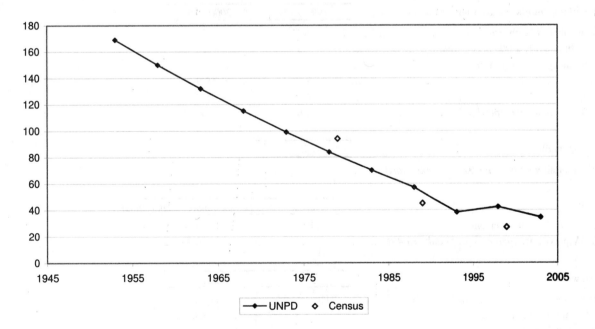

Indicator	Period					
	Earlier year				Later year	

I. Data and estimates from national and other sources

General mortality

	Year	Value			Year	Value		
Annual number of deaths *(thousands)*	1970	68.5			2003	118.6		
Annual number of deaths under age one *(thousands)*	1970	19.4			2002	7.6		
Crude death rate *(per 1 000 person-years)*	1970	6.6			2003	5.0		

	Year	Male	Female		Year	Male	Female	
Life expectancy *(years)*								
at birth..	1974	64.5	69.4		1995-2000	68.6	74.5	
at age 15..	1974	54.5	58.9		1995-2000	56.9	62.3	
at age 60..	1974	16.9	18.9		1995-2000	17.9	20.8	
Survival probability								
from birth to age 15...	1974	0.93	0.94		1995-2000	0.95	0.96	
from age 15 to age 60...	1974	0.76	0.84		1995-2000	0.81	0.89	
from age 60 to age 80...	..	..	..		1995-2000	0.45	0.59	

Infant and child mortality

	Year	Male	Female	Both sexes	Year	Male	Female	Both sexes
Infant mortality rate *(per 1 000 live births)*	1975	51	41	46	1995-2000	24	20	22
Mortality from age 1 to age 4 *(per 1 000 live births)*	1975	14	14	14	1995-2000	20	6	13
Under-five mortality rate *(per 1 000 live births)*	1975	64	54	59	1995-2000	43	26	35

II. Data and estimates from United Nations sources

United Nations Population Division estimates

	1990-1995	2000-2005
Annual number of deaths *(thousands)*	101	127
Crude death rate *(per 1 000 person-years)*	5	5
Life expectancy at birth *(years)*		
Male...	68.7	69.9
Female..	74.5	75.8
Under-five mortality rate *(per 1 000 live births)*	30	29

Maternal mortality

	2000
Maternal mortality ratio *(deaths per 100 000 births)*	96

HIV/AIDS

	2003	*[Low estimate - high estimate]*
Number of HIV-infected persons, ...	110 000	[47 000 - 170 000]
Adult HIV prevalence *(percentage of adults 15-49)*	0.7	[0.4 - 1.2]

Policy views

	1976	2003
Life expectancy...	Unacceptable	Acceptable
Under-five mortality..		Unacceptable
Maternal mortality..		Unacceptable
Level of concern about AIDS...................................		Major concern

Life Expectancy at Birth

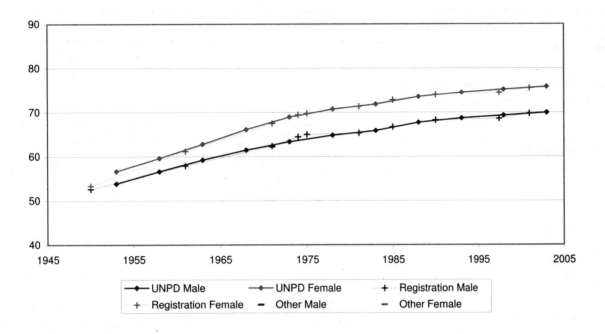

Infant Mortality Rate

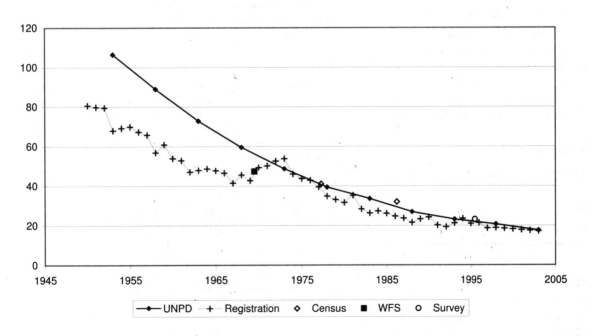

Indicator	Period			
	Earlier year		Later year	

I. Data and estimates from national and other sources

General mortality

	Year	Value	Year	Value
Annual number of deaths *(thousands)*	..	..	..	..
Annual number of deaths under age one *(thousands)*	..	..	..	..
Crude death rate *(per 1 000 person-years)*	..	..	..	..

	Year	Male	Female	Year	Male	Female
Life expectancy *(years)*						
at birth..	1979	63.7	67.9	..	..	..
at age 15..	1979	55.0	59.2	..	..	..
at age 60..	1979	16.0	19.4	..	..	..
Survival probability						
from birth to age 15.................................	..	..	..	..	..	..
from age 15 to age 60...............................	..	..	..	..	..	..
from age 60 to age 80...............................	..	..	..	..	..	..

Infant and child mortality

	Year	Male	Female	Both sexes	Year	Male	Female	Both sexes
Infant mortality rate *(per 1 000 live births)*	1985	40	34	37	1992-2002	25	25	25
Mortality from age 1 to age 4 *(per 1 000 live births)*	1985	15	16	16	1992-2002	10	7	8
Under-five mortality rate *(per 1 000 live births)*	1985	55	49	52	1992-2002	34	31	33

II. Data and estimates from United Nations sources

United Nations Population Division estimates

	1990-1995	2000-2005
Annual number of deaths *(thousands)*	520	496
Crude death rate *(per 1 000 person-years)*	7	6
Life expectancy at birth *(years)*		
Male..	64.6	68.4
Female..	68.5	72.4
Under-five mortality rate *(per 1 000 live births)*	60	39

Maternal mortality

	2000
Maternal mortality ratio *(deaths per 100 000 births)*	130

HIV/AIDS

	2003	*[Low estimate - high estimate]*
Number of HIV-infected persons, ...	220 000	[110 000 - 360 000]
Adult HIV prevalence *(percentage of adults 15-49)*	0.4	[0.2 - 0.8]

Policy views

	1976	2003
Life expectancy...	Unacceptable	Acceptable
Under-five mortality...		Acceptable
Maternal mortality...		Unacceptable
Level of concern about AIDS.................................		Major concern

Life Expectancy at Birth

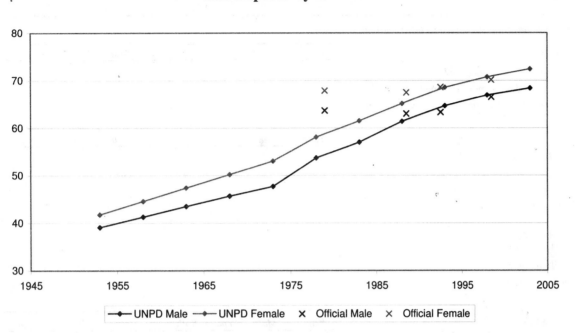

Infant Mortality Rate

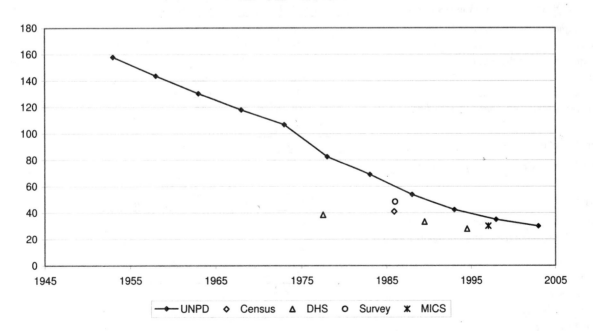

Indicator	Period			
	Earlier year		Later year	

I. Data and estimates from national and other sources

General mortality	Year	Value	Year	Value
Annual number of deaths *(thousands)*	..	..	..	..
Annual number of deaths under age one *(thousands)*	..	..	..	..
Crude death rate *(per 1 000 person-years)*	..	..	..	..

	Year	Male	Female	Year	Male	Female
Life expectancy *(years)*						
at birth...	..	..	..	..	..	..
at age 15..	..	..	..	..	..	..
at age 60..	..	..	..	..	..	..
Survival probability						
from birth to age 15...	..	..	..	..	..	..
from age 15 to age 60...	..	..	..	..	..	..
from age 60 to age 80...	..	..	..	..	..	..

Infant and child mortality	Year	Male	Female	Both sexes	Year	Male	Female	Both sexes
Infant mortality rate *(per 1 000 live births)*	..	..	..	..	..	..	..	..
Mortality from age 1 to age 4 *(per 1 000 live births)*	..	..	..	..	..	..	..	..
Under-five mortality rate *(per 1 000 live births)*	..	..	..	..	..	..	..	..

II. Data and estimates from United Nations sources

United Nations Population Division estimates	1990-1995	2000-2005
Annual number of deaths *(thousands)*	2	2
Crude death rate *(per 1 000 person-years)*	10	8
Life expectancy at birth *(years)*		
Male..	57.3	62.2
Female..	60.6	65.7
Under-five mortality rate *(per 1 000 live births)*	106	70

Maternal mortality	2000
Maternal mortality ratio *(deaths per 100 000 births)*	..

HIV/AIDS	2003	*[Low estimate - high estimate]*
Number of HIV-infected persons, ...	..	..
Adult HIV prevalence *(percentage of adults 15-49)*	..	..

Policy views	1976	2003
Life expectancy..	..	..
Under-five mortality..		..
Maternal mortality..		..
Level of concern about AIDS......................................		..

Life Expectancy at Birth

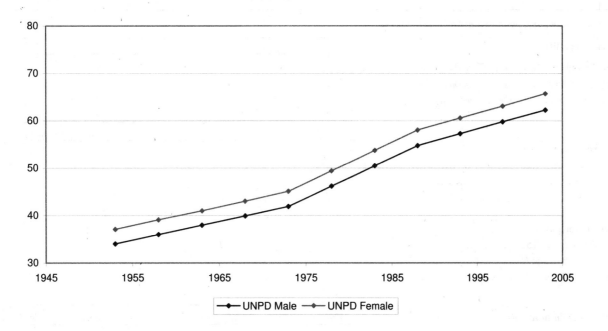

Infant Mortality Rate

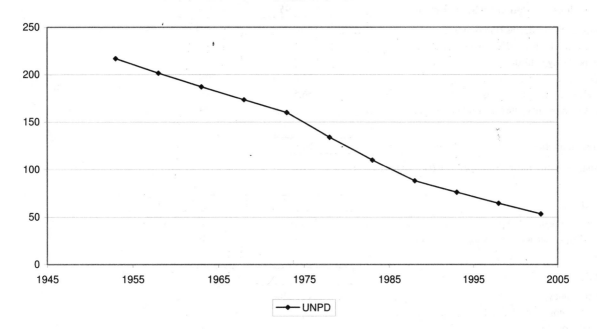

Indicator	Period							
	Earlier year				Later year			

I. Data and estimates from national and other sources

General mortality

	Year	Value			Year	Value		
Annual number of deaths *(thousands)*	..	..			..	..		
Annual number of deaths under age one *(thousands)*	..	..			..	..		
Crude death rate *(per 1 000 person-years)*	..	..			..	..		

	Year	Male	Female		Year	Male	Female	
Life expectancy *(years)*								
at birth	..	..	..		..	..	..	
at age 15	..	..	..		..	..	..	
at age 60	..	..	..		..	..	..	
Survival probability								
from birth to age 15	..	..	..		..	..	..	
from age 15 to age 60	..	..	..		..	..	..	
from age 60 to age 80	..	..	..		..	..	..	

Infant and child mortality

	Year	Male	Female	Both sexes	Year	Male	Female	Both sexes
Infant mortality rate *(per 1 000 live births)*	1975	165	146	156	1987-1997	98	80	90
Mortality from age 1 to age 4 *(per 1 000 live births)*	1975	113	124	118	1987-1997	33	36	35
Under-five mortality rate *(per 1 000 live births)*	1975	259	252	256	1987-1997	128	114	121

II. Data and estimates from United Nations sources

United Nations Population Division estimates

	1990-1995	2000-2005
Annual number of deaths *(thousands)*	161	169
Crude death rate *(per 1 000 person-years)*	12	9
Life expectancy at birth *(years)*		
Male	54.8	59.1
Female	56.5	61.7
Under-five mortality rate *(per 1 000 live births)*	130	95

Maternal mortality

	2000
Maternal mortality ratio *(deaths per 100 000 births)*	570

HIV/AIDS

	2003	*[Low estimate - high estimate]*
Number of HIV-infected persons,	12 000	[4 000 - 24 000]
Adult HIV prevalence *(percentage of adults 15-49)*	0.1	[0.0 - 0.2]

Policy views

	1976	2003
Life expectancy	Unacceptable	Unacceptable
Under-five mortality		Unacceptable
Maternal mortality		Unacceptable
Level of concern about AIDS		Major concern

Life Expectancy at Birth

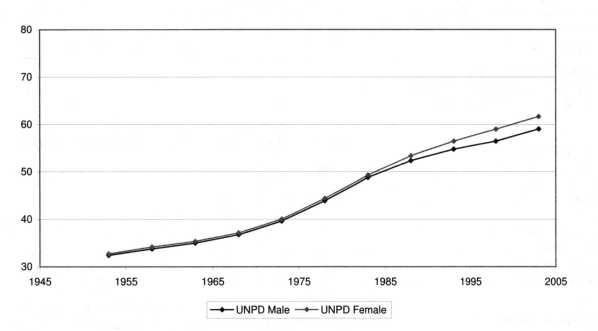

Infant Mortality Rate

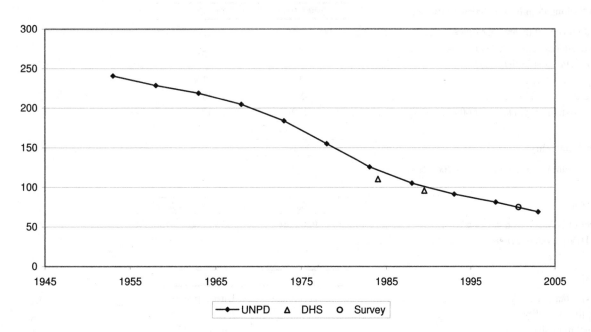

Indicator	Period			
	Earlier year		Later year	

I. Data and estimates from national and other sources

General mortality

	Year	Value	Year	Value
Annual number of deaths *(thousands)*	..	..	..	..
Annual number of deaths under age one *(thousands)*	..	..	..	..
Crude death rate *(per 1 000 person-years)*	..	..	..	..

	Year	Male	Female	Year	Male	Female
Life expectancy *(years)*						
at birth	1980	50.7	53.0	..	..	..
at age 15	1980	48.1	50.3	..	..	..
at age 60	1980	14.9	15.8	..	..	..
Survival probability						
from birth to age 15	1980	0.79	0.80	..	..	..
from age 15 to age 60	1980	0.64	0.69	..	..	..
from age 60 to age 80	1980	0.29	0.34	..	..	..

Infant and child mortality

	Year	Male	Female	Both sexes	Year	Male	Female	Both sexes
Infant mortality rate *(per 1 000 live births)*	..	..	..	..	1991-2001	95	93	94
Mortality from age 1 to age 4 *(per 1 000 live births)*	..	..	..	..	1991-2001	89	74	82
Under-five mortality rate *(per 1 000 live births)*	1973	179	171	175	1991-2001	176	160	168

II. Data and estimates from United Nations sources

United Nations Population Division estimates

	1990-1995	2000-2005
Annual number of deaths *(thousands)*	172	255
Crude death rate *(per 1 000 person-years)*	19	23
Life expectancy at birth *(years)*		
Male	42.0	37.9
Female	45.0	36.9
Under-five mortality rate *(per 1 000 live births)*	179	173

Maternal mortality

	2000
Maternal mortality ratio *(deaths per 100 000 births)*	750

HIV/AIDS

	2003	[Low estimate - high estimate]
Number of HIV-infected persons,	920 000	[730 000 - 1 100 000]
Adult HIV prevalence *(percentage of adults 15-49)*	16.5	[13.5 - 20.0]

Policy views

	1976	2003
Life expectancy	Unacceptable	Unacceptable
Under-five mortality		Unacceptable
Maternal mortality		Unacceptable
Level of concern about AIDS		Major concern

Life Expectancy at Birth

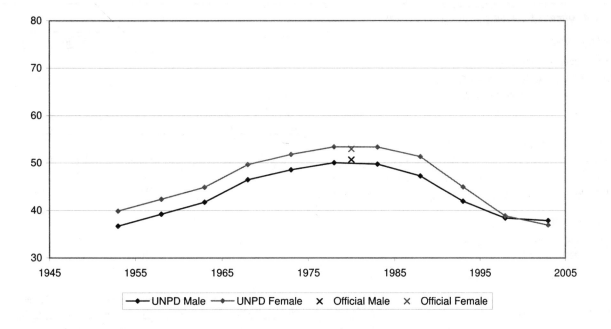

Infant Mortality Rate

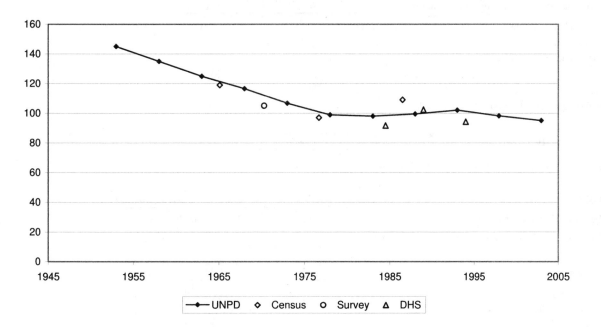

Indicator	Period				
	Earlier year			Later year	

I. Data and estimates from national and other sources

General mortality	Year	Value		Year	Value	
Annual number of deaths *(thousands)*	..	..		..	..	
Annual number of deaths under age one *(thousands)*	..	..		..	..	
Crude death rate *(per 1 000 person-years)*	..	..		..	..	

	Year	Male	Female	Year	Male	Female
Life expectancy *(years)*						
at birth.............	..	..	..	1990	58.0	62.0
at age 15.............	..	..	..	1990	50.9	53.9
at age 60.............	..	..	..	1990	14.9	16.7
Survival probability						
from birth to age 15.............	..	..	..	1990	0.88	0.90
from age 15 to age 60.............	..	..	..	1990	0.70	0.76
from age 60 to age 80.............	..	..	..	1990	0.28	0.36

Infant and child mortality	Year	Male	Female	Both sexes	Year	Male	Female	Both sexes
Infant mortality rate *(per 1 000 live births)*	..	..	..	..	1989-1999	63	56	60
Mortality from age 1 to age 4 *(per 1 000 live births)*	..	..	..	..	1989-1999	35	31	33
Under-five mortality rate *(per 1 000 live births)*	1975	127	113	120	1989-1999	95	85	90

II. Data and estimates from United Nations sources

United Nations Population Division estimates	1990-1995	2000-2005
Annual number of deaths *(thousands)*	117	291
Crude death rate *(per 1 000 person-years)*	10	23
Life expectancy at birth *(years)*		
Male.............	53.4	37.5
Female.............	59.7	36.9
Under-five mortality rate *(per 1 000 live births)*	85	117

Maternal mortality	2000
Maternal mortality ratio *(deaths per 100 000 births)*	1 100

HIV/AIDS	2003	[Low estimate - high estimate]
Number of HIV-infected persons, ...	1 800 000	[1 500 000 - 2 000 000]
Adult HIV prevalence *(percentage of adults 15-49)*	24.6	[21.7 - 27.8]

Policy views	1976	2003
Life expectancy.............	..	Unacceptable
Under-five mortality.............		Unacceptable
Maternal mortality.............		Unacceptable
Level of concern about AIDS.............		Major concern

Life Expectancy at Birth

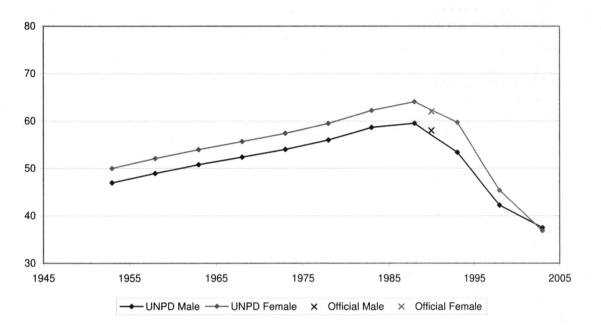

Infant Mortality Rate

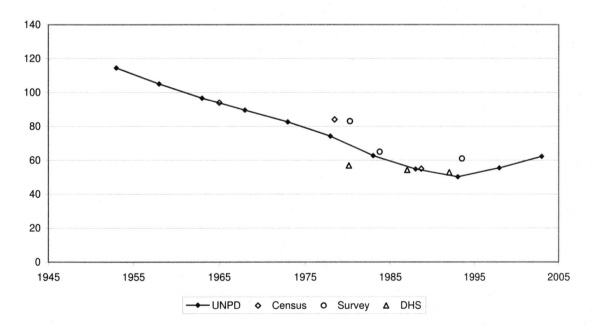